THE LIFE OF

JESUS CHRIST

My Friend and Savior

Tom D. Wilcox

ACKNOWLEDGEMENTS

I appreciate those who helped and encouraged me over the six years plus it has taken me to write this book. I have taken some of their advice and have re-written it twice. I owe my wife a debt of gratitude for the hours I have taken from her and put into this book.

Jeannie Worthen was kind enough to edit it for me. Her website is http://otherworlddiner.blogspot.com/. It reads much better, thanks to her touch.

The picture on the cover was done by Hilarie Couture, a very prolific artist and teacher. I highly recommend her. Her website is https://hcouturearts.com/.

My sister Sherri Moe, her daughter, Marci Cardon, my friend Ed Steck, as well as Paul Yearout, and DeWaine George, have had a hand in making this book a reality.

Most important of all, I could not have done it without the Lord's help.

INTRODUCTION

I have written this for those who don't have a relationship with Christ and may not be Christians, but those who have a strong religious affiliation can also profit. I have combined the four Gospels chronologically to make it easier to understand Christ's teachings. All faiths should bring people to God and I want this book to help you know Christ better, no matter your faith or lack of it.

There is a war going on around us in which we are involved, and most of us don't even know it. It's a war against evil and ignorance. How is that possible?

Many of us have the priority of a big home, a new shiny car, taking care of the earth, reducing global warming, or a strong and healthy body. I could go on and on. What is wrong with these things? Nothing, but for many of us, these things have become our gods. While we are chasing these things, we feel happy and fulfilled, which is good, but our lives can come crashing down around us because we have no moral foundation. That foundation needs to be built on principles that will withstand the test of time.

Individuals have a God-given sense that drives them to want to be happy, so we look for things we think will do that. We are not issued a handbook on life at birth, except that which is given to us by our parents, which may or not be helpful. It is very difficult to find our way along the pathway to happiness, without guidance. I believe the best handbooks on life are the scriptures. Why is that?

There are several, but I think the best is because numerous surveys have found religious people to be the happiest over time. If you don't believe in God, it doesn't mean he doesn't exist. He is still there for those who believe. I believe, and He is there for me and others I know. He can be there for you, too, but you need to look. It's not hard, but it does take some effort. Is happiness worth some effort? I surely hope so.

A little about myself. I am a 79-year-old ex-businessman and have been retired for 22 years, which has allowed me to be a volunteer fireman, serve on boards, including fire, water, homeowner, mediation, and to serve my church in many different ministerial positions.

I was raised a Methodist, and because I was blessed with caring and loving parents, I was taught early to believe in God and because he answered my prayers, I knew Him. I read the Bible through for the first time when I was about 13 and have been doing it ever since. I have probably read it 40 or 50 times along with other

LDS scriptures. I find it interesting that people often say, "It is in the Bible," or "The Bible says," when those things are not there.

In my late teens and early twenties, I found there were several things I didn't understand. For answers, I attended many other churches and read about other faiths, but to no avail. Finally, they were answered when I found "The Church of Jesus Christ of Latter-day Saints" and I have been a member for 49 years.

I have recently been told that my brain is full of amyloid protein, the precursor of Alzheimer's disease. Fortunately, you don't have to be dead to obtain that diagnosis today. My brain still works, and I hope it continues to do so until I pass on. I have joined with 1600 fellow sufferers who have the same diagnosis in a pharmaceutical drug test to see if their new drug will cure us. I have no idea if I am getting a placebo, but hopefully, it will be a cure for some. If you are likewise suffering, talk to a neurologist, there are many new things happening.

The friend portion of this book's title comes from John 15:14, when Christ is speaking to His disciples and says, "You are my friends if you do whatever I command you." I don't claim to fully follow this all the time, but I try to live my life by this principle. I believe this book exists because Christ wanted me to write it, for what reason I don't know.

As some of Abraham's family relations can be confusing, I have included a chart showing his genealogy to help the reader understand them.

I have used fictional dialogue to bring some characters more fully to life. I believe this dialogue could have been true. Footnotes and regular script document what is factual or scriptural and italics the fictional and what I cannot document. There are a few instances where things of general knowledge are not footnoted.

Most of the scriptures in this book are taken from the Bible, but a few are from "The Book of Mormon" and other LDS scriptures, which are footnoted. Joseph Smith the founder of The Church of Jesus Christ of Latter-day Saints and its first prophet, made a translation of the Bible and I have used (JST) to identify those, (BM) for "The Book of Mormon", (PGP) for "The Pearl of Great Price," and (D&C) for "The Doctrine and Covenants." I have used the standard designations for the Bible. I have underlined a few items I thought special.

In the table of contents, you will see this book has four main parts. If you are familiar with the Old Testament, you could skip Part 2, but I don't recommend it. Happy reading.

TABLE OF CONTENTS

Part 1. Mary and Joseph 1
    Mary and Joseph Marry 3
    The Savior Born 15
    The Wise Men... 20
    Egypt and Home 26
Part 2. The Jews 31
    Diagram - Genealogy of Abraham.......................... 32
    Abraham... 33
    Isaac and Jacob 38
    Joseph... 57
    Moses and the Miracles 75
    Wandering the Desert 92
    Joshua.. 137
    Samuel, Saul, and David.. 153
    Solomon 168
Part 3. The Ministry of Jesus 179
    The Temple 181
    The Death of Joseph... 194
    John the Baptist.. 196
    His Disciples and Galilee....................................... 205
    Sermon on the Mount and Capernaum 222
    Death of John the Baptist and Parables................. 230
    The Twelve Sent Out 238
    Passover Time Again and Transfiguration 244
    Feast of the Tabernacles... 253
    Roman Uprising 268
    The Feast of Dedication 280
    Betrayed and Trial.. 300
    Christ in the Spirit World....................................... 323
Part 4. After the Resurrection 327
    The Resurrected Christ 329
    The Road to Emmaus 333
    Christ and the Nephites 339
    Jesus in Galilee 342
    The Apostles After the Atonement 352
    Apostasy and Renaissance 359
    The Second Coming and Millennium 362
Epilogue 367

PART 1
MARY AND JOSEPH

MARY AND JOSEPH MARRY

Summer had come in all its beauty. The hills behind the village of Nazareth were green and dotted with blooming flowers.

Nazareth was a small, sleepy village about an hour's walk from Sepphoris, the large city where one of Herod the Great's palaces stood.[1]

In this day, the father of a young woman who would be married would give a gift or dowry to the family of the groom to help the couple get started. This union was agreed between the families and the engagement was expected to end in the wedding ceremony. Divorce was the only way to break the agreement. If the young woman was to get pregnant by another man, she could be stoned to death.

Two sisters sat on the grass enjoying the beautiful day.

Esther playfully threw a handful of grass at her sister, Mary, as she said, "You are so lucky. Joseph is a great guy. All the girls have been eyeing him and you are engaged to him."

Mary brushed the grass off her cotton shift. " I just wish we didn't have to wait a year to live together. It's only been three months... Nine more sounds like forever, but Joseph is making a place for us to live and working, too. That takes time."

Esther said, "Most of the other girls have been talking about the Messiah, wondering when he will come, and hoping he will be theirs. You and Joseph both have royal lineage. You could be the mother of the Messiah."

Mary laughed and said, "You know the Messiah is going to be born in Bethlehem.[2] It's a long way from Nazareth. There is no way I could be his mother living here. Besides, he'll probably be born to a rich family."

"I suppose that's true. This isn't a very exciting place," Esther said, her voice sad. Then she brightened. "But wouldn't you like to be his mother?"

"It would be a big responsibility, but if God wanted me to do it, I suppose I would. Remember, I am marrying Joseph and it would be his baby, too.

That night, as the family was eating; Esther asked Heli, her dad, "Dad, all the girls are saying the Messiah is going to be born

---

[1] Brown & Holzapfel. (2002). *Between the Testaments from Malachi to Matthew.* Salt Lake City, UT. Deseret Book. pg. 243-244
[2] Micah 5:2

MARY AND JOSEPH MARRY

soon. Do you think that's really going to happen?"

Her father shook his head. *"I'm sure I don't know. The prophets have told us it is going to happen, but I don't know when."*

"Some of the girls say Joseph would be the king if the Romans weren't running the country. Is that so?"

"Joseph has the royal Davidic lineage[3], but whether he would be king is another story. There are a lot of men who claim to be the rightful king, but they'd better not let King Herod hear it."

***

That night, Mary was awakened by a light in her room. It got brighter and brighter until it was as bright as noon. She looked over to her siblings sleeping in the same room, but they were still sound asleep.

She felt no fear, but a peaceful feeling filled her. Immediately, an angel was standing beside her. He was standing in the air, for his feet did not touch the floor. He was adorned in a loose robe that shone exquisitely white. His hands were bare, and his arms also, a little above the wrist. Also, his feet and his legs were bare, a little above the ankles.[4]

The angel spoke, "Mary, you are highly favored; the Lord is with you, for you are chosen and blessed among women."

She wondered what this meant, but the angel went on; "Fear not, Mary: you have found favor with God. You will conceive and have a son and shall call his name Jesus. He will be great and will be called the Son of the Highest, and the Lord God will give to him the throne of his father David. He will reign over the house of Jacob forever and of his kingdom there will be no end."

Puzzled, Mary asked the angel, "How can this be, since I'm a virgin?"

He answered, "It is of the Holy Ghost and the power of the Highest. Therefore, that holy child which you will have shall be called the Son of God. *As you know*, your cousin Elisabeth, who couldn't have children, is pregnant with a son in her old age, and this is the sixth month. With God, nothing is impossible."

Mary thought a moment and, with a sigh, said, "I accept the Lord's will, let it happen as you have said," and the angel departed.[5]

Mary listened to see if anyone else was awake, but could only hear normal breathing. She couldn't get back to sleep, tossing

---

[3] Matthew 1:1-17
[4] PGP Joseph Smith---History, 1:30-31. Joseph Smith's description of the angel Moroni, who came to him in answer to prayer. Notice, no wings..
[5] Luke 1:26-38

MARY AND JOSEPH MARRY

and turning on her mat. It didn't seem possible she would be the mother of the Messiah.

What would Joseph say? How could she tell him? How would she tell her family? What would the family friends say when they saw she was pregnant? She tried to remember what she had learned about the Messiah; what he would do. She prayed to God for help to understand what she should do and to know what the role of the Messiah would be.

Mary had met her cousin Elisabeth at Passover several times. She didn't know her very well, but she was old. It hardly seemed possible she could be giving birth. As for herself, had she really talked to an angel? Was she really going to have a baby?

It all seemed so unreal. The next day, she went through her daily chores almost in a daze. She desperately wanted to confide in her sister, Esther, with whom she was close. She didn't know how she could ever tell Joseph. How could she tell Esther and not tell Joseph?

That afternoon she decided to tell her mother. She waited until Esther and her other siblings were outside and said to her mother, "Mom, last night an angel appeared to me, right in my room. He told me I was going to give birth to the Messiah."

Her mother laughed and put her arms around Mary and said, " Nobody has angels appearing to them. You were just dreaming. You just got to thinking about the Messiah after what Esther said last night. Don't be silly; you're not going to have the Messiah."

"They say Zacharias saw an angel in the temple a few months ago."

Her mother held her at arm's length to look at her. "People say a lot of things, Mary. I wouldn't believe it unless Zacharias told me about it himself, and then I still might not believe it," she said. "You'd better get back to your work."

Mary went back to what she had been doing. That night she was exhausted and soon fell asleep.

The next day, when Mary rose, she decided she should go to visit her cousin Elisabeth who lived in Juttah, a small town about 120 miles from Nazareth.[6] She could stay there until the baby was born, where nobody knew her. It would be much easier.

She was afraid to tell anyone. She'd prayed fervently to her Lord for guidance, and to visit Elisabeth seemed like the right thing

---

[6] Talmage, James. (1981). *Jesus the Christ.* Salt Lake City, UT. The Church of Jesus Christ of Latter-day Saints. Pg. 82

MARY AND JOSEPH MARRY

to do. Elisabeth had a miracle happen to her; maybe she would understand Mary's predicament. When she made this decision, a weight seemed to be lifted from her shoulders.

At breakfast, she said, "I have decided to go visit Elisabeth."

Her family looked at her in stunned silence.

"Mary, you must be out of your mind," her dad said in a stern voice. "Why would you want to do that? You're engaged to Joseph; you can't just decide to run off."

Mary lifted her chin. "I know it sounds strange, but I've prayed about it and think it is the right thing to do. I'll carry just a few clothes. People provide travelers food and shelter all the time. I'll be fine."

Her mother said, "It's that dream about the angel and the Messiah, isn't it?"

Mary sighed. "Yes, Mother, but it wasn't a dream. He was really there. Dad, I'm sure Mom told you about it. Do you believe me?"

"I'm not sure what to believe, but I wish you wouldn't go." Her father frowned. "You need to tell Joseph what you're doing."

"Dad, how can I tell Joseph? If you don't believe me, how will Joseph? Please tell him. Just say I had to go see my cousin Elisabeth. He'll understand. I think it will be easier to talk to him when I come back. Please," she said, with a smile that melted her dad's heart.

He shook his head, but said, "Okay, I'll tell him, but I think you should be the one."

They tried their best to dissuade her, but they could not change her mind. She made a little pack of clothes and left.

It took her four days to make the trip. Perhaps she should have been concerned about the journey, but she felt a peace come over her that took her worries away. As she journeyed, she thought about what the angel had told her. When she had a chance to talk to somebody, she always asked what they thought the Messiah would do. Most said he would be their king and make their country great. She talked to many people, and it amazed her how much she learned.

As she walked, many thoughts raced through her mind. It didn't seem possible she would become pregnant, especially since she'd not been with a man. How could that be? Would she go to Bethlehem? How could she possibly resolve things with Joseph when he found out?

The third night, she met a kind elderly woman who gave her shelter and food. This woman had a different view of the Messiah.

She said, "He will be our Savior and free us from sin. He will pull down the tyrants who lead us now. The humble will be exalted."

That evening, Mary prayed with real conviction for guidance.

The next morning, she awoke with a feeling of peace. As she continued her journey, she thought about what a responsibility it is to be the mother of the Messiah, but also what a privilege to be chosen to bear this holy being.

It was late in the day on her fifth day of walking when she got to Juttah. After asking directions, she made her way to Elisabeth and Zacharias's home, where she knocked on the door.

When Elisabeth opened the door, Mary said, "I'm sorry to surprise you, but I had to come for a visit."

When Elisabeth saw Mary, she was filled with the Holy Ghost and threw her arms around Mary, gave her a big hug, and said, "I knew you were coming; *the Spirit told me*. You are the most blessed of women and blessed is your child who will be born. Why am I privileged to have the mother of my Lord come to me? When I heard your greeting, my baby jumped in my womb for joy. You are blessed for believing the promises you received from the Lord, for they shall be fulfilled."

When Mary heard this, it seemed like words were put in her mouth and she answered, "I praise God and rejoice in the Lord, my Savior, because God has seen my poverty and now all generations shall call me blessed. For God, who is mighty, has done great things to me, and his name is holy. He extends his mercy to those who obey Him from generation to generation. He has shown his strength and has overthrown the proud with the thoughts of their hearts. He pulls down the mighty from their seats of power and exalts the humble. He fills those that hunger and thirst for righteousness; but sends away the rich, empty. He has helped his servant Israel to remember mercy, just as he taught to our fathers, to Abraham, and to his posterity, forever."[7]

Elisabeth welcomed her. "Mary, come in. "Forgive Zacharias; he is deaf and can't speak. I'll tell you all about that in a minute, but now I want to hear about what's happened to you. I'll write the highlights for him later."

They sat down and Mary said, "I was worried about how I would be greeted, but I see the Spirit prepared the way."

---

[7] Luke 1:39-55

MARY AND JOSEPH MARRY

Elisabeth nodded. "Yes, Mary. We knew you were coming; tell us the details. Don't keep us waiting."

Mary told her about Joseph, her espousal and said, "I was sleeping one night and was awakened by a light in my room. It got brighter and brighter until it was as bright as noon. I looked over at my siblings sleeping in the same room, but they stayed sound asleep. I felt no fear, just peace. An angel stood beside me. He said, 'Mary, you are highly favored, the Lord is with you, for you are chosen and blessed among women.' I immediately wondered what this was about, but the angel went on; 'Fear not, Mary: you have found favor with God. You will conceive and have a son and shall call his name Jesus. He will be great and will be called the Son of the Highest and the Lord God will give to him the throne of his father David. He will reign over the house of Jacob forever and of his kingdom there will be no end.'

"I asked the angel, 'How can this be, since I'm a virgin?'

"He answered, 'It is of the Holy Ghost and the power of the Highest. Therefore, that holy child which you will have shall be called the Son of God.'"

When Mary was finished, Elisabeth said, "What an experience. What do you think the angel meant when he said, 'It is of the Holy Ghost and the power of the Highest and the child shall be called the Son of God?'"

Mary shook her head. "I don't know what it means, except somehow God or the Holy Ghost is the father, because I am still a virgin."

Elisabeth said, "I need to think and pray about that for a time. We also have had a great experience. Last winter, when Zacharias' course (a group of priests who served in the temple for a given time) was serving in the temple, the lot fell to him to minister within the Holy Place. That had never happened to him before and it is a great honor. Some priests never have that opportunity all their lives. He felt very fortunate to have been chosen. Mary, I want to make sure you understand what happens there. The priest leaves the people praying and enters the Holy Place in which are the golden altar of incense, the golden candlestick and the table of shewbread. It is separated from the Holy of Holies by the veil of the temple. The priest enters the Holy Place and burns incense on the altar of incense. When he is finished, he goes out to the people and dismisses them.[8]

---

[8] Bible Dictionary. *Tabernacle.* (1979). The Holy Bible, Authorized King James Version. Salt Lake City, UT. The Church of Jesus Christ of Latter-day Saints.

"On his day of service, he entered the Holy Place and there, standing on the right side of the altar of incense, was an angel of the Lord. He was really surprised and scared; he didn't know what to make of it. But the angel said to him, 'Fear not Zacharias, your prayer has been heard. Your wife, Elisabeth, will bear you a son and you shall call his name John. You will have joy and gladness and many will rejoice at his birth. He will be great in the sight of the Lord and shall not drink wine or strong drink. He will be filled with the Holy Ghost from his mother's womb. Many of the children of Israel will he turn to the Lord their God. He will go before the Lord in the spirit and power of Elias, to turn the hearts of the fathers to the children and the disobedient to the wisdom of the just; to make ready a people prepared for the Lord.'

"He still couldn't believe what was happening, so he asked him, 'How will I know this? I am an old man and my wife past childbearing.'

"He answered, 'I am Gabriel who stands in the presence of God and am sent to speak to you and give you these glad tidings. Because you didn't believe my words, which shall be fulfilled in their time, you will be deaf and not able to speak until the day these things shall be performed.'[9]

"At this point, he seemed to disappear. Zacharias went ahead and burned the incense and went out to the people. He tried to tell the people he had seen an angel, but he couldn't speak. He made motions to try to tell them what happened to him. He wrote out what had happened for the other priests, but he still doesn't know how many believed it. It has been a long time since anyone in Israel has had a vision such as he had. As soon as his course was finished, he came home. When he told me, I believed him, but it was hard for me to understand how I was going to get pregnant since I was past bearing. Soon after that, I found I was with child. It has been about six months now."

Mary smiled. *"That's amazing, Elisabeth. You're carrying John, who will be the Elias, preparing the way for the Messiah I carry. Sometimes I have trouble believing this is real."*

Elisabeth took Mary's hand. *"I feel the same way. I hope you will stay with us at least until John is born. It is going to be hard for you to go home pregnant and face all the questioning looks. I'm sure Joseph will understand. He must be a good man and God will want a good man to be an example for the Messiah."*

---

[9] Luke 1:7-22

MARY AND JOSEPH MARRY

"I hope you're right." Mary squeezed Elisabeth's hands. *"Thank you."*

***

Finally, the time came for Elisabeth to be delivered, and John was born. The extended family came together on the eighth day to celebrate, circumcise the child, and give him a name. The family wanted to call the baby Zacharias after his father, but Elisabeth said firmly, "No, he is going to be called John."

But they wouldn't let it go. "There is no one in your family called John."

They made signs to Zacharias and asked him what he should be called. They were surprised when he wrote, "His name is John!" in big letters.

As soon as Zacharias wrote this, his mouth and ears were opened and he prophesied: "Blessed be the Lord God of Israel, for he has visited and redeemed his people and has raised up a horn of salvation for us in the house of his servant David, as he spoke by the mouth of his holy prophets, ever since the world began. That we should be saved from our enemies and from the hand of all those who hate us and to perform the mercy promised to our fathers and to remember His holy covenant; the oath which He swore to our father Abraham, that He would grant to us, that we being delivered out of the hand of our enemies might serve Him without fear, in holiness and righteousness before Him, all the days of our lives. And you, child, shall be called the prophet of the Highest. For you shall go before the face of the Lord to prepare His ways and to give knowledge of salvation to His people by baptism for the remission of their sins, through the tender mercy of our God. Whereby, the dayspring from on high has visited us, to give light to them who sit in darkness and in the shadow of death, to guide our feet into the way of peace."[10]

While Mary was at Elisabeth's home, she discovered she was pregnant. She had some problems with morning sickness, which ended by the third month. She helped for a few days after John's birth, but decided she needed to return and face whatever was in store for her at home. After bidding Elisabeth and her family goodbye, she walked the four days home without incident and arrived about dinner time. Her family welcomed her with open arms.

---

[10] Luke 1:59-79

They gathered around her, and she told them, "As you probably can see, I am pregnant and carrying the Messiah, just as the angel said before I left."[11]

Mary went on, "I had no problems on my way to Elisabeth's. I met some great people along the way and learned a lot about what the Messiah will do. When I got to Elisabeth's home, she was expecting me. The Spirit had told them I was coming. She was about six months along in her pregnancy, just as the angel told me. When I greeted her, she was filled with the Holy Ghost.

She then told her family what she and Elisabeth had told each other. After which, she then told them what had happened to Zacharias and about his being deaf and dumb until the naming of his son John.

"What are you going to tell Joseph?" asked her mother.

"I am not sure. I suppose I will tell him the same things I just told you," Mary said.

The next day, she went to Joseph's carpentry shop. "Hi, Joseph," *she said sheepishly, standing just inside the door.*

Joseph stopped what he was doing at the sound of her voice, and looked up. "Hello, Mary. I'm glad to see you," *he said walking toward her with a big smile on his face. He said,* "I have been worried about you," *as he took her in his arms with a big hug. He stood back and looked at her and said,* "Your dad came by and said you went to visit your cousin Elisabeth. Why didn't you tell me yourself? You're espoused to me. Why did you do such a strange thing and not let me know?"

Mary looked at the ground and drew a circle with her right toe as she said, "Well, I was confused and didn't know what I could say."

"What were you so confused about, you couldn't share with me," *he said smiling at her.* "It can't be that bad."

Mary looked away from him and said, "I didn't think you would believe me."

"Mary, I love you and I can't think of anything you would say I wouldn't believe," *he said as he gave her a questioning look.*

Mary looked down at the ground again and then up at him and said, "I hope you believe me. An angel appeared to me one night just before I left. He told me I would be the mother of the Messiah and now I am over three months pregnant with the Messiah."

---

[11] Luke 1:28-37

MARY AND JOSEPH MARRY

  Joseph felt like he had been struck with a thunderbolt. He gasped, stepped back from Mary, and said, "You're pregnant with someone else's baby?"
  "Yes, with the Messiah."
  Joseph just stood there with his mouth open.
  Mary said, "Do you believe me?"
  "I want to believe you, but it just seems preposterous. Nobody sees angels. I am just a poor, hardworking man. Why would we have the Messiah? It just doesn't make sense. As much as I want to believe you, I . . . I just can't."
  "Joseph, you just have to believe me. The Lord wants us to raise him. It is a big responsibility, but you will be a great father."
  Joseph looked at her sadly and said, "Mary, I am not going to raise someone else's baby.
  Mary desperately wanted to convince him and raising her voice said, "Joseph, an angel really did appear to me! He came right into my room in the middle of the night and told me!"
  Joseph said dejectedly, "Mary, just leave and please don't come back."
  Mary turned and ran away from him, tears streaming down her cheeks. When she got home, she hurried inside and threw her arms around her mother, buried her head in her mother's shoulder and said, "Mother, he doesn't want me. I tried so hard to tell him, but it just didn't go well. I just know he's going to divorce me."
  "There, there, calm down." *Mary's mother gently pushed her away and looked at her face. She brushed a lock of hair out of Mary's eyes and said,* "You have told me several times you are carrying the Messiah and you know the Lord wants Joseph to help raise him. I know you well enough to know what you are saying is true. It will all work out, I'm sure! The Lord wouldn't want his Messiah not to have a father. I'll have your dad talk to Joseph. I love you, Mary, and am so happy for you. Everything will work out."
  Mary smiled through her tears. " I feel like a little kid, coming to you this way, but I feel better already."
  That evening, after supper, Mary's mother told her husband, Heli, "You need to go talk to Joseph tomorrow and tell him about Mary. If you tell him what happened, I think he will believe you."
  Heli looked up from the fire, concerned. "I'll go talk to him . . . I hope you're right and he believes us -- He is a good and caring man. I'll do my best."

***

  Early the next day, Heli went to Joseph's home.

MARY AND JOSEPH MARRY

Joseph was just coming out, and said, "Hi, Heli. I'm sure you came here to talk to me about Mary. I'm on my way to see her. I am embarrassed. I got upset when she came and talked to me yesterday. It didn't go well – for some reason I didn't believe her. I know her better than that. After our conversation, I decided I would have to divorce her. Later, I decided to put her away privately, so there wouldn't be a trial of divorce. I didn't want there to be a lot of notoriety. Then last night while I was thinking about it, I had a vision. An angel of the Lord appeared to me and said, 'Joseph, son of David, don't be afraid to take Mary to be your wife, for the baby she is carrying is conceived of the Holy Ghost. She will have a son and you shall call his name Jesus: for he will save his people from their sins. This is what the prophet said, 'A virgin shall be with child and shall bring forth a son and they shall call his name Emmanuel, meaning God with us.' I'll walk back with you and apologize to Mary. We'll want to complete the marriage right away."[12]

"Thank you, Joseph. I knew you were a good man. I'm so happy to have you for a son-in-law. Mary will be thrilled," Heli said, slapping Joseph on the back.

Joseph and Heli walked back to Heli's house, each lost in their own thoughts. When they got there, Joseph turned to Heli. "Please tell Mary I'm not angry and would like to talk to her."

Heli went into his house and told Mary, "I went over to Joseph's to talk to him, but met him just as he was starting on his way over to see you. He had a dream last night and feels bad about the way things went yesterday. He's outside waiting to talk to you."

"Thanks, Dad. I can't wait to see him," she said, grabbing a shawl for warmth and hurrying out to Joseph. As she went out the front door, she remembered her pregnancy and started feeling shy, but she faced him with her head held high. "Good morning, I'm glad to see you, I was really worried."

He replied, "I'm sorry, Mary. I was very upset yesterday. I don't know what got into me. I should have believed you. Let's go for a walk. Last night I had a dream. An angel of the Lord appeared to me and said, 'Joseph, son of David, don't be afraid to take Mary to be your wife, for the baby she is carrying is conceived of the Holy Ghost. She will have a son and you shall call his name Jesus: for he will save his people from their sins. This is what the prophet said about this, 'A virgin shall be with child and shall bring forth a son and they shall call his name Emmanuel, meaning God with us.'"

---

[12] Matthew 1:19-24

MARY AND JOSEPH MARRY

Mary said, "I told you an angel appeared to me. It wasn't a dream; he was actually in my room. Let me tell you the whole story. Just before I left Nazareth, the angel came to me, right in the room where we all were sleeping. He woke me up, but all my siblings went right on sleeping. He said to me, 'Hail, you are highly favored, the Lord is with you; blessed are you among women.'" I was really surprised and wondering what this was all about, but the angel went on; 'Fear not, Mary: you have found favor with God. You will conceive in your womb and bring forth a son and shall call his name Jesus. He will be great and will be called the Son of the Highest and the Lord God will give to him the throne of his father David. He will reign over the house of Jacob forever and of his kingdom there will be no end.'"Since I was a virgin, I asked him how that was possible and he said, "It is of the Holy Ghost and the power of the Highest. Therefore, that holy child which you will have shall be called the Son of God. *As you know*, your cousin Elisabeth, who couldn't have children, is pregnant with a son in her old age and this is the sixth month. With God, nothing is impossible."

"I didn't find it scary having an angel talk to me. But, when an angel is asking you to do something, it is hard to say no. All the girls have talked about having the Messiah, and I had thought about it before, but it's different when it's really happening to you. I do want to do what the Lord asks of me. This is what our nation has been waiting for, for so long. All the prophets have testified of His coming. He is the Son of God. Joseph, you will be a great father to him."

Joseph said, *"I hadn't thought of it in that light. I was just thinking about you. I guess I was jealous yesterday, thinking there was some other guy. It's hard for me to get my head around the idea we'll be raising the Messiah. I am humbled God would give me the responsibility of raising His son. It is just hard for me to get used to it."*

Mary said, *"I know. I have had that problem, too."*

"Mary, we need to finish the marriage right away. I don't want anyone to make fun of you being pregnant and not married. Also, it is important the Messiah be of the royal line. I am of the royal line, though I'm not the father. I will give him a name and legally make him my son; thus, he will be a royal heir."

At this, Mary looked up at Joseph with a look of adoration and said, "Thank you, Joseph; that's very thoughtful. I love you and can't wait until the marriage is completed."

Joseph said, "One other thing you need to understand, Mary. I don't plan to consummate our marriage until after the baby is born."

"I do understand, Joseph. Thank you, that makes perfect sense."

THE SAVIOR BORN

One day in mid-afternoon, after they were married, Joseph came in from his carpenter's shop and told Mary, "You have been telling me for months we were going to go to Bethlehem, because that's where the prophet said the Messiah would be born. Well guess what? A notice of a decree was just put up on the public board announcing Caesar Augustus is requiring a tax. All Jews need to go to their ancestral homes for it.[13] Both of our families are of the house of David, which means all of us need to go to Bethlehem and we have to do it right away. That's a trip of about ninety miles. *I think both of our families ought to go together. It would be safer and we could help each other. You know what that is like from your trip to Juttah. Jesus is due in about a month. Do you think you could make the trip?"*

Mary nodded. "I know I can. The Lord will provide, though it's getting harder for me to walk. I've been thinking I look like a funny duck, waddling along. It would be nice to go sooner than later. Do you think there is any way I could ride? I know ninety miles is a long way."

Joseph smiled, putting his arm around her. "I would hope so, Mary. And you don't look like a duck."

The families all agreed going together would be a good idea. It took about a week for them to get ready. Jacob and Joseph had projects they needed to finish for customers. They put Mary on a cart with the things they needed for the trip. Things went smoothly until just about three miles out of Bethlehem. It was early afternoon on a warm spring day. Joseph was leading the ass pulling the cart. He was thinking about how busy the road was and how good the Romans were at building roads, when the cart hit a big pothole he hadn't

---

[13] Luke 2:1, 3

THE SAVIOR BORN

noticed. There was a crack and the right wheel fell off. The cart lurched to the side and stopped.

Mary called down to Joseph, "What happened?"

"The wheel came off, "Joseph said as he walked back to inspect the situation. After checking he said, "Actually, the axle broke."

Jacob walked back and joined his son. While they were checking it, Mary said, "I'm having labor pains. I didn't want to say anything because we were getting so close. The pains aren't very close together, but I don't know what to do."

Jacob looked at Joseph, who had a blank, helpless look on his face. "Joseph, you can be in Bethlehem in about an hour if Mary can ride. That should be fine. Firstborns usually don't come too fast. I can get some wood and make an axle. It'll take some time, so we will camp here for the night. You need a midwife who knows what to do. Find an inn, and then get a midwife. You can find one in Bethlehem, I'm sure."

"Thanks, Dad. That sounds like a plan," said Joseph, relieved.

He and Mary got to Bethlehem with no problem, but Bethlehem was full of people. The streets were crowded and busy. When Joseph saw how many people were there, he told Mary, "This isn't what I expected. I don't know why I didn't. There were a lot of people on the road; they had to be going somewhere. I guess this is somewhere. I hope we can find a place to stay."

He decided to try the first inn they came to. He went in and told the proprietor, "My wife is ready to deliver a baby and we need a place to stay right away."

The proprietor, a kindly old man, looked at Joseph and shook his head. "Good luck. I'm sorry, but I don't have any place at all and I don't know anybody that does. I guess you will just have to keep asking until somebody takes pity on you."

Before going into the third place, he told Mary, "Let's ask God to help us find somewhere to go. It's his son, the Messiah; he should want him to have a place to be born."

They bowed their heads and sent a simple heartfelt plea to God. Joseph then went and told the proprietor, "My wife is in labor. I have to have a place for her to stay. Please, I need something, anything!"

This man looked at Joseph with sympathy. "We are so crowded; all my rooms are full. There is the cave where I have my stable. You are welcome to use that. You can check it out. If that will

THE SAVIOR BORN

work for you, let me know. My wife is a good midwife. I'll send her out to help you."

Joseph grabbed his hand, shook it hard and said, "Thanks. I'm sure the stable will be great. Please have your wife come. I can't tell you how much I appreciate it. My family is coming tomorrow. I'm going to tie my ass outside in the morning, so they will know where we are. Please send them to the stable when they come."

The other man waved him away, smiling. "Don't worry, I'll send my wife out and tell your family where you are."

With that, they made their way to the cave. The front part of the cave was about twenty feet wide, but it narrowed toward the rear to about fifteen feet. They could tell it ran into the hillside quite a distance, but because there was no light, they didn't know how far. It had a curved ceiling and, along one side, stalls were cut into the side of the cave.

Mary looked around and said, "Look, Joseph, there's clean hay. We can make a place for the baby in this empty stall. We can lay him on hay on the ledge at the front of the stall." She grimaced as a labor pain hit. "I'm glad the midwife is coming. I don't know how much longer it will be."

"I hope she hurries" he responded. "Are you okay?"

"I'll be fine. The pains aren't close yet. I'm anxious to get this over, though," she replied.

The midwife came in shortly after they'd gotten settled. She examined Mary, then told Joseph, "It probably will be a couple of hours. Go up to the inn and get something to eat. Bring your wife back something to eat later."

Joseph left the midwife in charge. The delivery proceeded with no problems and, when Joseph came back just after dark, he found baby Jesus wrapped in swaddling clothes (a square of cloth wrapped tightly around the baby with bandages to hold the cloth in place), *with Mary resting peacefully.*

***

Meanwhile, a short distance out of Bethlehem, shepherds were in the field on this warm spring evening tending their flock. (Flock, not flocks. Might this flock have been used for temple sacrifices?) *The were sitting around enjoying the evening and telling stories, while watching the sheep,* when an angel from God came to them. His glory shone about them and they were very afraid. The angel said to them, "Fear not, because I bring you good, joyous news, which will be to all people. For this night is born in the City of David a Savior, who is Christ the Lord. This is the way you will find the

THE SAVIOR BORN

baby; he is wrapped in swaddling clothes and lying in a manger. Suddenly, there was with the angel a multitude of the heavenly host praising God and saying, 'Glory to God in the highest and on earth peace, goodwill to all people."[14]

When the angels left, the shepherds looked at one another, and Ittai said, "That was unbelievable. Did that really happen?"

Ram, the tallest of the group, replied, "I know what you mean. I have had a hard time believing some of the miracles that have happened to our forefathers, but this has made a believer out of me. I want to go and find this baby."

A murmur of approval went up and they began to gather their things. "Let's go."

"How are we going to find the baby?" asked Ittai.

Ram answered, "The angel said we would find it in a manger. There are only a few inns that have mangers. Let's check those out first and, if we can't find him, we'll ask around. Who would like to stay here and make sure the sheep are safe in the sheepfold?"

No one wanted to stay. "Let's cast lots," Ram said.

When the lot fell to Tomer, he let out a few expletives, but he agreed to stay. The others thanked him before hurrying off in search of the child.

When they got to Bethlehem, the first inn they went to happened to be the one where the baby was. They found Mary and Joseph and the baby lying in the manger just as the angels had foretold. When they had seen him, they went about Bethlehem and the surrounding area telling all the people what had happened.

Those who heard them were amazed and wondered what it meant. Mary too pondered about what had happened. The shepherds returned to their sheep glorifying and praising God for all they had heard and seen.[15]

The next morning, just before noon, Jacob came into the stable. The first thing he said was, "Good morning, let me see my grandson." He admired Jesus, picking him up and saying, "I'm glad to see you're doing well. I'm looking forward to making a carpenter out of you."

Joseph said, "Dad, that's my job. Grandfathers get to spoil grandsons. I get to teach him... Just kidding. I'm sure you'll have lots of opportunities to teach him."

Jacob said, "He looks healthy. How did it go last night? The town is full of talk that the Messiah was born."

---

[14] Luke 2:7-14
[15] Luke 2:16-20

THE SAVIOR BORN

Joseph replied, "It was amazing. We hardly got any sleep. First, there came a bunch of shepherds, who said angels came to them last night to tell them the Savior was going to be born in Bethlehem. After they left, they must have told everyone, because it seemed like half the town was here last night wanting to see the baby."

Jacob said, "We are camping just on the outskirts of Bethlehem. I brought the cart. I'll help you get Mary and Jesus on the cart and we'll join the family. Everybody is anxious to see you and hear what happened."

The families decided to stay in Bethlehem until the time of Jesus' circumcision. After that, Mary and Joseph would stay until it was time to present Jesus in the temple after Mary's purification, since it was only about five miles from the temple. When the eighth day arrived, the families gathered together for the circumcision and the baby was formally named Jesus.

When the forty days of Mary's purification was finished, in accordance with the Law of Moses, Joseph, and his family went to Jerusalem to present Jesus to the Lord. The law said every firstborn male of beast or man should be called holy to the Lord and a sacrifice of turtledoves or two young pigeons was required.

As they walked into the temple, a man approached them and said, "I am Simeon. The Holy Ghost revealed to me I should not die before I had seen the Lord's Christ. Today the Spirit told me to come here and has whispered to me this is the child." He picked Jesus up in his arms, blessed God and said, "Lord, now let your servant depart in peace, as you told me previously. For my eyes have seen your salvation, which you have prepared in the sight of all people: A light to lighten the Gentiles and the glory of your people Israel."

Joseph and Mary looked at each other and shook their heads in astonishment. Simeon went on and blessed them and told Mary, "This child shall cause the fall and rising again of many in Israel and shall be spoken against that the thoughts of many will be revealed. A sword shall pierce through your own soul also."

After Simeon left, Mary said to Joseph, "I don't understand what he told me, do you?"

"No... No, I don't. I also don't understand why all these wondrous things keep happening. I don't know the reasons for them. One thing, though; after listening to Simeon, I don't think our Jesus is going to have an easy time."

Mary replied, "I do think the Lord wants the world to know the Messiah, our Savior, has been born. I wonder how long this will last. Herod isn't going to be happy to know the Messiah is here."

Also in the temple that day was Anna, a prophetess, the daughter of Phanuel of the tribe of Asher. She was very old and had been a widow for about eighty-four years, ever since her husband died seven years after their marriage, which was in her youth. She didn't leave the temple, but served God with fasting and prayer night and day.

She came to Mary and Joseph and gave thanks to the Lord for showing her the Messiah. She then told others there he would be their redeemer. After visiting the temple, Mary and Joseph returned to their home in Nazareth.[16]

THE WISE MEN

When Jesus was about a year old and saying a few words, wise men came to King Herod's palace in Jerusalem from the east. They were well dressed and came with a large entourage. They traveled mostly at night, as they were following a star, which their prophets had foretold and for which they had been looking. Their ancestors had left Salem when Melchizedek, king of Salem, was just beginning to rule. They were feeling cramped in Salem and wanted to find a less crowded area in which to live. They went east and found some good land and prospered.

At one of their stops, two of them were talking. The older said, "I wonder where this star is leading us. I can't help but marvel at the way it behaves. Stars normally move with the night sky or go shooting through it. This one has its own track."

Another said, "Well, isn't that why we're following it? Our prophets have told us it will be bright and rise and move differently than any other star. They say it will lead us to the Son of God; He who will lay down his life for our sins, that after this life we can become clean and are able to return and live again in our Heavenly Father's presence."

The first replied, "I know all that, but I have trouble getting my mind around it. Inside, I do know it's true but, for some reason, I keep questioning it. Where do you think we're going? We've traveled a long way already. I didn't expect we'd be gone this long."

---

[16] Luke 2:21-39

THE WISE MEN

The second wise man shook his head. "I know what you mean. It is a long time. We're getting close to Edom, Samaria and Judea. I don't know much about them, but I'm going to use my Greek and see what I can learn."

A little later he came back to their group and another wise man said, "I saw you talking and you really seemed excited. I bet you found out something interesting."

"I sure did. Those living in Judea are called Jews and they worship the same God we do. They don't have the greater priesthood, but the lesser priesthood. They call it the Priesthood of Aaron. Do you remember reading in our scriptures how Abraham paid tithes to Melchizedek? [17] *The Jews are descended from Abraham."*

As they neared Jerusalem, the eldest said, "I am looking forward to meeting Herod. I'm still sure the star we're following is leading us to Judea. I am excited to see the Savior. For hundreds of years, all our prophets have testified to us about this event and, finally, it is here. They have told us the Son of God would be born and would save us from our sins and the government would be on his shoulder.

Another wise man asked him, "What do you expect Herod will be like?"

He answered, "With all his problems, he seems to have done a good job of ruling. Judea is peaceful and prosperous, even though there are heavy taxes. I don't imagine we will get to spend much time with him, since his health is not good. I suppose he will be pretty much like other kings we have met."

Another said, "That's true, but he seems bloodthirsty, killing off anybody when there is even a glimmer of a threat to his throne, including his sons and wives. Do you think there is any chance he would kill the king we're coming to worship?"

"If he could, I am sure he would. I don't think there is any possibility he will be able to do so."

When they got to Jerusalem and Herod's palace, the eldest wise man walked up to the guard that met them and said in Greek, "We have come to worship he who is born King of the Jews. We have seen his star in the east. [18] *We want to ask Herod where the child is."*

The guard said, "Wait here. I will tell Herod of your arrival."

---

[17] Genesis 14:18, 20
[18] Matthew 2:1-3

THE WISE MEN

The guard then passed the information on to Herod's administrative assistant, who went to Herod and said, "Some wise men from the east have come seeking a child. They say he is born King of the Jews and they have come to worship him. They want you to tell them where he is." Herod frowned. "That is very interesting. I will receive them. Also, have the chief priests and scribes come. I want to hear what they have to say about this. I am the King and yet somebody from the east has to come to tell me a new king has been born."

He started yelling as he looked around at his assistants, "Tell me why I didn't know about this. How can some foreigner come and tell me a king has been born in the country I rule and no one knows anything about it? I am troubled and when I get troubled, someone can lose their life. You'd better find out where this child king is."

His assistant smiled, looked at him and said, "Don't get so excited, your highness. Just ask them, when they find him, to come back and tell you where he is, so you can go and worship him, too."

"Thanks, that's a great idea. I'll go and worship him with a sword." Herod laughed.

The wise men were then shown into the receiving chamber. They bowed as they entered the chamber with its lavish trappings. The king said to them through their interpreter, "I understand you are seeking one who is born King of the Jews."

One of them responded, "We have traveled a long way and look forward to ending our journey soon. Tell us where he is."

Herod shook his head. "I would love to tell you. Unfortunately, this is the first I have heard about the birth. I have called the chief priests and scribes to come here to ask them where he would be born. I am sure they will know. Help yourselves to food and wine while we wait, and tell me about your trip and when the star appeared," said Herod.

The wise men ate and drank and told him about their journey following the star of prophecy.

When the chief priest and scribes arrived, Herod asked them, "Where do the prophets say the Messiah will be born? These wise men have come to worship him, following a star out of the east."

The chief scribe responded, "That is easy, it is said, 'Bethlehem, which is in the land of Judah, in you shall be born a

THE WISE MEN

Prince, which is not the least among the princes of Judah: for out of you shall come the Messiah, who shall save my people Israel.'"[19]

Herod turned to the wise men and said, " Bethlehem isn't far from Jerusalem, so your trip won't be long. Go seek the child and when you have found him, bring me word that I may come and worship him also." [20]

The chief wise man inclined his head. "Thank you for your hospitality and kindness. We must be on our way." With that, the wise men bowed and left.

After they left, they talked amongst themselves about their experience with Herod. One said, "Herod looked terrible. I don't think he is long for this life."

Another nodded. "I think you're right. I'm glad I'm not in his sandals. He has quite a palace, though." He looked around at his companions. "They told us he was born in Bethlehem and it is not very far. *They certainly have great roads. We should be there tomorrow."*

One of them said, "I don't think we should just head to Bethlehem. I would like to wait until night and keep following the star. When we came here, we thought Herod would know where the child was, but he didn't. Maybe the child isn't in Bethlehem."

Another responded, "I hadn't thought about that. I agree we ought to follow the star. Are we all in agreement?"

They were.

He added, "We seem to be getting close to the end of our journey. How do you think the star will show us in which building the child is? It is one thing to follow the star in the distance and just keep going. Do you think it will sit on the roof? Will it stop over the building and shine a beam on to the roof?"

Another answered, " Our prophecy about a star appearing said the star would announce the birth of the Savior of the world. It also said some men should follow that star and greet the Savior. We prayed about that and set out on this journey. The star has continued to guide us to the spot where prophecy is being answered. We just need to continue praying and to exercise our faith. When we come to where the child is, somehow the star will show us the spot."

Since the day was about over and they were tired, they decided to wait until the following day to leave.

The next night, as they were following the star, one said, "This doesn't look like the way to Bethlehem. From the directions we

---

[19] Matthew 2:6 and JST Matthew 2:6
[20] Matthew 2:8

THE WISE MEN

received, we should be heading toward the south and we are going north. We will just have to keep following it, wherever it goes. Hopefully, it will let us know when we get there."

After several days, they approached Nazareth. They had camped not very far away and the night was still young. It was a pleasant evening, with almost a full moon.

One said, "The star seems to be getting lower in the sky and I think we are coming to a village. Do you suppose the child is here?"

After a while, another spoke, "Look, the star appears to be right over that roof. It's almost like it is sitting on top of it. I have never seen it look so low in the sky. The roof seems like it is glowing."

They approached the home with the glowing roof. "This must be the place. Let's make camp outside of town and come back during the day."

Again, the eldest spoke, "No, I think we ought to knock on their door tonight. The village is quiet and everybody seems to be asleep. If we visit during the day, everybody will see us and it will create a stir. I think it will be better for the child if we visit while it's quiet. Let's make camp away from the village and come back on foot. It is still several hours before daybreak."

After making camp and returning to Nazareth, they quietly knocked at the door. After a few minutes, a sleepy male voice asked, "Who's there?"

One of the wise men answered, "We have come from afar to worship the child."

With that, some low voices were heard, and then the door opened. A man carrying a candle stepped out and looked at them in the moonlight. "Please come in," he said. After they were in, he closed the door and said, "I'm Joseph, and this is my wife, Mary."

The wise men introduced themselves, and one of them said, "We have come from the east following a star. Prophecies foretold of a star that would arise, signaling the birth of the Savior of the world. We have followed that star to your home."

Joseph glanced at Mary and saw her mouth was agape and her eyes wide open. That's also the way he felt.

The wise man continued, "We have brought him gifts of gold, frankincense, and myrrh. May we see the child?"

THE WISE MEN

With that, Mary led them over to the corner where Jesus slept. The wise men fell to their knees and worshiped him. When they arose, they presented their gifts to Joseph and left.[21]

As Joseph closed the door, he took Mary by the hand and walked over to where Jesus was sleeping. They looked down at the sleeping child. "I keep forgetting he is the Messiah. But then something amazing like tonight happens and I realize a lot is expected of us. I hope we can do the job the Lord expects."

Mary put her hand on the back of his neck and pulled his head down, giving him a kiss. " The Lord picked the right man to raise him. I am proud of who you are." With that, she gave him another kiss.

Meanwhile, the wise men went back to their camp to get a little sleep before daylight. They arose a few hours after sunrise for breakfast. As they were sitting around the fire, one of them said, "I had a strange dream this morning. An angel appeared to me and told me we shouldn't go back and tell Herod what we found."[22]

Another said, "That's strange. I had the exact same dream."

"Me too," another said, and they returned home another way.

***

The next morning, after the visit of the wise men, when Joseph awoke, he turned to Mary and said, "I had a strange dream last night. The same angel came to me and told me I should marry you, came to me again last night. He said, 'Arise and take the young child and his mother and flee into Egypt. Be there until I bring you word, for Herod will seek the young child to destroy him.'"[23]

Mary responded, "Oh, Joseph, that's such a long way. I don't want to leave all our friends."

Joseph said, "I know how you feel, Mary. But we must keep Jesus safe. We've been given a gift from the Lord and we need to do our part. The gifts of the wise men will be useful. I have wondered why the wise men were sent to Jesus. I think the Lord wanted to tell Herod and those at his court the Messiah was here, just like he told those in Bethlehem, through the shepherds. Also, their gifts will help us get to Egypt and to be able to provide things for Jesus as he grows. If he is going to be the Messiah, he will need wise teachers. I think we will have opportunities to get things that will help him do that."

---

[21] Matthew 2:11
[22] Matthew 2:12
[23] Matthew 2:13

Mary replied, "I know you're right. We must go, but I'm not looking forward to it ... Actually, it might be kind of fun. I would like to see Egypt. After all, it is where Israel was for 400 years".[24]

Joseph told Mary, " I think we need to make our way to Egypt right away. We should pack up everything and leave tonight. Let's only tell our parents where we are going and ask them to keep it close. We need to protect Jesus. I don't want Herod sending someone after us into Egypt."

They packed their things and left for Egypt that night.

EGYPT AND HOME

After they arrived in Egypt and found a place to live, Mary and Joseph talked about what they should do. Joseph said to Mary, "I have been thinking about what we will need to raise Jesus to be the Messiah. He will need to read and learn about the prophets. I have met some very learned men here. I don't know what the situation will be when we return to Israel, and someday we must do so. To be the Messiah, I am sure Jesus will need to be in Israel. We have the gifts from the wise men to use. Depending on where we end up in Israel, it might be hard to find a good teacher for him. These men are willing to teach me and we have enough to pay for it. I could then teach Jesus and the rest of our children. If we go back to Nazareth, I don't know how we would find a teacher. Sepphoris is too far away for our children to go there and there is nobody in Nazareth that could do it, I am sure."

Mary said, "How long do you think it would take for you to get enough knowledge to be able to teach Jesus?"

Joseph said, "I am not sure, but I think somewhere around one year. I don't expect to know everything in one year, but if I can learn the basics, I can get materials from which I can continue to learn and they will be available for you and the other children also. That way we all can learn. As our children come along, we can teach them. It will be difficult, but I think I can learn and still do some work. I think we have enough money from the wise men's gifts to pay for it."

Joseph studied as well as worked for about a year, when he had another dream. When he awakened, he found Mary was already up getting breakfast. He went over to her, gave her a kiss and said,

---

[24] Genesis 15:13

EGYPT AND HOME

"I had another dream last night. The angel came again and told me, 'Arise and take the young child and his mother and go into the land of Israel. Herod and those who sought the young child's life are dead.'[25] *We should leave soon. Where do you think we should go?"*

Mary asked, "Didn't the angel say anything about where to go?"

He shook his head. "No, he just said what I told you. Go into the land of Israel."

"Joseph, I really don't want to go. We have just gotten settled and are making good friends. People are finally coming to you to make and repair things. I'm expecting again. The birth is only about three months away. It's not an appropriate time to travel."

"I know, Mary, but Jesus needs to grow up in Israel. We need to follow what the Lord tells us to do and it will work out."

Mary sighed. "That's true. We do need to follow the Lord. Since he is the Messiah, I think it would be good for Jesus to be close to Bethlehem, as it is not far from Jerusalem and it would be easy for him to go to the temple. The Messiah will need to be at the temple. That should be a good place for your work also."

Joseph replied, "Let's pray about it, but right now I think that sounds good. I am caught up with my work. In just a couple of days, I should be able to finish my backlog. I won't be able to do that project I was going to do for Abel, but he can get somebody else. I think I have learned enough so I can teach our family the things they need most and they can finish their own education."

They immediately started preparing to leave and, three days later, left. About a week after leaving, as they were camped for the evening, they were sharing a fire with another family. While their wives were cooking, the men were talking and the other man, Eliab, told Joseph, "We decided to leave Jerusalem and are moving to Egypt."

Joseph said, "That's just the opposite of what we're doing. When I heard Herod the Great was dead, we decided to return and go to Bethlehem. It is our city."

Eliab said, "I hope it works out. I know it is your city, but when Herod decided to kill all the children under two, we lost my first and only son. Because of that, we started planning to leave. When Herod died, we thought about staying. But then his son, Archelaus, took over, and we just had to get out."

---

[25] Matthew 2:20

EGYPT AND HOME

Joseph said, "We feel fortunate we left. It must be tough to put that behind you."

"It is tough. I think of my son all the time. He would be about the same age as your Jesus. I wouldn't go anywhere near Jerusalem, if I were you."

"I hear you." Joseph kicked up some dust with his sandal. "We might just go to Nazareth."

Eliab said, "You said your son was born in Bethlehem. My grandfather died about a year and a half ago. He served in the temple many years and shortly before he died, he told us he had seen the Messiah. He always told us the Messiah would be born in Bethlehem, because that is what the prophets say. He also said he thought he would live in Nazareth, because the prophets said he would be a Nazarene.[26] Nazareth can't be a very big place; maybe your son will be the Messiah."

Joseph said, "I guess we will just have to wait and see."

Later that evening Joseph told Mary what had taken place. "Can you imagine what it would be like to have the soldiers come through town, killing all the babies? Herod must have been mad. I just can't imagine anything like that. How could the Lord allow that? We must make sure nothing happens to Jesus. When he is the King, things like that won't happen."

Mary replied, "If the angel hadn't told you to return, I would turn right around and go back to Egypt. Let's go back to Nazareth. It sounds a lot safer to me than Bethlehem. Let's ask the Lord if that is the right thing to do. You had a lot of work in Sepphoris when we were living there before. It's an hour's walk and that makes for a long day. We will miss you those two hours, but it is work and the pay is good."

Joseph put his arm around her. "Mary, I think you're right about getting work there, but I don't like the place. It's not like Jerusalem. I just don't like the way the place feels, it isn't Jewish - - there are too many foreigners. I was looking forward to living in Bethlehem. It's close to Jerusalem, and I thought it would be good for Jesus to be near the temple and the place of Jewish power. Nazareth is very small; I don't see how he will ever get noticed in such a place. I don't like Sepphoris, but Herod has a castle there. Maybe that counts for something. Do you think Nazareth would be a good place to raise our kids?"

---

[26] Matthew 2:23

EGYPT AND HOME

Mary replied, "I've been thinking a lot about Jesus and this Messiah thing. I always thought the Messiah would be born in the palace, be a son of the King. With the kings we have now, I see why that doesn't work. Yet, I don't understand how Jesus is going to get from our poor village of Nazareth to be King. I guess the Lord can make that happen, if he wants. Maybe it is important to be near Sepphoris. I do think Nazareth is a good place to raise children. I don't know what will happen if Jesus is the Messiah, though. How will that affect our other children?"

"I know what you mean. I have been wondering about the same thing. I can't believe we are bringing up a king."

Mary gave birth to her second child about two months after arriving in Nazareth. They named him James. About every 18 months, another child was born. After James came Joses, then Simon, then Sara, *then Judas and* then Anna.[27]

One day, when Jesus was seven, Jesus was watching Joseph use an adze to finish a beam he was making. He watched for a while and said, "Father, may I try to do that?"

Joseph replied, "This adze is pretty big; even though you are big for your age, it will be hard to control it."

Jesus would not give up. "Please, let me try."

"Okay, you can try it, but be careful. I don't want you cutting yourself."

Jesus smiled. "Father, you know I'll be careful; I think things through and never lose my temper. I know I can do this."

"Straddle the beam and just let the adze swing freely. You hold it like this. You don't have to do it hard; you just want to take out small chips. . . That's good. The adze is a little big for you, but you're making it work. You're doing a great job."

"Father, this is fun. I want to be a carpenter just like you when I grow up," said Jesus.

That night Joseph said to Mary, "As you know, Jesus has been watching what I do and helping out a bit. Today he used the adze very well. I think he is old enough and strong enough he can do more to help me in my work. I have that project I need to install in Sepphoris. It would be very helpful to have someone to assist me there. With a little help from him, it should only take three days. As we travel there I will teach Jesus some of our history. It will be good for him as well as myself."

---

[27] Matthew 13:55-56

EGYPT AND HOME

Mary said, "That sounds great. Jesus needs to start learning more of our history and I am sure he will love the work and you will love teaching and working with him."

PART 2
THE JEWS

GENEALOGY OF ABRAHAM

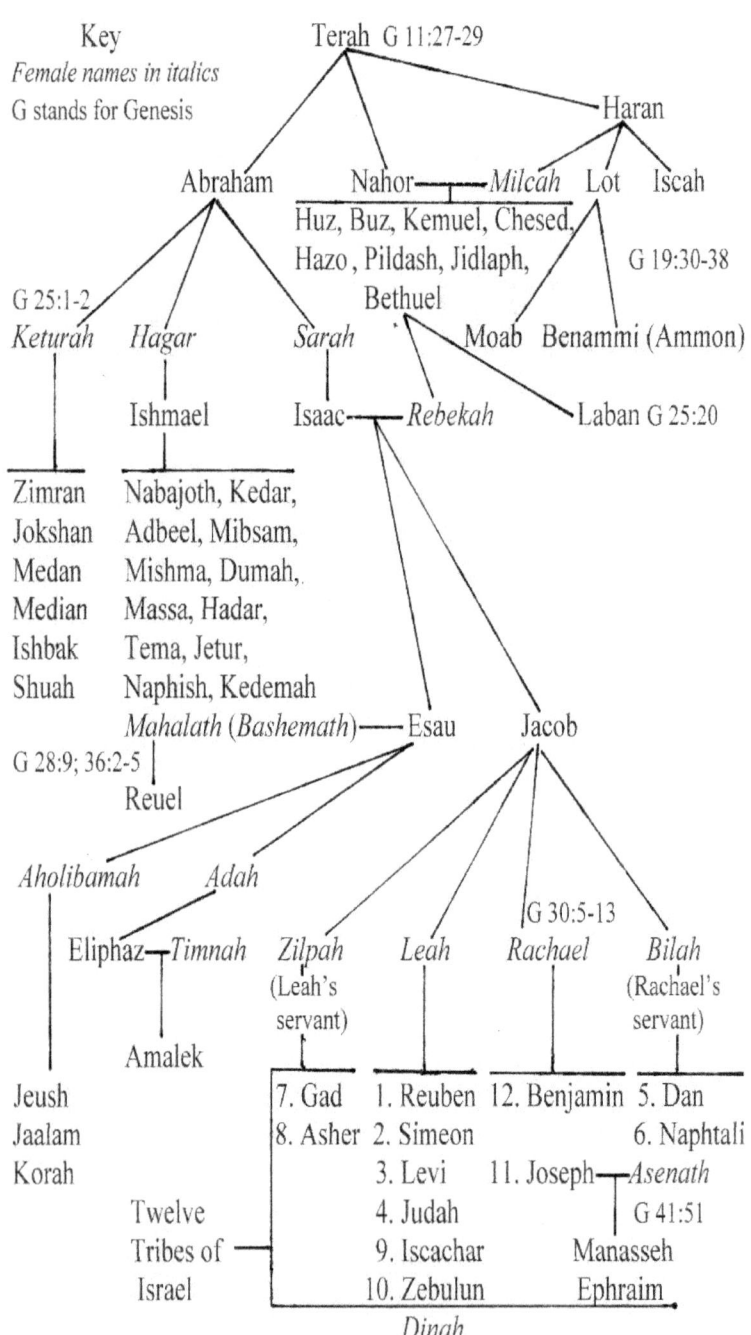

ABRAHAM

When he had a few minutes, Joseph reviewed some scrolls and planned what he would teach. A few days later, Joseph and Jesus loaded their cart and started off to Sepphoris. Joseph started his teaching.

All of us need to study the prophets, as it is one of the best ways to know about God. I have been studying hard since before you were born. You are going to need to know the prophets well. Your mother and I want to prepare you the best we can. There are scrolls you can study yourself later. But now I want to teach you a little history and about the Children of Israel and Moses. We are going to start this morning and will continue as I am able with the time we have. This work I have in Sepphoris will take three days, so it is a great opportunity to make use of our travel time.

As you know, all Jews are descended from Abraham. He lived in Ur of the Chaldeans and was the son of Terah and had two brothers, Haran and Nahor. His name was originally Abram, but God changed it to Abraham, because he was righteous and worshipped the Lord. He sought the priesthood to receive greater knowledge and be more righteous. His father, Terah, was not righteous and worshipped the Gods of Egypt to which men, women, and children were sacrificed. The priest of Elkenah wanted to sacrifice Abram on the altar and tried to tie him up, but Abram prayed to the Lord. He had a vision of God and an angel stood by him. His bands were loosened and he escaped. A voice said, 'My name is Jehovah and I have come to deliver you and take you from your father's house into another land. Because they worship the gods of Egypt and are trying to take away your life, I will destroy them. As it was with Noah, so shall it be with you. Through your ministry my name shall be known in the earth forever, for I am your God.' The Lord broke down the altars of the Egyptian gods and killed the priest.[28]

Jesus said, "I can't imagine killing children for a sacrifice to some god. How could any father do that?"

---

[1] PGP Abraham 1: 2-20

ABRAHAM

"I feel the same way, but both King Ahaz and King Manasseh did it and it is one of the reasons the Lord allowed Jerusalem to be conquered by Babylon."[29]

Joseph went back to his teaching.

After this, there was a famine in the land of Ur and Haran died from the famine. The Lord told Abram to leave and go to the land of Canaan. He took his wife, Sarai, and his nephew, Lot, the son of Haran, with him. They left and, when they came to a land they called Haran, the famine abated and they stayed there. Terah followed them to Haran.

The Lord again appeared to Abram, and promised him he would give the land of Canaan to his children, but because there was still a famine in the land, they went down to Egypt.[30]

After spending some years in Egypt, they returned to Bethel in Canaan, the land the Lord promised Abram. Both Abram and Lot were rich with livestock and the land couldn't support them. There was fighting between Lot's and Abram's herdsmen, so they decided to separate so there would be no fighting between their herdsmen.

Abram told Lot, "The whole land before us is unsettled, pick which direction you want to go and I will go the other way."

Lot looked out over the land and saw the plain of Jordan was well watered and chose to live there. He also chose to live there in Sodom, a very wicked city. They separated themselves and Abram lived in the land of Canaan.

After they were separated, the Lord said to Abram, "Look out over the land north, south, east and west. All the land which you see I will give you and your children forever. I will make them as the dust of the earth; so many they can't be counted."

A group of kings attacked Sodom and Gomorrah, capturing the people and took all their food and goods, including Lot and his family and all that he had. When Abram heard of it, he armed his trained servants and pursued the kings. He rescued Lot and his family with all their goods and returned everything he had taken. On his

---

[29] 2 Kings 21:6; 2 Chronicles 28:1-4; Jeremiah 32:35-36
[30] Genesis 12:1-16; 20:12; Abraham 1:29-31; 2:1-15

ABRAHAM

return from the battle, he was met by Melchizedek, King of Salem, with bread and wine. Melchizedek was a priest of God and Abram paid tithes to him of all he received, after returning the goods to all those to which they belonged, and Melchizedek blessed him.[31]

Jesus said, "I have heard of Lot and Abraham, but never of Melchizedek. Who was he?"
Joseph said, "Not much is known about him, but he seems to have made Salem a very righteous city. Let's go on.

Abram had a vision in which God told Abram he was pleased with him. Abram told God he was disappointed because he had no children. In fact, the steward of his house was not a relative, but Eliezer of Damascus, who he thought would be his heir. God told him Eliezer would not be his heir, but his children would be as the stars of heaven in number. Abram believed God and his faith in God was considered as righteousness. Because those living in Canaan were not totally unrighteous, he was told his children would be strangers in a land that was not theirs and serve those of that land for four hundred years. After that time, they would leave with great wealth to come back to this Promised Land. God made a covenant with Abram and said, "To your children I have given this land, from the river of Egypt to the great river Euphrates."[32]

Abram's wife, Sarai, continued to be barren. She deeply regretted this and gave her maid, Hagar, to Abram as another wife. This was an accepted custom. When Hagar found she was pregnant, she looked down on Sarai. Sarai went to Abram about this problem and asked him what she should do. Abram told her it was her maid and her problem. She dealt harshly with Hagar, who then ran away. When Hagar was by a fountain of water in the wilderness, an angel of God came to her and asked her why she was there and where she was going. She said she was running away from her mistress Sarai. The angel advised her to return and submit to Sarai, and promised her she would have a huge posterity. He also told her from her pregnancy a son would

---

[31] Genesis 13,14
[32] Genesis 15

ABRAHAM

be born and she should name him Ishmael. He would be at odds with all men and they would be at odds with him. Abram was eighty-six years old when Ishmael was born.[33]

When Abram was ninety-nine years old, God appeared to him and made a covenant with him. If Abram and his future children would keep his commandments and live righteously, he would multiply him and he would be a father of many nations. He would give him and his future children the land of Canaan where they were and which he had promised him previously, as an everlasting possession. Also, Abram would be called Abraham and his wife would be called Sarah. As a token of this covenant, all males would be circumcised when they were eight days old. God said that Sarah would have a son and be a mother of nations and kings of people would be of her.

When Abraham heard this, he laughed and said to himself, "Shall a child be born to a man who is one hundred years old and has a wife who is ninety years old?"

"God replied, 'Sarah, your wife, will indeed bear a son and you will call him Isaac. I will make my covenant with him, an everlasting covenant, and with his children after him. As for Ishmael, I have blessed him and will make him fruitful and multiply him exceedingly. I will make him a great nation. But my covenant will be with Isaac, which Sarah will have next year.'[34]

Sarah had the child at the appointed time and they called him Isaac. Abraham was one hundred when Isaac was born. Isaac was circumcised when he was eight days old.

Abraham had a great feast on the day Isaac was weaned. Sarah saw Ishmael mocking Isaac, so she went to Abraham and told him to cast out Ishmael and Hagar. This grieved Abraham, as he loved Ishmael, so he asked God if he should do it. God told him not to be grieved because of Ishmael and Hagar, but to do what Sarah had asked, because his lineage would be considered to come through Isaac. He also said he would make Ishmael a great nation, because Ishmael was his child.

Abraham got up early the next morning and gave Hagar food and water and sent her and Ishmael away. They

---

[33] Genesis 16
[34] Genesis 17

ABRAHAM

wandered in the wilderness of Beth Sheba and, when the water was gone, Hagar expected they would die. But Ishmael prayed and God heard him. An angel appeared to Hagar and showed her a well of water and told her God would make Ishmael a great nation. Ishmael grew in the wilderness and became a great archer. His mother took a wife for him from Egypt.[35]

When Isaac was a lad, the Lord tried Abraham. God called to him and told him to take his only son, whom he loved, and make a burnt offering of him on a mountain which God would show him. The next morning, Abraham rose early, along with Isaac and two of his servants. They took wood for the fire and started for the place God had told him to go. When they saw the place in the distance, Abraham had his servants wait there. He put the wood on Isaac to carry and with a knife and fire they started off.

Joseph looked up at Jesus and said, "To have Isaac carry all the wood, he must have been fairly old, probably around twelve. It must have been very hard for Abraham to do this, since he once escaped from being sacrificed by the priest of Pharaoh."

Jesus said, "My Father is asking a lot of Abraham; he must be a very special man. Go on, I would like to hear more."

Joseph went on.

Isaac asked his father, "We have fire and wood, but where is the lamb for the burnt offering?"

Abraham said, "God will provide the lamb."

When they came to the place which God had shown him, Abraham built an altar. He laid the wood in order and bound his son and laid him on the altar and took a knife to kill him.

A voice from heaven called to Abraham and told him not to kill him, because now God knew Abraham was obedient. When Abraham looked up, he saw a ram caught in a thicket by its horns. They took the ram and used it for the burnt offering instead of Isaac.

---

[35] Genesis 21:1-21

Again, the Lord called to Abraham from heaven and told him, "Because you have done this thing and have not withheld your son, your only son, I will bless you and multiply your descendants as the stars of heaven and as the sand of the seashore. Your posterity shall possess the land of their enemies and in your posterity, all the nations of the earth shall be blessed, because you have obeyed me."[36]

Sarah died when she was one hundred twenty-seven. Abraham bought a cave as a grave site for her from those who lived in the land, the sons of Heth, and they buried her there.[37]

ISAAC AND JACOB

Abraham was getting old and wished to get a wife for Isaac. He didn't want one of the Canaanites who lived there, but one of his kindred. He went to his servant, who was over all he had and asked him to swear by the Lord, the God of heaven, and the God of the earth, that he would go to get a wife for Isaac. His servant asked what he should do if the woman wouldn't come with him. Abraham told his servant this was the Lord's will and everything would work out, but if not, the servant would no longer be obligated to do more. His servant then swore he would do it.

Taking ten camels, the servant went to Nahor in Mesopotamia. When he got there, he had his camels kneel by a well in the evening when the women went to draw water. He prayed saying, "O Lord God of my master Abraham, send me good speed this day and show kindness to my master Abraham. When the daughters of the city come out to draw water, let it come to pass the young woman to whom I say, 'Would you please give me water from your pitcher, that I may drink;' will say 'Drink and I will also give your camels water.' Let her be the one you have selected for your servant Isaac. Then will I know you have shown kindness to my master."

Before he finished praying, Rebecca came, the daughter of Bethuel, a cousin of Isaac. She had a pitcher on

---

[36] Genesis 22:1-19
[37] Genesis 23

her shoulder and was a beautiful woman and a virgin. She went down to the well and filled her pitcher. As she came up from the well, the servant ran to meet her and said, "Would you please let me drink a little water from your pitcher."

She let down her pitcher and said, "Drink, my lord," and let him drink until he was finished. When he was done, she said, "I will draw water for your camels until they have enough to drink," and hurried to empty her pitcher into the trough and ran to draw water for his camels.

The servant watched and wondered if the Lord had made his journey successful. When she was done, he put a gold ring of about four ounces on her hand and gave her two bracelets of about five pounds. He asked, "Whose daughter are you? Please tell me if there is room in your father's house for us to lodge."

She said, "I am the daughter of Bethuel, the son of Milcah and Nahor (Abraham's brother). We have both straw and food for the camels and room in which to lodge."

The servant said, "Blessed be the God of my master Abraham, who has not left my master Abraham without his mercy and truth, but has led me to his family."

Rebecca hurried to her home and told them what had happened. They saw the ring and bracelets on her arms and prepared to receive guests. Laban, Rebecca's brother, ran to the well and told the servant, "Come, blessed of the Lord, we have prepared the house and have room for the camels."

The man told him, "I am Abraham's servant. The Lord has blessed my master greatly. He has become great and the Lord has given him flocks and herds, silver and gold, menservants and maidservants and camels and asses. Sarah, my masters' wife, bore a son to my master when she was old and my master has given everything to him." He proceeded to tell them of his oath and what had happened at the well, and then went on to say, "Now, if you will deal kindly with my master and give him a wife, tell me. If not, tell me, that I may do something else."

Then Laban and Bethuel said, "The thing is from the Lord, what can be said? Rebecca is here, take her and go and let her be Isaac's wife, as the Lord said."

ISAAC AND JACOB

The servant worshiped the Lord, bowing himself to the earth. He took out jewels of silver and gold and raiment and gave them to Rebecca, to her brother and to her mother, very precious things. They ate and drank and the servant spent the night.

In the morning, he said, "Let me go to my master," but Laban and her mother wanted him to wait ten days before leaving. Since the servant wanted to leave right away, Laban and her mother suggested he ask Rebecca.

They called Rebecca and asked her, "Will you go with this man now?"

She said, "I will go."

When the servant returned home, he told Isaac what he had done. Isaac brought Rebecca into his mother's tent and she became his wife and he loved her.[38]

After Sarah died, Abraham married Keturah, who bore him Zimran, Jokshan, Medan, Midian, Ishbak, and Shuah, but Abraham gave all he had to Isaac. To his other sons, he gave gifts and sent them away from Isaac. Abraham died when he was one hundred seventy-five years old, and Isaac and Ishmael buried him in the cave with Sarah.[39]

Isaac was forty years old when he married Rebecca. He and Rebecca had no children for twenty years, so Isaac prayed to the Lord and the Lord blessed them and Rebecca became pregnant. The pregnancy felt strange to her and she asked the Lord what was happening. He told her there were twins in her womb and their offspring would become two different nations. One would be stronger than the other and the older would serve the younger.

When she delivered, the first came out red all over, like a hairy garment and they called him Esau. The second had hold of his brother's heel and was called Jacob.

They grew and Esau became a cunning hunter, while Jacob was a complete man. Isaac loved Esau, but Rebecca loved Jacob. One day, Jacob made red pottage (boiled lentils). Esau came in from the field feeling hungry. He told Jacob, "Feed me some of your pottage, for I am faint from hunger."

Jacob said, "I will give it to you for your birthright."

Esau said, "If I die, of what value is my birthright?"

---

[38] Genesis 24: 1-58
[39] Genesis 25:1-10

Jacob said, "Swear to me this day you will give me your birthright for this pottage."

Esau swore to it and Jacob gave it to him.

Jesus said, "What is a birthright?"

Joseph replied, "In Abraham's day, as in ours, there is a patriarchal order. The firstborn son is the heir and inherits the responsibility of caring for the family; because of this, they inherit a double portion.[40] Under the law of Moses, the firstborn belongs to God and ordinances are provided for his redemption.[41] As is the case with Abraham and Jacob, sometimes a wife's maid also would be given a man to marry. Children of that union would be considered as children of the woman the maid served, but the birthright would go to the firstborn that was not a son of the maid. In the case of Abraham, since Ishmael was the son of Hagar, Sarah's maid, when Isaac was born, Ishmael lost his firstborn designation and it went to Isaac.[42] (Today, many Muslims who are descendants of Abraham through Ishmael believe they are heirs of the Abrahamic covenant through Ishmael,[43] but the Bible is very clear it went to Isaac.)

Jesus said, "I wonder why Esau would value his birthright for so little?"

Joseph said, "I don't know. Maybe he didn't want the responsibility that goes with it."

Joseph continued, "There was another famine in the land and Isaac thought to go to Egypt, but the Lord appeared to him and told him not to go there, but to go to Gerar and Abimelech, king of the Philistines. He said if Isaac would do this, he would be with Isaac and bless him and give him all the area around him. He would multiply his offspring as the stars of heaven and by them all the nations of the earth would be blessed. Isaac planted there and received a

---

[40] Deuteronomy 21:15-17
[41] Bible Dictionary, *Firstborn*. (1979). The Holy Bible, Authorized King James Version. Salt Lake City, UT. The Church of Jesus Christ of Latter-day Saints.
[42] Genesis 21:12
[43] Wikipedia. https://en.wikipedia.org/wiki/Ishmael. 3/17/2017

ISAAC AND JACOB

hundred-fold of what he planted. He continued to grow and became very great, with herds and flocks and servants.

When Esau was forty years old, he married Judith, a Hittite. This disappointed his parents, as they wanted him to marry within their family.[44]

When Isaac was old and couldn't see, he called for Esau. He said, "I do not know the day of my death, but I am old. Take your bow and arrows and go get a deer. Then make me my favorite meat dish and I will bless you before I die."

Esau left to go hunting.

Rebecca overheard Isaac ask Esau for this. She told Jacob about this and asked him to get two young goats from the flock. She said she would make Isaac his favorite meat dish and then he could take it to Isaac, who would bless him instead of Esau. Jacob told his mother, "Esau is hairy and I am smooth. Perhaps father will feel me and think I am trying to deceive him and curse me instead of blessing me."

His mother said, "The curse will be upon me, just obey me and fetch me the goats."

Jacob brought her the goats and she made the meat dish Isaac loved. She took some of Esau's clothes she had and Jacob put them on. Then she put goatskins on his arms and on the smooth of his neck and gave him the meat dish she had made. Jacob went to Isaac and said to him, "Father, I am here."

Isaac said, "Who are you?"

Jacob said, "I am Esau, your firstborn. I have done what you asked. Come eat of the venison I have made, that you may bless me."

Isaac said, "How is it you found it so quickly, my son?"

Jacob said, "Because the Lord your God brought it to me.'

Isaac said, "Come here, my son, that I may feel you, whether you are my very son Esau or not."

Jacob went near him and his father felt him and said, "The voice is Jacob's voice, but the hands are the hands of Esau. Are you Esau?"

---

[44] Genesis 26:1-5; 12-16; 26-35

Jacob said, "I am." Because his hands were hairy, Isaac didn't realize it was Jacob.

Isaac said, "Bring it here and I will eat of my son's venison, that my soul may bless you."

Jacob brought it to him with some wine, and he ate and drank. Isaac then said, "Come here and kiss me, my son."

Jacob came to him and kissed him. Isaac smelled the smell of his clothing and blessed him, saying, "The smell of my son is the smell of a field which the Lord has blessed. Therefore, God give you of the dew of heaven and the fatness of the earth and plenty of grain and wine. Let people serve you and nations bow down to you. Be lord over your brothers and let your mother's sons bow down to you. Cursed be every one that curses you and blessed be he that blesses you."

As soon as Isaac had finished blessing Jacob and he had scarcely left, Esau came in from hunting. He also had made his father's favorite meat dish and said to his father, "Come, my father, and eat of my venison, that your soul may bless me."

Isaac said, 'Who are you?'

Esau said, "I am your son, your firstborn, Esau."

Isaac trembled and said, "Who? Where is he that has taken venison and brought it to me? I have eaten before you came and have blessed him. Yes, and he shall be blessed."

When Esau heard this, he cried with a bitter cry and said, "Bless me, even me also, my father."

Isaac said, "Your brother came subtly and has taken away your blessing."

Esau said, "Is not he rightly named Jacob (meaning usurper). He has supplanted me these two times. He took away my birthright and now he has taken away my blessing. Have you not reserved a blessing for me?"

Isaac said, "Esau, I have made him your lord and all his brothers have I given to him for servants. With grain and wine, I have sustained him. What shall I do now for you, my son?"

Esau said, "Have you but one blessing, father? Bless me, even me also." And Esau lifted his voice and wept.

ISAAC AND JACOB

Isaac blessed him, "Your dwelling shall be the fatness of the earth and of the dew of heaven from above. By your sword, you shall live and shall serve your brother. It shall come to pass when you shall have the dominion, you shall break his yoke from off your neck."

After that, Esau hated Jacob because of the blessing and said in his heart, "When my father dies and is being mourned, I will kill my brother Jacob."

Rebecca was told of this and she called Jacob in and told him, "Esau is comforting himself with thoughts of killing you. Listen to me and flee to Laban, my brother, in Haran. Stay there until your brother's fury and anger turn away from you and he forgets what you have done. Then I will send for you. Why should I lose both of you in one day?"

Rebecca went to Isaac and said, "I don't think the daughters of Heth, which are the daughters of this land, are suitable for Jacob to marry and it would break my heart if he would marry one of them."[45]

Isaac called Jacob to him and said, "You shall not marry a daughter of Canaan. Go to Padan Aram, to the house of Bethuel, your mother's father and take a wife from one of the daughters of Laban, your mother's brother. God, bless you and make you fruitful and multiply you, that you may be a multitude, with the blessing of Abraham for you and your posterity and you may inherit the land wherein you are a stranger, which God gave to Abraham."

Isaac sent Jacob away to Laban. As he was going, he stopped to spend the night. He made a pillow of stone and lay down to sleep. He dreamed of a ladder that stretched from the earth to heaven, and he saw the angels of God ascending and descending on it. The Lord stood above it and said, "I am the Lord God of Abraham, your father, and the God of Isaac. The land where you lie, I will give to you and your posterity. They will be as the dust of the earth and you shall spread abroad to the west, the east, the north and the south. In you and in your posterity, all the families of the earth will be blessed. I am with you and will keep you in all places where you go and will bring you again into this land.

---

[45] Genesis 27

I will not leave you, until I have done all which I have spoken to you."

Jacob awoke and said, "Surely the Lord is in this place and I didn't know it. This is a sacred place, the house of God and the gate of Heaven."

He arose early in the morning and set the stone he used for a pillow as a pillar and poured oil on the top of it and called the name of the place Bethel, which means God's house. Before this it had been called Luz. Jacob made a vow saying, "If God will be with me and will keep me in the way I go and will give me food to eat and clothes to put on, so I can come again to my father's house in peace; then shall the Lord be my God. This stone, which I have set up for a pillar, shall be God's house and of all you shall give me, I will surely give the tenth to you."[46]

Jacob continued to Padan Aram and stopped at a well in a field. There were three flocks of sheep lying around it. Out of the well, they watered the flocks, and a great stone was upon the well's mouth. When all the flocks were gathered, they rolled the stone from the well's mouth and watered the sheep. When they were done, they rolled the stone back. Jacob asked them, "Where do you live?"

They replied, "Haran."

Jacob said, "Do you know Laban, the son of Bethuel, the son of Nahor (the brother of Rebecca)?"

They said, "Yes, we know him."

Jacob said, "How is he?"

They said, "He is well. Look! There is his daughter coming with the sheep."

Jacob said, "The sun is still high in the sky, it is not time the sheep should be gathered for the night. Water them that they may be fed some more."

They said, "We cannot until all the flocks be gathered together. Then the stone will be rolled away so we can water the flocks."

While he was speaking, Rachel came with her father's sheep, for she was the keeper of them. When Jacob saw Rachel and Laban's sheep, he went and rolled the stone from the well's mouth and watered the flock. He looked at Rachel and wept. He told her he was her father's brother-in-

---

[46] Genesis 28: 1-5, 10-22

law and Rebecca's son. When Rachel heard this, she ran to tell her father. When Laban heard, he ran out to meet Jacob and embraced him, kissed him and brought him to his house.

Jacob stayed with him one month and worked for him. Laban said, "You are my brother-in-law, you shouldn't work for me for free. What should your wages be?"

Laban had two daughters; the older one was Leah and the younger one Rachel. Leah wasn't very good looking, but Rachel was beautiful and Jacob loved Rachel. He told Laban, "I will work for you seven years, if you will give Rachel to me to marry."

Laban said, "It is better for me to give her to you in marriage, than to someone else. Stay and work for me."

Jacob worked for Laban for seven years for Rachel's hand in marriage and they seemed but a few days to him for his love of her. When he had worked seven years, he said to Laban, "Give me Rachel for my wife, for the seven years are up."

Laban said, *"You're right. Seven years have come and gone.* I'll invite everybody in the area and we will have a feast and celebrate the marriage." *During the wedding feast, he made sure Jacob was given wine that was made extra strong. Just as Rachel was beginning to get dressed, he brought her and Leah to him with their maids, Zilpah and Bilhah, and said, "I am going to have Jacob marry Leah tonight instead of Rachel."*

At this, Rachel said, *"Father you can't; you have promised me to Jacob. You know I love him and we have waited seven years to be married."*

Laban said, *"Rachel, be quiet. I can and I will.* You know it is the custom to marry the oldest daughter first. *This is the only way I will get a dowry for Leah. Jacob has worked for seven years for your hand, but if he is stupid enough to get so drunk he marries Leah, he will get what he deserves. I don't need your help. Leah's voice and yours are almost the same."*

He turned to Leah and said, *"I expect you to help me do this. Would you like to be married to Jacob?"*

'Jacob is a good man and he is handsome. I would love to marry him and I will do whatever you ask," she said, glancing at Rachel with a look of glee and triumph.

In a weak, plaintive voice, Rachel asked, "What will happen to me?"

Laban said, "That depends on what Jacob does. I expect to get a good dowry for you, too."

Turning to Zilpah, he said, "Dress Leah in the clothes Rachel was going to wear and put on her Rachel's bracelets and rings. Bilhah, I want you to fix Leah's hair just like you were going to do Rachel's and use her hair combs."

He turned to one of his sons and said, "Make sure this gets done. I'm going back to the party."

When it came time for the vows, Leah was brought in dressed in Rachel's clothes and wearing a heavy veil.

The ceremony was started and Laban asked, "Jacob, will you take my daughter to be your wife?"

Jacob said, "I will."

He then asked, "Daughter, will you take Jacob to be your husband?"

Leah said, "I will."

They were pronounced husband and wife. After a short time, they were led outside in the darkness to another tent that was unlit and left alone and expected to consummate the marriage.

In the morning, as the early sunlight found its way into the tent, Jacob awakened with a bad headache and turned to look at his bride. He was startled to see Leah. It only took him a moment to realize what had happened. Knowing the answer, he said, "Leah, what are you doing here?"

She said, "My husband, I have been here all night enjoying you."

Jacob gave her a scathing look and, without saying anything, jumped up, threw on some clothes, and angrily went to find Laban.

When he found Laban, he said, "What have you done to me? Didn't I serve you for Rachel? Why have you tricked me?"

Laban said, "In my country, you marry off the older, before the younger. Live with her a week, and then I will give Rachel to you for a wife and you can serve me another seven years for her."

Even though he had been tricked, Jacob could see no way out and agreed to do what Laban demanded. He spent a week with Leah, and then was married to Rachel, but Jacob loved Rachel more than Leah. Laban gave Zilpah, his maid, to Leah to be her maid, and gave Bilhah to Rachel, for her maid.

Leah conceived and had a son and named him Reuben (meaning 'look, a son'). She said, "The Lord has seen I am not loved. Now Jacob will love me."

She conceived again and had another son and said, "Because the Lord has heard I was hated, he has also given me this son," and called him Simeon (meaning hearing).

She conceived the third time and had a son again and said, "Now this time will my husband be joined in love to me, because I have given him three sons." She called him Levi (meaning joined).

Again, she conceived, and had a fourth son and said, "Now will I praise the Lord," and called him Judah (meaning praise). After Judah, she stopped conceiving.[47]

Rachel hadn't conceived and she envied her sister. She said to Jacob, "Give me children or else I will die."

Jacob got angry and said, "Do you think I am God and can withhold children from you."

She said, "There is Bilhah, my maid. Marry her and she shall give you children upon my knees, that I may have children by her."

She gave Jacob Bilhah, her handmaid, for a wife and Jacob married her. (In this time, it was customary for men to marry their wife's maid and children from the union were considered as children of the wife who had the maid.) Bilhah conceived and gave Jacob another son. Rachel said, "God has judged me and has also heard my voice and has given me a son."

She called him Dan (meaning he has judged).

Bilhah conceived again and bore Jacob her second son. Rachel said, "With great effort, I have wrestled with my sister and have prevailed." She called him Naphtali (meaning my wrestling).

When Leah saw she had stopped bearing, she gave Jacob her maid, Zilpah, to wife and they were married.

---

[47] Genesis 29

ISAAC AND JACOB

Zilpah also gave Jacob a son, and Leah said, "A troop is coming," so she named him Gad, (meaning troop or good fortune). Again, Zilpah conceived and had her second son. Leah said, "I am happy because the daughters will call me blessed," and called him Asher, (meaning happy or blessed).

During the time of wheat harvest, Reuben was in the fields and found some mandrake plants which often grow in wheat fields. Their fruit was thought to help one conceive, so he picked some for his mother, Leah. Rachel saw them and said to Leah, "Please give me some of your son's mandrakes."

Leah said to her, "You have taken my husband and you want to take my mandrakes, too?"

Rachel replied, "If you will give me some of your mandrakes, you can sleep with Jacob tonight."

When Jacob came out of the field that evening, Leah met him and said, "You must come with me, because I have hired you with mandrakes Reuben picked." He slept with her that night and God answered her prayers and she conceived, giving Jacob his fifth son. She said, "God has given me a reward, because I gave my maid to my husband." She called his name Issachar (meaning recompense).

Leah conceived again and had her sixth son. She said, "God has given me a good dowry, now my husband will live with me, because I have borne him six sons." She called him Zebulun (meaning exalted abode). Next, she had a daughter and called her Dinah.

God answered the prayers of Rachel and she conceived and had a son. She said, "God has taken away my reproach. The Lord will add to me another son." She called him Joseph (meaning to add, to take away, and to gather).

When Rachel had Joseph, Jacob said to Laban, "Send me away that I may go to my own land and to my country. Give me my wives and my children for whom I have served you and let me go. You know the service I have done for you."

Laban said to him, "Please, won't you stay here. I have found by experience the Lord has blessed me for your sake, but tell me what I owe you and I will pay it."

ISAAC AND JACOB

Jacob said, "You know how I have served you and how your livestock were with me. It was little you had before I came and it has increased to a multitude and the Lord has blessed you since my coming. When shall I provide for my family?"

Laban said, "What shall I give you?"

Jacob said, "You will not give me anything, if you will do this for me. I will again keep and feed your flock. I will go through your flock today and remove all the spotted and speckled from among the goats and all the brown from among the sheep. These shall be my wages. I will separate them from yours and in the future, to show my honesty, any that are found in my flock that are not speckled and spotted among the goats and all that are not brown among the sheep, will be counted as stolen with me."

Laban agreed to the plan and Jacob removed the ringstraked and spotted from among the goats and all that had some white on them. He took all the brown from among the sheep. The flocks of Laban and the flocks of Jacob were separated by a three-day journey and Jacob fed Laban's flocks.[48]

One day, much later, Jacob heard Laban's sons saying, "Jacob has taken away all that was our father's and because of it, he has gotten all this glory."

Jacob looked at the face of Laban and it was not like it had been before. The Lord said to him, "Jacob, return to the land of your father and to your kindred and I will be with you."

Jacob called Leah and Rachel to him in the field and said to them, "I see your father's countenance is not toward me as before, but the God of my father has been with me. You know with all my power I have served your father. He has deceived me and changed my wages ten times. But, God has kept him from hurting me. If he said the speckled shall be your wages, then they all bore speckled. If he said the ringstraked shall be your wages, then they all bare ringstraked. Thus, God has taken away those of your father and given them to me.

"I had a dream and the angel of God spoke to me and said, "Lift your eyes and see all the livestock that it is

---

[48] Genesis 30: 1-36

ISAAC AND JACOB

ringstraked, speckled and grizzled, for I have seen all that Laban has done to you. I am the God of Bethel, where you anointed the pillar and where you vowed a vow to me. Arise and get out from this land and return to the land of your kindred."

Rachel and Leah answered him, "Is there any inheritance for us in our father's house? Are we not considered strangers by him? He has sold us and has devoured our money. All the riches which God has taken from our father, is ours and our children's. Whatever God has said to you, do."

Jacob gathered all his livestock, packed his tents and all they needed and took his family and started back to Canaan and to his father, Isaac. When they were packing, Rachel stole her father's idols and, when Laban went to shear his sheep, he found them missing.

Jacob didn't tell anyone they were leaving and it wasn't until the third day after they left that Laban was told about it. When he heard they were gone, he got a group of his kindred and they went after them. It took them seven days to catch up. They both camped on Mount Gilead. That night, Laban had a dream in which he was told to be careful of how he spoke to Jacob and not to be too harsh.

When they met, Laban said to Jacob, "What are you doing? You left without telling me and have taken my daughters with a sword like a kidnapper. Why did you flee away secretly? Tell me! I would have liked to send you away with laughter, with song and music of the tambourine and lyre. I didn't get to kiss my grandchildren and say goodbye to my daughters. You have done foolishly. It is in my power to harm you, but the God of your father appeared to me last night and told me not to harm you. I know you longed to go to your father's house, but why then have you stolen my gods?"

Jacob said, "I did this because I was afraid. I thought you might by force take your daughters from me. I didn't take your idols. Search through our things and whoever has stolen them, let them be killed." Jacob didn't know Rachel had taken them.

Laban went and searched Jacob's tent and didn't find anything. Then he searched Bilhah and Zilpah's tents. Next, he went to Leah's tent without finding anything.

Lastly, he went to Rachel's tent. Rachel had hidden them in the camel's saddlebags and sat on them. Laban searched the whole tent, but didn't find anything. Rachel said, "Forgive me if I don't get up, it's my woman's time of the month."

Laban left without finding the images.

Jacob was displeased with Laban. He asked him, "What have I done wrong? Why is it you have so hotly chased me? You have searched all my stuff. What have you found of all the household stuff? Put it here before us that we may make a judgment of what is right. I have worked for you twenty years. Your ewes and goats have not lost their young. I have not eaten the rams of your flock. That which was killed by wild animals, I have not brought to you, but I have withstood the loss of them, as you required, whether stolen by day or night. I suffered in the heat of the day and the frost of the night and often went without sleep. I have been with you twenty years and have served fourteen years for your two daughters and six years for your livestock. You have changed my wages ten times. Except for the God of my father, the God of Abraham, warning you and the fear of Isaac, you would have sent me away empty. God has seen my problem and the labor of my hands and rebuked you last night."

Laban replied, "These daughters are my daughters and these children are my grandchildren and these sheep and goats are mine and all you see is mine. But there is nothing I can do today about that. Let's make a covenant and it will be a witness between you and me."

Jacob set up a stone for a pillar and they took other stones and made a pile and called it Galeed.

Laban said, 'Look at this pile and pillar which is set up between you and me. This pile and this pillar are witnesses that I will not come over this pile to you and you will not pass over this pile to me for harm. The God of Abraham, and the God of Nahor, the God of their father, judge between us.'

Jacob swore by the God of Isaac, his father, and offered sacrifice on the mountain. They ate and spent the night on the mountain. In the morning, Laban arose and kissed his daughters and grandchildren goodbye and returned home.[49]

Jacob sent messengers before him to Esau, his brother, to the land of Seir in Edom to tell him he was coming. He told them to say, "Your servant Jacob has told us to say to you, 'I have been living with Laban until now. I have oxen, asses, flocks, menservants and women servants. I am doing this to find grace in your sight.'"

The messengers returned and told Jacob, "We went to your brother, Esau, and he is coming to meet you with four hundred men."

When Jacob heard this, he was afraid and greatly distressed. He divided the livestock and people that were with him into two bands. He said, "If Esau comes to the first company and attacks it, the other company will escape."

Then Jacob prayed, "O God of my father Abraham and God of my father Isaac, the Lord, who said to me, 'Return to your country and to your kin and I will deal well with you,' I am not worthy of the least of your mercies and of all the truth you have shown to me. With my staff, I passed over Jordan and am now two bands. Deliver me, I pray, from the hand of my brother, Esau. I fear he will attack me and the mothers with the children. You said, 'I will surely do you good and make your posterity as the sand of the sea, which cannot be numbered for the multitude.'"

Jesus said, "Jacob has seen angels and the Lord has told him he will have a lot of children. Why is he so fearful? Why doesn't he believe the Lord?"

Joseph answered, "I think he believes the Lord, but sometimes it is hard to overcome our fears and it is nice to have some reassurance. It also takes a lot of faith to move ahead in life when things are difficult. Jacob was very smart in what he did next. The Lord wants us to do all we can first and then rely on him, which is just what Jacob did." He spent the night there and, in the morning, separated out a present for Esau of two hundred she goats, twenty he goats, two hundred ewes, and twenty rams. Also, thirty milk camels with their calves, forty cows and ten bulls, twenty

---

[49] Genesis 31

ISAAC AND JACOB

she-asses and ten foals. He put them into the hands of his servants, each group by itself. He said to his servants, "Go before me and put a space between each group. When Esau, my brother, meets you and asks, 'Whose are these and where are they going?' Tell him, 'They are your servant, Jacob's, and are a present to my lord Esau. Your servant, Jacob, is behind us.'" He commanded each group to say the same thing so he would appease his brother.[50]

That night he sent his family over the brook Jabbok, but he stayed behind. God appeared to him in the night and said, "Your name is Jacob, but you shall not be called anymore by that name, but by Israel. I am God Almighty and I tell you to be fruitful and multiply. A nation and a company of nations shall be from you and kings will come from you. The land which I gave to Abraham and to Isaac, I give to you and to your posterity.'

This was the same place where God had appeared to him before and Jacob had set up a pillar of stone and called it Bethel.[51]

As they rounded a small hill, Joseph said, "Look Jesus, there is Sepphoris. We will be there in a few minutes. You will find it very different from Nazareth. It has an entirely different feel."

Jesus said, "I can hardly wait. I am excited about working with you and seeing the new city. I have been to Jerusalem, but don't know anything about Sepphoris."

Joseph said, "We had better get back to Jacob:

The next day, when he saw Esau and his four hundred men in the distance, he divided the children to Leah, Zilpah, Bilhah, and Rachel, with Rachel and Joseph last. He went before them and bowed himself to the ground seven times until he got near his brother. Esau ran to meet him and embraced him and they hugged, kissed and wept.

Esau looked and saw the women and children and said, "Who are these with you?"

Israel said, "The children which God has graciously given your servant."

---

[50] Genesis 32: 1-23
[51] Genesis 35: 9-15

Then Bilhah and Zilpah came forward with their children, then Leah with hers, and then Rachel with Joseph, and they all bowed.

Esau asked, "What do you mean by all the livestock I met?"

Israel said, "These are to find grace in your sight."

Esau said, "I have enough, my brother. Keep what you have for yourself."

Israel said, "No. I pray you, if I have found favor in your sight, accept my present. I have seen your face as though I had seen the face of God and you were pleased with me. Take the blessing I brought to you. God has been good to me and I have enough."

Esau replied, 'Thank you, my brother, I will accept your gifts. Let's leave and I and my men will go in front of you."

Israel said, "My lord, you know the children are young and the flocks and herds with me have many young. If the men will drive them too hard, many will die. My lord, please go before us and I will lead out slowly after you have left, as the livestock and children can endure and travel to Seir."

Esau said, "Let me leave with you some of the men that are with me."

Israel said, "Thank you for the offer, but we can manage."

Esau said, "Very well," and Esau and his men returned to Seir.

Israel followed and made corrals for his livestock and built a house and called it Succoth, which means corrals.[52]

Later, God came to him and said, "Go up to Bethel and live there. Make there an altar to God, who appeared to you when you fled from Esau, your brother."

Israel said to his household, "Put away the idols that some of you have, change your clothes and be clean in body and spirit. Let us go up to Bethel. I will make there an altar to God, who answered me in my distress and was with me in what I did."

---

[52] Genesis 33:1-17

ISAAC AND JACOB

His household gave to Israel all the images which they had and all their earrings that were in their ears. Jacob buried them under an oak tree. They all went to Bethel, previously called Luz, in the land of Canaan

Israel built an altar there in a place he called El Bethel, because God appeared to him there when he was fleeing from Esau. There Deborah, Rebecca's nurse, died and was buried under an oak. They left and went toward Ephrath, which is Bethlehem.

On the way, Rachel went into hard labor. Her midwife said, "Don't be afraid; you will have this son also." She died and, as she was dying, she called her son Benoni (meaning son of my distress), but Israel called him Benjamin (meaning son at the right hand). She was buried and Jacob set a pillar on her grave.

They went on to Ephrath and then to the city of Arbah, which is Hebron, where Abraham and Isaac lived. On the way, Reuben went to bed with Bilhah, one of Israel's wives. Because Reuben sinned against his father, Israel disinherited him and the birthright went to Joseph.

Isaac died at the age of one hundred eighty, and Israel and Esau buried him there in Hebron.[53]

Joseph said, "Just up here is where we will be working. We are going to install the shelves and cupboards I have been making. I am sure you will enjoy doing the work. You like to make things and do nice work. Have you enjoyed what I told you on the way here?"

Jesus said, "Very much. I enjoy listening to you and learning about the prophets and what happened to them, but I am really excited to see this house and what we will be doing."

Joseph said, "Don't get too excited. The first few days we are not going to do much installing. We need to tear out the old and make room for the new. We both are going to get dirty, but you will have fun. You can take the sledge hammer and see how many swings it takes to knock the old out, but we don't want to damage them much, because I want to reuse them for the widow Moriah."

They worked hard and at the end of the day, they were both tired. After they had the cart loaded, with what they had removed they started home and Joseph said, "On the way home, I am going to tell you more about Joseph, Israel's son.

---

[53] Genesis 35

JOSEPH

Because Joseph was born when Israel was old and he was the only son of Rachel, who had died, Israel loved him more than any of his other sons and made him a long coat with sleeves. Joseph's brothers hated him because of this, and wouldn't talk to him without making fun of him. When Joseph was seventeen years old, he dreamed a dream and told his brothers about it, and they hated him even more.

He said, "Last night I had a dream; we were tying sheaves in the field. My sheave rose and stood upright. Your sheaves stood around mine and bowed to it."

His brothers said, "Do you think you are going to reign over us? Do you think you are going to tell us what to do?" and they hated him even more after this.

Again, he had a dream and told it to his brothers, saying, "I had another dream last night. This time I saw the sun, the moon and eleven stars and they all bowed down to me."

He also told it to his father, who rebuked him and said, "Shall I and your mother and your brothers all bow down to you? I don't think so." But later he remembered Jacob telling him of the dreams. His brothers envied him for the love Israel showed and hated Joseph because of it.

One day, Israel said to Joseph, "Your brothers are feeding the flock in Shechem. I want you to go to them."

Joseph said, "I'm happy to go; what do you want me to do?"

Israel said, "I want to find out how things are going. I want to know if everything is all right with the flocks and with your brothers. Go and bring me word."

Joseph left Hebron and went to Shechem looking for his brothers. A man found him wandering in a field and said, "What are you looking for?"

Joseph replied, "I am looking for my brothers, who are feeding their flock. Have you seen them?"

The man said, "They were here, but they left. I heard them say they were going to Dothan."

Joseph went to Dothan and found them. When he was some distance away, they saw him and said, "Look! Here comes the dreamer. Let's kill him and throw his body

JOSEPH

into some pit and say a wild beast killed him. We shall see what becomes of his dreams."

Reuben said, "Let's not kill him. Let there be no bloodshed but throw him into this pit here in the wilderness." He said this to save his brother.

When Joseph came to his brothers, they stripped off his new coat and put him into a pit, which was empty of water. They sat down to have lunch and when they looked up, they saw a company of Ishmaelites coming from Gilead with their camels on their way to Egypt with spices, balm, and myrrh. Judah said to his brothers, "What do we gain if we kill our brother and hide his blood? Let's sell him to the Ishmaelites. Let's not physically hurt him, for he is our brother and part of our family."

The brothers all agreed. They lifted Joseph out of the pit and sold him to the Ishmaelites for twenty pieces of silver.

They killed a goat kid and dipped the new coat into the kid's blood. They took the coat to Israel and said, "We have found this coat. Do you know if it is Joseph's?"

He knew it and said, "It is Joseph's coat. A wild beast has eaten him. No doubt, Joseph is torn to pieces."

Israel tore his clothes and put on sackcloth, as the custom was to do when there was a great tragedy (sackcloth is a material that is rough and itchy.) He mourned for Joseph many days.

The rest of his children tried to comfort him, but he wouldn't be comforted. He said, "I will go to my grave mourning for my son," and he continued to cry and mourn for his son.[54]

The Ishmaelites took Joseph to Egypt, where he was sold to Potiphar, captain of the guard and an officer of Pharaoh, the king. The Lord blessed Joseph for his righteousness and Potiphar saw the Lord was with him, as whatever he did prospered. For this reason, he made him overseer for all he had. From that time forth, all Potiphar did prospered, for the Lord blessed him for Joseph's sake. He left all his business in Joseph's hand and didn't concern himself with any business, except what he ate. The Lord continued to bless Potiphar and Joseph.

---

[54] Genesis 37:1-28, 31-36

JOSEPH

One day, Potiphar's wife came up to Joseph from the rear, put her arms around him in a big hug, and whispered in his ear, "I am really attracted to you; come to bed with me."

Joseph stepped forward, breaking the hug and said, "My master has put everything into my hands and there is none greater in this house than I am. He has not held anything back except you, because you are his wife. How could I do such an evil thing to him? Also, I would be breaking the commandments of my God."

As the days went by, she repeatedly kept trying to get Joseph to sleep with her, but Joseph continued to refuse.

One day, Joseph went into the house on business and there was no one in that part of the house, except Potiphar's wife. She grabbed his robe and tried to pull him down to the floor with her. Joseph bolted from her, leaving his robe in her hands.

He had spurned her once again and she was angry. She realized she had his robe in her hands and she yelled, 'Help! Help!' at the top of her lungs.

When some of the men came to help, she showed them Joseph's robe and said, "My husband could have hired anybody to be an overseer, but just to spite me, he hired one of those awful Hebrews. See what that Hebrew did. He tried to rape me. When I yelled for help, he ran away; he ran away so fast he left his robe."

When Potiphar came home, his wife repeated the story to him and he was livid. He had Joseph thrown in prison, where the king's prisoners were kept. But the Lord continued to bless Joseph. The captain of the guard for the prison put Joseph in charge of all the prisoners. Whatever was done there, Joseph did it. All that Joseph did prospered, because the Lord blessed him for his righteousness.[55]

Later, the butler and the baker of the king of Egypt offended their lord the king, and he was angry with them. He had them put in the prison where Joseph was, and the captain of the guard put Joseph in charge of them. After some time, the butler and the baker each had a dream the same night. In the morning, when Joseph saw them, he said, "Why are you looking sad this morning?"

---

[55] Genesis 39

JOSEPH

They said, "We each have dreamed a dream, but there is no one to interpret the dreams for us."

Joseph said, "Don't interpretations belong to God? Why don't you tell me the dreams?"

The chief butler went first and said, "In my dream I saw a vine with three branches. The three branches budded and blossoms shot forth and turned into ripe grapes. I took the grapes and squeezed the juice into Pharaoh's cup and gave it to him."

Joseph said to him, "This is the interpretation. Within three days, Pharaoh will free you and return you to your chief butler's place. You will put Pharaoh's cup into his hand as you did before when you were the chief butler. Please show me kindness and mention me to Pharaoh and free me from prison. I was stolen away out of the land of the Hebrews and have done nothing wrong that I should have been imprisoned. Don't forget to think of me when you are restored to your position."

When the chief baker saw the interpretation for the butler was good, he said, "I also dreamed about myself. I had three white baskets on my head. In the top basket were all kinds of baked items for Pharaoh, but the birds ate them out of the basket on my head."

Joseph said, "This is the interpretation. The three baskets are three days. Within three days, Pharaoh will cut off your head and hang your body on a tree and the birds will eat your flesh."

The third day was Pharaoh's birthday and he made a feast for all his servants. He restored the butler to his butlership and he gave Pharaoh his cup as before, but he forgot to tell Pharaoh about Joseph. Pharaoh hanged the baker as Joseph had interpreted.[56]

After two full years, Pharaoh dreamed a dream. He was by a river and seven cows came up out of the river. They were fat and healthy looking. They went to a meadow and started grazing. Seven other cows came up out of the river. They looked thin and sickly. They walked to the meadow and ate the seven fat cows and Pharaoh awoke.

He slept again and dreamed again. This time seven heads of grain grew up on one stalk, large and good. Seven

---
[56] Genesis 40

JOSEPH

thin heads of grain sprang up after them, thin and wind blasted. The seven thin heads devoured the seven big ones. Pharaoh awoke again and it was a dream.

In the morning, the dream troubled him; he could not get it out of his mind. He called for all the magicians and wise men of Egypt and told them of his dream, but there was no one that could interpret it. The chief butler spoke to Pharaoh and said, "I remember my faults now. You were angry with your servants and you put me and your chief baker in prison. We each dreamed a dream one night, each a different dream. In prison with us was a young man, a Hebrew, which was a servant to the captain of the guard. We told him our dreams and he interpreted them. It happened to each of us as he interpreted. He restored me to my office and the baker to hang."

The Pharaoh sent for Joseph to fetch him out of the dungeon. Joseph shaved, changed from his prison garb, and came before Pharaoh. Pharaoh said to Joseph, "I have dreamed a dream and there is no one that can interpret it. I have heard you can understand and interpret dreams."

Joseph answered, "It is not I that interpret. God will give Pharaoh his answer."

Jesus said, "Joseph has real faith and is not afraid to rely on it."

Joseph said, "That's true. You are very perceptive to have seen that."

Pharaoh said, "In my dream I stood on the bank of the river. There came up out of the river seven cows, fat and good looking. They went and fed in a meadow. Seven more cows came up after them, but they looked thin and sickly. I have never seen any in Egypt that looked as bad as those. They ate up the fat and good-looking cows and, after eating them, they were still as thin and sickly looking as they were before. Then I awoke.

"I went back to sleep and dreamed again. This time I saw seven heads of grain grow up on one stalk. They were full and good. Seven more heads of grain grew up after them. They were thin and wind blasted. The thin heads devoured the full heads. I told this to the magicians, but they couldn't tell me what the dream meant."

JOSEPH

Joseph said, "The two dreams are one. God has showed Pharaoh what he is about to do. The seven good cows are seven years and the seven good heads of grain are seven years. The two dreams are one. The seven thin cows and the seven empty heads of grain are seven years of famine. As I said, what God is about to do, he is showing to Pharaoh. There will come seven years of great plenty throughout all of Egypt and after them will come seven years of famine. All the years of plenty will be forgotten in the land of Egypt and the famine shall consume the land. The good years will not be remembered, because the famine following will be so hard. The dream was doubled to Pharaoh, because it is God's plan and he will soon bring it to pass.

"Now, let Pharaoh look for a man that is knowledgeable and wise and put him in charge throughout the land of Egypt. Have him appoint officers over the land and gather up a fifth of the harvest in the years of plenty and store it in the cities. This will provide for the people in the years of famine, that those in the land don't starve."

This sounded good to Pharaoh and he said to his servants, "Can we find anyone as good as this man, one in who is the Spirit of God?"

Pharaoh said to Joseph, "Since God has shown you all this, there is none as knowledgeable and wise as you are. You shall be over my house and by your word shall all my people be ruled; only in the throne will I be greater than you."

Pharaoh took off his ring and put it on Joseph's hand, dressed him in fine linen and put a gold chain around his neck. He made him ride in the second chariot and they cried before him, "Bow the knee." He made him ruler over all the land of Egypt. Pharaoh called Joseph "Zaphnath-Paaneah" and he gave him Asenath to be his wife, who was the daughter of Potipherah, priest of On. At the age of thirty, Joseph was ruler over all of Egypt.

In the seven plenteous years, the land yielded food by the handfuls. Joseph gathered it up throughout Egypt and stored it in the cities close to where it was grown. He gathered grain like the sand of the sea; there was so much they stopped counting it.

During the time of plenty, Joseph's wife, Asenath,

bore him two sons. The first was Manasseh and the second Ephraim. When the seven years of plenty ended, the seven years of famine started, as Joseph had said. The famine was in all the lands around Egypt, but in Egypt there was food. When the crops failed, they asked Pharaoh for food and he told them to go to Joseph and do whatever he says. Joseph opened the storehouses and sold food to those who needed it.[57]

When Israel saw there was food in Egypt, he said to his sons, "Why do you look at one another like you don't know what to do? I have heard there is food in Egypt, go down and buy food for us that we may live and not die."

Ten of Joseph's brothers went to Egypt to buy food, but they left Benjamin at home, because Israel was worried something might happen to him. Joseph was the governor, and it was he that sold to the people of the land. Joseph's brothers came to him and bowed down themselves before him. Joseph saw them and knew them, but he didn't want them to recognize him, so he tried to make his voice different and disguise himself. He spoke roughly to them through an interpreter, saying, "Where do you come from?"

Joseph's brothers didn't recognize him. He said to them, "You are spies. To find out the weakness of this country you have come."

They said, "No, my lord. Only to buy food are your servants come. We are all brothers, the sons of one man. We are honest men and true. We are not spies."

He said, "No! To find out the weakness of the country you have come."

They said, "We are twelve brothers, the sons of one man, from the land of Canaan. Our youngest brother is with our father in the land of Canaan and one has died."

Joseph said, "You are spies, as I said before. This is the way I will know if you are telling the truth. One of you go home and fetch your younger brother. I will keep the rest of you here in prison until your younger brother comes. If you won't do this, surely you are spies."

He put all of them in prison for three days. The third day, he went to them and said, "Do this and live, for I serve God. If you are honest men, let one of you stay in prison

---

[57] Genesis 41

JOSEPH

and the others take food to your home for the famine. Then bring your youngest brother to me. Thus, will your story be verified and you shall not die." They said to one another, "We are guilty concerning our brother. We saw his anguish when he pleaded for his freedom, but we didn't listen to him. That is why this has come on us.

Reuben said, "Didn't I say to you not to do that to him? But you wouldn't listen. Now we have to pay the price."

Joseph went a distance away from them and wept. They didn't realize Joseph could understand what they were saying. Drying his eyes, he returned and talked some more with them through the interpreter, and then bound Simeon in front of them.

Joseph commanded his servants to fill the brother's sacks with grain and to put each brother's money into the sack. He also commanded them to provide provisions for the trip home. On the way home, one of the brothers opened his sack to give his ass some grain and saw his money in the sack on top of the grain. He said, "My money is in my sack." They were faint-hearted and afraid, because they knew they would probably have to go back someday.

When they got back to Canaan, they told Israel all that had happened to them. When each brother opened his sack, he found his money in the sack. Again, they were fearful, knowing they might have to go back to Egypt for more food. Also, they couldn't go back without Benjamin. Israel said, "I am bereaved of my children. Joseph and Simeon are dead and now you will take Benjamin."

Reuben said, "Let me take Benjamin and I will bring him back safe and sound. Kill my two sons if I don't."

Israel said, "Benjamin will not go to Egypt with you. His brother is dead and he is the only son of Rachel I have. If something should happen to him and I would lose him too, it would bring me down to the grave."[58]

The famine continued and they used up all the food they had brought from Egypt. Israel said, "Go to Egypt and buy us some more food."

Judah said, "The Egyptian said, 'You shall not come to see me, unless your brother is with you.' If you will

---

[58] Genesis 42

send Benjamin with us, we will go and buy food. If not, we will not go, because he said we had to bring our brother. The man asked us about our family. He said, 'Do you have another brother? Is your father yet alive?' We answered truthfully. How would we have known he would say, 'Bring your brother down to me?' Send Benjamin with me and we will go, that we may live and not die; we, you and our little ones. I will be surety for him. If I don't bring him home to you, then let me bear the blame forever. If we had not lingered, we could have been home by now."

Israel said to them, "I see it must be done. Take of the best fruits we have and make the man a present, a little balm, a little honey, spices, myrrh, almonds, and other nuts. Also, take double money. The money that was placed in your sacks could have been an oversight. Take your brother and go down to the man, that he might release Simeon. God Almighty give you mercy before him. If I am bereaved of my children, I am bereaved."

The brothers took the present, double money, Benjamin, and went to Egypt.

When they stood in front of Joseph, Joseph saw Benjamin and told the servant over his house to take the brothers to his house and prepare a meal, because he would eat with them at noon.

The servant did as he was told and brought the brothers to Joseph's house. The brothers were concerned about this and thought it had something to do with the money being returned in the sacks. They were afraid Joseph might be planning to harm them in some way, so they went up to the servant and said, "Indeed we came down the first time to buy food, but when we came to the inn and opened our sacks we found our money in the sacks, all our money, every bit of it. We have brought it back with us. We have brought other money to pay for the food. We have no idea how the money got to be in our sacks."

The servant said, "Don't be afraid, your God and the God of your father has given you the money. I had your money."

Then he brought Simeon out to them. He brought the brothers into Joseph's house and gave them water and they washed their feet. He also fed their asses and told them they would eat with Joseph when he came home at noon.

JOSEPH

They made ready their present to give to Joseph. When he came, they bowed themselves to him down to the earth. Joseph asked them, "How are things going at home? Is your father still alive?"

They answered, "Your servant, our father, is in good health and still alive." They bowed again and made obeisance.

Joseph looked up and saw Benjamin and said, "Is this your younger brother of whom you spoke to me?"

They said, "Yes."

He said, "God be gracious to you, my son." He then rose hurriedly and went into another room, where he wept. After he recovered, he washed his face and went out to them and said, "Let's eat."

Joseph ate by himself, the brothers by themselves and the Egyptians by themselves. It was against the customs of the Egyptians to eat with a Hebrew. They served the food to each of the brothers by his birthright, starting with the oldest down to the youngest. This amazed the brothers, as they had not told anyone their birth order. Benjamin was served five times as much food as any of the other brothers. They all drank and had an enjoyable time.[59]

Joseph commanded the steward of his house to fill the brothers' sacks with as much food as they could carry. He also said to put their money into their sacks and to put his silver cup into the sack of the youngest with his money. His steward did as he was commanded.

The next day, when dawn broke, the brothers left. A little later, Joseph said to his steward, "Follow those men and ask them, 'Why have you rewarded evil for good by stealing my master's silver cup? It is what my master drinks from and uses to divine. You have done evil in stealing it.'"

The steward left and caught up with the brothers and told them what Joseph had commanded. The brothers replied, "God forbid we, your servants, should do such a thing. We brought back the money we found in our sacks in Canaan. Why then would we steal out of thy lord's house silver or gold? Whomever the cup is found with, let him die and we also will be your lord's bondmen."

---

[59] Genesis 43

The steward replied, "As you said, let it be, except whom it is found with will be my servant and the others will be blameless." He started searching the bags with the oldest, down to the youngest, where it was found in Benjamin's sack.

The brothers tore their clothing as a sign of distress, loaded their things and returned to the city. Judah and his brothers went to Joseph's house, and he was still there. They fell before him on the ground.

Joseph said, "What have you done? Didn't you know such a man as I am can certainly divine?"

Judah said, "What can we say? How can we clear ourselves? God knows our sins. We are your servants, both we and Benjamin."

Joseph replied, "God forbid you should be my servants. Only he that had the cup shall be my servant. Get up and go to your father in peace."

Then Judah came near him to speak, "My lord, let me speak a word to you and don't be angry with me, for you are as Pharaoh. You asked us if we had a father or a brother at home. We said we had a father, an old man, and a child of his old age. His brother is dead and he is the only son of his mother. His father loves him dearly. You told us last time, when we returned, to bring him with us. We told you the lad cannot leave his father, for if he should, his father would die. Then you said, if you don't bring him with you, don't bother to come. When we returned to our father, we told him what you said. Our father told us to come back again to buy some more food. We told him we wouldn't come again unless we brought our youngest brother. Our father said, 'You know my wife bore me two sons. One is surely torn in pieces and I haven't seen him since. If you take this other from me and something happens to him, that will bring me down to the grave.'"

He continued, "Now if we go home without him, when our father sees he is not with us and since his life is bound up in the lad's, our father will die. We will have brought him down to the grave with sorrow. I told my father I would be surety for my brother. I said, 'If I don't bring him back, I shall bear the blame forever.'

"Let me be a bondman to my lord instead of the lad and let him return with my brothers to our father. How can

JOSEPH

I return to my father, if the lad is not with me? I couldn't bear to see the evil that would come."[60]

At this, Joseph could no longer contain his love for his brothers and he started to cry. He asked all the servants to leave the room and then he said to his brothers, "I am Joseph. Is my father still alive?"

His brothers did not answer because they were surprised and didn't know what to think.

Joseph then said, "Come here near to me." And they did.

He said, "I am Joseph, your brother, who you sold into Egypt. Don't be unhappy with yourselves or concerned about selling me here. God sent me before you to preserve life. For two years, the famine has been in the land and yet there are five years in which crops shall not be grown or harvested. God sent me before you to preserve you and your posterity and to save your lives by a great deliverance. So, it was not you that sent me here, but God. He has made me a father to Pharaoh and lord of his entire house and a ruler throughout all of Egypt. Hurry and go up to my father and tell him I am alive, and God has made me lord of all of Egypt. He wants you to hurry and come down to him in Egypt. You will live in the land of Goshen and be near me. You and your children and your grandchildren, your flocks and herds, and all you have. There I will nourish you, lest you come to poverty, for there are still five years of famine left."

He went on, "I see in your eyes and the eyes of my brother, Benjamin, you know it is I, Joseph, that is speaking to you. You shall tell my father of all my glory in Egypt and of all you have seen. You shall hurry and bring my father here."

He put his head on Benjamin's neck and wept and Benjamin wept. He kissed all his brothers and they wept together. After that, his brothers talked with him.

The news that Joseph's brothers had come spread rapidly and Pharaoh heard it. It pleased him as well as his servants. He told Joseph to tell his brothers, "Load your animals and go to the land of Canaan and bring your father and his household to me. I will give you the good of the land

---

[60] Genesis 44

of Egypt and you shall eat of the fat of the land. I command you to take wagons out of Egypt for your little ones and for your wives and bring your father and come. You don't have to worry about your things for the good of all the land of Egypt is yours."

Joseph gave his brothers wagons and provisions for the way as Pharaoh commanded. He gave each man a change of clothes, but to Benjamin, he gave three hundred pieces of silver and five changes of clothes. To his father, he sent ten asses loaded with all the good things of Egypt and ten she-asses loaded with grain, bread, and meat for his father by the way. He sent his brothers away with the warning not to have an argument and falling out on the way home.

When they got home, they told Israel, "Joseph is alive and is governor over all of Egypt."

He wouldn't let himself believe it. When they told what had happened and showed him all the wagons and goods he had sent, his spirit revived and he said, "It is enough. Joseph is yet alive. I will go and see him before I die."[61]

Israel left on his Journey with all he had. When he came to Beer Sheba, he offered sacrifices to the God of his father Isaac. In a vision that night, God spoke to him and said, "Jacob, Jacob."

Jacob said, "I am here."

God said, "I am God, the God of your father. Don't be afraid to go to Egypt, for there I will make of you a great nation. I will go down with you into Egypt and be with you and your posterity. Your posterity will certainly return to Canaan. Joseph will care for you in Egypt until you die."

Israel continued and sent Judah ahead to meet Joseph, so they could be directed to Goshen. When Judah met him, Joseph went up in his chariot to meet his father. When they met, they hugged and each wept.

Israel said, "Now I have met you, I can die in peace, because you are still alive."

The years of famine continued, and Joseph fed his family as they needed. There was no food in all the land of Egypt, except that which was stored by Joseph. Joseph sold

---

[61] Genesis 45

JOSEPH

the food for money and brought the money to Pharaoh until the money failed in Egypt and Canaan.

The people came to Joseph and said, "Give us food that we don't die, but we have no money."

Joseph then traded food for their horses, their flocks, their asses and their cattle that year. The next year they came to Joseph and said, "We have no money and no animals. All that is left is our bodies and land. We will sell our bodies and land for food and seed that we don't die.'"

Because of the famine, all Egypt sold their land to Pharaoh, except the priests, because they had food provided to them by Pharaoh.

Joseph told the people, "I have bought you and your land for Pharaoh. Here is seed for you, go sow it. Give one-fifth of the increase to Pharaoh, the rest shall be yours."

The children of Israel lived in the land of Egypt, in Goshen, and built their homes there. Their numbers grew rapidly. Israel lived fifteen years there until he died at one hundred and forty-seven years of age. When he saw he would soon die, he said to Joseph, "If you would be so kind, swear to me when I die you won't bury me in Egypt, but bury me with my fathers in Canaan."

Joseph swore he would do it.[62]

One day, they told Joseph his father was sick. He took his sons, Manasseh and Ephraim, to see him. Israel was told they were on their way, so he prepared himself and sat up on the bed. When Joseph arrived, his father said, "God Almighty appeared to me at Luz in the land of Canaan and blessed me. He said, 'I will make you fruitful and multiply you and I will make you a multitude of people. I will give this land to you and your posterity for an everlasting possession.' Your two sons, Ephraim and Manasseh, which were born to you in Egypt, I will adopt and they will be mine, as Reuben and Simeon are mine, with all the blessings pertaining thereto. Any other children you have will be yours and be called after the name of their brothers in their inheritance."[63]

"When the God of my fathers appeared to me in Luz, he swore to me he would give to me and my posterity the land for an everlasting possession. Thus, he has blessed

---

[62] Genesis 47
[63] Genesis 48: 1-6

me in raising you up to be a servant to me, in saving my house from death and in delivering my people, your brothers, from famine which was sore in the land. Wherefore, the God of your fathers shall bless you and your posterity. They shall be blessed above your brothers and above your father's house. You have prevailed and your father's house has bowed down to you, even as it was shown to you before you were sold into Egypt by your brothers. Wherefore, your brothers shall bow down to you and your posterity from generation to generation forever. You shall be a light to my people to deliver them from bondage in the days of their captivity and to bring salvation to them when they are altogether bowed down under sin."[64]

Israel's eyes were dim with age, so he could not see well. He saw Joseph's sons and asked, "Who are these?"

Joseph said, "They are my sons, who God gave me in this place."

Israel said, "Bring them here and I will bless them."

Joseph brought them to him, and Israel kissed them and hugged them. He said to Joseph, "I thought I would never see you again and now God has shown me your children."

Joseph moved Ephraim in his right hand toward Israel's left hand and Manasseh in his left hand toward Israel's right hand. Israel stretched out his right hand and laid it upon Ephraim's head, who was the younger, and put his left hand upon Manasseh's head, crossing his hands wittingly, as Manasseh was the firstborn.

He started to bless them. "God, before whom my fathers, Abraham and Isaac walked, the God who fed me all life-long to this day, the Angel which redeemed me from all evil, bless the lads and let my name be named on them, the name of my fathers, Abraham and Isaac and let them grow into a multitude amid the earth."

It displeased Joseph when he saw his father laid his right hand on the head of Ephraim and he held up his father's hand to move it from Ephraim's head to Manasseh's head. He said, "Not so, my father, this is the firstborn, put your right hand on his head."

His father said, "I know it, son. I know it. He also

---

[64] JST Genesis 48: 7-11

shall become a people and he also shall be great, but truly his younger brother shall be greater than he and his posterity shall become a multitude of nations."

He finished his blessing saying, "In you shall Israel be blessed. God make you as Ephraim and as Manasseh" and he put Ephraim before Manasseh.

He said to Joseph, "I am dying, but God shall be with you and bring your progeny again to the land of your fathers. I have given to you one portion more than your brothers, which I took out of the hand of the Amorite with my sword and with my bow."[65]

Israel called his sons to his bedside, saying, "Gather yourselves together so I can tell you what will happen to you in the last days."

Jesus, Israel blessed each of his sons. Some of them are hard to understand today. *I think they are very interesting, but I think they are something you can study on your own later. I think those for Joseph and Judah are the most important. Perhaps, it is because my name is Joseph I think he is important and we are of the tribe of Judah, so Judah's is important to us.*

He told Judah, "You will be praised by your brothers. Your hand will be on the neck of your enemies. Your father's children shall bow down before you. Judah is a lion's cub, from the prey, my son, you are gone up. He stooped down; he couched as a lion and as an old lion. Who shall rouse him up? The scepter shall not depart from Judah or a law-giver from between his feet, until Shiloh comes. To him shall the gathering of the people be. Tying his foal to the vine and his son's colt to the choice vine, he washed his clothes in wine and his clothes in the blood of grapes; his eyes shall be red with wine and his teeth white with milk."[66]

"Judah is obviously a good man. It shows in his willingness to take the place of Benjamin and be a slave to Joseph. So, he will be praised. The Lord is showing Israel a vision of the future. He will overcome his enemies, because he will have them by the neck. I think in the rest of it he is comparing Judah to a fierce lion, the king of the jungle. First, he is young, the cub. Then he is a teenager and gets the prey. He gets older and stoops and sleeps. Who will rouse him up? He is still a fierce lion and somebody or something will need to rouse him in the end, so Judah can be kept strong. A scepter is a

---

[65] Genesis 48:7-22
[66] Genesis 49:8-12

symbol of authority, so Judah will be in charge which is borne out in our history, as most of us living here are descended from him. When our children are young and shy, they tend to stay between our feet. Next, I think he is saying a lawgiver or ruler shall not stop being over Judah until this Shiloh comes. I don't know who Shiloh is, maybe it is the Messiah, you. But then why would the scepter depart? I don't know. I am going to go on to Joseph.

"Joseph is a fruitful bough, even a fruitful bough by a well with branches running over the wall. The archers have greatly distressed him, shot at him and hated him. But his bow kept its spring and his arms and hands were made strong by the hands of the mighty God of Jacob from who comes the Savior. Even by the God of your father, who shall help you and by the Almighty, who shall bless you with blessings of heaven above, blessings of the deep that lies under, blessings of the breasts and of the womb. The blessings of your father have prevailed over the blessing of my fathers, to the utmost bound of the everlasting hills. They shall be on the head of Joseph and on the crown of the head of him that was separate from his brothers.[67]

"Joseph is fruitful. Israel blessed him with the blessings of the breasts and the womb and said he was a fruitful bough. He has fruitful branches running over a wall by a well. That certainly means he will have a posterity elsewhere separated from the rest of the family. A well signifies water and a wall a boundary. So, the branch is separated by a large body of water. The archers have shot at him, but not hurt him and they hate him. Israel might be talking about Joseph's brothers here, but I think he is talking about others. Joseph must have a lot of enemies someplace, but he has stayed strong and they can't destroy him, because he is made strong by his God. He gave Joseph more blessings than did his fathers; everlasting blessings on not only those in the land of Israel, but also on those that are on the other side of the water."

What do you think of these, Jesus?"

Jesus frowned, deep in thought. *"I think these are more prophecies than blessings, though blessings are mentioned in Joseph's. It is interesting that these were given many years ago and today it is still true about Judah, but I don't think we know where the tribe of Joseph is today."*

Joseph said, *"Nor do I know about the tribe of Joseph. If they exist today, they are obviously separated from Judah, because*

---

[67] Genesis 49:22-26

JOSEPH

we don't know where they are. Maybe they are out there somewhere across some water. Let's continue on with Israel." (If you go to the section "Christ and the Nephites," you will find where the tribe of Joseph is today.)

He said, "I want to be buried with my people in the cave that is in the field of Ephron the Hittite. It is in the field of Machpelah before Mamre in the land of Canaan. Abraham bought the field of Ephron the Hittite for a burying place. Buried there are Abraham and Sarah, his wife, Isaac and Rebecca, his wife, and there I buried Leah. The purchase of the field and of the cave that is there was from the children of Heth." When Israel finished commanding his sons, he lay down on the bed and died. [68]

Joseph hugged his father and wept on him and kissed him, then commanded his physician servants to embalm his father, and they did so. Embalming takes forty days, which was the time of mourning for the Egyptians. When the days of mourning were over, Joseph spoke to Pharaoh, saying, "If it pleases you, my father made me swear to him I would bury him in the land of Canaan. Let me go bury my father and I will return."

Pharaoh said, "Go bury your father as he made you swear to do."

When Israel died, his brothers were worried Joseph would take revenge on them for selling him into Egypt. They sent a messenger to him saying, "Your father commanded us before he died to tell you, 'Forgive the trespass of your brothers, for they did you a great evil. Please forgive them the sin they did.'"

Joseph wept when he heard that.

His brothers then went to see him and they bowed down to the ground to him and said, "We are your servants."

Joseph said, "Don't be afraid. Am I God? You thought evil against me, but God turned it to good, to save many people's lives, as it is today. Don't be afraid, I will nourish you and your little ones." He spoke kindly to them and comforted them.

Joseph lived to a hundred and ten. He lived to see Ephraim's children of the third generation and Machir, Manasseh's son. His children were raised on his knees.

---

[68] Genesis 49:29-33

He said to his family, "When I die, God will surely bring you out of this land to the land which he swore to Abraham, Isaac, and Jacob." Joseph had them swear to take his bones with them when they went.[69]

At this point, Joseph said to Jesus, "We are getting close to home and I think that is enough for today. Would you like to hear more tomorrow?"

Jesus said, "Yes, please, Father. I have enjoyed learning about Abraham, Isaac, and Israel."

"Good! Tomorrow I want to tell you about Moses. He was a great prophet and did many miracles. I think you will enjoy learning about him and Israel. You won't believe how slow Israel is to learn about the Lord."

MOSES AND THE MIRACLES

The next day as they started for Sepphoris, Joseph commenced telling Jesus about Moses. The children of Israel were very fruitful and multiplied, becoming a large group of people, more populous than the native Egyptians. After Joseph died, a new Pharaoh arose over Egypt who did not know him. He said, "The children of Israel are more populous and stronger than we and, if a war comes, they may fight against us. Let's be wise and prevent that." So, they made the Israelites slaves who built treasure cities for Pharaoh, Pithom, and Ramses. Their lives were difficult with hard bondage, as they worked with mortar and brick.

The Pharaoh spoke to the two Hebrew midwives and said, "When you act as a midwife to the Hebrew women and they are giving birth and a son is born, kill him. If it is a girl, let her live."

The midwives loved God and did not do what the Pharaoh commanded, but saved the males. He asked the midwives, "Why haven't you done as I commanded."

They said, "Because the Hebrew woman are not as the Egyptian women, but are toughened with work and, before we can get there, have already delivered."

---

[69] Genesis 50

The midwives were blessed and the people continued to multiply.

Pharaoh commanded the Hebrews, "Every son that is born shall be thrown in the river and every daughter saved."[70]

A woman and a man of the house of Levi married and had a son. He was a goodly child and she hid him three months. When she could no longer hide him, she made a basket of bulrushes, daubed it with slime and pitch and put the child in it. She placed it in the river among reeds and had his sister, *Miriam,* stand some distance away to see what would happen.

The daughter of Pharaoh came down to the river to wash. She walked along the river with her servants and, when she saw the basket among the reeds, she had one of her maids fetch it. When she opened it, she saw the child and he was crying. She felt sorry for the baby and said, "This is one of the Hebrew's children."

The baby's sister came up to her and said, "Shall I go and get a nurse of the Hebrew woman to nurse the baby for you?"

Pharaoh's daughter told her to do that and she went and got her mother. The mother came to Pharaoh's daughter, who told her, "Take this baby away and nurse it for me, and I will pay you." His mother took him and nursed him.

The child grew and she brought him to Pharaoh's daughter and he became her son. She called him Moses, which means 'to draw out' in Hebrew, because she said, "I drew him out of the water."

*Moses knew he was adopted and of Hebrew lineage. One day, w*hen he was grown, *he was curious* and went out to see his people and saw what they had to do as slaves. He saw an Egyptian hitting one of the Hebrews. He looked around and, when he didn't see anybody, he killed the Egyptian and hid his body in the sand. When he went back the next day, two Hebrew men were fighting. He said to the one that was in the wrong, "Why did you hit this man?"

---

[70] Exodus 1

MOSES AND THE MIRACLES

The man asked him, "Who made you a prince and a judge over us? Are you going to kill me, as you killed the Egyptian?"

When he heard this, Moses was afraid, because he thought his crime must be known and he fled to the land of Midian. When Pharaoh heard about it, he sought to kill Moses, but he couldn't find him.

In Midian, Moses sat down by a well. The priest of Midian had seven daughters and they came and drew water and filled the troughs to water their father's flock. When they were filled, other shepherds came to drive them away to water their flock. Moses didn't think that was right and helped the daughters to water their flock. When they went home to their father, Jethro, he said, "Why are you home so soon?"

They said, "An Egyptian saved us from the shepherds and drew water and helped to water the flock."

Their father said, "Where is he? Why did you leave him? Call him that he may eat with us."

They invited him to their home and Moses was content to live there with Jethro. Jethro gave him his daughter, Zipporah, for his wife. She bore him a son and he called him Gershom, which means, "a sojourner there," because he had been a stranger in a strange land.

After a while, Pharaoh died and the Israelites were very unhappy because of their bondage. They cried to God and he heard their cries and remembered the covenant he had made with Abraham, Isaac, and Jacob.[71]

Moses was keeping the flock of Jethro, his father-in-law, the priest of Midian, and had led the flock to the backside of Horeb, the mountain of God. He saw a bush burning, but it was not consumed. He decided to go see why the bush was not destroyed by the fire. When he started toward the bush, God called to him out of the midst of the bush and said, "Moses, Moses."

Moses said, "I am here."

God said, "Don't come here, but take off your shoes, for where you stand is holy ground. I am the God of your father, the God of Abraham, the God of Isaac and the God of Jacob."

---

[71] Exodus 2

Moses covered his face, because he was afraid to look on God.

God went on, "I have seen the affliction of my people in Egypt, have heard their cry because of their taskmasters, and I know their sorrows. I have come down to deliver them from the Egyptians and to bring them out of that land to a good land and a large one. A land flowing with milk and honey, to the place of the Canaanites, Hittites, Amorites, Perizzites, Hivites, and Jebusites. I hear the cry of the children of Israel and see the oppression with which the Egyptians oppress them. I will send you to Pharaoh so you can bring my people, the children of Israel, out of Egypt."

Moses said, "Who am I, that I should go to Pharaoh to bring the children of Israel out of Egypt?"

God said, "I will certainly be with you, and this burning bush shall be a token to you that I have sent you. When you have brought the people out of Egypt, you shall serve God upon this mountain."

Moses said, "When I come to the children of Israel and they ask me who has sent me, what shall I say?"

God said, "You shall say, 'I AM has sent me. He is the Lord God of your fathers, the God of Abraham, the God of Isaac and the God of Jacob.' This is my name forever and is my memorial to all generations. Gather the elders of Israel together and tell them, 'The Lord God of your fathers, the God of Abraham, of Isaac and of Jacob has visited you and has seen what has been done to you in Egypt. He will bring you out of the affliction of Egypt to the land of the Canaanites, Hittites, Amorites, Perizzites, Hivites, and Jebusites, a land flowing with milk and honey.'

"They will listen to you and follow you. You and the elders of Israel shall go to the king of Egypt and you shall tell him, 'The Lord God of the Hebrews has met with us and now let us go three days' journey into the wilderness, so we may sacrifice to the Lord our God.'

"I am sure the king won't let you go, no, not by a mighty hand. I will stretch out my hand and smite Egypt with all my wonders, which I will do in the sight of all, and after that, he will let you go. I will cause the Egyptians to honor and fear my people, that when you leave, you will not go empty. But every woman shall borrow of her Egyptian

MOSES AND THE MIRACLES

neighbors, jewels of silver and gold and clothing. You shall put them on your sons and daughters and you shall spoil the Egyptians."[72]

Moses said, "They will not believe me, but will say I did not see you."

The Lord said, "What is in your hand?"

"A rod."

"Toss it on the ground."

Moses tossed it on the ground and it became an asp, and he ran from it.

The Lord said, "Pick it up by the tail."

Moses obeyed and it became a rod in his hand.

The Lord said, "Do this, so they will believe the Lord God of their fathers, the God of Abraham, Isaac, and Jacob has appeared to you. Put your hand on your chest under your clothing."

Moses did and, when he pulled it out, his hand was leprous as snow.

The Lord said, "Put your hand to your chest again."

Moses did and, when he pulled it out, it was normal.

The Lord continued, "If they will not believe you after the first sign, they will believe you after the next sign. If they will not believe you after these two signs, then you will take water from the Nile and pour it on to the dry land. The water you take out of the Nile shall become blood upon the dry land."

Moses said, "I have never been eloquent and have a speech impediment."

The Lord said, "Who made man's mouth? Or who makes the dumb or deaf or the seeing or blind? Have not I the Lord? Now, go and I will be with your mouth and teach you what you shall say."

Moses argued, "My Lord, please, send someone else. They will be able to do it."

The Lord's anger was kindled against Moses and he said, "Aaron the Levite is your brother! I know he can speak well. He will come to meet you and, when he sees you, he will be glad. You shall talk to him and put words in his mouth and I will be with your mouth and his mouth and I will teach you what you shall do. He shall be your

---

[72] Exodus 3

MOSES AND THE MIRACLES

spokesman to the people and he shall be to you instead of a mouth and you shall be to him instead of God. You shall take this rod in your hand, with which you shall do signs.

"When you go to Egypt, be sure to do all those wonders before Pharaoh which I have given you. But he will harden his heart and shall not let the people go. You shall say then, 'The Lord says, Israel is my son, even my firstborn. Let my son go, if not, I will kill your son, even your firstborn.' You can return safely to Egypt, for those who sought your life are dead."

Moses went to his father-in-law and said, "Let me go, I pray you, and return to my people which are in Egypt and see if they are still alive."

Jethro told him, "Go in peace."

The Lord told Aaron to go into the wilderness to meet Moses.

Aaron went and met him in the mount of God, where God appeared to Moses.[73]

Moses told Aaron all the words of the Lord who had sent him and all the signs which he had commanded him.

Moses and Aaron went and gathered together all the elders of the children of Israel. Aaron told them all the Lord had said and did the signs in the sight of the people.

The people believed and, when they heard the Lord had visited the children of Israel and was aware of their affliction, they bowed their heads and worshipped,[74] *for they were sure somehow, Pharaoh would let them go.*

Moses and Aaron went and told Pharaoh, "The Lord God of Israel says, 'Let my people go, that they may hold a feast to me in the wilderness.'"

Pharaoh said, "Who is the Lord that I should obey his voice to let Israel go? I don't know the Lord; neither will I let Israel go."

They told him, "The God of the Hebrews has met with us. Let us go three days' journey into the desert and sacrifice to the Lord our God, lest he fall upon us with disease or the sword."

Pharaoh said, "You have many people and you make them rest from their labors. I am going to command my taskmasters and your foremen not to give your people

---

[73] JST Exodus 4:24-27
[74] Exodus 4: 28-31

straw to make brick, as we have done before, but let them gather straw for themselves. The number of bricks will not be reduced, but kept the same, because they are idle and cry, 'Let us go and sacrifice to our God.' Let more work be given them that they may have something to do, so they don't have time for vain words." (Bricks were made by mixing mud and straw.).

The taskmasters went out and told the Hebrew foremen, "Pharaoh will not give you straw. Now, go and get straw where you can find it. The number of bricks you are required to make will not be reduced."

The people scattered throughout all of Egypt to gather stubble instead of straw.

The taskmasters told the Hebrew foremen, "Get all your work done, the same as when there was straw."

The taskmasters beat the foremen because they didn't make enough brick, saying, "Why have you not fulfilled your work in making brick today and yesterday as you did before?"

The Hebrew foremen went to Pharaoh and said, "Why are you doing this to us, your servants? No straw is given to us, yet we are told to make brick. But we can't make all the brick and then are beaten. The fault is in your own people."

Pharaoh said, "You are idle and say, 'Let us go and sacrifice to the Lord.' Go now and work. There shall be no straw be given you, yet you shall deliver the same number of bricks."

When Pharaoh said he would not diminish the number of bricks, the Hebrew foremen of the Children of Israel saw they were in a tight spot. They met Moses and Aaron, who were standing on the path as they were leaving Pharaoh, and said to them, "May the Lord look on you and punish you, because you have made us look bad in the eyes of Pharaoh and be hated in the eyes of his servants. You have put a sword in their hand to slay us."

Moses went to the Lord and said, "Lord, why have you evilly treated this people? Why did you send me? Since I came to Pharaoh to speak in your name, he has done evil

MOSES AND THE MIRACLES

things to this people. You haven't delivered your people at all."[75]

Jesus said, "Moses doesn't seem to have much faith in the Lord at this point. He must develop it, because I have heard what a great prophet he was."

Joseph answered, "He was a great prophet and had great faith. I think it shows how all of us can develop great faith."

Joseph went on with his story.

The Lord said, "Now, you shall see what I will do to Pharaoh. With a strong hand, he shall let your people go and, with a strong hand, he shall drive them out of his land. I am the Lord. I appeared to Abraham, to Isaac, and to Jacob. I am the Lord God Almighty; the Lord JEHOVAH. I have established my covenant with them, which gives them the land of Canaan, the land of their ancestors where they were strangers. I have also heard the groaning of the children of Israel, whom the Egyptians keep in bondage, and I have remembered my covenant with them. Say to the children of Israel, 'I am the Lord and I will bring you out from under the burdens of the Egyptians and I will free you of their bondage and redeem you with a stretched-out arm and with great judgments. I will take you to me for a people and I will be to you a God. You shall know I am the Lord your God, that brings you out from under the burdens of the Egyptians. I will bring you into the land, the land I did swear to give to Abraham, to Isaac, and to Jacob and I will give it to you for a heritage. I am the Lord.'"

Moses told this to the children of Israel, but they would not listen to him because of their anguish and cruel bondage.

He then spoke to the Lord. "The children of Israel have not listened to me, how will Pharaoh listen to me with my speech impediment?"[76]

The Lord said to Moses, "I have made you a god to Pharaoh and Aaron, your brother, shall be your prophet. You shall say all that I command you and Aaron shall speak to Pharaoh, so he will send the children of Israel out of his land. As I told you, Pharaoh will harden his heart and I will

---

[75] Exodus 5
[76] Exodus 6: 1-12

MOSES AND THE MIRACLES

multiply my signs and wonders in the land of Egypt. Pharaoh shall not listen to you, that I may lay my hand on Egypt and bring out my armies and my people, the children of Israel, from the land of Egypt by great judgments. The Egyptians shall know I am the Lord, when I stretch out my hand upon Egypt and bring out the children of Israel from among them."

Moses was eighty years old and Aaron eighty-three years old when they spoke to Pharaoh. The Lord said to Moses and Aaron, "Pharaoh shall tell you to prove yourself by showing him a miracle. You shall have Aaron take his rod and toss it before Pharaoh and it shall become an asp."

Moses and Aaron went to Pharaoh and did as the Lord commanded. Aaron tossed down his rod before Pharaoh and his servants, and it became an asp.

Pharaoh called the wise men and the magicians of Egypt and they also threw down their rods and they became asps, but Aaron's asp swallowed up their asps. Pharaoh hardened his heart and didn't listen to them, as the Lord had said.

The Lord told Moses to tell Aaron, "Take your rod and stretch out your hand on the waters of Egypt, on their streams, their rivers, and their ponds and their pools of water that they become blood. That there may be blood throughout all of Egypt, both in vessels of wood and stone."

Moses and Aaron did as the Lord commanded in the sight of Pharaoh and his servants. All the water in the river was turned to blood. The fish that were in the river died and the river stunk. The Egyptians could not drink the river water and there was blood throughout all of Egypt.

Pharaoh called for the magicians and they did the same with their enchantments. Pharaoh hardened his heart and did not listen to Moses, as the Lord had said. He turned and went into his house and didn't think any more about it. The Egyptians dug near the river for drinking water, as they could not drink the river water.

After seven days passed,[77] the Lord said to Moses, "Go to Pharaoh and say, 'The Lord says to let my people go, that they may serve me. If you refuse to let them go, I will cause all the land within your borders to be covered

---

[77] Exodus 7

with frogs. The river will bring forth lots and lots of frogs. They will come up into your house and into your bedroom and onto your bed and into the house of your servants and all the people. They will come into your ovens and your kneading troughs. They will be on you, on all your people, and all your servants."

Pharaoh turned a deaf ear to Moses, so the Lord told Moses to have Aaron stretch forth the rod, which Aaron did. The frogs came up as the Lord had said.

Pharaoh summoned his magicians and they also caused frogs to come up. Later, Pharaoh called for Moses and Aaron and said, "Ask the Lord to take away the frogs from me and from my people and I will let the people go that they may offer sacrifice to the Lord."

Moses said, "When should I ask the Lord to destroy the frogs for you, your servants and all your people, that they may remain in the river only?"

Pharaoh said, "Tomorrow."

Moses said, "Be it as you have asked, so you may know there is none like the Lord our God."

Moses and Aaron left and Moses asked the Lord to remove all the frogs from Egypt, except in the river. The frogs all died that were in Egypt and the Egyptians gathered them together in heaps and the land stunk.

When Pharaoh saw there was relief from the frogs, he hardened his heart and didn't let the people go.

Next, the Lord told Moses, "Stretch out your rod and tap the dust of the land that it becomes lice throughout the land of Egypt."

Moses did that, and there were lice on man and beast throughout all of Egypt.

The magicians told Pharaoh, "This is the finger of God," but Pharaoh hardened his heart and would not listen, as the Lord had said.

The Lord told Moses to say, "The Lord says to let my people go, that they may serve me. If not, I will send swarms of flies on you, your servants, and your people. There will be swarms of flies in your houses and the houses of the Egyptians and they shall cover the ground where they walk. I will separate the land of Goshen, where my people live, so no swarms of flies shall be there, that you may know I am the Lord."

MOSES AND THE MIRACLES

And swarms of flies came as the Lord had told Moses, and Goshen was free of them.

Pharaoh said he would let the people go and Moses went out and asked the Lord to remove the swarms of flies. The Lord did as Moses asked and removed all the flies from Pharaoh, his servants, and his people. There remained not one.

Again, Pharaoh hardened his heart and would not let the people go.[78]

Jesus said, "Pharaoh doesn't learn very fast. He must really want the Egyptians as slaves."

Joseph told him, "I think he wanted them to build monuments to him. Without them, he probably thought he couldn't build as big a monument. It is very easy to get so caught up in our importance that we lose track of what is really important."

Next, the Lord caused a plague to kill the livestock of the Egyptians, but none of the Hebrew's died.

Again, Pharaoh said he would bow to the Lord's will, but changed his mind and would not let them go.

After this, the Lord caused boils to be on the Egyptians and their livestock. Their magicians could not stand because of the boils. Once more, Pharaoh changed his mind and would not let the people go.

The Lord said, "Now, I will stretch out my hand, that I may afflict you and your people with pestilence. You shall be cut off from the earth. Indeed, for this cause have I raised you up to show in you my power, that my name may be declared throughout all the earth. Do you yet exalt yourself over my people that you will not let them go? Tomorrow about this time, I will cause a very damaging hail storm, such as has not been in Egypt since the beginning of time. Go now and gather in all your cattle and all you have in the field. Every man and beast which shall be left in the field and shall not be brought in, the hail shall kill."

He that heeded the word of the Lord among the servants of Pharaoh had their servants and cattle flee into houses. Those that didn't regard the word of the Lord left their cattle and servants in the field and they were killed.

---

[78] Exodus 8

MOSES AND THE MIRACLES

Pharaoh sent for Moses and Aaron and said, "I have sinned this time. The Lord is righteous and I and my people are wicked. It is enough. Ask the Lord to stop, so there is no more thunder and hail. I will let you go and you shall stay no longer."

The flax and barley were destroyed, but the wheat and spelt were not grown. Moses did as he told Pharaoh, and the thunder, rain, and hail stopped.

When Pharaoh saw they had ceased, he sinned more because he hardened his heart and would not let the children of Israel go, as the Lord had said.[79]

The Lord spoke to Moses, "Go to Pharaoh, for he has hardened his heart and the hearts of his servants. Therefore, I will show my signs to him that you may tell them to your son, and your son tell them to his son, that all may know I am the Lord."

Moses and Aaron went to Pharaoh and said, "The Lord God of the Hebrews, says, 'How long will you refuse to humble yourself before me and let my people go, that they may serve me? If you refuse to let my people go, tomorrow I will bring locusts into your land. They shall cover the ground so it can't be seen. They shall eat all that was left by the hail and shall devour all that you grow in the field. They shall fill your houses, those of your servants, and the houses of all the Egyptians. It will be like nothing your fathers and grandfathers have seen since man was on the earth.'"

They turned and left Pharaoh.

Pharaoh's servants said to him, "How long shall this man do these things? Let the people go that they may serve the Lord, their God. Don't you know yet Egypt is destroyed?"

Pharaoh hardened his heart and would not let the people go.

The Lord said to Moses, "Stretch out your hand over the land of Egypt for the locusts that they may come and eat everything in the land, all that the hail has left."

Moses stretched out his rod and the Lord brought an east wind on the land all that day and all that night. When it was morning, the east wind brought the locusts. The

---

[79] Exodus 9

MOSES AND THE MIRACLES

locusts came up over all the coasts of Egypt. They covered the face of the whole earth that the land was darkened and they ate every green thing and all the fruit the hail had left. There remained not any green thing in the trees and nothing in the field, through all the land of Egypt.

Pharaoh called for Moses and Aaron in haste and said, "I have sinned against the Lord your God and against you. Now, please forgive me just this once and ask the Lord your God to take away this death."

Moses went out and asked the Lord to take away the locusts. There was not one locust left in all of Egypt. But, again, Pharaoh hardened his heart and would not let them go.

The Lord said to Moses, "Stretch out your hand toward heaven that there may be darkness over the land of Egypt, even a darkness which may be felt."

So, Moses stretched out his hand toward heaven, and there was a thick darkness in all the land three days. They didn't see one another and no one left their houses for three days, except the children of Israel who had light in their homes.

Pharaoh called for Moses and said, "Go serve the Lord, take your little ones with you, but leave your flocks and herds."

Moses said, "You must also allow us to have sacrifices and burnt offerings, that we may sacrifice to the Lord our God. Thus, our cattle must also go with us; there shall not be a hoof left behind. We must take them to be able to serve the Lord our God. We won't know what we need to serve the Lord until we get there."

Pharaoh hardened his heart and would not let them go.[80]

The Lord said to Moses, "I will yet bring one more plague on Pharaoh and Egypt. Afterwards, he will let you go." He explained what he would do to the Egyptians and told Moses to tell it to Pharaoh.

Moses turned to Pharaoh and said, "The Lord says about midnight, I will go out into the midst of Egypt. All the firstborn in the land of Egypt shall die, from the firstborn of Pharaoh who sits on his throne to the firstborn of the

---

[80] Exodus 10: 1-27

maidservant that is behind the mill and all the firstborn of beasts. There shall be a great lament throughout all the land of Egypt. There has been none like it, nor shall there be any more like it. To the children of Israel nothing shall happen, nothing; that you may know the Lord recognizes a difference between the Egyptians and Israel. All these around us here, your servants, and those who follow you will come to me, bow down themselves to me and say, 'Get out.' After that, we will go."[81]

Pharaoh said, "Get away from me. Take care you don't see me again, because if you do, you will die."

Moses said, "Let it be as you say. I will not see you again." and he went from Pharaoh very angry.[82]

The Lord said to Moses, "Pharaoh did not listen to you that my wonders may be multiplied in the land of Egypt. When he lets you go, he shall thrust you out in one group. Let every man and woman ask their Egyptian neighbors for jewelry of silver and gold."[83]

The Lord said to Moses and Aaron, "This month shall be the first month of the year to you, the beginning of months. Talk to the congregation of Israel and say, 'In the future, on the tenth day of this month, every household shall take a lamb without blemish, either a sheep or goat. If the household is too small for a lamb, let them go together with their neighbor, based on the number of people and how much they can eat. You shall keep the animal until the fourteenth day of the month. The whole congregation of Israel shall kill it the same evening. They shall take of the blood and streak it on the two side posts and on the upper door post of the houses where they shall eat it. You shall eat it that night, roasted with fire and not boiled. You shall eat the head and the legs and other edible parts. Anything that is left over shall be burned and not left until morning.'

"You shall eat it dressed in your traveling clothes, with your shoes on and your staff in your hand. You shall eat it in haste. It is the Lord's Passover. I will pass through the land of Egypt this night and will kill all the firstborn in the land of Egypt, both man and beast. Against all the gods of Egypt, I will execute judgment. I am the Lord.

---

[81] Exodus 11: 1, 4-8
[82] Exodus 10: 28, 29
[83] Exodus 11: 9

"The blood shall be a token on the houses where you are. When I see the blood, I will pass over you and the plague shall not destroy you. This day shall be to you a memorial and you shall keep it for a feast by ordinance forever. Seven days you shall eat unleavened bread. The first day you shall take leaven out of houses, for whoever eats leavened bread from the first day until the seventh day shall be cut off from Israel."[84]

Moses called for all the elders of Israel and said, "Select a lamb based on the size of your household and kill the Passover. Drain the blood into a basin. Take a bunch of hyssops and dip it in the blood and streak the lintel and the two side posts with the blood. None of you shall go out of the door of his house until the morning. You shall observe this as an ordinance to you and your sons forever. When you come to the land, which the Lord will give you as he has promised, you shall keep this service. When your children ask, 'Why do we do this?' you shall say, 'It is the sacrifice of the Lord's Passover, who passed over the houses of the children of Israel in Egypt, when he killed the Egyptians and delivered us.'"

The people bowed their heads and worshipped and did as they were commanded.

At midnight, the Lord killed all the firstborn in the land of Egypt, from the firstborn of Pharaoh who sat on his throne to the firstborn of the captive in the dungeon and all the firstborn of cattle. Pharaoh got up in the night, as did all his servants and all the Egyptians. There was a great lament in Egypt, for there was not a house where there was not one dead.

Pharaoh called for Moses and Aaron by night and said, "Get up and come out from among my people, you and the rest of the children of Israel and go serve the Lord as you have asked. Take your flocks and your herds as you asked and be gone; bless me also."

The Egyptians urged the people to get going in a hurry, because they said, "We are all dead men."

The children of Israel borrowed from the Egyptians jewelry of silver and gold and clothing, as Moses had told them to do. The Lord gave them favor with the Egyptians

---

[84] Exodus 12: 1-15

MOSES AND THE MIRACLES

and the Egyptians gave what the children of Israel asked and they despoiled them.

The children of Israel traveled from Ramses to Succoth. There were about six hundred thousand males traveling on foot, not counting children. A mixed group of people traveled with them. There were also flocks and herds, a lot of livestock.

They baked unleavened cakes of dough, which they brought out of Egypt, because they were thrust out and had no time to leaven it and had prepared no food to take with them. They had spent four hundred and thirty years in Egypt.[85]

The Lord said to Moses, "Consecrate to me the firstborn, whatever opens the matrix, whether man or beast, the males shall be mine. You shall redeem with a lamb, every firstborn of an ass. If you won't redeem it, then you shall break its neck. All the firstborn of man among your children, you shall redeem. When your son asks you in the future, 'Why is this?' you shall tell him how the Lord brought you out of Egypt and how He killed the firstborn of man and beast. Thus, you sacrifice to the Lord all that open the matrix, being males, but all the firstborn of your children, you redeem."

When Pharaoh let the people go, God didn't lead them through the land of the Philistines, although that was closer, because God thought, the people would be afraid when they see war and return to Egypt. God led them through the wilderness of the Red Sea and they went dressed for war.

Moses took the bones of Joseph with him because Joseph had his children swear to him they would take his bones when the Lord had them leave Egypt. They left Succoth and camped in Etham on the edge of the wilderness. The Lord went before them in a pillar of a cloud by day and in a pillar of fire by night, to give them light and to lead them.[86]

The Lord told Moses to tell the children of Israel to camp before Pi Hahiroth, because Pharaoh would think the children of Israel had gotten bogged down in the wilderness and would harden his heart and follow them. The Lord

---

[85] Exodus 12: 1-40
[86] Exodus 13: 12-21

would receive glory from Pharaoh and his entire army and the Egyptians would know He is the Lord.

Pharaoh was told the people had fled and his heart and the hearts of his servants were turned against the children of Israel, and they said, "Why have we done this and let Israel go from serving us?"

Pharaoh made ready his chariot and his army. He took not only his six hundred best chariots, but all the rest of them, with captains over everyone and pursued after the children of Israel with all his chariots, horsemen, and army. He overtook them encamped by the sea beside Pi Hahiroth.

When he got close and the children of Israel saw them marching after them, they were very afraid and cried out to the Lord.

They said to Moses, "Why have you taken us away to die in the wilderness? Why did you do this? Weren't we better off in Egypt? Didn't we tell you in Egypt to leave us alone, that we may serve the Egyptians? It would have been better for us to serve the Egyptians, than that we should die in the wilderness."

Moses went to the Lord, "We can't fight all those chariots, what are we going to do now?"

The Lord said, "Why are you crying to me? Tell the children of Israel to go forward. Lift your rod and stretch out your hand over the sea and divide it. The children of Israel shall go through the midst of the sea on dry ground. The Egyptians will harden their hearts and follow you into the sea, and I will receive glory when Pharaoh and his entire army are lost. The Egyptians shall know I am the Lord."

Moses said to the people, "Don't fear! Stand still and see the salvation of the Lord, which he will now show you. The Egyptians whom you have seen today, you will never see again. The Lord shall fight for you and you shall be quiet."

The angel of God, which went before the camp of Israel, went from the front of them to the back of them, as did the pillar of the cloud. The cloud came between the camp of the Egyptians and the camp of Israel. It was a cloud and darkness to the Egyptians, but gave light to the Israelites, that they did not come near to one another the whole night.

Moses stretched out his hand over the sea and the Lord caused the sea to go back by a strong east wind all that night, making the sea dry land and dividing the water.

The children of Israel went into the midst of the sea upon the dry ground and the water was a wall on their right hand and on their left. The Egyptians pursued them into the midst of the sea, with all of Pharaoh's horses, his chariots, and horsemen.

The Lord caused trouble for the Egyptians. The wheels of their chariots came off and the chariots were hard to drive on the loose ground. The Egyptians said, "Let us flee from Israel for the Lord is fighting for them against us."

The Lord said to Moses, "Stretch out your hand over the sea that the waters may come together upon the Egyptians, their chariots, and their horsemen."

Moses did so and the waters returned and covered the chariots, the horseman and all the army of Pharaoh who came into the sea after them. There remained not so much as one of them. But the children of Israel walked upon dry land amid the sea and the water were a wall on their right hand and their left. Thus, the Lord saved Israel that day out of the hand of the Egyptians and Israel saw the Egyptians dead upon the seashore. The people feared the Lord and believed the Lord and his servant Moses.[87]

Jesus said, "Pharaoh had it coming to him. The Lord gave him every chance. But I can't help but feel sad for all the others who were killed; all the wives who lost their husbands and all the children who lost their fathers."

WANDERING THE DESERT

Joseph said, "Today, we will get into what happened to the Israelites in the wilderness after they left Egypt.
And Jesus sat at his feet, eager to hear more.

Moses brought Israel from the Red Sea and they went into the wilderness of Shur three days and found no water. When they came to Marah, which means bitterness,

---
[87] Exodus 14

they could not drink the water because it was bitter. They murmured against Moses, saying, "What shall we drink?"

Moses prayed to the Lord, and the Lord showed him a tree which, when he threw it into the water, removed the bitterness. The Lord said, "If you will listen to my voice and do that which is right and keep all my commandments and statutes, you will not get any of the diseases which the Egyptians have, for I am the Lord that heals you."

Next, they came to Elim, where there were twelve wells of water and seventy palm trees. They encamped there by the waters.[88]

They left and traveled to the wilderness of Sin and encamped there about a month. There the congregation murmured against Moses and Aaron. They said, "We wish we had died in the land of Egypt, where we sat by our cooking pots and had plenty of food. You have brought us into this wilderness to kill us all with hunger."

Jesus said, "They have only been away from Egypt a little over a month and they have already forgotten how tough it was in Egypt. It is hard to believe."

Joseph said, "That is true. You will see a lot of that as we go on." And he went on with his tale.

The Lord said to Moses, "I have heard the murmurings of the children of Israel. Have Aaron tell them, 'This evening you shall eat flesh and in the morning I will rain food down from heaven for you. You shall go out every morning except the seventh day and gather a certain portion that I may test you, whether you will keep my law or not. On the sixth day, you shall prepare that which you bring in and it shall be twice as much as you gather the other days.'"

Aaron spoke to the children of Israel and told them what the Lord said and then said to them. "Why do you complain to us? We are not God. You are not complaining to us, but against God." As he spoke, the multitude looked toward the wilderness and the glory of the Lord appeared in the clouds.

That evening, quail came and covered the camp. In the morning, the dew lay round about the camp. When the

---

[88] Exodus 15:22-27

dew had evaporated, on the ground lay a small round thing as small as the hoar frost. When the children of Israel saw it, they said one to another, "It is manna," for they didn't know what it was. (The meaning of manna in Hebrew is "What?")

Moses said, "This is the food which the Lord has given you to eat. The Lord has commanded every person to gather it based on how much they want; an omer (perhaps about a gallon) for each person in the household. Don't leave anything for the next morning."

They gathered it and measured it with an omer. Those that gathered a lot had nothing left over and they which gathered little, had no lack. Each gathered based on what they wanted.

Some didn't listen to what Moses said and left it until morning. It bred worms and stunk and Moses was angry with them. They gathered it every day, each person based on what they wanted. When the sun was hot, it melted.

On the sixth day, they gathered twice as much, two omers per person. The rulers came and told Moses they were gathering twice what they ordinarily did.

Moses said, "That is what the Lord said to do. Tomorrow is the rest of the holy Sabbath. Bake what you will today and boil that which you will boil. What is left, keep until the morning."

They kept it and, in the morning, it did not stink and there were no worms in it. Moses told them, "Eat the leftovers today, for it is the Sabbath to the Lord and there will not be any in the field. Six days you shall gather it, but on the seventh day, which is the Sabbath, there shall be none."

Some of the people didn't listen and went out to gather it, but they didn't find any. The Lord said to Moses, "How long will they refuse to keep my commandments and my laws?"

Moses said to the people, "The Lord has given you the Sabbath; therefore, on the sixth day he gives you the food for two days. Everybody stay in your tent and not go out on the Sabbath." So they rested on the Sabbath.

The house of Israel called, manna, God's gift and it was white like coriander seed and tasted like wafers made with honey.

The Lord commanded Moses to fill a pot with an omer of manna and put it before the Testimony, to be kept for future generations to see. Aaron did so. The children of Israel ate manna for forty years until they came to the border of Canaan.[89]

They left the wilderness of Sin and pitched in Rephidim, and there was no water to drink. The people complained to Moses, saying, "Give us water so we can drink."

Moses said, "Why do you complain to me? Put the Lord to the test."

The people were thirsty and continued to complain to Moses, saying, "Why have you brought us out of Egypt to kill us, our children, and our cattle with no water?"

Moses went to the Lord and asked, "What should I do? They are almost ready to stone me."

The Lord said, "Go before the people and take with you the elders of Israel and your rod with which you struck the river. I will stand before you upon the rock in Horeb and you shall strike the rock. Water shall come out of it that the people may drink."

Moses did it in sight of the elders of Israel. He called the place Massah (meaning trying or testing), and Meribah (meaning complaint), because of the complaining of the children of Israel and because they tempted the Lord by saying, "Is the Lord among us?"

After this came the people of Amalek to fight with Israel in Rephidim. Moses said to Joshua, "Choose men and go fight with Amalek. Tomorrow, I will stand on the top of the hill with the rod of God in my hand to see the battle.'

Joshua did as Moses commanded him and fought with Amalek. Moses, Aaron and Hur went up to the top of the hill. When Moses held up his hand, Israel prevailed and when he let down his hand, Amalek prevailed.

But Moses' hands got heavy, so they took a stone for him to sit on, while Aaron and Hur held up his hands, one on each side. His hands were steady until the sun set,

---

[89] Exodus 16: 1-35

WANDERING THE DESERT

and Joshua defeated Amalek and his people with the edge of the sword.

The Lord said to Moses, "Record this in a book for a memorial and tell Joshua I will utterly blot out the remembrance of Amalek."[90]

Moses had sent his wife and children back to live with Jethro, the priest of Midian, Moses' father-in-law. When he heard all God had done for Moses and how the children of Israel had been brought out of Egypt, he decided it was time for Moses' wife, Zipporah, and his two sons to return, so Jethro took them to him.

The name of the oldest was Gershom and the other was Eliezer, meaning the God of help. Moses named him that because he said, "The God of my father was my help and delivered me from the sword of Pharaoh."

Moses was told they were coming and went out to meet them. He kissed Jethro and they told each other what had happened. Jethro said, "Blessed be the Lord, who has delivered the people from out of the hand of the Egyptians. The Lord is greater than all gods as he has shown by overcoming the proud Egyptians and their gods.

The next day, Moses sat to judge the people and they stood by Moses all day. When Jethro saw this, he said to Moses, "What is this you are doing? Why do you sit by yourself and the people stand by you all day long?"

Moses said, "When the people have a problem, they come to me to ask of God and I judge between them and another. I teach them the statutes of God and his laws."

Jethro said, "What you are doing is not good. You will wear out and the people who are with you. This is too heavy for you; you shouldn't do it by yourself. Listen to me and I will give you counsel and God will be with you. You represent the people before God. Teach them ordinances and laws and show them what must be done and how to do it. Find from the people able men that obey God, men of truth that hate covetousness and make them heads of thousands, hundreds, fifties and tens. Let them judge the people throughout the year. Every great matter they shall bring to you, but every small matter they shall judge. This will make it easier for you, as they shall bear the burden

---

[90] Exodus 17

with you. If you do this, and God will command you to do so, then you will survive and all these people will have peace."

Moses listened to Jethro and did all he suggested. He chose able men out of all the people and made them heads over the people. They judged the people throughout the year. The hard decisions they brought to Moses, but the small matters they judged themselves. Jethro left and went home.[91]

Jesus said, "I need to remember that when I am the leader. One must let others do some of the work, if you are going to get things done."
Joseph nodded and continued.

Two months after they left Egypt, the children of Israel came to the wilderness of Sinai and camped before the mountain. Moses went up the mountain and the Lord called to him and told him to tell the house of Jacob and the children of Israel, "You have seen what I did to the Egyptians and how I brought you on eagle's wings here to me. If you will obey me and keep my covenant, then you shall be a peculiar treasure to me above all other people, for all the earth is mine. You shall be a kingdom of priests and a holy nation."

Moses gathered the elders of the people and told them all that the Lord commanded. All the people answered together and said, "All that the Lord has said, we will do."

Moses reported this back to the Lord.

The Lord said, "I will come to you in a thick cloud, that the people may hear when I speak with you and believe you forever. Go hallow the people today and tomorrow and have them wash their clothes. The third day, I will come down in the cloud which will be in sight of all the people on Mount Sinai. You shall set boundaries around the area for the people, that they don't go up higher on the mount or touch the border you set. Whoever touches the border on the mount shall surely be put to death. They will be stoned or shot through and shall not live. When the trumpet sounds long, they shall come up to the mount."

---

[91] Exodus 18

Moses went down from the mount and sanctified the people and they washed their clothes. He told them to be ready on the third day. In the morning of the third day, there was thunder and lightning and a thick cloud on the mount. The sound of the trumpet was very loud, so all the people in the camp trembled.

Moses brought the people out of the camp to meet with God at the foot of the mount. Mount Sinai was covered with smoke everywhere, because the Lord descended on it in fire. The smoke went up like the smoke of a great furnace and all the ground shook. When the trumpet sounded long and got louder and louder, Moses spoke and God's voice could be heard answering him. He called for Moses to come up to the top of the mount.

Moses went up and the Lord told him, "Go back down and make sure the people don't come up to see me and perish. Also, have the priests which come near to me cleanse themselves, lest they also perish."

Moses told the Lord, "The people can't come up, because we set boundaries for them as you told us."

The Lord said, "Away with you, go down. When you come back up, bring Aaron with you, but make sure the priests and people don't come up, lest they perish."

Moses went down and spoke with the people.[92] They had seen the lightning and heard the thunder and the trumpet sounding and they also saw the mountain smoking. This was very frightening to the people and they went down and stood some distance away.

They said to Moses, "You can talk to us and tell us things, but don't have God speak to us, so we don't die."

Moses said, "Don't be afraid. God is testing you. Because you have had this experience, you will always respect God and won't sin."

Jesus said, "I don't understand why they didn't want the Lord to speak to them. If I had been there, I would want to hear from God myself."

Joseph said, "I agree with you. I too would like to be respected enough to have the Lord take his time to speak with me. There are a lot of things I would like to ask Him."

---

[92] Exodus 19

The people stood some distance away and watched Moses walk back into the thick cloud where God was.

The Lord told Moses to tell the children of Israel, "You shall not make gods of silver or gold. You shall make me an altar of earth on which to sacrifice your burnt offerings, your sheep and oxen. You shall do this in all the places where I command you to do it and I will come to you and bless you. You can also make me an altar of stone, but don't make it of hewn stone, for if you use tools on it, you have polluted it."[93]

The Lord proceeded to give Moses the rules and laws by which the children of Israel should live. Then he told them how they would come into the Promised Land. He said, "I will send a fear of me before you and will destroy all the people to whom you shall come and I will make all your enemies flee before you. I will send hornets before you, which shall drive out the Hivite, the Canaanite and the Hittite before you. I will not drive them out from before you in one year so the land does not become desolate and wild beasts take over. Bit by bit, I will drive them out from before you, until you have increased and inherited the land. I will set your boundaries from the Red Sea even to the sea of the Philistines and from the desert to the river. I will deliver the inhabitants of the land to you and you shall drive them out before you. You shall make no covenant with them or with their gods. They shall not dwell in your land, lest they make you sin against me. If you serve their gods, it will be a snare to you.[94] Now, go down and return with Aaron, Nadab, Abihu, and seventy of the elders of Israel and worship me from a distance. You only shall come near to me."

Moses went down and told the people all that the Lord had told him, including all the laws and rules. All the people answered with one voice and said, "All that the Lord has said, we will do."

Moses wrote all the words the Lord had said. He arose in the morning, built an altar at the foot of the mountain, and set up twelve pillars, one for each of the twelve tribes of Israel. He had young men of the children of Israel offer burnt offerings and sacrifice peace offerings of

---

[93] Exodus 20: 18-24
[94] Exodus 23: 27-33

oxen to the Lord. He took half of the blood of the offerings and put it in basins. The other half he sprinkled on the altar. He took the book of the covenant and read it in an audience of the people.

They said, "All that the Lord has said, we will do and be obedient."

Moses took the rest of the blood in the basins and sprinkled it on the people and said, "Behold, the blood of the covenant, which the Lord has made with you concerning all he has said."

Joseph said, "As you can see we are almost to our work site. I think I will stop here and tell you what happened next to Moses and the children of Israel on the way home."

***

They spent another day of hard work, removing the last of the old and installing the new. After they had walked a short distance, Jesus said, "Aren't you going to tell me what happened next."

Joseph said, "I am sorry Jesus, I was thinking about what we need to do tomorrow and what other tools we might need. I am glad you want to know more.

Moses, Aaron, Nadab, Abihu and seventy of the elders of Israel went up the mountain. They saw the God of Israel and there was under his feet a paved area that looked like sapphire stone, as clear as the sky. Nothing happened to the elders, but they saw God from a distance and ate and drank.

Later, the Lord said to Moses, "Come up the mount and bring Joshua with you. I will give you tables of stone with a law and commandments which I have written on them, so you can teach them."

Moses told the elders of Israel that Joshua and he were going farther up the mount and to wait in camp for their return. If there were matters to take care of, Aaron and Hur would be available for that. The glory of the Lord was on Mount Sinai and the cloud covered his glory six days, while Moses and Joshua waited on the mount.

On the seventh day, the Lord called out of the midst of the cloud for Moses to come up. Moses left Joshua, and went into the cloud and up to the top of the mount of God. He was in the mount forty days and forty nights.[95]

The Lord said to Moses, "Tell the children of Israel to bring me an offering. You may take it from every person who gives it willingly. The offering may be gold, silver, brass, blue, purple, scarlet, fine linen, goat hair, rams' skins dyed red, badgers' skins, acacia wood, oil for the light, spices for anointing oil and sweet incense, onyx stones, and stones to be set in the ephod and breastplate. Let them build me a sanctuary that I may dwell among them. I will show you the patterns for the tabernacle and the furniture, equipment, and utensils that go in it. Make it after the pattern I will show you."[96]

The Lord showed him the pattern for the tabernacle, the Ark of the Covenant, the mercy seat, the altars for incense and the burnt offerings, the decorations of the tabernacle, the instruments, and the holy garments of the priests. He explained the rites that would be performed.[97]

The Lord told Moses, "I have selected Bezaleel, the son of Uri, the son of Hur of the tribe of Judah. He is filled with the spirit of God, in wisdom, understanding, knowledge, and all kinds of workmanship. He can work in gold, silver, and brass. He can cut stones and set them and carve wood. I have selected Aholiab, the son of Ahisamach of the tribe of Dan to work with him.

"Tell the children of Israel, "You shall keep my Sabbaths. It is a sign between me and you throughout your generations that you may know I am the Lord that sanctifies you. You shall keep the Sabbath, for it is holy to you. Six days may work be done, but the seventh is the Sabbath of rest, holy to the Lord. Everyone that defiles it or does any work on the Sabbath day shall be put to death.

"Therefore, the children of Israel shall keep the Sabbath to observe it throughout their generations, for a perpetual covenant. It is a sign between me and the children of Israel forever. In six days, the Lord made heaven and earth, and on the seventh day he rested and was refreshed."

---

[95] Exodus 24
[96] Exodus 25: 1-9
[97] Exodus 25: 10 to Exodus 30: 38

God gave Moses two stone tablets of testimony, written with his finger.[98]

At the bottom of the mount, the people were waiting for Moses to return. When he didn't, they went to Aaron in a group and said, "This Moses, the man who brought us out of Egypt, has not returned and we don't know what has happened to him. Make us gods which shall lead us, because we don't know what has happened to Moses."

Aaron said, "Take off the gold earrings that are in the ears of your wives, sons, and daughters and bring them to me."

They did so and he took the gold, melted it, formed it over wood into the shape of a calf, and used an engraving tool to finish it.

They said, "These are your gods, O Israel, which brought you out of Egypt."

When Aaron saw this, he built an altar before it and proclaimed, "Tomorrow is a feast to the Lord."

The people arose early the next day and offered burnt offerings and peace offerings. They sat down to eat and drink and rose to play.

The Lord said to Moses, "Go down to your people, whom you have brought out of Egypt, for they have corrupted themselves. They have turned aside quickly from what I commanded. They have made them a molten calf and have worshipped it and sacrificed to it.

"I have seen this people and they are a stiff-necked people. Now, let me alone that my anger may wax hot against then, that I may consume them. I will make of you a great nation."

Moses said, "Lord, why does your anger wax hot against your people, which you have brought out of the land of Egypt with great power and a mighty hand? Why should the Egyptians say, 'For mischief their God brought them out, to kill them in the mountains and to consume them from the face of the earth?' Turn from your fierce anger. Your people will repent of this evil; therefore, don't be against them. Remember Abraham, Isaac, and Jacob, your servants, to whom you swore, yourself, and said to them, 'I will multiply your posterity as the stars of heaven. All this land

---

[98] Exodus 31

I have spoken of will I give to your seed and they shall inherit it forever.'"

The Lord said, "If they will repent of the evil which they have done, I will spare them, and turn away my fierce anger; but you shall execute judgment upon all who will not repent of this evil today. Therefore, see you do what I have commanded you, or I will do all I had thought to do to my people."

Moses turned and went down from the mount with the two tablets of testimony in his hands. The tables were written on both sides. The tablets were the work of God, as well as the writing.

When he got to where Joshua was, Joshua said, "There is a noise of war in the camp."

Moses said, "It is not the sound of them who shout for mastery, nor the sound of those being overcome, but the sound of singing."

As soon as they came near the camp, they saw the calf and dancing, and Moses was angry. He threw the tablets out of his hands and they broke at the bottom of the mount. He took the calf they had made and burnt it in the fire, ground it to powder, strewed it on the water, and made the children of Israel drink it.

Moses said to Aaron, "What did this people do to you that you have brought such a great sin upon them?"

Aaron said, "Don't get angry. You know the people are set on mischief. They said to me, 'Make us gods which shall lead us; because we don't know what has happened to Moses.' I said to them, 'Whoever has any gold, let them take it off.' They gave it to me and I threw it in the fire and out came this calf."

Moses saw the people were riotous and Aaron had made them so to their shame. He stood in the gate of the camp and said, "Who is on the Lord's side? Let him come to me."

All the sons of Levi gathered themselves together to him.

He said to them, "The Lord God of Israel says, 'Every man take his sword and go in and out from gate to gate throughout the camp and slay his brother, his friend, and his neighbor.' Serve the Lord today, even if it's your son or your brother, that the Lord will bless you today."

The children of Levi did that and about three thousand men were killed.

The next day Moses said to the people, "You have sinned a great sin. Now, I will go up to the Lord; maybe I can make an atonement for your sin."

Moses went up the mount and said to the Lord, "These people have sinned a great sin and have made them gods of gold. Yet, if you will, please, forgive their sin; if not, please blot me out of the book which you have written."

The Lord said, "Whoever has sinned against me, I will blot out of my book. Now, go and lead the people to where I have told you. My angel shall go before you; nevertheless, when it's time to punish, I will punish them for their sin."

The Lord plagued the people, because of the calf Aaron made.[99]

The Lord said to Moses, "Make two other tables of stone, like the first and I will write on them also, the words of the law, according as they were written at the first on the tables which you broke, but it shall not be like the first. I will take away the higher priesthood out of their midst. Therefore, my holy order, and the ordinances thereof, shall not go before them, for my presence shall not be in their midst, lest I destroy them. But I will give to them the law as at the first, but it shall be after the law of a carnal commandment, for I have sworn in my wrath, they shall not enter my presence, nor into my rest, in the days of their pilgrimage. Therefore, do as I have commanded you and be ready in the morning and come up Mount Sinai."[100]

Moses hewed two tables of stone like the first and he rose early in the morning and went up Mount Sinai, as the Lord commanded him, carrying the two tables of stone. The Lord descended in the cloud and stood with him there and proclaimed the name of the Lord. He passed by before Moses and proclaimed, "I am The Lord God, merciful and gracious, longsuffering, and abundant in goodness and truth. Giving mercy to thousands, forgiving iniquity, transgressions, and sin. Visiting the sins of the fathers on the children, and on the children's children, to the third and fourth generation."

---

[99] Exodus 32
[100] JST Exodus 34:1-2

Moses bowed his head toward the earth and worshipped. He said, "If now I have found grace in your sight, O Lord, let my Lord go among us, for it is a stiff-necked people. Pardon our iniquity and our sin and take us for your inheritance."

The Lord said, "I make a covenant and before all your people I will do marvels such as have not been done in all the earth or in any nation. All the people you are among shall see the work of the Lord, for it is a terrible thing I will do with you. I will drive out before you the Amorite, the Canaanite, the Hittite, the Perizzite, the Hivite, and the Jebusite. Take heed you don't make a covenant with the inhabitants of the land where you go, so they won't be a snare in your midst. You shall destroy their altars, break their images, and cut down the groves where they worship."

Moses brought down from the mount the two tables of stone. On them were the Ten Commandments as follows:[101]

"I am the Lord your God, who has brought you out of the land of Egypt, out of the house of bondage.

1. You shall have no other gods before me.

2. You shall not make any graven image or any likeness of anything that is in heaven above, that is in the earth beneath, or that is in the water under the earth. You shall not bow down to them or serve them. I the Lord your God, am a jealous God, visiting the iniquity of the fathers on the children to the third and fourth generations of them who hate me, but I show mercy to thousands of them who love me and keep my commandments.

3. You shall not take the name of the Lord your God in vain, for the Lord will not hold them guiltless who take his name in vain.

4. Remember the Sabbath day to keep it holy. Six days shall you labor and do all your work, but the seventh day is the Sabbath of the Lord your God and in it you shall not do any work, you, your son, your daughter, your manservant, your maidservant, your cattle, or a stranger who is within your gates. In six days the Lord made heaven and earth, the sea, and all that in them is and rested the

---

[101] Exodus 34:3-13, 29

seventh day. Wherefore the Lord blessed the Sabbath and hallowed it.

5. Honor your father and mother, that your days may be long upon the land which the Lord your God gives you.

6. You shall not kill.

7. You shall not commit adultery.

8. You shall not steal.

9. You shall not bear false witness against your neighbor.

10. You shall not covet your neighbor's house, your neighbor's wife, his manservant, his maidservant, his ox, his ass, or anything that is your neighbor's."[102]

Jesus said, "I wonder what was on the first two stone tablets. What would it be like if we were living under a higher law than the Ten Commandments?"

Joseph shook his head. "We probably will never know, but it would be interesting. Now, we will get into some of the law. You will need to know the law in depth, but right now, I am just going to talk about it in general terms. We will go over it in detail later after we cover the prophets."

While Moses was in the mount and after he came down, the Lord gave him other laws besides the Ten Commandments, so the people would know how to live their lives. These things pertained to the treatment of servants, laws of marriage, including ones pertaining to those with more than one wife, the death penalty, a neighbor's animal being injured or injuring one of yours, usury or, in short, all the things one experiences in everyday living. He also was given the laws pertaining to sacrifices. The people were to sacrifice the first-born male of all clean animals, but their children were to be redeemed with a payment to the Lord. Sacrifices were made to the Lord of an animal without blemish so they could be redeemed from their sins; these were sin offerings. Other offerings were made, including the first fruits of a harvest.[103]

They built the tabernacle of the congregation, which was a portable temple. The Israelites donated the

---

[102] Exodus 20: 2-17
[103] Exodus 21-23; 29-31; Leviticus 1-7, 11

cloth, gems, gold, and everything it was built with to the Lord for the tabernacle. They had their most skilled workers and artists do the sewing, engraving, carpentry, and castings. When it was finished and erected, a cloud rested on it during the day and fire rested on it by night. When the cloud was taken up from over the tabernacle, the children of Israel traveled, but if it was not taken up, they stayed where they were. Moses and his sons were brought to the door of the tabernacle of the congregation and washed with water. Moses put on them the holy garments that had been made and anointed them and sanctified them that they might minister in the priest's office. Their anointing was to an everlasting priesthood throughout their generations.[104]

To hallow the tabernacle and to have a remission of sins for the children of Israel, Moses and Aaron were commanded to make offerings over an eight-day period. When they were done and the people had gathered to the tabernacle, the glory of the Lord appeared to all the people and fire came out from the Lord and consumed the burnt offering and the fat upon the altar.[105]

Later, the oldest two sons of Aaron, Nadab, and Abihu, took their censers, put fire in them, put incense on them, and offered strange fire before the Lord, which they had not been commanded to do. Fire went out from the Lord, killing them, and they died before the Lord. Moses said to Aaron, "This is what the Lord spoke to us, saying, 'Those who come near me, must respect me or I will be glorified before all the people.'"

Aaron said nothing to this, and Moses called the sons of Uzziel, the uncle of Aaron, Mishael, and Elzaphan, and said, "Carry your brothers from before the sanctuary out of the camp," and they did so.

Moses said to Aaron and his other sons, Eleazar and Ithamar, "Don't uncover your heads nor rend your clothes as you would normally do to show sorrow in such a situation, that you don't die and wrath doesn't come on the people, but let your brothers, the whole house of Israel, bewail the burning which the Lord has done."

Aaron and his other two sons continued the priestly duties and offered the sin and burnt offerings. The goat of

---

[104] Exodus 35-40; Leviticus 8
[105] Leviticus 9

the sin offering was for them to eat, but they burnt it instead of eating it, which was what was to be done when there was too much for the priests to eat. Moses looked for the goat meat and found they had burnt it instead of eating it. He was angry with Aaron and his two sons which were left for doing this, and said to them, "Why have you not eaten the sin offering in the holy place, seeing it is most holy and God has given it to you to bear the iniquity of the congregation and make atonement for them before the Lord? The blood of it was not brought within the holy place. You should indeed have eaten it in the holy place, as I commanded."

Aaron said to him, "This day they have offered their sin offering and their burnt offering before the Lord and terrible things have happened to me. If I had eaten the sin offering today, should it have been accepted in the sight of the Lord?"

When Moses heard this, he was content.[106]

Jesus said, "That must have been very sad for Aaron and his other sons. I wonder what his other sons were thinking when they used strange fire."

Joseph said, "I don't think we will ever know.

The Lord revealed more of his laws to Moses. He told him which animals were clean and could be eaten and which were unclean and could not be eaten. He was told rules relating to when and how a carcass of an animal could make clean things unclean. After giving birth, women had to be purified for a set time to become clean, and rules were given for that. Rules were given for determining what was and was not leprosy in people, as well as in buildings and clothing, and how they were to be cleansed. Rules were given for other types of uncleanness. Rules for the sacrifice of a goat for the sins of the people and a scapegoat were given. The people were told to bring their sacrifices to the tabernacle and not offer them elsewhere and not to eat blood. Rules relating to which relatives you could marry were given, as well as rules pertaining to homosexuality, bestiality, and other things.[107]

---

[106] Leviticus 10
[107] Leviticus 11-23, 25-27

The Lord told Moses, "Command the children of Israel to bring you pure olive oil beaten to burn for light in lamps continually. Outside of the veil of the testimony, in the tent of meeting, Aaron shall set it from the evening until the morning for a statute forever in your generations. He shall set the lamps on the branches of the candlestick of pure gold, before the Lord continually.

"You shall take fine flour and bake twelve loaves. You shall set them in two rows, six in a row, on the table of pure gold before the Lord. You shall put pure frankincense on each row that it may be on the bread for a memorial, even an offering made by fire to the Lord. Every Sabbath he shall continually set it before the Lord, taken from the children of Israel by an everlasting covenant. It shall be Aaron's and his sons' and they shall eat it in the holy place, for it is most holy to him of the offerings of the Lord made by fire by a perpetual statute."

The son of a woman of Israel, whose father was an Egyptian, went out among the children of Israel. This son and a man of Israel fought together in the camp. This son blasphemed the name of the Lord and cursed, so they brought him to Moses. This son's mother's name was Shelomith, the daughter of Dibri, of the tribe of Dan. They put him under guard that the mind of the Lord might be shown them.

The Lord spoke to Moses. "Bring him who cursed out of the camp and let all that heard him lay their hands on his head and let the entire congregation stone him.

"You shall say to the children of Israel, 'Whoever curses their God shall bear their sin. Those that blaspheme the name of the Lord shall surely be put to death and the entire congregation shall certainly stone them. This is true for the stranger, as it is true for those that are born in the land. When they blaspheme the name of the Lord, they shall be put to death.

"They who kill any person shall surely be put to death. Those who kill a beast shall make it good, beast for beast. If a person causes a blemish in his neighbor as they have done, so shall it be done to them. Breach for breach, eye for eye, tooth for tooth; as they have caused a blemish in a person, so shall it be done to them again. You shall have one manner of law for the stranger as for one of your own country; for I am the Lord, your God."

Moses told this to the people and the son who had cursed was brought out of the camp and stoned to death.[108]

Jesus shook his head. "That makes me sad, but I know the Lord had his reason, so others would be more inclined to keep the law."

Joseph said, "I think that is right. If a lot of people are doing wrong things, it makes it easier for others to be lazy and not do the right things."

The people continued to gather manna every day except the Sabbath, but they began to lust for flesh. They said, "Who shall give us flesh to eat? We remember the fish, the cucumbers, the melons, the leeks, the onions, and the garlic we had in Egypt. Our soul has dried away because there is nothing at all, except this manna."

The Lord was angry with the people and Moses was also displeased with them. Moses went to the Lord and said, "These people weep to me saying, 'Give us flesh to eat. I am not able to bear this entire people alone; it is too heavy for me.'"

The Lord told him, "Gather me seventy men of the elders of Israel, whom you know to be the elders of the people, and officers over them. Bring them to the tabernacle of the congregation that they may stand there with you. I will come down and talk with you there, and I will take of the spirit which is on you and will put it on them. They shall bear the burden of the people with you, that you bear it not by yourself."

"Say to the people, 'Consecrate yourselves for tomorrow and you shall eat flesh. You have wept in the ears of the Lord; therefore, the Lord will give you flesh and you shall eat. You shall not eat one day, or two days, or five days, or ten days, or twenty days, but for a whole month. You shall eat until it comes out your nostrils and it is loathsome to you, because you have despised the Lord who is among you and said, 'Why did we come out of Egypt?'"

---

[108] Leviticus 24

Moses said, "My people are six hundred thousand warriors and you said you would give them flesh to eat for a whole month. Should the flocks and herds be slain for them, to provide for them? Shall all the fish of the sea be gathered for them?"

The Lord said, "Is the Lord's hand weak? You shall see now whether my word shall come to pass to you or not."

Moses went and told the people what the Lord had said and gathered the seventy men of the elders of the people and set them about the tabernacle. The Lord came down in a cloud and spoke to him and took of the spirit that was on him and gave it to the seventy elders. When the spirit rested on them, they prophesied and did not stop.

A wind came up and brought quail from the sea and they fell by the camp, a day's journey on each side, about three feet high on the ground. The people spent all that day, that night, and the next day gathering quail. While they were eating the quail, the wrath of the Lord was kindled against the people and they were hit with a great plague.

Later, Aaron and Miriam were speaking against Moses because of the Ethiopian woman he had married. They said, "Has the Lord spoken only by Moses? Has he not spoken by us also?"

The Lord heard this and spoke to Moses, Aaron, and Miriam, "Come out to the tabernacle of the congregation."

The three came out. The Lord came down in the pillar of the cloud and stood in the door of the tabernacle and called Aaron and Miriam. They came out and he said, "Hear my words. If there is a prophet among you, I the Lord will make myself known to him in a vision and will speak to him in a dream. Moses is very meek, above all the men which are on the earth. There is none as faithful as he is. I speak to him clearly and not with riddles. The likeness of the Lord he sees, then why were you not afraid to speak against my servant Moses?"

The Lord was angry with them and he left and the cloud departed from the tabernacle. Miriam became leprous, white as snow. Aaron looked at Miriam and saw she was leprous. Aaron said to Moses, "Alas, my lord, I beg you, lay not the sin on us, in what we have done foolishly and in which we have sinned. Let her not be as one dead, of

WANDERING THE DESERT

whom the flesh is half eaten when they come out of their mother's womb."

Moses prayed to the Lord, saying, "Heal her now, O God, I beg you."

The Lord said, "If her father had spit in her face, should she not be ashamed seven days? Let her be shut out from the camp seven days and after that let her be brought in again."

Miriam was shut out of the camp for seven days and the people didn't travel until Miriam was healed and brought in again. They then moved to the wilderness of Paran.[109]

Jesus said, "I am glad Miriam was healed. It would be sad if she had to spend the rest of her life outside of camp."

Joseph said, "That is true Jesus, but there are a lot of people who have leprosy and have to live away from family, friends, and other people until they die. It is a very sad life."

Jesus said, "Are those people all sinners?"

Joseph said, "We are all sinners. Some do worse things than others, but I don't think those who have leprosy, as a rule, are any more sinners than I am. I don't know why they have leprosy. Let's go on."

Jesus said, "Please wait. Why do bad things happen to good people?"

Joseph said, "I can't answer that. I think sometimes the Lord gives us problems to help us grow and learn things, but I don't really know. I imagine you will find out someday. Let me know what you learn."

The Lord spoke to Moses and said, "Send men to search the land of Canaan, which I give to the children of Israel. You shall send one from each of the tribes of their fathers, every one a ruler among them."

Moses told them, "See the land, what it is and the people who live there, whether they are strong or weak and how many. Check the land where they live, whether it is good or bad, the cities where they live and what they live in, tents or strongholds. Find out if the land is fat or lean and if there is wood. Be of good courage and bring of the fruit of the land."

---

[109] Numbers 11-12

It was time for the first ripe grapes.

After forty days, they returned. They reported back to Moses and the people. They showed them the fruit, a cluster of grapes so large two of them had to carry it, pomegranates, and figs. They said it was a land that flowed with milk and honey. But the people were strong and the cities were walled and very great. They also saw giants, the children of Anak.

Caleb quieted the people and said, "Let us go up at once and possess it, for we are well able to overcome them."

Others gave an evil report of the land, saying, "The land through which we have gone is a large land that one can get lost in. All the people we saw were very large men. We saw giants, the sons of Anak, and we were like grasshoppers to them. We are not able to go up against the people, for they are stronger than we."[110]

All the people raised their voice and cried and wept. They complained against Moses and Aaron. The people said, "We wish we had died in Egypt or the wilderness!" They also said, "Let us make a new leader and return to Egypt."

Joshua and Caleb, who had gone to explore the land, argued with them. They said, "The land we saw is a very good land. If the Lord delights in us, then he will bring us into this land and give it to us. It is a land which flows with milk and honey. Don't rebel against the Lord, or fear the people of the land. They are bread for us and their defense is departed from them. The Lord is with us, don't fear them."

The people wanted to stone them, but the glory of the Lord appeared in the tabernacle before all the people. The Lord said to Moses, "How long will this people provoke me? How long will it be before they believe me, after all the signs which I have shown among them? As truly as I live, all the earth shall be filled with the glory of the Lord. Because all these which have seen my glory and my miracles, which I did in Egypt and in the wilderness and have tempted me now ten times and have not listened to me, surely, they shall not see the land which I swore to their fathers, nor shall any of them who provoked me see it. Only

---

[110] Numbers 13

my servants Caleb and Joshua will see it, because they have another spirit with them and have followed me fully. I will bring them into the land and their children shall possess it.

"Tomorrow turn around and go into the wilderness by way of the Red Sea. How long shall I bear with this evil congregation, who complain against me? I have heard their complaints. Say to them, 'Your carcasses shall fall in the wilderness, all of you, from twenty years old and up, which have complained against me. You surely shall not come into the land, which I swore to give to you to live in, except Caleb and Joshua. Your little ones, which you said should be a prey, they will I bring in, and they shall know the land which you have despised. But your carcasses shall fall in this wilderness. Your children shall wander forty years in the wilderness and bear your whoredoms until your carcasses are wasted. After the number of days in which you searched the land, even forty days, each day for a year, shall you bear your iniquities, even forty years and you shall know my breach of promise due to your disobedience."

Moses told this to the children of Israel and they mourned greatly. They arose early the next morning and went up to the top of the mountain and said, "We will go up to the place which the Lord has promised, for we have sinned."

Moses said, "Why now do you transgress the commandment of the Lord, it shall not prosper? Don't go up, for the Lord is not with you and you will be defeated by your enemies. The Amalekites and the Canaanites are there before you and you shall fall by the sword, because you have turned away from the Lord and thus the Lord will not be with you."

They still went up, but the Ark of the Covenant of the Lord and Moses stayed in the camp. The Amalekites and the Canaanites which lived there destroyed them and chased them.[111]

Jesus said, "I don't know why so many of them can't obey the Lord. They are very headstrong. It just doesn't make any sense to me."

---

[111] Numbers 14

Joseph said, "Nor does it make sense to me. Next, I am going to tell you something else you won't be able to make sense of."

After this, two hundred and fifty of the princes of the children of Israel, famous in the congregation and men of renown, led by Korah of the tribe of Levi and Dathan and Abiram of the tribe of Reuben, rebelled against Moses and Aaron and said, "You take too much on yourselves. Since the entire congregation is holy, every one of them, and the Lord is among us, then why do you lift yourselves up above the rest of us?"

When Moses heard this, he bowed down and said to Korah and the rest, "Tomorrow, the Lord will show who are his and who is holy. He will cause them whom He has chosen to come near Him. Take your censers and put fire and incense in them before the Lord tomorrow. Those whom the Lord chooses shall be holy."

Then Moses said to Korah, "Hear, I pray you, you son of Levi: Because you are a Levite, you have been chosen to stand before the Lord in the service of the tabernacle and to stand before the congregation to minister to them. Does that seem like a small thing to you? He has brought you near to Him and all the brothers of Levi with you and do you seek the priesthood also? For this cause this company is gathered together against the Lord. What complaints do you have against Aaron?"

Moses called Dathan and Abiram to come up to him, but they would not and they said to Moses, "Is it a small thing you have brought us up out of a land that flows with milk and honey to kill us in the wilderness, unless you make yourself a prince over us? You have not brought us into a land that flows with milk and honey or given us inheritance of fields and vineyards. Will you put out the eyes of these men? We will not come up."

Moses was very angry and told the Lord, "Don't respect their offering. I have not taken one ass from them, nor have I hurt one of them."

Moses said to Korah, "You and all your company be here tomorrow before the Lord, and Aaron will be here also. Every one of you take your censer with incense, two hundred and fifty censers and Aaron also."

The next day they all took their censers, put fire in them, and laid incense on them. Korah gathered all those who were against Moses and Aaron to the door of the tabernacle of the congregation with Moses and Aaron and the glory of the Lord appeared to the entire congregation.

The Lord spoke to Moses and Aaron, saying, "Separate yourselves from among this group, that I may consume them in a moment."

They bowed themselves and said, "O God, the God of the spirits of all flesh, shall one man sin and will you be angry with all the people?"

The Lord said, "Speak to the congregation and say, 'Move away from the tents of Korah, Dathan, and Abiram.'"

Moses went to the tents of Korah, Dathan, and Abiram and the elders of Israel followed him. They had the people move away from their tents, but Korah, Dathan, and Abiram stood in the door of their tents with their wives and children,[112] but their wives and children were ordered to move away from them.[113]

Moses said, "You shall now know that the Lord has sent me to do all these works, for I have not done them of my own mind. If these men are visited by death as all men are, then the Lord has not sent me. But if the Lord makes a new thing and the earth opens her mouth and swallows them up, with all that appertains to them, and they go down quick into the pit, then you shall understand that these men have provoked the Lord."

When Moses was finished speaking, the ground separated and the earth opened her mouth and swallowed them up, with all that appertained to them, and the earth closed upon them and they perished from among the people. All who were round about them fled at their cry, lest the earth would swallow them up also. Then fire came out from the Lord and consumed the two hundred and fifty men who offered incense.

The Lord told Moses, "Have Eleazar, son of Aaron the priest, pick up the censers out of the burning and scatter the fire over there, for the censers are hallowed. Use them to make a covering for the altar, for they offered them before

---

[112] Numbers 16: 1-33
[113] Numbers 26: 9-11

the Lord and they are hallowed. They shall be a sign to the children of Israel and a reminder that no one, unless they are authorized, should come near to offer incense before the Lord; otherwise they may become like Korah and his company."

The next day, all the congregation of the children of Israel complained to Moses and Aaron, saying, "You have killed the people of the Lord."

Jesus said, "You were right, this doesn't make any sense. All these have just died because they didn't keep the Lord's commandments, and now they are blaming Moses. I can't believe it."

Joseph said, "Nor can I."

When the people were gathered against Moses and Aaron, they looked toward the tabernacle and the cloud covered it and the glory of the Lord appeared. Moses and Aaron came before the tabernacle and the Lord spoke to Moses, saying, "Get up from among this people that I may consume them in a moment."

Moses and Aaron bowed, and Moses told Aaron, "Take a censer and put fire in it from off the altar, put on incense, and go quickly to the congregation. Make atonement for them, for wrath has gone out from the Lord and a plague has begun."

Aaron did as Moses commanded and ran into the midst of the people. The plague had begun and he stood between the dead and the living and the plague was stayed. Those who died in the plague were fourteen thousand and seven hundred, beside those who died in the matter of Korah.[114]

After this, the Lord spoke to Moses and said, "Tell the people to have each tribe's leader take a rod and write on it their name. You shall put them in the tabernacle before the testimony, where I will meet with you. The rod I shall choose shall blossom and I will make to cease the complaining of the people against you."

Moses spoke to the leaders and each of the twelve tribes gave him a rod and he laid them in the tabernacle of

---

[114] Numbers 16: 34-50

witness. The rod with Aaron's name on it for the tribe of Levi was among the twelve. The next day, Moses went into the tabernacle and the rod with Aaron's name had budded, bloomed, and brought forth almonds. He brought them out of the tabernacle and each man took his rod.

The Lord said to Moses, "Place Aaron's rod again before the testimony, to be kept for a token against the rebels. This shall take away their complaints from me, so they don't die."[115]

The Lord said to Aaron, "You and your sons and your father's house have been given the responsibility of the priesthood and the sanctuary and, if it is not done properly, iniquity will accrue for those responsible. Your brothers also of the tribe of Levi, the tribe of your father, bring them with you that they may minister with you, but you and your sons shall minister before the tabernacle of witness. They shall keep your commands and do the duties of the tabernacle; they shall not come near the vessels of the sanctuary and the altar, that neither they nor you die. You shall take charge of the sanctuary and the altar; that there is no wrath any more on the children of Israel.

"I have taken your brothers, the Levites, from among the children of Israel; to you they are given as a gift for the Lord, to do the service of the tabernacle of the congregation. Therefore, you and your sons shall keep your priest's office and serve for everything of the altar and within the veil. I have given your priest's office to you for a gift of service and the unauthorized person who comes near shall be put to death."

The Lord also said to Aaron, "I also have given you the charge of my heave offerings of all the hallowed things of the children of Israel. *(There were numerous offerings made by Israel. Burnt offerings were made at times and the entire animal was burned. There were other offerings such as sin, peace, thanksgiving, and trespass, where only the fat and other parts that were not usually eaten, were burned. Most of the animal went to those who had offered the animal, but the skin and some other parts were the priest's and his family's. These other parts, depending on what they were, were given to the Lord and then given back to the*

---

[115] Numbers 17

priest, through a waving motion or a heaving motion, hence the name of the offering, wave or heave.) I have given them because of the anointing and to your sons, by an ordinance forever. This shall be yours of the holiest things, kept from the fire. Every oblation of theirs, whether a meat offering, a sin offering or a trespass offering, which they shall render to me, shall be most holy for you and your sons. In the holiest place shall you eat it and it shall be holy to you. This is yours, the heave offering of their gift, with all the wave offerings of the children of Israel. I have given them to you and to your sons and daughters with you, by a statute forever. Every one who is clean in your house shall eat it.

"All the best of the oil and all the best of the wine, and of the wheat, the first fruits of them which they shall offer to the Lord, them have I given you. Whatever is first ripe in the land, which they shall bring to the Lord, shall be yours; every one who is clean in your house shall eat it.

"The firstborn of everything which the people bring to the Lord, whether it is of men or beasts, shall be yours. Nevertheless, the firstborn of man shall you redeem and the firstling of unclean beasts shall you redeem. Those who are to be redeemed from a month old shall you redeem, by your estimation, for the money of five shekels, after the shekel of the sanctuary. But the firstling of a cow, a sheep, or a goat you shall not redeem. They are holy and you shall sprinkle their blood on the altar and shall burn their fat for an offering made by fire, for a sweet savor to the Lord. The flesh of them shall be yours, as the wave breast and as the right shoulder are yours. All the heave offerings of the holy things, which the children of Israel offer to the Lord, have I given you and your sons and daughters with you, by a statute forever.

"You shall have no inheritance in the land, nor shall you have any part among the children of Israel. I am your part and your inheritance among them. I have given the children of Levi a tenth of all the offerings of Israel for an inheritance, even the service of the tabernacle of the congregation. The children of Israel henceforth must not come near the tabernacle of the congregation, lest they bear sin and die. The Levites shall do the service of the tabernacle of the congregation and they shall bear the responsibility for doing it correctly. It shall be a statute forever throughout your generations that among the children of Israel they have no inheritance. But the tithes of the children of Israel, which they offer as a heave offering to the Lord, I have given to the Levites to inherit. Therefore, I have said to them, 'Among the children of Israel, they shall have no inheritance.'"

The Lord said to Moses, "Speak to the Levites and tell them, 'When you take of the tithes of the children of Israel, which I have given you for your inheritance, then you shall offer up a heave offering of it for the Lord, even a tenth part of the tithe. This heave offering shall be reckoned to you, as though it were the grain of the threshing floor or as the fullness of the winepress. Thus, you also shall offer a heave offering to the Lord of all your tithes which you receive of the children of Israel, and you shall give thereof the Lord's heave offering to Aaron the priest. Out of all your gifts you shall offer every heave offering of the Lord of all the best thereof, even the hallowed part thereof out of it. You shall eat it in any place, you and your households, for it is your reward for your service in the tabernacle of the congregation. You shall bear no sin because of it, when you have heaved from it the best of it, neither shall you pollute the holy things of the children of Israel, lest you die.'"[116]

The whole congregation of the children of Israel went into the desert of Zin in the first month and they abode in Kadesh. Miriam died and was buried there. There was no water for the people and they gathered together against Moses and Aaron.

The people contended with Moses and said, "We wish we had died when our brothers died before the Lord! Why have you brought up the congregation of the Lord into this wilderness, that we and our livestock should die here? Why have you made us to come up out of Egypt, to bring us into this evil place? It is no place of seed, figs, vines, or pomegranates, nor is there any water to drink."

Moses and Aaron went from the presence of the assembly to the door of the tabernacle of the congregation and bowed their faces to the ground and the glory of the Lord appeared to them. The Lord said to Moses, "Take the rod and gather the assembly together, you and Aaron your

---

[116] Numbers 18

brother, and speak to the rock before their eyes. It shall give forth its water and you shall bring forth to them water out of the rock for them and their beasts to drink."

Moses took the rod from before the Lord, as he commanded him. Moses and Aaron gathered the congregation together before the rock and he said to them, "Hear now, you rebels, must we fetch you water out of this rock?"

Moses raised his hand and, with his rod, he smote the rock twice and the water came out abundantly and the congregation drank and their beasts also.

The Lord spoke to Moses and Aaron, "Because you believed me not, to honor me in the eyes of the children of Israel, by not speaking to the rock, but striking it, therefore, you shall not bring this congregation into the land which I have given them." This is called the water of Meribah (strife), because the children of Israel strove with the Lord and he was sanctified in them.

Jesus said, "That is really sad. I am sure Moses would have loved to see the promised land He was the prophet and leader. He above all should not have let his anger rule him and have forgotten to keep the commandments and do his Heavenly Father's will. I need to remember that in my life."
Joseph said, "Very good thinking."

Next, Moses sent messengers from Kadesh to the king of Edom, saying, "Thus says your brother Israel, You know all the trials that have befallen us: How our fathers went down into Egypt and dwelled a long time; and the Egyptians vexed us and our fathers. When we cried to the Lord, he heard us and sent an angel and has brought us out of Egypt. We are now in Kadesh, a city very close to your border. Let us pass through your country. We will not pass through the fields or the vineyards; neither will we drink of the water of the wells. We will go by the king's highway; we will not turn to the right hand or to the left, until we have passed your borders."

The king of Edom said, "You shall not pass by me or I will come out against you with the sword."

The children of Israel replied, "We will go by the highway and if I and my cattle drink of your water, then we will pay for it. We will only go through by foot."

Edom said, "You shall not go through," and came out against Israel with many people and with a strong hand. Thus, Edom refused to give Israel passage through their border, and Israel turned away from them.

They journeyed from Kadesh to Mount Hor.

The Lord spoke to Moses and Aaron in Mount Hor by the coast of the land of Edom, saying, "Aaron shall be gathered to his people, for he shall not enter the land which I have given to Israel, because you rebelled against my word at the water of Meribah. Take Aaron and Eleazar, his son, and bring them up to Mount Hor. Strip Aaron of his garments and put them on Eleazar. Aaron shall be gathered to his people and shall die there."

Moses did as the Lord commanded, and they went up into Mount Hor in the sight of all the people. Moses stripped Aaron of his garments and put them on Eleazar, his son. Aaron died there in the top of the mount, and Moses and Eleazar came down. When all the people saw Aaron was dead, they mourned for Aaron thirty days.[117]

On their way through the Negev Desert, Israel was attacked by Canaanites under the king of Arad and the Canaanites took some prisoners. Israel vowed a vow to the Lord and said, "If you will deliver these people into my hand, then I will utterly destroy their cities."

The Lord did as they asked and they destroyed them and their cities, naming the place Hormah.

They skirted the land of Edom by way of the Red Sea and were very discouraged because of the difficulty of traveling that way. The people complained to God and Moses, saying, "Why have you brought us this way out of Egypt to die in the wilderness? There is no bread or water and we hate this light bread."[118]

The Lord sent fiery flying serpents among the people and they bit the people and many died. The people came to Moses and said, "We have sinned, because we have spoken against the Lord and against you. Pray to the Lord so he will take away the serpents from us."

Moses prayed for the people and the Lord said to Moses, "Make an image of a fiery serpent and set it on a

---

[117] Numbers 20
[118] Numbers 21:1-5

pole. When someone is bitten, if they will look at the serpent on the pole, they will be healed."

Moses made a serpent of brass and put it on a pole. If a serpent had bitten someone, when they looked at the serpent of brass, they were healed. But because of the easiness of the way, many hardened their hearts and wouldn't look and thus perished.[119]

Jesus said, "I can't imagine how anyone would not look at something if it would save their life. Some of these Israelites are something else. Don't you think so, too, Father?"
"I do, son."

The Israelites continued their journey until they came to Mount Pisgah, which overlooked the land where they were going. They sent messengers to Sihon, king of the Amorites, saying, "Let us go through your land. We will not go into your fields or your vineyards and we will not drink of your well water, but we will go by the king's highway, until we are past your borders."

Sihon would not allow Israel to pass through, but gathered all his people together and fought with Israel in the wilderness, coming to Jahaz. Israel smote him with the edge of the sword and possessed his land from Arnon to Jabbok. Israel took all the cities of the Amorites, including Heshbon and the surrounding villages, and lived in them.

Moses sent a group to spy out Jazer, and they drove out the Amorites who were there, capturing it and its villages. Israel next went up to Bashan and Og. The king and all his people went out to fight them at Edrei.

The Lord said to Moses, "Don't fear him, for I have delivered him into your hand, along with all his people and his land. Do to him as you did to Sihon, king of the Amorites." They smote him, his sons, and all his people, until there was not one left alive and they possessed his land.[120]

After this, the children of Israel moved forward and pitched their tents in the Plain of Moab on the east of the Jordan by Jericho.

---

[119] Numbers 21:6-9; BM 1 Nephi 17:41-42
[120] Numbers 21

Balak, the son of Zippor and the King of the Moabites, saw what was done to the Amorites and was very afraid of Israel, because there were many of them. An ally of Moab was the neighboring country of Midian, so he told the elders of Midian of his concern, saying, "This people shall conquer all that are around us."

Balak decided to ask the help of Balaam, the son of Beor of Pethor (a prophet, but not of Israel). He sent the elders of Moab and Midian to Balaam with rewards for him to curse Israel, and they told him, "There is a group of people who have come from Egypt. They cover the face of the earth and they are now next to us. Come now, I beg, curse this people, for they are too mighty for us. Perhaps we shall prevail, that we may smite them and drive them out of the land. We know that those whom you bless are blessed and those whom you curse are cursed."

Balaam said, "'Spend the night and I will tell you in the morning what the Lord tells me."

That night, God came to Balaam and said, "What men are these with you?"

Balaam told God, "Balak, the king of Moab, says, 'A people have come from Egypt, which cover the face of the earth. Come and curse them for me. Perhaps I shall be able to overcome them and drive them out.'"

God said, "You shall not curse them, for they are blessed."

In the morning, Balaam said to the princes, "Go home; for the Lord refuses to let me go with you."

The princes returned to Balak and said, "Balaam refused to come with us."

Balak sent more princes and more honorable ones than at first. They came to Balaam and said, "Balak, the son of Zippor, says to let nothing, we beg you, keep you from coming to me. I will give you great honors and whatever you want. I beg you, come curse this people."

Balaam said, "If Balak would give me his house full of silver and gold, I cannot go against the Lord, my God. Stay this night and I will again ask the Lord what I can do."

God came to Balaam and said, "If the men ask you again, get up and go with them, but the word I shall say to you, that shall you do."

Balaam went with the princes in the morning.

God was angry with him because he went with them. The angel of the Lord stood in the way as an adversary to him. He was riding on his ass and his two servants were with him. The ass saw the angel of the Lord standing in the way with his sword drawn. The ass turned aside and went into a field.

Balaam struck the ass to turn her back on the path. The angel of the Lord moved ahead and stood in the path in a vineyard, with a wall on each side. When the ass saw the angel of the Lord, she thrust herself into the wall and crushed Balaam's foot against the wall and he struck her again.

The angel of the Lord moved ahead again into a narrower place, where there was no room for the ass to turn. When the ass saw the angel of the Lord again, she laid down under Balaam. Balaam was angry and struck the ass with a staff.

Balaam thought he heard the ass speak, saying, "What have I done to you that you have struck me these three times?"

Balaam said, "Because you have not obeyed me. I wish there was a sword in my hand, for I would kill you."

The ass seemed to reply, "Am not I your ass, on which you have ridden ever since I was yours until now? Did I ever do this?"

He said, "No."

The eyes of Balaam were opened and he saw the angel of the Lord standing in the path, with his sword drawn, and he bowed his head to the ground.

The angel of the Lord said, "Why have you struck your ass three times? I am here to oppose you, because you have not been obedient. The ass saw me and turned away or I would have slain you."

Balaam said, "I have sinned, for I knew not you stood in the way against me. If I displease you, I will return home."

The angel said, "Go with the men, but only the word of the Lord shall you speak to them."

Jesus said, "I don't understand what is happening. Balaam was told by the Lord to go with the men, if they asked him. Didn't they ask him?"

Joseph said, "I don't know if they asked him or not. They may have, but it doesn't really matter. Balaam had already asked God if he could curse Israel and was told they were blessed. There was no need to ask again. Just because they came with more rewards for Balaam didn't change what was right and wrong. He knew what he was asking was not good, but he asked anyway. When we pray for things, we should be careful and ask only what is good for us. If we ask for something not good, we usually are protected and don't get it, but sometimes we do, and it is not good for us when that happens. Does that make sense to you?"

Jesus said, "It does, but did his ass really speak?"

Joseph said, "What do you think?"

Jesus said, "If my Father wanted it to speak, it could. Ah. . . It probably doesn't make any difference what happened, as long as Balaam thought the ass was talking. It is funny he didn't seem to think the ass talking was strange."

When Balaam came to Moab, Balak went to meet him and said to Balaam, "Didn't I send for you? Why didn't you come? Am I not able to reward you handsomely?"

Balaam said, "I have come to you, but I have no power to say anything except the word God puts in my mouth."

They went to Kirjath Huzoth and, in the morning, Balak took Balaam up into the high places of Baal, that he might overlook and see all the children of Israel.[121]

Balaam said to Balak, "Build me seven altars here and prepare seven oxen and seven rams for sacrifice."

Balak did as Balaam asked, and Balaam offered on every altar an ox and a ram.

Balaam said to Balak, "Stand by the altars and I will go to meet the Lord and, whatever he shows me, I will tell you."

The Lord met him and said, "Return to Balak and tell him what I tell you."

Balaam returned to Balak and told him and those with him, "Balak, you have told me to curse Jacob and defy Israel. How can I curse whom God has not cursed? Or how can I defy whom the Lord has not defied? From the top of the rocks I see Israel and from the hills I behold them."

---

[121] Numbers 22

Then Balaam blessed Israel.

Balak said, "What have you done to me? I asked you to curse my enemies and you have blessed them."

Balaam answered, "I must speak the words the Lord has put in my mouth."

Balak said, "Please come with me to another place where you can see them. You won't see them all, just a portion of them. Curse them for me from there."

Balak brought him to the top of Pisgah and built seven altars there. He offered an ox and a ram on every altar.

Balaam said to Balak, "Stand here by the burnt offering, while I meet the Lord."

The Lord met Balaam and told him what to say to Balak.

Balaam returned to Balak who was standing by the burnt offering with the princes of Moab. Balak asked, "What did the Lord say?"

Balaam said, "Balak, God is not a man who lies, neither the son of man who needs to repent. What he says he will do, he does. I have been commanded to bless. He has blessed and I cannot reverse it. He has not seen iniquity in Jacob, neither has he seen perverseness in Israel. The Lord is with Israel and the shout of a king is among them. God brought them out of Egypt; they have the strength of a wild ox. Surely there is no enchantment against Jacob, neither is there any divination against Israel. It shall be said of Jacob and of Israel, "What has God wrought!" The people shall rise as a great lion and lift themselves as a young lion. He shall not lie down until he eats of the prey and drinks the blood of the slain."

Balak said to Balaam, "If you can't curse them, don't bless them."

Balaam said, "Didn't I tell you, what the Lord says, I must do?"

Balak said, "Please, I will bring you to another place. Maybe it will please God that you may curse them for me from there."

Balak brought Balaam to the top of Peor.

WANDERING THE DESERT

Balaam told Balak to build seven altars and prepare seven oxen and seven rams. Balak did that and offered an ox and a ram on every altar.[122]

When Balaam saw it pleased the Lord to bless Israel, he didn't go as he did at other times to seek for enchantments, but he set his face toward the wilderness. He lifted his eyes and blessed Israel.

Balak was angry with Balaam. He struck his hands together and said, "I called you to curse my enemies and you have blessed them these three times. Therefore, flee to your place. I thought to promote you to great honor, but the Lord has kept you back from honor."

Balaam said to Balak, "Didn't I tell your messengers, 'If Balak, would give me his house full of silver and gold, I cannot go beyond the commandment of the Lord, to do either good or bad myself, but what the Lord says, that I must speak?' I am going to my home now."

Balaam turned to leave, as did Balak.[123] As Balaam thought about the honor and riches he had missed out on, an idea came to his mind.

He turned about and went to Balak. He said, "I know how you can get Israel to curse themselves. Invite them to the sacrifices of your god Baal Peor. They will eat and fornicate, which will cause them to sin in the eye of their god."[124]

Balak rewarded Balaam for this advice, though not as richly as he would have, had he not blessed Israel first.

Israel abode in Shittim and the Israelites began to commit whoredoms with the daughters of Moab. They invited the Israelites to the sacrifices of their gods. They came and ate and bowed down to their gods. Israel joined themselves to Baal Peor and the anger of the Lord was kindled against Israel.

The Lord said to Moses, "Take all the chief men of the people who have joined themselves to Baal Peor and hang them up before the Lord facing the sun, that the fierce anger of the Lord may be turned away from Israel. They have bowed down to the sun, they should be hanged facing it."

---

[122] Numbers 23
[123] Numbers 24
[124] Revelations 2:14

Moses said to the judges of Israel, "Slay every one of your men who were joined to Baal Peor."

One of the children of Israel, Zimri, the son of Salu, a prince of a chief house among the Simeonites, brought into the camp a Midianitish woman, Cozbi, the daughter of Zur, head over a people and of a chief house in Midian. This was done in the sight of all the congregation of the children of Israel, who were weeping before the door of the tabernacle of the congregation about the problem with Baal Peor.

Phinehas, the son of Eleazar, the son of Aaron the priest, saw it. He got up from among the people and took a javelin in his hand. He went after the man of Israel into the tent and thrust both through, the man of Israel and the woman through her belly. So the plaque was stayed from the children of Israel. Those who died in the plague were twenty-four thousand.

The Lord spoke to Moses and said, "Phinehas has turned my wrath away from the children of Israel, that I didn't consume the children of Israel in my jealousy. I gave to him my covenant of peace. He shall have it and his seed after him, even the covenant of an everlasting priesthood, because he was zealous for his God and made atonement for the children of Israel."

Continuing, the Lord said, "Vex the Midianites and smite them. They vexed you with their wiles and have beguiled you."[125]

They were now at their home and Jesus said, "It is good to be home. It looks mighty nice. I am glad we live in Nazareth and not Sepphoris. It is too busy."

Joseph said, "I feel the same way. We will start where we left off tomorrow."

The next day Joseph said,

"After the plague, the Lord told Moses and Eleazar to number the men of Israel, from twenty years old and up, all who are able to go to war. The numbers by tribe were Reuben 43,730; Simeon 22,200; Gad 40,500; Judah 76,500; Issachar 64,300; Zebulun 60,500; Manasseh 52,700;

---

[125] Numbers 25

Ephraim 32,500; Benjamin 45,600; Dan 64,400; Asher 53,400; Naphtali 45,400 for a total of 601,730.

The Lord told Moses, "To these the land shall be divided for an inheritance based on the number of names. The more names, the more land you shall give them. The fewer names, the less you shall give them. To every one shall his inheritance be given based on those who were numbered. Nonetheless, the land shall be divided by lot."

The tribe of Levi was also numbered, males from one month of age up. They were not numbered with the others, as there was no inheritance given them among the children of Israel, except the priesthood. Their number was 23,000.

Among those who were numbered were none Moses and Aaron numbered, when they numbered them in the wilderness of Sinai, except Caleb, the son of Jephunneh, and Joshua, the son of Nun. The Lord had told the rest of them they would surely die in the wilderness and they did.[126]

The Lord told Moses, "Go up into Mount Abarim and see the land which I have given the children of Israel. When you have seen it, you also shall be gathered to your people as Aaron your brother was gathered. You rebelled against my commandment in the desert of Zin, in the strife of the congregation, to honor me at the water before their eyes. That is the water of Meribah in Kadesh in the wilderness of Zin."

Moses said to the Lord, "Let the God of the spirits of all flesh set a man over the congregation. One who will lead them well, so they are not as sheep which have no shepherd."

The Lord said, "Take Joshua, the son of Nun, a man in who is the spirit, and lay your hands on him. Set him before Eleazar, the priest, and before the entire congregation and give him a charge in their sight. You shall put some of your honor on him that all the congregation of the children of Israel may be obedient. At his word, shall they go out and come in, both he and all the congregation of the children of Israel with him."

---

[126] Numbers 26

Moses laid his hands on him and gave him a charge as the Lord had commanded, before the entire congregation.[127]

The Lord spoke to Moses and commanded the children of Israel to give Him his sacrifices by fire for a sweet savor to him. There were morning and evening offerings, Sabbath offerings, offerings at the beginnings of their months, offerings for Passover, for harvest, and for various feasts. Offerings were made of lambs, rams, bullocks, goats, birds, flour, wine, fruits, etc.[128]

The Lord spoke to Moses, "Avenge the children of Israel of the Midianites and, after this, you will be gathered to your people."

Moses had the people pick one thousand warriors from each tribe, for a total of twelve thousand, telling them to be armed for war. They went to war with Phinehas, the priest, who had the holy instruments and the trumpets to blow.

They slew all the males of the Midianites and their kings. They also killed Balaam, the son of Beor, with the sword. They took all the women of Midian captive, with their little ones. They took all their cattle, their flocks, and all their goods as a spoil. They burned all their cities where they lived, as well as their strongholds. They brought all the captives, livestock, and goods to Moses, Eleazar, and the congregation where they camped in the plains of Moab, by the Jordan near Jericho.

Moses, Eleazar, and the princes of the congregation went out to meet them. Moses was angry with the captains which came from the battle. He said to them, "Have you saved all the women alive? These caused the children of Israel, through the counsel of Balaam, to commit trespass against the Lord in the matter of Peor. There was a plague among the congregation of the Lord, because of it.

"Kill every male among the little ones and kill every woman who has had sex with a man. But all the female children who are virgins, keep alive for you. Whoever has killed anyone, or touched any slain, stay out of the camp for seven days. Purify both yourself and your captives on the third day and on the seventh. Purify all your

---

[127] Numbers 27
[128] Numbers 23-29

clothing and all that is made of skins, all things of goat hair, and all things made of wood."

Eleazar, the priest, told them, "This is the law which the Lord commanded Moses. Gold, silver, brass, iron, tin, lead, and anything else that will withstand the fire, you shall make go through the fire and it shall be clean. Nevertheless, it shall also be purified with the water of purification, as will anything that will not withstand fire. You shall wash your clothes on the seventh day and you shall be clean and then you shall come into camp."

The Lord told Moses, "Take the total of the spoil and divide it into two parts. One half is for those who were in the war and went into battle; the other half is for the congregation. Levy a tribute of one in 500 (0.2 %) on what the men of war have, both of persons, cattle, asses, and sheep. Take it from their half and give it to Eleazar for a heave offering of the Lord. Of the children of Israel's half, take one in 50 (2%) of the persons, the cattle, the asses, the flocks, and all manner of beasts and give them to the Levites, which keep the charge of the tabernacle of the Lord."

The total of the spoil that was taken was 675,000 sheep, 72,000 cattle, 61,000 asses, and 32,000 young females.

The officers and the captains of the men of war came to Moses and said, "We have taken a head count of all our men and not one was lost in the war. Thus, we have brought an oblation for the Lord, from what every man has gotten, jewels of gold, chains, bracelets, rings, earrings, and tablets to make an atonement for our souls before the Lord." All the gold that was offered up to the Lord was about four hundred twenty pounds. Moses and Eleazar took the gold and brought it into the tabernacle for a memorial for the children of Israel before the Lord.[129]

The Children of Reuben and of Gad had a lot of livestock. When they saw the land of Jazer and of Gilead was a great place for livestock, they spoke to Moses, Eleazar, and the princes of the congregation, saying, "The land which the Lord captured before the congregation of Israel, is a land for livestock and we have a lot of livestock.

---

[129] Numbers 31

If we have found grace in your sight, let this land be given to us for a possession and bring us not over Jordan."

Moses said, "Shall your brothers go to war and you sit here? Why discourage you the heart of the children of Israel from going over into the land which the Lord has given them? Thus, did your fathers, when I sent them to spy out the land which the Lord had given them. When they went up and saw the land, they discouraged the heart of the children of Israel that they should not go into the land which the Lord had given them. The Lord's anger was kindled the same time and he swore, 'Surely none of the men who came up out of Egypt, from twenty years old and up, shall see the land which I swore to Abraham, Isaac, and Jacob, because they have not wholly followed me. That is except Caleb, and Joshua, for they have wholly followed the Lord. The Lord was angry with Israel and he made them wander in the wilderness forty years, until all the generation that had done evil in the sight of the Lord was consumed. You have grown up in your father's stead, an increase of sinful men, to augment yet the fierce anger of the Lord toward Israel. For if you turn away from following Him, he will yet again leave them in the wilderness and you shall destroy this entire people.'"

The children of Gad and Reuben came near to Moses and said, "We will build sheepfolds here for our livestock and cities for our little ones. We will go armed before the children of Israel, until we have brought them to their place and our little ones shall dwell in the fenced cities because of the inhabitants of the land. We will not return to our houses until the children of Israel have inherited every man his inheritance. We will not inherit with them on the other side of Jordan, because our inheritance has fallen to us on this side of the Jordan."

Moses said, "If you will all go over the Jordan armed before the Lord, until the Lord has driven out His enemies from before Him and the land is subdued before the Lord, then afterward you shall return and be guiltless, and Israel and this land shall be your possession. But if you will not do so, you have sinned against the Lord and your sin will find you out. Build your cities for your little ones and folds for your sheep and do what you have said."

They said, "Your servants will do as my lord commands. Our little ones, our wives, our flocks, and all our cattle shall be there in the cities of Gilead, but your servants will pass over, every man armed for war, before the Lord to battle, as you said."

Moses commanded Eleazar, the priest, Joshua, and the chief fathers of the tribes of the children of Israel, "If the children of Gad and the children of Reuben will pass over the Jordan with you, then you shall give them the land of Gilead for a possession. But if they will not pass over with you armed, they shall have possessions among you in the land of Canaan."

Moses gave to them, even the children of Gad, Reuben, and the half tribe of Manasseh, the son of Joseph, the kingdom of Sihon king of the Amorites and the kingdom of Og, king of Bashan, the land with the cities thereof.[130]

The Lord spoke to Moses, "Say to the children of Israel, 'When you have passed over Jordan into the land of Canaan, you shall drive out all the inhabitants of the land. You shall destroy all their stone figures, their molten images, and pull down all their high places. You shall dispossess the inhabitants of the land and live there, for I have given you the land to live in. The land shall be divided by lot for an inheritance among your families. The more people, the more land you shall give them. The fewer people, the less land you shall give them. Everyone's inheritance shall be where his lot falls.

"But if you do not drive out the inhabitants of the land, then it shall come to pass those which you let remain shall be pricks in your eyes and thorns in your sides. They shall vex you in the land where you live. It shall come to pass that I shall do to you what I thought to do to them."

The Lord went on to define the borders of Israel and told him how to divide the land among the tribes.[131] "Command the children of Israel that they give to the Levites of their inheritance cities to live in. Also, give the Levites suburbs around the cities. They shall live in the cities, and the suburbs shall be for their cattle, their goods, and for their beasts. The suburbs shall reach from the wall of the city out a thousand cubits all around the city. To have

---

[130] Numbers 32
[131] Numbers 33:52-56; 34

this, measure out from the city on the east, south, west, and north side two thousand cubits. The city shall be in the midst.

"Among the cities which you shall give to the Levites, there shall be six cities for refuge, which you shall appoint for the manslayer. There shall be three cities on this side of Jordan and three in Canaan. Everyone who kills a person accidentally may flee there. The congregation shall judge whether the slayer is guilty of murder or if it was manslaughter. If the person is guilty of murder, the revenger of blood, probably a relative, will kill the murderer wherever he meets him. If he is not guilty of murder, the congregation will restore him to the city of refuge where he fled. He shall live there until the death of the high priest, which was anointed with the holy oil, at which time he may return to his home. But if the slayer shall at any time come without the border of the city of his refuge and the revenger of blood find him without the borders of the city, the revenger of blood will not be guilty of blood if he kills him, because he should have stayed within the city. Don't defile the land which you shall inhabit, where I dwell, for I dwell among the children of Israel."[132]

Jesus said, "If it was an accident and somebody was killed, why should they have to spend the rest of their life, or until the High Priest dies, in the city of refuge?"

Joseph said, "Human life is precious. We should not do anything that will endanger someone's life. If we killed someone, even accidentally, we were probably doing something we should not have been doing."

Jesus said, "Why do they have to stay in the refuge city until the death of the High Priest?"

Joseph said, "I am not sure, but it may be somewhat like a sacrifice. Somehow life is tied in to the death of the High Priest making a sacrifice for the sin or mistake of the killer.

In the fortieth year of their leaving Egypt, on the first day of the eleventh month, when he was one hundred and twenty years old, Moses spoke to the children of Israel. He rehearsed to them their Journey from Egypt to the

---

[132] Numbers 35

Promised Land and the problems he and they experienced on the way. He reminded them to keep the commandments they had made and if they would do so they would be blessed in the land, otherwise they would be scattered among all nations.

He reminded them of the covenant they made in Horeb with God; it was with them not their fathers and they heard the voice of God. He went over the Ten Commandments and told them, "The Lord, our God, is one Lord and you shall love the Lord, your God, with all your heart, your soul, and your might." He reminded them while they were in the wilderness for forty years, their clothes didn't wear out and their feet didn't swell. He told them about the abundance of good things they did not have to work for that they would find in the Promised Land.

He told them they must teach their children the laws of God and to teach them to be obedient to Him. If their children were not obedient in future generations, the wrath of God would be upon them. They would be conquered by stronger nations. They would suffer with disease, pestilence, crime, and their children would be taken from them by force. Some would be in besieged cities and the tender, delicate woman, who would not adventure to set the sole of her foot on the ground for delicateness and tenderness, should have her eye for evil toward her husband and her children; for she should eat her own children.

Moses called Joshua to him in the sight of all Israel and told him, "Be strong and of good courage. You must go with this people to the land which the Lord has sworn to their fathers to give them and you shall cause them to inherit it. The Lord will go before you and be with you. He will not fail you, nor forsake you; fear not, neither be dismayed."

Moses blessed the tribes, but blessed Joseph above the rest, saying to Joseph, "Blessed of the Lord be his land: For the precious things of heaven, for the dew and for the deep that lies beneath; For the precious fruits, brought forth by the sun and for the precious things put forth by the moon; For the chief things of the ancient mountains and for the precious things of the lasting hills; For the precious things of the earth and fullness of it; For the goodwill of him who dwells in the bush.

"Let the blessing come upon the head of Joseph and upon the top of the head of him who was separated from his brothers. His glory is like the firstling of his bullock and his horns are like the horns of the wild ox. With them he shall push the people together to the ends of the earth. They are the ten thousands of Ephraim and the thousands of Manasseh."

Moses went up from the plains of Moab to the mountain of Nebo, to the top of Pisgah, near Jericho. The Lord showed him all the land of Gilead to Dan and all of Naphtali, the land of Ephraim, Manasseh, and Judah to the farthest sea. He also showed him the south and the plain of the valley of Jericho.

Moses, the servant of the Lord, died there in the land of Moab, as the Lord said, but no one knows of his sepulcher. The children of Israel wept for Moses in the plains of Moab for thirty days.

Joshua, the son of Nun, was full of the spirit of wisdom, because Moses had laid his hands on him. The children of Israel listened to him and did as the Lord commanded Moses.

Moses was a mighty prophet whom the Lord knew face to face. His might was shown by all the signs and wonders the Lord sent him to do in the land of Egypt to Pharaoh, to all his servants, and his land.[133]

JOSHUA

At this point, Joseph stopped and said to Jesus, "That is enough for today. Would you like to hear more tomorrow?"

Jesus said, "Yes. I have really enjoyed learning about this history."

The next afternoon, Joseph started where he left off,

After the death of Moses, the Lord spoke to Joshua and said, "Moses, my servant is dead; now go over Jordan, you and the children of Israel, into the land which I give them. Every place you will walk, I have given to you, as I said to

---

[133] Deuteronomy, Recap of

JOSHUA

Moses. From the wilderness of Lebanon to the great river Euphrates, all the land of the Hittites to the great sea toward the west, shall be yours. There shall not any man be able to stand before you all the days of your life. As I was with Moses, so I will be with you. I will not fail you, nor forsake you. Be strong and of a good courage, for to this people shall you divide the land for an inheritance, which I swore to their fathers to give them.

"Observe and do all the law, which Moses, my servant, commanded you. Turn not from it to the right hand or to the left, that you may prosper wherever you go. This book of law shall not depart out of your mouth, but you shall meditate therein day and night, that you may observe to do all that is written therein. Then your way shall be prosperous and you shall have success, for the Lord your God is with you wherever you go."

Joshua commanded the officers of the people to pass through the host and command the people to prepare food, for within three days they would pass over Jordan and go in to possess the land which the Lord, their God, would give them.

Joshua sent two men to secretly spy out the land of Jericho. They went and came to a harlot named Rahab and lodged in her house. The king of Jericho was told, "Men came here tonight of the children of Israel to search out the country."

The king sent to Rahab, saying, "Bring the men who have come to you, for they have come to search the country."

The woman took the two men and hid them, and told the king, "Men came to me, but I don't know where they are. About the time of shutting the gate, when it was dark, the men left. Where they went, I don't know. Go after them quickly and you will catch them."

Then she took the men up to the roof of the house and hid them with the stalks of flax which she had on the roof. The king's men pursued them to the fords of Jordan, and they shut the gate as soon as the pursuers had left.

Before the spies had lain down, Rahab came to them on the roof and said, "I know the Lord has given you the land and your terror has fallen on us and all the inhabitants of the land faint because of you. We have heard how the Lord dried up the water of the Red Sea for you when you came out of Egypt. Also, what you did to the two kings of the Amorites

JOSHUA

who were on the other side Jordan, Sihon and Og, whom you destroyed.

"As soon as we heard these things, our hearts did melt, neither did there remain any courage in any man, because of you. For the Lord, your God, he is God in heaven above and in the earth beneath. Therefore, I pray you to swear to me by the Lord, since I have shown you kindness, you will also show kindness to my father's house and give me a true token. A token that you will save alive my father, my mother, my brothers and sisters, and all they have and deliver us from death."

The men answered her, "Our life for yours, if you don't tell our business. It shall be, when the Lord has given us the land, we will deal kindly and truly with you."

She let them down by a cord through the window, for her house was built on the town wall. She said to them, "Go to the mountain, lest the pursuers meet you. Hide yourselves there three days, until the pursuers have returned, and then you may go on your way."

The men told her, "We will be blameless of this oath which you have made us swear, unless you tie this line of scarlet strands in the window which you let us down with. You shall bring your father, mother, brothers, and your entire father's household home to you. It shall be whoever shall go out of the house into the street, their blood shall be on their own head and we shall be guiltless. Whoever shall be with you in the house, their blood shall be on our head, if any hand be on them. If you tell anyone our business, then we will be quit of the oath which you have made us swear."

She said, "According to your words, so be it," and sent them away.

They went to the mountain and stayed there three days, until the pursuers had returned. The pursuers sought them all along the way, but didn't find them. After the three days, the spies returned to Joshua and told him what had happened to them. They said, "Truly, the Lord has delivered into our hands all the land, for all the inhabitants of the country faint because of us."[134]

Joshua and all of Israel rose early in the morning and moved their camp from Shittim to Jordan. After three days,

---

[134] Joshua 1, 2

JOSHUA

the officers went through the host and commanded the people, "When you see the Ark of the Covenant of the Lord, your God, and the Levite priests bearing it, begin to move, you shall follow it. Keep a space between you and it of about four thousand feet. Don't come near it to see where to go, because you have not come this way before. Consecrate yourselves, for tomorrow the Lord will do wonders among you. You shall know the living God is among you and that without fail, he will drive out the Canaanites, the Hittites, the Hivites, the Perizzites, the Girgashites, the Amorites, and the Jebusites from before you."

The next day Joshua told the priests, "Pick up the Ark of the Covenant and go over before the people."

The Lord told Joshua, "This day I will begin to magnify you in the sight of all Israel, that they may know, as I was with Moses, so I will be with you. Command the priests who bear the ark to stand still when they come to the brink of the water of Jordan. When the soles of their feet rest in the water, the waters of Jordan shall be cut off from the waters that come down from above, and shall stand in a heap."

When the priests carrying the Ark of the Covenant came to Jordan and their feet dipped in the brim of the water (the river was overflowing its banks as it does at the time of harvest), the water coming down from upstream stopped and rose in a heap for a long distance away. There was no water going downstream and the people went right over next to Jericho.

The priests carrying the ark stood firm on dry ground amid Jordan, and all the Israelites passed over on dry ground until all the people had passed over.[135]

When all the people had gone over Jordan, the Lord said to Joshua, "Take twelve men from the people, one from each tribe, and command them to take out of the midst of Jordan, where the priests' feet stood, twelve stones. They shall carry them over with you and leave them where you lodge this night."

The children of Reuben, of Gad, and the half tribe of Manasseh, passed over armed before as Moses had commanded. About forty thousand prepared for war passed over before the Lord to battle on the plains of Jericho.

---

[135] Joshua 3

The Lord magnified Joshua in the sight of all Israel and they feared him as they feared Moses, all the days of his life.

The Lord said to Joshua, "Command the priests that bear the ark to come up out of Jordan."

Joshua did so and, when the priests came up out of Jordan and the soles of their feet were placed on the dry land, the waters of Jordan returned to their place and flowed over the banks as they had before.

When they came up, the children of Israel did as commanded and Joshua set up the twelve stones from out of Jordan where they lodged that night. He told them in the future it would be a sign among them that when their children asked their fathers, "'What do these stones mean?", you shall say, "Israel came over this Jordan on dry land. The waters of Jordan were cut off before the Ark of the Covenant of the Lord. The Lord, your God, dried up the waters from before you, until you had passed over, as the Lord, your God, did to the Red Sea. That all the people of the earth might know the hand of the Lord is mighty and might fear the Lord their God forever." These stones shall be for a memorial to the children of Israel forever.[136]

When all the kings of the Amorites and the Canaanites heard the Lord had dried up the waters of Jordan so the children of Israel could pass over, their hearts melted and there was no spirit in them anymore.

Then the Lord said to Joshua, "Make sharp knives and circumcise again the children of Israel."

Joshua did this, and circumcised the children of Israel at the hill of the foreskins. This was done because all the men of war who were born in the wilderness as they came out of Egypt had not been circumcised. But all the males who came out of Egypt had been circumcised, and they walked forty years in the wilderness until they all had died on the way. This was because they didn't obey the voice of the Lord. He swore he would not show them the land, the land which he swore to their fathers he would give them, a land that flows with milk and honey.

When all the males were circumcised, they stayed in their places until they were healed. The Lord then told Joshua,

---

[136] Joshua 4

"This day I have rolled away the reproach of Egypt from off you." Thus, they called the place Gilgal (rolling in Hebrew).

They kept the Passover on the fourteenth day in the plains of Jericho at Gilgal. The day after the Passover, they ate of the previous year's grain in the unleavened bread and parched grain they had. The next day the manna ceased, but they then ate of the fruit of the land of Canaan.

With Israel near, Jericho had its gates closed and no one came in or left. The Lord said to Joshua, "I have given Jericho into your hand and their king and their mighty men. You shall go around the city once, all the men of war. You shall do this six days. Seven priests shall go before the ark with trumpets of rams' horns. The seventh day, you shall go around the city seven times, and the priests shall blow with the trumpets. When they make a long blast with the ram's horn and when you hear the trumpet, all the people shall shout with a great shout and the wall of the city shall fall down so it is flat. All the people shall go up every man straight before him."

Joshua called the priests and said, "Take up the Ark of the Covenant and let seven priests carry seven trumpets of rams' horns before the Ark of the Lord."

He told the army, "Go around the city with the army in front of the Ark of the Covenant."

When Joshua spoke to the people, the seven priests carrying the seven trumpets of rams' horns went on before the Lord and blew with the trumpets. The Ark of the Covenant of the Lord followed them. The army went before the priests that blew with the trumpets and the rearguard came after the ark, with the priests blowing the trumpets.

Joshua had commanded the people, saying, "You shall not shout, nor make any noise with your voice, neither shall any word come out of your mouth, until the day I bid you shout. Then you shall shout."

The first morning, Joshua rose early and the priests took up the Ark of the Lord. Seven priests, each continually blowing a rams' horn trumpet, went before the Ark of the Lord, with the army in front of them, followed by the rear guard. They circled the city once and returned to camp. They did the same thing for six days.

On the seventh day, they rose early, about dawn, and went around the city as before, but this time they went around it seven times. Joshua said to the people, "On the seventh day, when you hear the priests blow a blast on the trumpet, shout, for the Lord has given you the city. The city is accursed to the Lord, it and all that are in it. Only Rahab, the harlot, shall live, she and all that are with her in the house, because she hid the messengers we sent. Kill all the living; people and animals. Keep yourselves from the banned things, lest you make yourselves accursed, by taking of the banned things and make the camp of Israel a curse and trouble it. All the silver and gold and the vessels of brass and iron are consecrated to the Lord and will come into the treasury of the Lord."[137]

Jesus said, "Father, why did they have to kill all the animals and people? That seems cruel to me."

Joseph said, "It doesn't sound very humane. But remember, the Lord told Abraham his children would not have this land for 400 years, until those living there had developed in iniquity and would be judged. When a people become unrighteous, they are destroyed and their land is given to those who are more righteous. The people living in Canaan were a depraved people. *Their religious rites were idolatrous and many sacrificed their children. When children grow up in a wicked, unrighteous environment, it is very hard for them to grow up to be good, righteous people.*

"Elohim wants all his children to have the opportunity to be righteous and to know Him. There is also the problem of what to do if they didn't kill them. From the Midianites alone they got 32,000 babies and young females. They can't just drive out the people living on the land, because they will want to come back at some future time and they will join with other people they have displaced.

"As for the livestock, they sometimes killed them and sometimes used them. I think it depended on the Israelites need at the time and how evil the people were. If you are fighting, you can't afford too many men of war taking care of excess animals."[138] Going on...

The people shouted a great shout when the Priests blew with the trumpets, and the wall fell down so it was flat. The men went up into the city, every man straight before him and they took the city. They destroyed all that was in the city, man and woman, young and old, ox, sheep, and ass with the edge of the sword.

---

[137] Joshua 6:1-19
[138] Genesis 15:13-14; 1 Nephi 17:31-35

JOSHUA

Joshua had told the two men who had spied out the country to go into the harlot's house and bring out the woman and all she had, as had been promised. They went in and brought out Rahab, her father, mother, her brothers, other relatives, and all she had. They left them outside of the camp of Israel and Rahab lived with Israel her whole life.

Joshua said, "Cursed be the man who comes and rebuilds this city, Jericho. He shall lay the foundation of it in his firstborn and. in his youngest son, he shall set up the gates of it."

The Lord was with Joshua and his fame spread throughout all the country.[139]

Achan, the son of Cormi of the tribe of Judah, took of the banned things and the Lord's anger was kindled against the children of Israel.

Joshua sent men from Jericho to Ai to view the country. They returned and said to him, "Don't make all the people go up, but only about two or three thousand men. All of us don't need to fight, because there are only a few people in Ai."

About three thousand men were sent up to take Ai and they fled before the men of Ai. The men of Ai smote about thirty-six men of Israel. They chased them from the gate of Ai to the quarries and struck them as they descended. The hearts of the people melted and became as water.

Joshua rent his clothes and fell with his face to the ground in front of the Ark of the Lord until eventide, with the elders of Israel. They all put dust on their heads. Joshua said, "Alas, O Lord God, why have you brought this people over Jordan to deliver us into the hand of the Amorites, to destroy us? I wish we had been content and lived on the other side Jordan! O Lord, what shall I say, when Israel turns their backs before their enemies! For the Canaanites and all the inhabitants of the land shall hear of it and shall surround us and cut off our name from the earth. What will you do to your great name?"

The Lord said, "Get up! Why do you lie on your face? Israel has sinned and has transgressed my covenant, which I commanded them. They have taken the banned

---

[139] Joshua 6:20-27

thing and have also stolen and deceived. They have put it with their own stuff. Therefore, the children of Israel could not stand before their enemies, but turned their backs before them, because they were accursed. Neither will I be with you anymore, except you destroy the accursed from among you. Get up, bless the people and tell them the Lord says, 'There is an accursed thing among you, O Israel. You cannot stand before your enemies, until you take away the accursed thing from you.'

"In the morning, you shall be brought by your tribes. It shall be that the tribe which the Lord selects shall come by families, and the family which the Lord shall select shall come by households. The household which the Lord shall pick shall come man by man. He who is taken with the banned thing shall be burnt with fire, he and all that he has, because he has transgressed the covenant of the Lord and because he has wrought folly in Israel."

Joshua rose early in the morning and brought Israel by tribes and the tribe of Judah was taken. He brought the family of Judah and the family of the Zarhites was taken. He brought them man by man and Zabdi was taken. He brought his household man by man and Achan, the son of Carmi was taken.

Joshua said to Achan, "My son, please give glory to the Lord God of Israel and make confession to him. Tell me now what you have done; don't hide it from me."

Achan said, "Indeed, I have sinned against the Lord God of Israel, and this is what I did. When I saw among the spoils a good Babylonish garment, five pounds of silver, and a wedge of gold of about twenty ounces, I coveted them and took them. They are hidden in the earth in the center of my tent with the silver under it."

Joshua sent messengers to run to his tent and they found them in his tent with the silver under it. They brought them to Joshua and to the children of Israel and set them before the Lord. Joshua and all Israel with him, took Achan, the silver, the garment, the wedge of gold, his sons, his daughters, his oxen, his asses, his sheep, his tent, and all that Achan had to the valley of Achor.

Joshua said, "Why have you troubled us? The Lord shall trouble you this day."

All Israel stoned him with stones and, after he was

JOSHUA

dead, they burned him and all that he had with fire, while his family watched. They raised over him a great heap of stones. So, the Lord turned from the fierceness of his anger.[140]

The Lord told Joshua, "Fear not and don't be dismayed. Take all the men of war and go up to Ai. I have given into your hand the king of Ai and all his people with his city and land. You shall do to Ai and her king as you did to Jericho and her king. Only the spoil and the cattle you shall take for yourselves. Lay an ambush for the city behind it."

Joshua and the men of war went up against Ai. Joshua chose out thirty thousand mighty men of valor and sent them away by night. He commanded them, "You shall lie in wait behind the city, though not far from it, but be ready. I and the rest of the men of war will approach the city and, when they come out against us as before, we will flee from them. When we have drawn them away from the city, because they think we are fleeing as before, you shall rise from the ambush and seize the city, for the Lord, your God, will deliver it into your hand. When you have taken the city, you will set it on fire as the Lord and I have commanded you."

Following the directions of the Lord, they took Ai, killing all those in it.

Joshua built an altar to the Lord God of Israel in Mount Ebal. He made the altar of whole stones, on which no man used any iron, as Moses had been commanded by the Lord. They offered there burnt offerings to the Lord and sacrificed peace offerings.

Joshua wrote on the stones a copy of the Law of Moses in the presence of the children of Israel. Afterward, he read all the law, the blessings and cursing as it is written in the book of the law. There was not a word of all Moses commanded, which Joshua didn't read before all the congregation of Israel, with the women, little ones, and the foreigners who were among them.[141]

All the kings on the west side of Jordan heard what was happening, so they formed a league to fight with Israel as one. When the inhabitants of Gibeon heard what was

---

[140] Joshua 7
[141] Joshua 8

JOSHUA

happening, they decided to save themselves with cunning. They took some men to be ambassadors. They dressed them in old patched footwear and old patched garments. They had food that was moldy and dry. Their asses had on them old sacks and old wineskins that were torn and patched. They went to Joshua at the camp at Gilgal and said to him, "We have come from a distant country. Make a pact with us."

The men of Israel said, "Perhaps you live among us. Why would we make a league with you?"

They said to Joshua, "We are your servants."

Joshua said, "Who are you? Where do you come from?"

They said, "We have come from a very faraway country, because of the name of the Lord, your God. We have heard the fame of Him and all he did in Egypt. Also, all he did to the two kings of the Amorites, Sihon, and Og, that were beyond Jordan. Our elders told us to take food for our journey and tell you, 'We are your servants, make a league with us.' This bread we took hot for our provisions from our houses on the day we left, but now it is dry and moldy. These skins of wine which we filled were new and now they are torn. Our clothing and our footwear is old because of our long journey."

The men of Israel tasted their food and didn't pray to the Lord their God for guidance, but made peace with them. They made a league to let them live, and the princes of the congregation swore so to them. At the end of three days, after they had made the league, they heard they were their neighbors and lived among them.

The children of Israel traveled and came to their cities on the third day. Their cities were Gibeon, Chephirah, Beeroth, and Kirjath-jearim. The children of Israel didn't kill them, because the princes of the congregation had sworn to them by the Lord God of Israel. The entire congregation complained to the princes, but the princes said, "We have sworn to them by the Lord God of Israel, so we may not touch them. This is what we will do; we will let them live, so wrath will not be on us, but they will be hewers of wood and drawers of water to all the congregation."

Joshua said to them, "Why did you trick us by telling us you were very far from us when you lived among us? Therefore, you are cursed and there shall none of you

JOSHUA

be freed from being bondmen and hewers of wood and drawers of water for the house of my God."

They said, "Because we were told how the Lord, your God, commanded his servant Moses to give you all the land and to destroy all the inhabitants of the land from before you. Therefore, we were afraid for our lives because of you and did this. We are in your hand. Do to us what seems good and right for you to do."[142]

When Adonizedek, king of Jerusalem, heard how Joshua had taken Ai and had destroyed it as he had Jericho and her king and now the inhabitants of Gibeon had made peace with Israel, he was very afraid. Gibeon was a great city, one of the royal cities and was greater than Ai with many mighty men.

Therefore, he sent to four of the Amorite kings around him, saying, "Come up with me and help me to smite Gibeon, because it has made peace with Joshua and the children of Israel."

So, the five kings of the Amorites went up with their armies and encamped before Gibeon and made war against it. The men of Gibeon sent to Joshua at the camp in Gilgal, saying, "We are your servants, come up quickly and save us, for all the kings of the Amorites that live in the mountains are gathered together against us."

Joshua went up from Gilgal and all the men of war. The Lord said to him, "Don't fear them, for I have delivered them into your hand. There shall not a man of them stand before you."

Joshua came to them suddenly, going up from Gilgal all night. The Lord put them to flight before Israel and they slew them with a great slaughter at Gibeon and chased them. As they fled before Israel going down to Beth Horon, the Lord cast down great hailstones from heaven, and more were killed by the hailstones than were killed by the sword. That day Joshua said in the sight of Israel, "Sun, stand still on Gibeon and you, moon, in the valley of Ajalon."

The sun stood still and the moon stayed put until the people had avenged themselves on their enemies. This is written in the book of Jasher. So, the sun stood still in

---

[142] Joshua 9

JOSHUA

heaven and didn't go down for about all day. There was no day like it before or after it. The Lord listened to the voice of a man, for the Lord fought for Israel.

Joshua told them, "Pursue after your enemies and smite the hindmost of them. Don't let them enter their cities, for the Lord, your God has delivered them into your hand."

When they had made an end of slaying with a great slaughter, all were consumed that had not made their way into fenced cities. Next, they fought against Libnah. The Lord delivered it also and its king. All those that were in it were killed.

From Libnah, they went to Lachish and fought against it. They took it on the second day and again killed all who were in it. as was done in Libnah. Horam, king of Gezer, came up to help Lachish, and Joshua smote him and all his people, leaving none remaining. From Lachish, they went to Eglon, then Hebron, and then Debir, fighting against each and killing all who were in them.

Joshua smote all the country around and all their kings. He left none remaining, but destroyed all that breathed as the Lord God had commanded. He smote them from Kadesh Barnea to Gaza and all the country of Goshen to Gibeon. All these kings and their land did Joshua take at one time, because the Lord God of Israel fought for Israel. Joshua returned and all Israel with him to Gilgal.[143]

When King Jabin of Hazor heard about this, he sent messengers to all the other kings in the whole area. The armies of these peoples came out as the sand on the seashore for multitude, with many horses and chariots. They met at the waters of Merom, to fight against Israel.

The Lord said to Joshua, "Don't be afraid of them. Tomorrow about this time I will deliver them up all slain before Israel. You shall hamstring their horses and burn their chariots with fire."

Joshua and all Israel came against them by the waters of Merom and suddenly fell on them. The Lord delivered them into the hand of Israel, who smote and chased them until none of them remained. Joshua did as he was commanded and hamstrung their horses and burned their chariots.

---

[143] Joshua 10

JOSHUA

Joshua turned back and took Hazor, killing the king who had before been the head of all those kingdoms. They killed all the souls who were in Hazor and burned it. They captured all the cities of those kings, killing all who were in them, but did not burn any of the cities except Hazor.

Israel took the livestock for their use. There was not a city that made peace with Israel, except the Hivites of Gibeon. Joshua also destroyed the Anakims (giants) in the land of Israel. Only those in Gaza, Gath, and in Ashdod remained. Joshua made war a long time with these kings and cities.[144]

Joshua had become old and stricken in years. The Lord said, "There still remains much land to be possessed. Divide this land for an inheritance to the nine tribes and the half tribe of Manasseh, as Moses gave the Reubenites, Gadites, and the half tribe of Manasseh their inheritance on the east of Jordan."

Joshua divided up the land by lot, giving each tribe their inheritance, except the Levites, as the sacrifices of the Lord were their inheritance and cities were given them amongst the other tribes.

Joshua gathered all the tribes to Shechem and called for the elders of Israel, their heads, judges, and officers to present themselves before God. Joshua said, "I am old and stricken with age. You have seen all the Lord, your God, has done to all these nations, because of you, for the Lord, your God, is He that fought for you. I have divided to you by lot these nations that remain, to be an inheritance for your tribes, from Jordan, with all the nations I have cut off, even to the great sea westward. The Lord your God shall expel them from before you and drive them out of your sight. You shall possess their land, as the Lord your God has promised you.

"Be very courageous to keep and to do all that is written in the book of the Law of Moses. Don't turn aside to the right hand or to the left. Don't come among those nations that remain among you. Neither mention the name of their gods, nor swear by them, neither serve them, nor bow yourselves down to them. But cleave to the Lord, your God, as you have done to this day. One man of you shall chase a

---

[144] Joshua 11

thousand, for the Lord, your God, fights for you as he has promised you.

"Take heed that you love the Lord, your God, or else if you in any wise go back and cleave to the remnant of these nations, even these that remain among you and shall make marriages with them, know for a certainty the Lord, your God, will no more drive out any of these nations from before you. They shall be snares and traps to you and scourges in your sides and thorns in your eyes until you perish from off this good land which the Lord, your God, has given you.

"When you have transgressed the covenant of the Lord, your God, which he commanded you and have gone and served other gods and bowed yourselves to them, then shall the anger of the Lord be kindled against you and you shall perish quickly from off the good land which he has given to you.

"Thus, says the Lord God of Israel: 'I have given you a land for which you did not labor, and cities which you didn't build and you live in them. You eat of vineyards and olive yards which you didn't plant.'

"Now fear the Lord and serve Him in sincerity and in truth. Put away the gods which your fathers served on the other side of the flood in Egypt and serve the Lord. If it seems evil to you to serve the Lord, choose you this day whom you will serve, whether the gods which your fathers served that were on the other side of the flood or the gods of the Amorites in whose land you live. But as for me and my house, we will serve the Lord."

The people answered, "God forbid that we should forsake the Lord, to serve other gods. The Lord, our God, he it is who brought us up and our fathers out of the land of Egypt and the house of bondage and which did those great signs in our sight and preserved us in all the way wherein we went and among all the people through whom we passed. The Lord drove out from before us all the people, even the Amorites which lived in the land. Therefore, will we also serve the Lord, for he is our God."

Joshua said, "You cannot serve the Lord, for he is a holy God and a jealous God. He will not forgive your transgressions, or your sins. If you forsake the Lord and

JOSHUA

serve strange gods, then he will turn and do you hurt and consume you, after he has done you good."

The people said, "No, but we will serve the Lord."

Joshua said, "You are witnesses against yourselves that you have chosen the Lord, to serve Him."

They said, "We are witnesses."

Joshua said, "Now, therefore, put away the strange gods which are among you and incline your heart to the Lord God of Israel."

The people said, "The Lord, our God, we will serve and his voice we will obey."

Joshua made a covenant with the people that day and set them a statute and an ordinance in Shechem. Joshua wrote these words in the book of the Law of God and took a great stone and set it up under an oak that was by the sanctuary of the Lord.

Joshua said, "This stone shall be a witness to us, for it has heard all the words of the Lord which he spoke to us. It shall be, therefore, a witness to you, lest you deny your God."

Joshua let the people depart and after this Joshua, the servant of the Lord, died, being a hundred and ten years old. They buried him in his inheritance in Mount Ephraim.

The bones of Joseph, which the children of Israel brought up out of Egypt, they buried in Shechem, in a parcel of ground which Jacob bought of the sons of Hamor, the father of Shechem for a hundred pieces of silver, and it became the inheritance of the children of Joseph.

Also, Eleazar died and they buried him in a hill that was his son, Phinehas', in Mount Ephraim.

Israel served the Lord all the days of Joshua and all the days of the elders who outlived Joshua and which had known all the works of the Lord, which he had done for Israel.[145]

---

[145] Joshua 23,24

SAMUEL, SAUL, AND DAVID

"That covers Joshua. Jesus, I want you to understand where we, as a people came from. I think what we covered from Abraham through Joshua should give you a basic knowledge of that."

After Joshua, Israel was governed by a series of judges. Israel was not really a country, but the twelve tribes acted as separate states, fighting amongst themselves instead of being one country. They never finished driving out or killing the inhabitants of their land. These people were idolatrous and a bad influence on Israel, and Israel would become unrighteous following their examples. The Lord would then punish them for not keeping his commandments. They would repent, a leader would come along, and rescue them from their enemy.

There were quite a few Judges, perhaps thirteen. The most famous are Deborah, the only female, Samson, Eli, and Samuel. I think of Eli more as a prophet than a judge. He was replaced by Samuel, whom he raised from a young child.[146]

When Samuel was old, the elders of Israel told Samuel they wanted to have a king to rule over them like the rest of the countries around them. Samuel tried to discourage them, but they insisted. He took it to the Lord, who told him to provide them a king. The Lord said, "They have not rejected you, but have rejected me."

Samuel told them what a king would do for them. "He will take your sons, and appoint them for himself, for his chariots, and to be his horsemen. He will appoint captains over thousands and over fifties. He will have them cultivate his ground, reap his crops, and make weapons of war. He will take your daughters to be perfumers, cooks, and bakers. He will take the best of your fields, vineyards, and your olive yards and give them to his servants. You will cry out in that day, because of your king and the Lord will not hear you."[147]

The Lord picked Saul, of the tribe of Benjamin, to be the first king. Saul was out looking for some asses that

---

[146] Judges 4;13-16; 1 Samuel 1-3
[147] 1 Samuel 6

had been lost, and went to Samuel, the seer, to ask where they were. When Samuel saw Saul coming, the Lord told him that Saul was the man he had picked to lead Israel. Samuel anointed Saul to be king.[148]

Initially, Saul proved to be a good man and an effective king, successful in battle against the Philistines and other enemies. As he became surer of himself, he did not do things the way the Lord commanded him. The Lord asked him to destroy the Amalekites and all their animals, because of what they did to the Israelites when they were coming into the promised land. Saul attacked the Amalekites, killing all the people including babies and children. However, he did not kill their king, Agag, and he didn't destroy the best of their livestock, because the people asked him not to kill the best of the livestock, *so they could offer them for a sacrifice and eat them.*

The word of the Lord came to Samuel, "I am sorry that I gave the kingdom to Saul, because he has decided not to obey my commandments."

This dismayed Samuel and he prayed to the Lord all night.

Samuel went to see Saul, and Saul told him, "I have performed the commandment of the Lord."

Samuel asked, "Then why do I hear the bleating of the sheep and the lowing of the oxen?"

Saul said, "The people have saved the best of the livestock for a sacrifice to the Lord and the rest we have destroyed."

Samuel said, "Last night the Lord told me, when you were little in your own sight, you were made leader over the tribes of Israel and anointed king. You were asked to go and destroy the Amalekites with everything they had. Why did you not destroy everything as the Lord asked?"

Saul said, "I did all the Lord asked. I destroyed the Amalekites and have brought Agag, their king. The people took livestock of the spoil for a sacrifice to the Lord, your God."

Samuel said, "Has the Lord as great a delight in burnt offerings and sacrifices as he has in obeying the voice of the Lord? To obey is better than sacrifice and to do is

---

[148] 1 Samuel 9-10

better than the fat of rams. Rebellion is as the sin of witchcraft and stubbornness is as sin and idolatry. Because you have rejected the word of the Lord, he has rejected you from being king."

Samuel did not see Saul anymore, but he mourned for Saul.[149]

The Lord said to Samuel, "How long will you mourn for Saul, seeing I have rejected him from reigning over Israel? Fill your horn with oil, and go to Jesse of Bethlehem of the tribe of Judah, because I have picked one of his sons to be king, and anoint him king. So Saul doesn't suspect what you are doing, tell them you are going there for a sacrifice, and invite Jesse and his family to it."

Samuel did so and, when they came, he looked at Eliab, the oldest and thought, this is surely the Lord's anointed, but the Lord said, "Don't look at his countenance or his height, because I have refused him. I don't see as man, who looks at the outward appearance, for I look at his heart."

Next, Jesse called Abinadab, and he passed before Samuel, but the Lord had not chosen him. Jesse had seven of his sons pass before Samuel, but the Lord did not choose any of them.

Samuel asked Jesse, "Are these all of your children?"

Jesse said, "I have one more, the youngest, who is keeping the sheep."

Samuel said, "Bring him here."

When he came, the Lord said, "This is the one; anoint him king."

Samuel anointed him amid his brothers.

The Spirit of the Lord departed from Saul and an evil spirit troubled him. Saul's servants said to him, "An evil spirit troubles you. Command your servants, which are before you, to seek out a man, who is an accomplished player on the lyre. Then, when the evil spirit is on you, he shall play with his hand and you shall be well."

One of the servants said, "I have seen a son of Jesse, the Bethlehemite, who is accomplished in playing the lyre, a valiant man, prudent in matters, a comely person, and the

---

[149] 1 Samuel 11, 15

SAMUEL, SAUL, AND DAVID

Lord is with him."

Then Saul sent messengers to Jesse and said, "Send me David, your son, which is with the sheep."

Jesse took an ass laden with bread, a bottle of wine, and a kid and sent them by David to Saul. David came to Saul and stood before him and Saul admired him greatly.

Saul told Jesse, "Let him stay with me, for I am pleased with David's playing."

When the evil spirit was upon Saul, David took a lyre and played, so Saul was refreshed and was well and the evil spirit departed from him.[150]

There was fighting between the Philistines and Israel every year, and the Philistines came to renew the conflict.

As they prepared for war, *the evil spirit departed from Saul and he sent David home to his father,* and his father had him feeding his sheep at Bethlehem. The Philistines gathered together their armies on one side of a mountain and Israel gathered theirs on another mountainside with a valley between them.

Daily a champion went out of the camp of the Philistines, named Goliath, whose height was about nine feet, nine inches. He had a helmet of brass on his head and he was armed with a coat of mail. The weight of the coat was about one hundred twenty-five pounds. He had shin armor on his legs and armor of brass between his shoulders.

The staff of his spear was like a weaver's beam and his spear's head weighed fifteen pounds. One bearing a shield went before him. He stood and cried to the armies of Israel and said, "Why are you come out to set the battle in array? Am not I a Philistine and you servants to Saul? Choose you a man for you and let him come down to me. If he can fight with me and kill me, then we will be your servants. But if I prevail against him and kill him, then you shall be our servants and serve us. I defy the armies of Israel this day. Give me a man that we may fight together."

When Saul and all Israel heard the words of the Philistine, they were dismayed and greatly afraid.

Just before this, Jesse had told David, "Take half a bushel of this parched grain and these ten loaves and run

---

[150] 1 Samuel 15-16

with them to your brothers in the camp. Take these ten cheeses to the captain of their thousand and see how your brothers fare and bring back news of them."

David rose early and left the sheep with a keeper, took what was requested, and went as Jesse had commanded. He reached the camp just as the army was moving out to fight and shouting for the battle.

David left his baggage in the hand of the baggage keeper, ran to the army, and greeted his brothers. As he talked with them, the champion, Goliath, spoke the same words as he always did and David heard them. When the men of Israel saw the man, they fled from him, for they were sore afraid.

The men of Israel where David was standing said, "Have you seen this man that is come up? Surely to defy Israel he has come up. It shall be that the man who kills him, the king will enrich, give his daughter to, and make his father's house free in Israel."

David spoke to the men that stood by him, saying, "Who is this uncircumcised Philistine, that he should defy the armies of the living God? Why doesn't somebody do something?"

Eliab, his oldest brother, heard what he said to the men and was angry with David, and he said, "Why did you come down here? With whom have you left those few sheep in the wilderness? I know your pride and the naughtiness of your heart. You have come down to see the battle."

David said, "What have I done? Don't you think there is a reason?"

He turned from him to another and said, "Why don't you do something?"

What David said was told to Saul and he sent for him.

David said to Saul, "Let no man's heart fail because of him. I will go and fight this Philistine."

Saul, who didn't recognize David, said, "You are not able to go against this Philistine to fight with him, for you are but a youth and he a man of war from his youth."

David said, "I kept my father's sheep, and there came a lion and a bear and took a lamb out of the flock. I went out after him and smote him and delivered it out of his mouth. When he arose against me, I caught him by his beard, and smote him and slew him. Your servant slew both the lion and the bear, and this uncircumcised Philistine shall be as one of them, seeing he has defied the armies of the living God. The Lord that delivered me out of the paw of the lion and the paw of the bear will deliver me out of the hand of this Philistine."

Saul said to David, "Go and the Lord be with you."

Saul armed David with his armor. He put a helmet of brass on his head and gave him a coat of mail. David girded his sword on his armor and tried to walk, but he could hardly do so, for he was not familiar with them.

He told Saul, "I cannot go with these, for I am not familiar with them," and took them off.

He took his staff in his hand and chose five smooth stones out of the brook and put them in his shepherd's bag. With his sling and staff in hand, he drew near to the Philistine.

The Philistine came toward him and, when the Philistine looked and saw David, he disdained him, for he was but a youth, ruddy and good looking. As he walked, the Philistine said to David, "Am I a dog that you come to me with staves?" Cursing David by his gods, he said, "Come to me and I will give your flesh to the fowls of the air and to the beasts of the field."

David said, "You come to me with a sword, a spear, and a shield, but I come to you in the name of the Lord of hosts, the God of the armies of Israel, whom you have defied. This day will the Lord deliver you into my hand. I will smite you and take your head from you. I will give the carcasses of the Philistine's army this day to the fowls of the air and to the wild beasts of the earth that all the earth may know there is a God in Israel. All this assembly shall know the Lord saves not with sword and spear, for the battle is the Lord's, and he will give you into our hands."

When the Philistine started toward David to meet him, David hurried and ran toward him. David put his hand in his bag, took out a stone, slang it, and hit the Philistine in his forehead. The stone sunk into his forehead and he fell on his face to the earth.

David prevailed over the Philistine with a sling and a stone. He smote the Philistine, drew his sword out of the sheath, and cut off his head with it. When the Philistines saw their champion was dead, they fled.

All the men of Israel and Judah arose, shouted, and pursued the Philistines, until they came to the gates of Ekron. The children of Israel returned from chasing the Philistines and they spoiled their tents. When David returned from the slaughter of the Philistines, Abner, the captain of the host, brought him before Saul with the head of Goliath in his hand.

Saul had not recognized David, though he had played his lyre for him and asked Abner, his chief general, to find out who he was.[151]

When David returned from the slaughter of the Philistines, women came out of all the cities of Israel, singing and dancing, to meet King Saul, with timbrels, joy, and with instruments of music. The women answered one another as they played, saying, 'Saul has slain his thousands and David his ten thousands.'

This saying displeased Saul and made him very angry. He thought, "They have given to David ten thousand and to me they have given only thousands, and what can he have more but the kingdom?"

Saul watched David from that day forward. The next day, the evil spirit came on Saul. David played the lyre as at other times and there was a javelin in Saul's hand. Saul thought, "I will smite David to the wall with this javelin," and threw it. David avoided the javelin and left his presence twice.

Saul was afraid of David, because the Lord was with him and was departed from Saul. Therefore, Saul sent him away from him by making him captain over a thousand men of war. He went to battle at the head of his men and returned. David behaved himself wisely in all he did and the Lord was with him.

Therefore, when Saul saw he behaved himself very wisely, he was more afraid of him. But all Israel and Judah loved David, because they saw him leading his troops.

Michal, Saul's daughter, loved David and they told Saul this and it pleased him. Saul thought, I will give her to him, that she may be a snare to him and that the hand of the Philistines may be against him.'

---

[151] 1 Samuel 17

Saul asked his servants to speak to David secretly, saying, "The king delights in you and all his servants love you, why not ask to be his son-in-law?"

David said, "Does it seem to you a light thing to be a king's son-in-law? I am a poor man and lightly esteemed."

The servants reported to Saul what David had said, and Saul told them to tell David, "The king doesn't want any dowry, but one hundred foreskins of the Philistines, to be avenged of the king's enemies."

Saul wanted David to fall by the hand of the Philistines.

When his servants told David these words, it pleased David well to be the king's son-in-law. He and his men went and slew of the Philistines two hundred men. David brought their foreskins and gave them in full tale to the king, that he might be the king's son-in-law. So Saul gave him Michal, his daughter, to wife.

Saul saw and knew the Lord was with David and that Michal loved David, and Saul became David's enemy continually. The princes of the Philistines went forth to battle and David behaved himself more wisely than all the other servants of Saul, so his name was adored.

David finally realized Saul wanted him dead, and fled from him to hide in the wilderness. Saul hunted him, but David eluded him. David had several chances to kill Saul, but he thought it wrong to kill the king.

On two occasions, David approached Saul as he slept in the wilderness and could have killed him, but did not, as the Lord had appointed Saul to be king. David was a fugitive for probably ten or fifteen years. During this time, it had become common knowledge that Samuel had anointed David to be king. Men flocked to David's side until he had about six hundred men with him.[152]

After several years, the Philistines again came to war against Israel. Israel lost and Saul was killed, with most of his sons. David mourned for Saul, even though they had been enemies. He also mourned for Saul's son Jonathan, to whom he had been very close. They had been like brothers. In fact, Jonathan was to be his right-hand man when David became king.[153]

---

[152] 1 Samuel 18-19
[153] 2 Samuel 1

David, who was still not in Israel, enquired of the Lord what he should do. The Lord told him to go to Hebron, which was in Judah. David did so and was anointed king over the house of Judah.

Abner was the chief general of Saul and had not been killed with him. He made Ishbosheth a son of Saul, king of Israel. Joab of Judah, David's nephew, was David's general. Joab and Abner, the general of Israel, took some of their army to Gibeon to talk. The talk wasn't fruitful and they started fighting. Joab had two brothers, Abishai and Asahel, who he trusted and depended on as his leaders. Joab's men defeated Abner's men in a long fight, but Abner killed Joab's brother Asahel, who was a fast runner and had been chasing Abner.

Ishbosheth was a weak ruler and criticized Abner for things in his personal life. Abner finally had enough and defected to David. They met and Abner agreed to bring Israel over to David. Shortly after this, Joab heard of what happened and was furious. He thought Abner had come as a spy and was deceiving David. He sent messengers to Abner, supposedly from David, telling him to return.

When he did, Joab killed him.

David mourned for Abner and made it clear to the people he had nothing to do with his killing. He said, "A great man has fallen today and, even though I am king, I am too weak to do anything about it."[154]

Jesus said, "Why could David not do something, if he is king?"

Joseph said, "He is king, but only of Judah. Joab is a mighty fighter, as is his brother Abishai. Also, though David is king, he is only the king of Judah. Joab's mighty men are probably a tight group and David needs all his men to overcome Israel. Does that make sense to you?"

"It does."

We are almost to the job. Are you ready for a good day's work?"

Jesus said, "Of course. And I am ready to hear more on our way home. I am enjoying this."

"I am glad to hear that. Let's get to work."

---

[154] 2 Samuel 2-3

It took a little longer than planned to finish, but finally, everything was done and it looked wonderful.

Jesus said, "I like the way everything looked when we were done. It was even fun cleaning up our mess. I can't wait until I can do those things myself. I want to work with you every day."

"We will see about that Jesus, but I too would like that."

Joseph continued his teaching as they went home.

When two of Ishbosheth's captains heard Abner was dead, they killed him, thinking David would reward them. They took his head to David, who had them executed for murder. This did lead to David being anointed king over Israel seven-and-one-half years after being king over Judah.

One of the first things King David did was to attack Jerusalem. It was a fortified city surrounded by Israel, where the Jebusites, the original inhabitants of the land, still lived. They were so sure they were impregnable, they said to King David, "You could not come in here, even if only the blind and lame were to defend it."

King David told his troops, "Whoever goes up the water canal and is the first to smite the Jebusites and their lame and blind (meaning their idols) that are hated of my soul, shall be chief and captain."

Joab went up first and the city was conquered. It was called the City of David and Joab continued to be chief and captain.

When the Philistines heard David was king, they were concerned David might be a strong leader, from what they knew of him from before. They came up to attack and get rid of him. When they came, David asked the Lord if he should attack them, and the Lord told him to do so. The Philistines were handily defeated.

They came up again and David asked the Lord again if he should go up against them. This time the Lord told him to go up around behind them and when they heard a noise in the tops of the mulberry trees, he should attack. They did this and defeated the Philistines again. [155]

David fought many battles with those around him until he had conquered most of them. Those that were not destroyed paid Israel tribute. With rest from his enemies,

---

[155] 2 Samuel 4, 5:1-9; I Chronicles 11:5-6

David wanted to build a temple to house the Ark of the Covenant of the Lord so it would have a place to rest.

Through Nathan, the prophet, the Lord told him, "You shall not build a house for my name, because you have been a man of war and have shed blood. Nevertheless, the Lord has chosen the house of Judah to be ruler forever and has chosen you to be king. When your days are fulfilled and you die, I will set up your son after you and establish his kingdom. He shall build a house for my name and I will establish the throne of his kingdom forever. If he sins, I will punish him with the rod of men and with the stripes of the children of men, but your throne shall be established forever."[156]

Because David's son was the one to build the temple, David prepared stones, imported cedar trees, gathered iron, and did all he could to have all that was needed to build the temple when his son was ready to do it.[157]

One evening, David couldn't sleep and arose from bed and walked on the roof deck of his house. He saw a very beautiful woman washing herself. David asked a servant who she was and was told it was Bathsheba, the wife of Uriah, the Hittite, who was one of David's soldiers. David had his people bring her to him and they spent the evening together. She became pregnant and told the king.

David sent a message to Joab and said, "Send Uriah to me."

When Uriah came, David asked him, "How are the soldiers doing and how is the war going?"

When they finished talking, the king said, "Go home, get cleaned up, and spend the night with your wife. I will send you over dinner from my kitchen."

David sent the food to him, but Uriah didn't go home and spent the night close to the king's house. David's servants told David this and he asked Uriah, "Why didn't you go home last night?"

Uriah said, "All the army of Israel and Judah are encamped in open fields. I wouldn't think of going to my house to eat and drink and lie with my wife when all of the rest can't."

---

[156] 2 Samuel 7:1-16
[157] I Chronicles 22:1-5

David told Uriah, "Stay here today and tomorrow and then you can depart."

David ate dinner with him that evening and got him drunk, but he would not go to his own home.

The next morning David wrote a letter to Joab and gave it to Uriah to carry to Joab. He said, "Put Uriah in the front of the hottest battle and leave him that he may be hit and die."

Joab put men where he knew the enemy was strong and Uriah was killed, along with some others. Joab sent a messenger to David to tell what had happened. He told the messenger, "When you give the king your message and if he gets angry tell him, 'Uriah was also killed.'"

David was angry when he heard how many had died, so the messenger told him, "Uriah was also killed."

When he heard this, he calmed down and told the messenger to tell Joab, "Let this not upset you, for the sword devours who it will. Fight harder and capture the city."

When Bathsheba was told her husband was dead, she mourned for him. After her mourning, David brought her to his house and married her, and she had a son, but what David did displeased the Lord.[158]

The Lord sent Nathan, the prophet, to David. Nathan told David, "There were two men; one rich and one poor. The rich man had many flocks and herds, but the poor man had nothing, except one little ewe lamb. He had bought and nourished it, together with his children. It was a pet to him and his family.

"A traveler came to the rich man and he needed to provide him food. He didn't want to take of his own flocks and herds, so he took of the poor man's, killed it, and prepared it for the traveler's dinner.

David was angry when he heard this and said to Nathan, "The man who has done this shall surely die and the lamb will be restored four-fold."

Nathan said, "You are the man. The Lord says, 'I anointed you king over Israel and protected you from Saul. I gave you your master's house, the house of Israel and Judah, and many wives. If that had been too little, I would have given many other things. Why have you despised the

---

[158] 2 Samuel 11

commandment of the Lord, to do evil? You have killed Uriah with the sword and has taken his wife for yours. Therefore, the sword shall never depart from your house and evil will come against it, because you have despised me. I will take your wives and give them to someone else. You did it secretly, but I will do it before all Israel.'"

David said, "I have sinned."

Nathan said, "You have not escaped punishment, but you will not die now. You have given occasion to the enemies of the Lord. Also, the child who is born will die."

Nathan left, and Bathsheba's son became very sick. David fasted and prayed to the Lord for him. Those in his house tried to cheer him, but he would not eat. On the seventh day, the child died. The servants were afraid to tell David, because he was so beside himself when the child was sick, what would he do when he was told the child was dead?"

David saw his servants whispering to one another and decided the child had died. He asked them, "Did the child die?" When they said yes, David got up, cleaned himself, dressed, went to the house of the Lord, and worshipped. Then he came home and ate.

His servants asked, "Why when the child was sick did you fast and pray, but when it died, you dressed and ate?"

He said, "While the child was alive, I fasted and wept, for who can tell whether God will be gracious to me, that the child might live? But now he is dead. Why should I fast? Can I bring him back again?"

David went to Bathsheba and comforted her. She became pregnant and bore Solomon.[159]

Absalom, one of David's many sons, was a handsome man. From head to toe there was not a blemish in him and his beauty was praised throughout the land. He went around to the people and told them they had no way to tell the king of their problems, but if he were king, he would be open to them to give them justice. This won the hearts of the people and Absalom conspired with David's advisers and leaders for their support.

He got permission from his father to go to Hebron

---

[159] 2 Samuel 12

to sacrifice there, but Hebron is where kings were crowned, and he really wanted to go there to be crowned king. He had sent spies around the country to proclaim him king when the trumpet sounded. It was a strong conspiracy.

David didn't find out about this until after the fact, and there was little he could do about it right then. He fled Jerusalem with his household, the six hundred men who had been with him when he was hiding from Saul, Zadok, the priest, with his son, and Jonathan, the son of Abiathar, another priest. Ahithophel, David's number one adviser, was with Absalom.

David sent back Zadok, with his son, and Jonathan to act as spies for him, so he would know what Absalom was doing. They met Hushai, another of David's advisers, as they were fleeing. He sent him back to try to defeat the advice of Ahithophel, if he could.

When they left Jerusalem, Shimei, of the tribe of Benjamin, called David names, cursed him, and threw stones at him. David's fighting men wanted to kill him, but David wouldn't let them.

He said, "Let him curse, because the Lord has told him, 'Curse David.' Who should then say, 'Curse him not?' My own son wants me dead, why shouldn't this Benjamite be allowed to curse me?"

Absalom came into Jerusalem and asked his advisers what he should do first. Ahithophel advised him to follow and attack David and his people while they were weak and unprepared. Hushai, to save David, advised him to wait because the people would flock to him and he would have such a big army that David would be crushed.

Absalom followed the advice of Hushai and waited. When Ahithophel heard this, he went to his home, put his affairs in order, and hanged himself. Absalom made Amasa general over his army. When Absalom finally attacked David, David's army had been strengthened more than his and David defeated him. The battle was fought in a wood and there was a great slaughter, with twenty thousand men slain.[160]

David had told his people not to kill Absalom when they fought, but to spare his life. During the battle, Absalom

---

[160] 2 Samuel 15, 16, 17

had been riding a mule, and somehow his head got caught in the fork of a limb, and his mule went out from under him. He was alive, but could not free himself.

A man saw him and told Joab. Joab said, "Why didn't you kill him? I would have given you ten shekels of silver."

The man said, "If you gave me a thousand shekels of silver, I would not kill him, because the king would kill me."

Joab went to the spot and killed Absalom. Because of this, David made Amasa general over his army instead of Joab.

The men of Judah took King David back to Jerusalem and made David king. The men of the other tribes took offense that they were left out of this and made Sheba king over Israel.

Amasa went out to organize the army to defeat Sheba, but it took longer than he planned. When he had not returned by the appointed time, David told Joab's brother, Abishai, his second general, to take the troops who were there to pursue Sheba. He was concerned Sheba would take over some walled cities and it would very difficult to defeat him.

The army left and, when Amasa later met them, he came up to Joab to greet him and Joab stabbed him to death with his sword and took over as general of the army.

Jesus said, "That is just plain murder. Could not David do something now?"

Joseph said, "Again, David is in a tricky situation. Joab is a smart man and sees David is in a tight spot and thinks he can get away with killing Amasa. David needs the army to beat Sheba. David had Joab kill Uriah for him. It was sneaky, not the out-in-the-open way Joab did, but it was the same thing. If he were going to remove Joab, who would he get to do it? Joab is getting older, but he is still a very able fighter, and the second in command is his brother, Abishai. It would be very difficult to get rid of Joab at any time, but with Sheba out there, it is not a good time. Do you have any thoughts about it?"

"No, I understand." Joseph went on with his story

Sheba took refuge in a walled city, as David thought he might, and Joab's army surrounded it. To keep from having her city destroyed, a wise woman made a deal with Joab. She said she would throw the head of Sheba over the wall, if Joab would leave them alone. Joab agreed and the women convinced the elders to kill Sheba instead of fighting. Sheba's head was thrown to Joab.

This ended the insurrection and all of Israel returned to David.[161]

SOLOMON

When David was old and feeble, he couldn't keep warm, even with a lot of bed clothes. His servants suggested he get a young woman who would cherish him and lie with him to keep him warm. They found Abishag, who married, cherished him, and lay with him, but they were not partners in sex.

During David's old age, his son Adonijah, a younger full brother of Absalom, exalted himself, saying, "I will be king." He had chariots, horsemen, and fifty men run before him. David did not question him at any time about why he was doing this.

Adonijah met with Joab, the general, and with Abiathar, the priest, and they helped him. But Zadok, the priest, and Benaiah, a general, and Nathan, the prophet, and some of his mighty men were not with Adonijah.

With the help of Joab and Abiathar, Adonijah planned a feast and invited the leaders of Judah and all his brothers, except Solomon, to whom the kingdom had been promised. He also did not invite Nathan, the prophet, Zadok, the priest, and Benaiah.

When Nathan heard of this, he went to Bathsheba, the mother of Solomon, and said, "Have you heard Adonijah is now king and David doesn't know it? To save your own life and the life of Solomon, go to King David and say, 'Didn't you promise me that Solomon, our son, would be king after you? Why then does Adonijah reign?' While

---

[161] 2 Samuel 18, 19, 20

you are still talking with the king, I will come in and confirm your words."

Bathsheba went into the king's chamber and bowed to the king.

King David said, "What do you want?"

She said, "Adonijah has been made king and you don't know it. He has prepared a feast and invited Abiathar, the priest, Joab, the general, and all your sons, except Solomon. They are now all with him. The eyes of everyone are on you to tell them who will replace you. If you don't do this, Solomon and I will be killed."

Just then, Nathan came in, bowed to the king and said the same things Bathsheba had just said.

David had Benaiah and Zadok, the priest, join them. He told them, "Have Solomon ride my mule to Gihon and have Zadok and Nathan anoint him king over Israel. Blow the trumpet and say, "God save King Solomon." Have him come back here and sit on the throne, for he shall be king in my stead."

They did this, and Zadok took a horn of oil out of the tabernacle and anointed Solomon king. All the people said, "God save King Solomon." The people followed him back to the palace, rejoicing as they went.

Adonijah and all those with him heard the noise. Joab asked, "Why is the city in an uproar?"

Just then, Jonathan, the son of Abiathar, came in and said, "David has made Solomon king. Zadok has anointed him and he has ridden on King David's mule. Nathan, the prophet, and Benaiah, the general, and a large group of people have gone back to the palace and Solomon is sitting on the throne."

When the guests of Adonijah heard this, they were afraid and left. Adonijah was also afraid and went to the altar. He said, "Let King Solomon promise me he will not kill me, and I will serve him."

Solomon said, "If he shows he is a good man, he will not be hurt, but if there is wickedness in him, he shall die."

Adonijah then came from the altar and bowed himself to King Solomon.[162]

---

[162] 1 Kings 1

SOLOMON

Before he died, David said to King Solomon, "I am about to die; keep the law of Moses and the commandments of the Lord. The Lord promised me if my children would keep the commandments and the law of Moses, they would be blessed in the land. Keep the commandments so your children and your children's children can keep them.

"You know what Joab did to me, how he killed Abner and Amasa; see that he does not go to his grave in peace. Also, you know how Shimei cursed me and threw stones at me when I fled, because of Absalom, your brother. You are a wise man and know what should be done, but do not hold them guiltless."

David died, and Solomon ruled in his place.

One day, Adonijah came to Bathsheba, the mother of Solomon. She said, "Hello, is everything all right?"

He said, "Yes, but I have a favor to ask of you."

She said, "What is it?"

He said, "Please speak to your son, Solomon, for he will not deny you anything. Since David's death, his wife Abishag has been lonely. I would like to marry her. Please ask him to give her to me to wife."

She said, "I will ask him."

She went in to see the king, and he arose to meet her and bowed to her. He sat down on his throne and had a seat put on his right side for her.

She said, "I have a small thing to ask of you."

He said, "Go ahead, ask me, for I will not deny you."

She said, "Give Abishag to your brother Adonijah to wife."

He said, "Why don't you ask for him the kingdom, too? He is my older brother! Don't just ask for him; ask for Abiathar, the priest, and for Joab, the general. God do so to me, if Adonijah has not spoken this against his own life. He will be put to death this day."

Jesus said, "Why is Solomon upset with Adonijah marrying Abishag?"

Joseph said, "It was the custom of the time to give the new king things the old king had. For instance, David put Solomon on his mule to be anointed king. Adonijah wanted to be king, and this sounds like the first step in his claiming the kingship again."

Jesus said, "I think I understand."
Joseph went on,

Solomon had his general put Adonijah to death.

To Abiathar, the king said, "You are worthy of death, but I won't kill you because you took part with my father in his trying times when he was escaping from Saul."

When Joab, who had supported Adonijah, heard what was happening, he fled to the altar. Benaiah, who Solomon had sent to execute him, asked him to come out of the tabernacle, but he would not.

Benaiah went to Solomon and asked what he should do, because Joab would not come out. Solomon told him to kill him there; the blood would be on Joab for the sins he had committed.

Solomon told Shimei, "Build a house in Jerusalem and live there, but don't leave the city. The day you leave is the day you will die."

Shimei said, "My Lord, that is good. I will do as you say."

After Shimei lived for three years in Jerusalem, two of his servants ran away to Gath and he went there to get them. When he returned, Solomon was told he had been away.

Solomon had Shimei brought to him and said, "You know all the wickedness that is in your heart, all the evil you did to my father when he was fleeing. The Lord shall turn that wickedness on your own head."

He had Benaiah, his general, slay him.[163]

Solomon made an alliance with the king of Egypt and took his daughter as his wife. Solomon offered a thousand burnt offerings on the altar in Gibeon. There the Lord appeared to him in a dream and said, "What would you like me to give you?"

Solomon said, "You showed great mercy to my father, David, as he walked in righteousness and uprightness with you. You were very kind to him in giving him a son to sit on his throne, as it is today. I am king today in place of my father, but I am a little child and don't know what to do. I am amid a great people that can't be counted,

---

[163] 1 Kings 2

SOLOMON

because there are so many. Therefore, give me an understanding heart, that I may discern between good and bad. Who is able to judge so great a people?"

The Lord said, "Because you have asked this, and not long life, riches, nor the life of your enemies, I have given what you asked, a wise and understanding heart, as well as the others."

Then Solomon awoke and realized it was a dream.

Solomon was reigning in Jerusalem, and two women who were prostitutes came to him. One woman said to him, "I and this woman share a house. A child was born to me there and, three days later, a child was born to this other woman. There was nobody else in the house, just the two of us. This woman's baby died in the night, because she laid on it and smothered it. She got up at midnight and took my son from me while I slept, and laid her dead child on my bosom and laid my child on her bosom.

"When I awoke in the morning and went to give my child my milk, behold, it was dead. When I had thought about it, I realized it was not my son that I held."

The other woman said, "That is not true! The living baby is my son and the dead is yours."

The other said, "Not true! The living is mine and the dead yours."

Solomon said, "You each say the living son is yours. I can't tell what is true. Bring me a sword."

So they brought him a sword. He said, "Divide the child in two and give half to one and the other half to the other."

Then the mother of the living child said, "No, Lord, give it to her, don't kill it," while the mother of the dead baby said, "Go ahead, divide it."

Solomon said, "The mother who said, 'No, Lord, give it to her, don't kill it,' is the mother of the living baby; give him to her."

All Israel heard of this judgment and they feared the king, for they saw the wisdom of God was with him.[164]

Jesus said, "That was pretty smart of King Solomon. He must have been very wise."

---

[164] 1 Kings 3

SOLOMON

"He was very wise, in fact, he was renowned for his wisdom, but in this life, it is very easy to lose our way. One needs to know where they want to go and what they want to be and do those things that will get them there. The Lord gave us commandments to guide us and make it easier for us to choose good things. You'll soon see how King Solomon lost his way and strayed from the path.

In the fourth year of Solomon's reign, he started building the temple of Solomon as a house for his God. He used what David, his father, had collected and added much to it himself. He hired artisans and, after seven years, he finished it. After finishing the house of the Lord, he built a house for himself, which took thirteen years.[165]

The temple or house of the Lord was dedicated and the Ark of the Covenant was placed in the temple. The Levites were singing, and trumpets and other musical instruments were playing in praising and thanking the Lord. The temple was filled with the cloud of the Lord, and the priests could not minister because of the glory of the Lord.

Solomon offered a dedicatory prayer, and there was a great feast lasting two weeks. He offered twenty-two thousand oxen and a hundred-twenty-thousand sheep as a peace offering.[166]

After Solomon finished the house of the Lord, the Lord appeared to him again. He said, "I have heard your prayers and supplications and have hallowed this house, which you have built. If you will walk before me, as David your father did, in integrity of heart and in righteousness, and keep my commandments and statutes, I will establish the throne of your kingdom on Israel forever, as I promised to your father.

"But if you shall turn at all from following me, either you or your children, and will not keep my commandments and statures, but go and serve other gods and worship them, I will cut off Israel from the land which I have given them, and this house, which I have hallowed for my name, will I cast out of my sight and Israel shall be a proverb and a byword among all people.

"Anyone who passes this ruined house shall see it and say, 'Because they forsook the Lord, their God, who

---

[165] 1 Kings 5-9; 7:1; 9:10; 2 Chronicles 2-5
[166] 1 Kings 8

SOLOMON

brought their fathers out of Egypt and have worshipped other gods and served them, they have caused all this evil to come on them.'"

Solomon taxed his people to build the Lord's house and his house. After they were done, he built cities for his chariots and his horsemen in all parts of his dominion. He made bondmen of the Amorites, Hittites, Perizzites, Hivites, and Jebusites, which Israel was not able to destroy. There were no Israelites that were bondmen. All the countries around them paid tribute to Israel.[167]

The queen of Sheba came to Israel with a great train and camels with spices and much gold and jewels. When she saw all he had, his house, his table, what was served, the apparel of his ministers, and how they attended him, she was impressed. She spoke to him at length and he answered all her questions and his wisdom amazed her.

She said, "I heard in my own country of your wisdom, splendor, and prosperity, but it was not half of what in reality is here. Blessed be the Lord, your God, who is delighted in you and has set you on the throne of Israel, to give the people judgment and justice."

She gave the king twenty talents of gold, an abundance of spices, and many jewels.

Everyone came to Solomon to hear the wisdom God had put in his heart and to see his glory. There was an abundance of everything in Jerusalem. Solomon had one thousand-four-hundred chariots and twelve thousand horsemen.[168]

Solomon had seven hundred wives and three hundred concubines. The first was the daughter of Pharaoh, king of Egypt, but he took wives of the Moabites, Ammonites, Edomites, Zidonians, and Hittites. These tribes Moses warned the Israelites about and told them to take no wives of them, for they would turn their hearts from their God. This is what they did to Solomon.

Solomon worshipped Ashtoreth, the goddess of the Zidonians and Milcom, the god of the Ammonites. He built a high place for Chemosh, the god of Moab, in the hill before Jerusalem and for Molech, the god of the children of

---

[167] 1 Kings 9
[168] 1 Kings 10

Ammon. He did this for all his foreign wives, burning incense and sacrificing to their gods.

The Lord was angry with Solomon, because his heart was not with the Lord, but turned away to other gods and was no longer keeping the commandments and statutes of the Lord. The Lord told him, "Because you have done this, I will rend the kingdom from you and give it to your servant. However, for David, your father's sake, I will not take it from you, but from your son. I will not rend away all the kingdom, but will give one tribe to your son for David, my servant's, sake and for Jerusalem, which I have chosen."

Jesus said, "I don't think Solomon was wise after all. I can't imagine how someone can have a thousand wives. And then to have so many that don't believe in Heavenly Father. What happened to him?"

Joseph said, "You'll see."

"Several people surfaced who were problems for Solomon, but in particular, there was Jeroboam. He was a very valiant fighter and very industrious. Solomon was impressed by him and put him in charge of the work the tribe of Joseph did.

One day, Jeroboam left Jerusalem and the prophet, Ahijah, who had put on new clothes, found him and just the two of them were there. Ahijah took his new garment and tore it into twelve pieces and told Jeroboam, "Take ten pieces, for the God of Israel says, 'I will rend the kingdom out of the hand of Solomon's son and give ten tribes to you, because they have worshipped Ashtoreth, the goddess of the Zidonians, Chemosh, the god of the Moabites, and Milcom the god of the children of Ammon, and have not walked in my ways and kept my statutes and judgments, and his heart has become as David, his father; but he has not repented as did his father, that I may forgive him. For my servant David's sake and Jerusalem's sake, I will leave him, Judah and Benjamin. Jeroboam, if you will follow all I command you and walk in my ways to do what is right in my sight, by keeping my statutes and commandments, I will be with you, and build you a sure house, as I did for David and will give Israel to you.'"

When word of this got back to Solomon, he sought

SOLOMON

to kill Jeroboam, much as Saul tried to kill David. Jeroboam fled to Egypt to escape Solomon.

Solomon reigned over Israel forty years and died, and Rehoboam, his son, reigned in his place.[169]

When Jeroboam heard of Solomon's death, he left Egypt and came to Israel. Israel called Rehoboam to come down to Shechem to make him king. Rehoboam came down, and they said to him, "Your father made our yoke hard, with hard service and taxes. If you will lighten our yoke, we will serve you."

Rehoboam told them, "Let me think about this for three days and then come back and I will tell you what I will do."

They left.

He consulted with the elders who had served his father, and they told him, "If you will be a servant and serve these people and tell them good things, they will be your servants forever."

He then consulted with those who had grown up with him, and they told him to tell the people, "My little finger shall be thicker than my father's yoke. Even though my father placed a heavy yoke on you, I will add to it. Though my father punished you with whips, I will punish you with scorpions."

Jeroboam and all the people came to Rehoboam the third day, and the king answered the people roughly and did not follow the elder's counsel, but those of his own age.

Israel said, "Rehoboam wants nothing to do with us. Let us all return to our tents." They did and made Jeroboam king of Israel.

Judah and Benjamin made Rehoboam king over them, and Rehoboam gathered an army of one-hundred-eighty-thousand chosen men to fight against Israel and bring them to him.

Shemaiah was a prophet, and the word of God came to him. "Tell Rehoboam and all of Judah and Benjamin, 'The Lord says not to go fight against your brothers, the children of Israel, but return to your homes.'"

They obeyed the prophet and returned to their homes.

---

[169] 1 Kings 11; JST 1 Kings 11:33

SOLOMON

In Israel, Jeroboam was worried. The temple was in Judah and, if his people went from Israel to Jerusalem in Rehoboam's land to sacrifice, they might revert to him. He needed to do something to prevent that. He counseled with his advisers and decided to make two gold calves; one to go in Dan and the other in Bethel.

He told his people, "It is too far for you to go to Jerusalem, here are your gods, which brought you up out of the land of Egypt."

This made it difficult for Israel to keep the commandments of the Lord, but Jeroboam made it worse by making shrines in high places, and compounded the problems when he ordained priests who were not Levites. Jeroboam also declared a feast on the fifteenth of the eighth month, like they had in Judah, and sacrificed to the golden calves and burned incense.[170]

Jesus said, "The prophet Ahijah told Jeroboam he would be king and, if he kept the Lord's commandments, he would be with him and build him a sure house. I think it should be obvious, since he was made king, that Ahijah was a true prophet. Why would he not follow the prophet's advice?"

Joseph said, "I imagine when he was made king, he forgot about what the prophet said and started thinking it was by his efforts he was made king. He then became worried about what would happen if his people went up to worship in Judah, and he didn't even consider what was righteous and what was sinful."

Jesus said, "What happened to him?"

Joseph said, "I'll tell you."

Things didn't go well. Jeroboam had a child who was very sick and he sent his wife to Ahijah, the prophet, to ask what would happen to the child. She went to Ahijah pretending to be someone else. By this time, Ahijah was blind in old age. The Lord told him who it was, and he said, "Come in, wife of Jeroboam who has come to ask about her sick child. Tell Jeroboam the Lord says, 'I exalted you from among the people and a made you a prince and king over Israel."'You have done more evil than any of those before you by making gods and images to provoke my anger.

---

[170] 1 Kings 12

Therefore, I will take away all your sons, leaving you with no posterity. None of them will be buried except the child who is sick and he will die as soon as your wife enters your home. I will scatter Israel out of this good land, because they have made images, provoking me to anger.'"

All this came to pass.[171]

Jesus said, "That is so sad. He could have had a great life and done a lot to help his people, but he lost his family and all else because he just thought of himself."

Joseph said, "I want to teach you some other things for a while, but first, just a little more history. Rehoboam wasn't a great king and did things he should not have done. The kings of Judah were more righteous, most of the time, than were the kings of Israel. It is interesting to me that when the kings were unrighteous, so were the people. When the kings were righteous, so were the people. The people seemed to follow the ruler. That is why righteous kings are important; it makes it easier for us to be righteous.

"After many prophets had warned Israel repeatedly, they were conquered by Assyria; the people were carried away to other countries and we no longer know where they are. Some years after Israel was conquered, Judah also was conquered and many died. Most of the survivors were carried to Babylon, where they lived for seventy years before they could return to their homeland and rebuild the temple." [172]

Joseph said. "I think I will stop here. We are almost home. The next thing I want to teach you is reading. Then you will be able to study the prophets on your own. I think you will enjoy that."

---

[171] 1 Kings 14:1-18
[172] 2 Chronicles 12-36

PART 3
THE MINISTRY OF JESUS

THE TEMPLE

Joseph continued teaching Jesus whenever he could make the time. Jesus was a fast learner and devoured everything he read, including the Talmud, the prophets, and the law. Joseph and Mary, with their children and other relatives, made it a point to go to Jerusalem and the temple for Passover every year.[173] Jesus was now twelve, *and they were on their way to the Passover with most of Nazareth. Jesus and his brother, James, were walking with their large company a little behind the rest of the family.*

Jesus said, "I'm really excited to be going to Passover this year. Now that I'm twelve and a son of the law, I can go to the temple and discuss things with the doctors of the law."

James said, "It would be exciting to go into the temple, but I don't know why you get excited about the law. It is so boring to me."

"Boring? It's not boring. The law is what guides us. It tells us what we can do and what we can't do. It should guide us back to our Father in heaven. The problem is the Scribes and Pharisees have made up so many laws about everything that what we should be doing has gotten lost.

"God gave us the law to help us live, so we can have a better life. There are so many laws now that keeping all of them is hard. We should just have the laws that will improve our lives and bring us closer to God."

"I'm not sure what you mean. Are you saying we ought to be able to decide what laws we should follow?"

Jesus said, "Kind of. We should know what the purpose of the law is and follow it for that purpose. Look! There's the widow Zeela. Her ass' pack is about to fall apart. See! She's leading it and I don't think she is aware of what's going on."

"Neat! Let's watch and see what happens," said James.

Jesus looked at James, his eyes wide and, with a sharp tone, said, "Come on, James! That's not nice. How would you feel if you were in her shoes? She's trying to feed her baby while walking and leading the ass. She doesn't need the pack falling apart and losing her stuff."

James sighed and said, "I guess you're right. We should help. But I still think it would have been neat to see what would have happened."

---

[173] Luke 2:41

THE TEMPLE

Jesus walked over to Zeela and said, "It looks like your pack is coming apart. I think I can get it tightened up as we are walking, if that's okay with you."

She said, " It's nice of you boys to notice and say something. Thank you very much."

They walked beside the ass while moving the straps and tightening them. Jesus then called out to the widow, "I think we have it all fixed."

"Thanks to you again," she called.

A little later, Jesus went up to Joseph and told him, "Father, I would like to walk around a bit and talk to some of my friends and see if anybody needs help. James and I helped the widow Zeela with a problem she had with her pack this morning. Maybe somebody else could use a hand. I like helping people."

Joseph replied, "That will be fine. I know you like to help, and we have everything under control here. Just be sure to come back when we stop for the night."

Jesus said, "Thanks, father," and went off.

It was several days later when they arrived in Jerusalem. They had made plans to meet Mary's cousin, Elisabeth, and her son, John, there. Elisabeth did not go every year and it had been several years since they had seen them. John was now of age, and Elisabeth wanted John to see and go into the temple.

The next morning, after everything was set up and they had eaten, Jesus asked Joseph, "Is it okay if I go and find Aunt Elisabeth and John? It has been about three years since I have seen John, and I would really like to see him again."

Joseph said, "That will be fine, but don't stay too long. We're going to get together later. Your mother and I want to see them, too, and we hope to have our Seder together."

Jesus found Elisabeth's camp where she had said it would be, tucked into some trees not too far from their campsite. When Elisabeth saw him, she said, "Hello, Jesus. My, how you've grown." Then with a bow, she said, "Welcome to my camp, Messiah."

Jesus looked down and shuffled his feet. "Why do you call me that? You're the only one who does."

She looked at him with steely grey eyes and said, "Look at me. I know it makes you uncomfortable, but you are the Messiah, the Son of God! You cannot afford to be shy. You need to take charge. You are twelve and of age. You can teach. Don't be afraid, but do the work your Heavenly Father has for you. I am one of the few who know you are the Messiah, and I want you to appreciate how *important that is. I don't say that when others are around, because they might not understand."*

Jesus looked at her intently and said, *"I will do what I need to do! I am not usually shy with people like I am with you. Is John around?"*

Elisabeth replied, *"I sent him out to do some errands. He won't be back for a while."*

Jesus frowned and said, *"I wanted to see him, but I need to get back to my father. He told me not to stay too long."*

Elisabeth replied quickly with a firm voice, *"Joseph is not your father; you should call him Joseph."*

"I know he is not my father, but he acts as my father and has told me to call him father, so I do."

"That's fine, but remember, you are the Son of God," she replied, emphasizing *"Son of God."*

Jesus replied, *"What does 'Son of God' mean to you?"*

"Have you read any of the writings of Abraham?"

Jesus said, *"No, I don't think we have any."*

Elisabeth said, *"I thought that might be the case, so I brought some for you to read. I will give them to you right now, but I want them back before we leave."*

Jesus said, *"Thanks, Aunt Elisabeth, that's very thoughtful of you."*

She went on, *"We're going to come over to see your family this afternoon. Why don't you come back for supper and spend the night with John? He would like that and you will see him tomorrow at our Seder."*

"I would love to. I am sure father will let me come," he said, emphasizing *father*. He started to leave, but then turned back and said, *"Aunt Elisabeth I have been wondering about what happened to Uncle Zachariah. Please tell me about it."*

"Haven't you talked to John about it?" she asked.

"Yes, but he doesn't have many details, and I'm wondering how it seemed to you."

"What did John tell you?" she asked.

Jesus looked down and then back up at her and said, *"He said an angel appeared to his father and said to take you and John into the desert away from people. That some soldiers tortured his father to find out where you and he were, but he didn't tell and they killed him. He doesn't seem to know much more than that."*

She replied, *"I guess we haven't talked much about it. I probably should tell him more. After seeing the angel in the temple*

THE TEMPLE

and becoming deaf and dumb, Zachariah became kind of a celebrity. Then, when he named his son John and could speak again, people got excited about who John was and what he would do. It seemed like the entire world wanted to talk to him. It had been a very long time since revelation had been received.

"The High Priest talked to him and wanted him to do some things for him. That is when the angel came to him. The angel told him Herod had heard about a king being born and would be killing babies about John's age and John needed to be protected. Zachariah didn't know how he could just leave and have nobody know where he had gone. He had met a nomad at the temple some years before and they had become good friends. He got word to him he would like to have John and me with them for a while. The story was my husband had been killed and I had no one to help, and my husband and the nomad had been very good friends. This was basically true and would become truer.

"Anyway, when Herod made the decree to kill all males under two years old, everybody knew about John. Where was he, they wanted to know? Of course, I wasn't there, so I don't know exactly what happened, but I assume Zachariah wouldn't tell them. I heard they tried to get him to tell through torture, but he never did, and they finally killed him. When I think about what he must have gone through to protect his son, it makes me sad, and yet proud he was so strong. He was such a good, loving man. I can't tell you how much I miss him," She said, wiping tears from her eyes.

Jesus said, "Thanks for sharing that with me. I don't understand how people can do such terrible things," he said with a sigh, and gave her a big hug.

When Jesus got back to their camp, he told Joseph, "I talked to Aunt Elisabeth, but John wasn't there. She invited me to come for supper and spend the night with them after their visit today. Is that okay?"

He said, "That will be fine. I know you are excited to go into the temple. We will go the day after our Seder. I think. Omri and Zadok will be going with us."

Jesus clapped his hands and said, "That's great! I can't wait to tell John. Can he come with us?"

"I don't see why not," replied Joseph.

"Aunt Elisabeth loaned me some writings of Abraham that I want to read right away, because she wants them back. She thinks I will find them very interesting. You might want to read them too."

"I am sure I will," said Joseph.

THE TEMPLE

When Jesus had a few minutes of free time, he started reading Abraham and this is part of what he read:

The Lord gave Abraham a Urim and Thummim when he was in Ur of the Chaldees, so he could receive revelation. He learned about the sun, moon, and stars and how the planets moved. The Lord also showed Abraham intelligences that were organized before the world was. The Lord stood among those who were spirits and said, "These I will make my rulers and Abraham, you are one of them. You were chosen before you were born."

Standing there was one who was like God. He said to those who were with him, "Let's go down, for there is space there and materials, and we will make an earth whereon these may live. We will test them to see if they will do all that Elohim commands them. They who keep their first estate shall have glory added on and those who don't keep their first estate, shall not have glory in the same kingdom with those who keep their first estate. They who keep their second estate shall have glory added on their heads forever and ever."

Elohim said, "Who shall I send?"

One answered like the Son of Man (*Man can be a synonym for God*): "Here am I, send me." Another answered, "Here am I, send me." Elohim said, "I will send the first." The second was angry and did not keep his first estate and many followed him.[174]

After reading this Jesus gave it to Joseph to read and then prayed about it. Later, Joseph and Jesus sat down together. Joseph asked Jesus, "What do you think Son of Man means?"

Jesus said, "I wasn't sure, so I prayed about that and I think that is me. I think the other one is the devil, but I don't understand it yet. Later. I think Elohim will help me understand it better."

Joseph said, "When I read it, I was reminded of something I was recently reading in Isaiah, but I don't know if it ties together. Let me read it to you, 'How have you fallen from heaven, O Lucifer, son of the morning? How are you cut down to the ground, who did weaken the nations? You have said in your heart, 'I will ascend into

---

[174] PGP Abraham 3

THE TEMPLE

heaven and I will exalt my throne above the stars of God. I will ascend above the clouds and I will be like God.' Yet you will be brought down to hell.[175]

He looked at Jesus. "What do you think of that?"

"I don't know. I am going to have to pray about it."

****

A few days later, as they neared the temple, Jesus said to John, "Every time I see the temple, I get this feeling. I don't know how to describe it. I feel peaceful, like everything is right with the world. I am filled with awe and wonder, but the peacefulness is the most important thing I feel. I want to keep feeling it forever. Do you know what I mean?"

"I know. I feel like that too. It's hard to explain," replied John.

Jesus said to John, "I love walking up to the temple. Holiness should be a goal in life for everyone, so the physical effort required in walking up the hill to a holy place seems right. Father took me into the second court before, but I have never been into the third court. It is reserved for clean men and now that we are twelve, we can go in. It will be exciting to see it."

Joseph, seeing Jesus' excitement, said, "Jesus, remember we can't stay long. We have food we need to get, and I need your help in setting up more of the things we are selling. If there is time later, we may be able to come again. I know how much you wanted to come here, so I made arrangements for today."

Jesus replied, "I understand, father, thank you."

After visiting the temple, Jesus and James were kept busy helping their father prepare more of the household items they had made and were selling. When they had restocked, Joseph told them they could go and be with their friends.

Jesus asked, "Is it okay for me to stay with Aunt Elisabeth and John?"

"That will be fine. Remember, we leave in two days."

"I know," said Jesus.

Jesus spent the next night with his aunt and John. That afternoon he told his aunt, "I think I should go to the temple. John and I are having fun being together, but I think I need to be about my Father's business. I think I would like to listen to some of the doctors and learn from them. I am sure you will see Joseph and my

---

[175] Isaiah 14:12-15

THE TEMPLE

mother before everybody leaves. Please tell them when I have finished my Father's business, I will come back."

His aunt replied, "That makes good sense to me. I will miss seeing you. You have a spirit about you that makes me want to be around you. You are a very special person; don't forget that."

Jesus said, "I know who I am and why I am here. I won't forget." He gave her a hug and said goodbye to John and left for the temple.

It was late afternoon when Jesus climbed up to the temple and went into the third court. "I should have left earlier in the day," he thought, "but I am here and can't wait to learn more about the law and how I can apply it in my life."

There were several small groups where Rabbis were teaching. Jesus walked over to some and listened for a while, then moved on to other groups. He went over to a corner where a Pharisee and a Sadducee were discussing the law. The Sadducee said, "Why do you say a person can only take so many steps on the Sabbath? How do you decide how many steps one should take?"

The Pharisee said, "I know you Sadducees only follow the five Books of Moses and not the prophets.[176] *But in the Ten Commandments, which Moses gave us; God tells us we shouldn't do any work on the Sabbath. It is obvious walking is work and we should keep it to a minimum. How will a person know how far they can walk without breaking that law unless they have a guide on how many steps they can take? As a leader, how can you judge someone on their righteousness unless you have some guidelines? Several of us have come together. We have counted the number of steps we need to take to do the necessary things on the Sabbath, such as eating, washing our hands, going to the synagogue, and other necessary things to be done. If we can do that, everybody else can, too."*

When Jesus heard this, he thought, "I came here to learn, but it is ridiculous to count your steps. My Father doesn't want me counting steps on the Sabbath; he expects me to know what the proper actions are for me to take."

He just had to voice his thoughts and said, "It's true we aren't to work on the Sabbath, but the purpose of the Ten Commandments is to guide us on what we should do. God wants us to understand the purpose so we can live our lives properly. By

---

[176] Richard N. Holzapfel and others. *Jesus Christ and the World of the New Testament.* ((2006). Deseret Book Company. Salt Lake City, UT. page 27

counting our steps, we become slaves to the law. Moses tells us God made the heaven and earth and all that is in them and rested the seventh day, blessed the Sabbath day and hallowed it.[177] *We, too, are to hallow the Sabbath day by not working, worshiping God, and doing good to others. When we go out and buy things on the Sabbath we are not hallowing it, because we are causing others to work. There are times when you need to do things on the Sabbath that require work. If a male child is eight days old, you circumcise him. If your field catches on fire, it needs to be put out. If someone is injured they need to be helped. The law is given to us to be a help, but you make it burdensome. It would be work to just count our steps. Why do you think God gave us the Ten Commandments and the rest of the Law?"*

The Pharisee answered, *"By living the Law, we become righteous and are able to live with God in the next life."*

Jesus responded, *"The Law cannot by itself make you holy so you can return to God. When you sin, you become unclean and no matter what you do you cannot make yourself clean. That is why the Messiah must come.* As Isaiah said, 'The Lord's hand is not weakened that it cannot save: nor His ear deaf that He cannot hear. But your iniquities have separated you and your God, that you can't feel Him nor hear Him.[178] The Redeemer shall come to Zion and to those that repent of Israel, says the Lord. This is my covenant with them; The spirit I give my children and the words that are given to them, shall not depart from them or from their children or from their grandchildren.'[179] *What God is telling us is that He is always there. He is not deaf, but hears us and because of our sin we cannot hear Him or feel Him. It is our sin that has separated us from Him. If we repent and obey Him, his spirit and words will stay with us and our children forever, if they will but obey Him. By living the law, we attune ourselves to God so we can follow His promptings. Look at our history, when our kings have been righteous, we have had peace and plenty. When they have worshiped other gods, we have had war, famine and sickness."*

The Pharisee said, *"If our righteousness will not save us, what will the Redeemer do that will save us?"*

Jesus replied, "Quoting again from Isaiah, 'He is despised and rejected by men; a man of sorrows and acquainted with grief. We hid our faces from Him as he was despised and we didn't value

---

[177] Exodus 20:10-11
[178] Isaiah 59:1-2
[179] Isaiah 59: 20-21

THE TEMPLE

Him. He bore our grief and carried our sorrow; yet we only valued Him as someone struck, punished by God and afflicted. But he was wounded for our sins, bruised for our mistakes; punished so we could have peace of mind and from His whipping we are healed. He was taken out of the land of the living for the transgressions of all of God's children. His grave was with the wicked and with the rich when He was buried. He had done no violence nor had He been deceitful. Yet it pleased the Lord to have Him suffer and give Him grief, so when we shall make an offering for sin and repent, we shall be His.'"[180]

The Sadducee interrupted and said, "I don't care what Isaiah said; I follow Moses and he didn't say anything about a Redeemer."

Jesus replied, "In Deuteronomy, he said, 'The Lord will raise up a prophet from the midst of Israel like me and will put words in his mouth and he shall speak to them all that I shall command him. And it shall come to pass that he who will not obey my words which are spoken in my name; I will require it of him. But the prophet who shall speak a word in my name, who I have not commanded him to speak or that shall speak in the name of other gods, shall die. If you say in your heart; "How shall we know the word which the Lord has not spoken?" When a prophet speaks in the name of the Lord, if the thing does not come to pass, the Lord has not spoken it. The prophet has spoken it falsely and you shall not be afraid of him."[181] *The prophet Moses says the Lord will raise up is the Redeemer, but he is also telling us how to recognize other prophets. Isaiah wrote for his day, our day and future days. We need to know his teachings, just as we know those of Moses and the teachings of Ezekiel, Joshua, Daniel, and the rest. What they are teaching is just as important as what Moses is teaching."*

Another Pharisee said, "When you quoted Isaiah about the Redeemer, you said he would suffer and be taken from the living. We know that, when the Messiah comes, his kingdom will last forever and he will rule it forever. It doesn't make sense that the Redeemer will die."

Jesus said, *"The Messiah will soon come and die for the sins of all. In the last days, he will return and rule forever."*

Jesus looked around and saw a crowd had formed. He could see others walking over to see what was so interesting. Suddenly, he felt nervous, but he went on, "As I was saying before, the law and

---
[180] Isaiah 53: 3-5, 9-10
[181] Deuteronomy 18: 18-22

THE TEMPLE

the prophets are a guide for us. Through them, we learn what our God desires us to do and how he would have us live. If we know what is proper to do, we won't have to worry about how many steps we take on the Sabbath. We will do things God wants us to do. The first and great commandment is from Deuteronomy, 'You shall love the Lord, your God, with all your heart and with all your soul, and with all your might.'[182] The second is from Leviticus, 'You shall love your neighbor as yourself.'[183] *If you will do these things, you won't need to count your steps and the Sabbath will be a pleasure to you, not a boring day that is burdensome."*

The Sadducee who'd been discussing with the Pharisee said, "It is getting late and I must be getting home. I hate to leave, but my wife will be looking for me."

"Me too," said the Pharisee, as he turned and walked away. With this, the crowd began to disburse until only a few were left.

One of the Pharisees, a kindly looking older man, well-groomed and dressed, asked Jesus, "Where are you from and where did you get your learning?"

He said, "I am from Nazareth and learned from my father."

The man shook his head. "You must have been a good student. You seem to know your scriptures. I assume your family is here for Passover. Where are you staying?"

"We are camped outside of town to the north," Jesus replied.

"It is getting late and it is quite a distance away. Do you think your parents would mind if you came to my house for the night? We have room and I would enjoy talking more with you," he said.

Jesus said, "I am sure that would be okay. My parents think I am with my aunt and they won't miss me tonight, but I do need to leave in the morning, as we will leave for home the following day."

Jesus spent a pleasant evening talking to the Pharisee and his wife, and went back to the camp the next day. When he got to the campsite, he found it deserted. "Oh, well," he thought, "they will miss me sooner or later and come back to find me. Mother will probably know I am at the temple. Where else would they expect me to be? I will ask the Pharisee if I can stay with him a few days more. I'm sure he won't mind. We can have some more discussions."

With that, he went back to the temple and spent several days listening, teaching, and spending nights with the kind Pharisee.

---

[182] Deuteronomy 6: 5
[183] Leviticus 19:18

THE TEMPLE

After Jesus left the campsite of Joseph and Mary, there was a discussion among the leaders of the Nazareth group. Business had been good for those selling things and most were sold out. The Passover was over and a majority wanted to return home a day early, so the decision was made to leave one day early. The word was passed around camp, but being off by themselves, Aunt Elisabeth didn't hear about it until the next day after Jesus had left. In fact, she didn't know about it until she saw others packing up.

"John!" she said. "Run over to the camp and see what is happening. It looks like everybody is leaving."

John ran over and asked, "Is everybody leaving?"

"That's right. Didn't you hear? Business was good this year there's very little left to sell. We might as well go home. You better hurry back and get packed if you're going with us."

"Mom, everybody's leaving. They said business was so good almost everybody's sold out, so they decided to go home."

Elisabeth said, "We'd better get packed up in a hurry. We don't want to be left here." With that, they scurried and packed. They were just about the last in line. "We'll get together with Joseph and Mary this evening," said Elisabeth.

That evening, shortly after they were stopped, Joseph came by. "Hi, Elisabeth. Is Jesus here?"

Elisabeth said, "No, he's not. He went into Jerusalem and didn't spend the night with us as we had planned."

"Well, I'd better check with others and see if he is with anybody else. He is usually so reliable, I don't worry about him, but Mary is going to be sick with worry."

Elisabeth smiled. "You'll probably have to go back, but he will be fine. He can take care of himself."

"I sure hope so. It's been good to see you and John. I hope we can get together again next year," said Joseph.

Joseph walked around and visited others they knew, but no one had seen Jesus. The next morning they went back to Jerusalem looking for him. After looking around the campsite, they went up to the temple, and there was Jesus, sitting amid the doctors, and they were hearing him and asking him questions.[184] And all who heard him were astonished at his understanding and answers.[185]

---

[184] JST Luke 2:46
[185] Luke 2:47

THE TEMPLE

When Mary saw Jesus, she was amazed and said, "Son, why have you done this. Your father and I have been looking for you and worrying about you."

Jesus said, "Why have you been looking for me? Didn't you know I must be about my Father's business?"[186]

Mary asked, "What do you mean, my father's business?"

Jesus replied, "This is my Father's house and I am here on His business."

Mary said, "Oh, I see what you mean."

The family returned to Nazareth.

Shortly after returning home, Jesus was again studying Isaiah, and thinking about what he had read in Abraham. He decided to pray about it in his favorite secluded spot. He went there and knelt. He asked his Father in Heaven, Elohim, to help him understand what he had read. As he prayed, an angel came down and spoke to him.

The next day, he told Joseph, "Last evening, I went to where I like to pray. I had been studying Isaiah and had questions about that and what we read in Abraham. As I prayed, an angel appeared. Maybe I should have been scared, but I wasn't. I just had a feeling of love and peace. Have you ever seen an angel?"

Joseph said, "No, but I have seen one in my dreams. What did he look like?"

"He was standing in the air; his feet didn't touch the ground. He had on a robe that was whiter than anything I have seen. It covered his shoulders, but his hands and arms were bare. Some people seem to think angels have wings, but they don't. His feet and ankles also were bare. He said, 'I am sent from your Father to help you understand the Messiah and what you will do as the Messiah.' Is that the way the angel you saw in your dreams looked?"

Joseph said, "That is pretty much the way I remember it. Your mother also has seen an angel. She doesn't talk much about it, but you should ask her to tell you. What did the angel say to you?"

"He said, 'Don't be afraid, I am a fellow servant of God (Elohim) and am his spirit child, just as you are. I want to explain what you read in Abraham and elaborate on it. You read in Abraham, That God (Elohim) stood among spirits who were organized before the world was and that there were many of the great and noble ones who he would make his rulers, among which was Abraham. There stood another one among them who was like

---

[186] Luke 2:48-49

THE TEMPLE

Elohim. Abraham is speaking of you there, Jesus. You are like Elohim. You are the one who led the other spirits down to make the earth you are living on, because there was space and materials to make it. You were the first spirit born to Elohim. It is you who created the world Abraham is telling us about, under the direction of your spiritual Father, Elohim. This earth you created is a testing place for Heavenly Father's children, to see if they will do all he commands.'[187]

"*We were originally intelligences and were spiritually born by our Heavenly parents. We saw they had physical bodies, and we wanted to be like them and experience and taste physical things we could not with spiritual bodies. Elohim had a plan for us. We would come to earth where we would receive a physical body and experience things we could not do in heaven with spiritual bodies. We would also learn how to handle our bodies and control the passions that come with a physical body. We would be free to choose how we would act and what we would do. When we sinned, we would become unclean and would not be able to return to heaven, because no unclean thing can be there. To overcome this, a savior would be provided. He would have to live without sin and then sacrifice himself once. Because he would be free of sin, he would pay the price of sin for each of us, so we would be clean and return to heaven to be with Elohim.* That is what you accepted Jesus.

"*In a conference, Elohim explained his plan to all of us spirits.* Besides you, Jesus, who in the spirit world is known as Jehovah, there was Lucifer, another of Elohim's leaders. *He was always jealous of you and* wanted to be more powerful than Elohim. When Elohim asked you to be the Savior, as was planned from the beginning, he put his own plan forward. He would have all go to a world where there is no opportunity to sin, because there would be no choice, and thus we would all return to heaven. Lucifer would take all the glory for this to himself. In contrast, you said all the glory would be Elohim's. This created a war in heaven, not a war with swords, but a war of words and ideas. A third of the spirits followed Lucifer and were thrust down to earth, where they try to influence all to do evil, *by whispering to everyone evil thoughts. If one allows themselves to be influenced by the thoughts, it leads to sin.*

"*This is what you and Joseph recently read in Isaiah.* 'How have you fallen from heaven, O Lucifer, son of the morning? How are you cut down to the ground, who did weaken the nations?

---

[187] PGP Abraham 3:22-24; D&C 29:39

You have said in your heart, 'I will ascend into heaven and I will exalt my throne above the stars of God. I will ascend above the clouds and I will be like God.' Yet you will be brought down to hell.[188]

"To start Elohim's plan, a male and female, Adam and Eve, would be placed on the earth and given physical bodies. Since Elohim would not force anyone to sin, which would then remove them from his presence, sin would have to be their choice.

"He placed Adam and Eve in the garden of Eden, where there were two special trees. One was the tree of knowledge of good and evil, the other the tree of life. God told Adam and Eve they could eat of every tree in the garden, except the tree of knowledge of good and evil, because when they ate it, they would become mortal and die.

"He also told them to be fruitful, multiply, and replenish the earth, which they could not do unless they were mortal.[189] If they had not eaten of the forbidden fruit and become mortal, Elohim's plan would not have worked, but Satan and his angels were there and they convinced Adam and Eve to eat of the forbidden fruit, putting the plan in motion. After eating of the tree of knowledge of good and evil, they were barred from the tree of life and removed from the garden. If they had eaten the fruit of the tree of life, they would have become immortal and Elohim's plan would have been defeated. Elohim's plan requires opposition so we can grow, and Satan's angels are a part of that plan.[190]

"Because of the sacrifice you will make, Jesus, all who live on earth will receive bodies. Those who live righteously can return and live with Heavenly Father. The third who became Satan's angels will never receive a body."

THE DEATH OF JOSEPH

When Jesus was about nineteen, he came into the shop after returning from working at a customer's home. He found Joseph sitting on a chair, slumped over a table on which he had been working, as if he were asleep. He went up to him and shook his shoulder, but there was no response. He was not breathing.

---

[188] Isaiah 14:12-15; PGP Moses 4:1-4
[189] Genesis 1:28; Genesis 2:8; Genesis 3:1-6, 24
[190] Genesis 1-3; D&C 29:34-39

THE DEATH OF JOSEPH

Jesus had become used to knowing when things were going to happen. He usually just knew when one of his siblings was hurting or was going to need help. This time, he had no forewarning whatever. It was a shock to him. Joseph was dead. Jesus knew he had only passed on to the next life, but he wouldn't see him in this life again. The tears started rolling down his cheeks. How would his mother, Mary, take this? How would his siblings? He would have to be the breadwinner for the family now.

Joseph was a great man. Jesus loved working with him. He was complementary, a good teacher, and he let Jesus make decisions himself on what was the right way to make something. Jesus loved to make things that had an inner beauty. They were useful, but also had a beauty to them. He would dearly miss the discussions they had about the law and practices of the time. Jesus sat there with Joseph thinking about these things, already missing this great father figure he had had. After a few moments, he realized it was time to tell his mother.

He left the shop and went into the house portion, put his arms around her and, before he could say anything, she said, with a frown on her face, "What's wrong?"

He said, "I'm sorry, mother, but father has died."

Her world seemed to collapse along with her legs. He guided her over to a stool, and she sat down, sobbing quietly. After a few minutes, she asked, "What happened?"

'I don't know, mother. When I got back from Amos' home, where I had been working, I found him slumped over the table he was making."

Mary said, "Take me in to see him."

Jesus walked in with Mary to the shop and over to Joseph's side. Mary touched him, and then put her arms around him and gave him a kiss. She said, "I am really going to miss him. He was a great man. Jesus, you always seemed to know when something bad was going to happen to one of your siblings and could be there to help them. I wish you could have been there for your father."

Jesus replied, "I do, too, mother. I usually can feel when something bad is going to happen, but this time I didn't have any such feeling. I just walked in and there he was, slumped over the table. I guess my Heavenly Father wants me to have some experience taking care of a family."

Mary wiped tears from her eyes and said, "I'm glad you're here, Jesus. Without you here to help, I don't know how I would be able to get along."

With that, she gave Joseph another hug and kiss, and Jesus walked out with her.

JOHN THE BAPTIST

One day, when Jesus was about 30, he was working in his shop when his mother came in. This was unusual for her to do.
He said, "Hi, Mother. What can I do for you?"
She responded, "Nothing is wrong. I just wanted to talk to you. I'm worried about how hard you work. I don't want what happened to your father to happen to you."
"Mother, you don't have to worry about that," he said with a big smile. "I promise you my working hard is not going to lead to my early death. I do wish you wouldn't call Joseph my father. While he was alive, I called him that because he wanted me to. I don't see any reason why we need to do it now."
Mary said, "I know you're right. Elisabeth keeps telling me the same thing. She tells me how lucky I am to be the mother of the Messiah, the Christ, or Emmanuel. She keeps calling you by different names. Don't say it; I know the prophets use different names and some of the things you have done are miracles, but I still worry. Your brother, James, is getting married in a few months. You're the eldest; you should find a nice girl and get married."
"I wish I could", he said as he put his hand to his chin and shook his head sadly. I gained mortality from you, but because Elohim is my Father, I can be eternal. Also, I will be starting my ministry soon and I wouldn't have much time to be with a wife."
Mary said with a smile, "There will always be time after your ministry."
Jesus said, "I don't think so. That's not the way I read Isaiah. Anyway, the reason I have been working so hard is to save enough money so during my ministry you'll have what you need. James is going to have a family to support, so he shouldn't have to be responsible for your care."
Mary said, "When do you think you will be leaving?"
Jesus replied, "I am not sure, but shortly after the wedding. John is baptizing beyond Jordan, and I need to go and have him baptize me. I will be gone for a while, but I will come back for a brief time."

JOHN THE BAPTIST

"I am going to miss you while you're gone. I hope this ministry won't go on for too long."

He replied, "I'll miss you too, Mother."

*His cousin, John, was preaching the baptism of repentance for the remission of sins and was baptizing people in the Jordan River. He preached as it is written in Isaiah, "*The voice of one in the wilderness. Prepare the way of the Lord, make his paths straight.*"*[191]

A little after this, the High Priest sent a group of three Pharisees to see what John was doing and to report back.[192] *The first, called Gamliel, said, "It is a hot one today. It doesn't feel like spring. I don't know why we're so lucky to be the ones picked for this back-to-nature experience. I can think of a thousand things I would rather be doing than walking out in the wilderness on a hot day to see some idiot."*

The second Pharisee, Nicodemus, said, "He might not be an idiot. He could be the Messiah or, as others say, the Christ. He is going to come one of these days! But I agree with you this guy is probably just another one of those claiming to be the Messiah. We certainly have had enough of them lately. There must be something in the air that makes people claim to be him."

The third, Aram, said, "You're right, Nicodemus. There must be something in the air, though I don't think there is much chance we're going to find the Messiah. . . I've been in this area before and I think the Jordan is just ahead."

Gamliel replied, "It can't be too soon for me."

As they walked around a bend, they could see the river, and he said, "Hey, there is a pretty big crowd. I didn't expect that many to be out here."

A few minutes later, as they got up to the crowd and could see and hear John, Aram said, "Wow, that's some classy outfit he's wearing. Not the latest fashion for sure."

Nicodemus said, "That's how the great prophet Elijah, the Tishbite, is said to have dressed. It's woven from camel hair and the big leather belt holds it all together. It doesn't look too comfortable to me, but it says he's a prophet. He supposedly lives on a diet of locusts and wild honey."

*They listened to John as he spoke, saying, "*I am come as the prophet Isaiah said, 'To prepare the way of the Lord and to make his paths straight. Every valley shall be filled and every mountain and

---

[191] JST Luke 3: 4-11
[192] John 1:24

hill shall be brought low. The crooked shall be made straight and the rough ways shall be made smooth and all flesh shall see the salvation of God.' You are a generation of vipers. You need to flee from the wrath of God which is coming by recognizing your sins and repenting.[193] Don't say to yourselves we are special because we are the children of Abraham and have kept the commandments of God and no one can inherit the promises of God to Abraham except his children. God is able from these stones to create children of Abraham."[194]

One in the audience asked, "Then what should we do?"

He answered, "If you have two coats, give them to those that have none. If you have food, do the same."

Some tax collectors asked him, "What should we do?"

He said, "Take no more than is owed."

Soldiers demanded of him, "What shall we do?"

He said, "Do violence to nobody, nor accuse anybody falsely, and be content with your pay."[195]

Nicodemus asked the question many were thinking. "Are you the Christ?"[196]

John answered, "I baptize you with water, but one is coming who is mightier than I. I am not worthy even to undo his shoes. He shall not only baptize you with water, but with fire and the Holy Ghost.[197] He will separate the wheat from the chaff; gather the wheat and burn the chaff with unquenchable fire.[198] *I am now ready to baptize anyone who is prepared to repent and change their lives."*

With that, he turned and went into the Jordan. He baptized a number of people, both men and women. John was standing in water about waist deep, and those desiring to be baptized would walk out to him. He would raise his right arm to the square and, calling them by name, would say, "Having authority of God, I baptize you in the name of Christ, that He might give you eternal life through His redemption, which has been prepared from the foundation of the world."

He would then take them by the arm and lower them into the Jordan until they were completely submerged.

---

[193] Luke 3:4-8
[194] JST Luke 3:8
[195] Luke 3:7-14
[196] John 1:19
[197] Mark 1:7-8
[198] Luke 3:17

JOHN THE BAPTIST

As he finished baptizing and was coming up out of the river, he saw his cousin, Jesus, coming from Galilee. He said, "Jesus, what are you doing here?"

Jesus said, "I am coming to be baptized by you, of course."

John said, "I can't baptize you, I need to be baptized by you. Why would you come to me?"

Jesus said, "Who else is there to baptize me who has authority? Baptize me so everything is done properly."

With that, John went back into the water and baptized Jesus as he had done the others. After Jesus was baptized and came out of the water, the heavens were opened and the Spirit of God descended in the sign of a dove and lighted on Jesus. A voice, which was heard by some, seemed to come from the heavens. It was not a loud voice, but was easily heard by those who did hear it. The voice said, "This is my beloved Son, in whom I am well pleased."[199]

John said, "I bear record that this is the Son and Lamb of God. He who sent me to baptize with water said, 'Upon whom you shall see the Spirit descending and remaining on him, is he who baptizes with the Holy Ghost."[200]

Nicodemus turned to Gamliel and said, "That's amazing. Can you believe that? The Messiah is here."

Gamliel said, "Just because some guy in a camel costume says, 'This is the Messiah,' doesn't make it so."

Nicodemus replied, "I suppose that's true. But what about that voice out of the sky saying 'This is my beloved son,' and wasn't it strange a dove landed on him?"

Both Aram and Gamliel looked at him with expressions of amazement, and Aram said, "A voice out of the sky? What are you talking about? I didn't hear any such voice, nor did I see a dove. This heat must be getting to you."

"You didn't hear a voice out of the sky, say something?"

This time, Gamliel said, "No, I didn't. A voice out of the sky? What have you been drinking?"

Nicodemus said, "Did you see the dove land on that Jesus guy?"

Aram said, "No, of course not. Did you?"

Nicodemus said, "I think so," as he scratched his head. "I think he's the Christ."

Gamliel said, "Nicodemus, you've got to be kidding me."

---

[199] Mark 1:11
[200] John 1:29, 33-34

Nicodemus said, "I am a little confused. I am not sure what I heard and didn't hear and saw and didn't see. I guess I'll just have to wait and see what happens. You did hear John say that he, John, wasn't the Christ, didn't you?"

Gamliel said, "Of course I heard him say that. I think we have heard enough and seen enough baptisms. Let's head back. I don't think we are going to learn any more."

They all agreed and started walking away.

Nicodemus asked, "What do you guys think of repentance? Is it important to get a remission of sins?"

Gamliel answered, "If we do what is proper and are righteous, we will please God and have a good life. If we make mistakes, not too much bad will happen. Just don't screw up something with the High Priest. I guarantee something bad will happen, if you do."

They all laughed.

Nicodemus said, "I thought I heard a voice from heaven say this Jesus guy was the son of God and saw a dove land on him. Maybe I was just too hot and dry and imagining things. After all, you two didn't see any such thing. Anyway, we are all agreed John is not the Christ. Right?"

Aram and Gamliel agreed.

Nicodemus went on, "Since we are all in agreement on that and I am not sure of the other, why don't the two of you make the report to the High Priest?"

Aram said, "That's fine with us," as Gamliel nodded yes.

***

After Jesus was baptized, he said, "John, thanks for baptizing me. I know you didn't think it was necessary, but it is one of the reasons you are here. You have the God-given authority to baptize through the Priesthood of Aaron. Baptism is the first gate a person needs to pass through to gain eternal life or, in other words, God's life. This is the start of my ministry. The Spirit is telling me I need to go into the wilderness to be with my Father to be taught more things to better prepare me for what lies ahead. I'll be sure to see you on my way back to Galilee."

John replied, "I plan to stay here baptizing. I'll look forward to seeing you then. I have some great disciples following me. When you come back, I will tell them about you. You're the one they should be following now. I know you must increase, but I must decrease.[201]"

---

[201] John 3:30

Following the promptings of the Spirit, Jesus went into the wilderness to be with his Father. He was there fasting for forty days and forty nights while communing with Him. When Jesus finished communing with his Father, he was hungry and was left to be tempted of the devil.[202] It is interesting that Moses went up to Mount Sinai and while fasting was taught for forty days and nights by Jehovah, the pre-mortal Jesus.[203]

Satan then appeared to Jesus and said, "Jesus, if you are the Son of God, you can command these stones to be made bread."

He thought about this for a moment and said, "Man shall not live by bread alone, but by every word that proceeds out of the mouth of God," *and put the thought out of his mind.*

Later, when Jesus was thinking about the temple in Jerusalem, the Spirit took him to the top of the temple. Satan again appeared to him and said, "If you are the Son of God, throw yourself down, because God has given his angels orders you are to be protected from being injured. *This would be a miracle that would make you famous.*

Jesus thought a moment and said, "You shall not tempt the Lord, your God," *and put it out of his mind.*

Next, Jesus was thinking about Israel and other countries of the world and the Spirit took him up to a very high mountain and showed him all the kingdoms of the world and the glory of them in vision.

Satan came again and said, "All these things will I give you, if you fall down and worship me." Jesus turned to him and said, "Leave me, Satan, for it is written, 'You shall worship the Lord, your God, and Him only shall you serve.'" After this Satan left and angels came and ministered to him.[204]

Jesus went back to see John. As Jesus came up to where John was baptizing, John saw him and said, "Behold, the Lamb of God, who will take away the sin of the world. This is he of whom I said, 'After me comes a man who is preferred before me; for he was before me.' I knew him and knew he should be made manifest to Israel; therefore, I am baptizing with water. When he was baptized of me, I saw the Spirit descending from heaven like a dove and it stayed on him. The same is he who baptizes with the Holy Ghost."[205]

---

[202] JST Matthew 4:1-2
[203] Deuteronomy 9:9
[204] JST Matthew 4:3-10
[205] JST John 1:30-32

JOHN THE BAPTIST

Jesus acknowledged his introduction and waved to the crowd. He sat off to the side listening to John. Several people from the crowd came to talk to him, but most continued to listen to John. He, after all, was the one they had come to see. After John was finished baptizing for the day, they spoke for a while and then parted for the night.

The next afternoon, Jesus came by to say goodbye, as he planned to leave for Galilee in a few days. Jesus said, "I have enjoyed visiting with you. I doubt we are going to meet again in this lifetime. Thank you for the testimony you have given of my mission."

John said, "I have enjoyed our conversation. I will continue baptizing here as long as I can. As I said before, I know you will increase, while I decrease. I look forward to hearing about your ministry."

They hugged and John called to his disciples as Jesus left and said, "Behold the Lamb of God."

A short time later, Jesus turned around and found two of John's disciples following him and said, "What do you want?"

They said, "Rabbi (a term of honor meaning Master), where are you staying?"

Jesus said, "Follow me and see."

The two of them followed him to where he was staying, and spent the night there. One was John, the son of Zebedee, not John the Baptist, and the other was Andrew, Simon Peter's brother.

Andrew left to find Simon. When he found him, he said, "We have found the Messiah! He is spending the night here. Come and see for yourself!"

Simon said, "Why do you think he is the Messiah?"

Andrew replied, "John the Baptist said so and, since I have talked to him, I am also convinced it is he. Come and see!"

Simon replied, "You do sound excited. I am sure you will keep asking me until I go, so let's go."

They got back to where Jesus was and, as they walked up to him, he said, "You are Simon, the son of Jonah: you shall be called Cephas[206] (which means a seer or stone in Aramaic the same as Peter)."

Peter replied, "I'm glad to meet you. I suppose Andrew told you Jonah is our father, but why do you call me Cephas?"

Jesus said, "Andrew didn't tell me your father is Jonah. My Father told me; just as He told me you will be a cephas or seer."

---

[206] John 1:42

Andrew said, "Simon, that's true. I never said anything to him about our father being Jonah."

Simon said, "You are a prophet! It's not only your knowing Jonah is our father, but I feel it in my heart and mind."

Jesus said, "Tomorrow I'm going to go into Galilee. Would you like to follow me?"

Simon said, "Yes, I would like to."

Jesus said, "Do you have somebody to take care of affairs in your absence? You are fisherman, aren't you?"

Simon responded, "Yes. We are fisherman and work with our father. He will be able to run things in our absence. I would like to follow you for a while and see what I can learn."

Andrew said, "We are from Bethsaida. Will you be going there?"

"I do plan to go there," said Jesus. "My brother, James, is being married Tuesday in Cana of Galilee. This is Thursday, and I plan to go to Bethsaida tomorrow and spend the Sabbath there, before going on."

Andrew said, "That's great. We have a friend there, Philip. I think he would love to meet you. When we get there, we will find him for you."

Jesus said, "Thank you. I would like to meet him."

The next day, they walked to Bethsaida and found Philip at his home mending nets.

When they walked up, Philip said, "Hello! It's good to see you."

Simon said matter-of-factly, "We'd like you to meet Jesus. He's the Messiah!"

Philip said to Simon, "The Messiah! That's interesting. How do you know?"

Simon said, "Andrew has been out with John in Bethabara. I will let Andrew tell you."

Andrew spoke up, "One day, when John was baptizing, Jesus came up to be baptized. After John baptized him, I saw the heavens open and the Spirit of God descending in the sign of a dove and lighting on him. I heard a voice out of the sky say, 'This is my beloved son, in whom I am well pleased. Hear him."[207]

John then said, "I bear record this is the Son and Lamb of God. He who sent me to baptize with water said, 'Upon whom you

---

[207] Mark 1:11

JOHN THE BAPTIST

shall see the Spirit descending and remaining on him, is he who baptizes with the Holy Ghost.'"[208]

"That was pretty impressive to me. We have been with Jesus for a few days and I am more sure than ever he is the Messiah."

Philip said to Jesus, "Master, you have pretty impressive credentials, I am glad to meet you."

Jesus replied, "I am here to do my Father's will. I hope you will follow me."

Philip answered, "I will. I have a friend, Nathanael, whom I would like you to meet."

Jesus said, "Great. I would like to meet him too. Why don't you go find him and bring him here?"

Philip said, "Stay here and I will bring him."

A short time later, Philip found Nathanael and said to him, "We have found Jesus of Nazareth, the son of Joseph, of whom Moses in the law and the prophets wrote."

Nathanael said, "Can any good thing come out of Nazareth?"

Philip said, "Come and see for yourself."

When Philip took Nathanael to Jesus, Jesus saw him coming and said to them, "Behold an Israelite, indeed, in who is no guile!"

Nathanael said to him, "How do you know me?"

Jesus answered, "Before Philip went for you, when you were under the fig tree, I saw you."

At this Nathanael said, "Rabbi, you are the Son of God, the King of Israel."

Jesus said, "Because I said to you, I saw you under the fig tree, you believe? You shall see greater things than these. Truly, hereafter you shall see heaven open and the angels of God ascending and descending to the Son of Man.[209] *Come follow me. My brother James is being married in three days in Cana of Galilee. We're going there for the wedding. Come along with us. You will learn a lot.*"

Nathanael said, "*It sounds good to me. I will get some things and be ready shortly.*"

John also brought his brother, James, to meet Jesus, and he also became a disciple.

The seven of them went to Cana, which was about thirty miles and took two days. They crossed the Jordan and went along the north shore of the Sea of Galilee, through Capernaum and Gennesaret. They left the Sea of Galilee and went inland to Cana.

---

[208] John 1:29, 33-34
[209] John 1:45-51

The wedding festival lasted a week. Toward the end of the festival, the wine was running out. Mary, the mother of Jesus, came to him and said, "There is no wine."

Jesus said, "Mother, whatever you want me to do for you, I will do it, because the time for my ministry has not yet come." Mary said to the servants, 'Whatever he says to you, see you do it.'

There were six waterpots of stone, after the manner of the purifying of the Jews. They contained about twenty-four gallons each.

Jesus said to the servants, "Fill the waterpots with water."

They filled them up to the brim.

Jesus told them to draw some out and take it to the head of the feast. The servants didn't tell the head of the feast where it had come from.

When he had tasted it, he called the bridegroom and said, "Usually, at the start of the feast, the good wine is put out, and then, after the guests have drunk much, the lesser wine is put out. But you have kept the good wine until now."

This was the beginning of the miracles Jesus did and the faith of his disciples was strengthened.[210]

HIS DISCIPLES AND GALILEE

After the wedding, Jesus and his family, his mother and siblings, as well as his disciples, went to Capernaum on the north shore of the Sea of Galilee about 25 miles. They stayed there a few days before Jesus and his disciples left to go down to Jerusalem for the Passover, about 85 miles.

As they walked into the city, Peter said to Jesus, "It always amazes me when I am here for Passover how many people come. The road is packed. It's hardly a road, more like a throng of humanity."

Jesus replied, "It is amazing, isn't it? I, too, can hardly believe the number of people. Are you looking forward to going to the temple?"

Peter said, "Yes, I am. I love to walk up the temple mount. The temple sits above you, with its imposing majesty. It gives me a feeling of awe. As I approach, tears come to my eyes."

Jesus said, "As I approach, I get that same feeling. How do you feel when you go inside?"

---

[210] John 2:3

HIS DISCIPLES AND GALILEE

Peter said, "I seem to lose that feeling. There is so much going on with all the livestock, birds, and money exchanging. There's the bleating of the livestock and those selling are calling out to potential buyers. It's a madhouse. One can hardly think straight. I don't think that's the way it should be."

Jesus stopped and turned to those following him and said, "The temple should be the House of the Lord. It should be a quiet place where one can feel the Spirit of God. It's important the animals and birds be ceremonial fit, but the selling should be done some other place. Moses said, 'Each person, for the ransom of his soul, shall pay half a shekel after the shekel of the sanctuary, for the service of the tabernacle of the congregation. The rich shall not give more and the poor shall not give less.'[211] *Those in charge decided that, since the Romans don't use shekels, it can't be paid with Roman coins. This allowed them to make a temple shekel and decide what it was worth. The purpose, as Moses said, was to provide for the service of the temple. They should have planned for a way that would have made it easy for all to fulfill that purpose and have the blessings of the temple. It would have been nice, if a price had been set in Roman coins, which would have just covered the cost of the temple service. But that's not what was done. Tomorrow we will go to the temple."*

The next morning, the seven of them, Jesus, Peter, John, James, Andrew, Philip and Nathanael, went up to the temple. As they entered the outer courts of the temple, they found the oxen, sheep, doves, and pigeons and those selling them, as well as the money changers.

Jesus turned to his disciples and said, "This is what I told you. These defile the temple. This needs to be done somewhere else."

Jesus looked like someone not to trifle with when he was angry. He made a whip of small cords and drove the sheep and oxen out of the temple and poured out the changers' money and overturned the tables. He told those selling doves to take them out. He said, "Don't make my Father's house a house of merchandise."

Later, his disciples remembered it was written, "The zeal of your house has consumed me." [212]

Two of the temple officials watched from a distance as Jesus cleared the temple. The first said, "Do you know who this man is? Is he a prophet? We've got to put a stop to this."

---

[211] Exodus 30:12-16
[212] John 2:13-17

The other said, "I have never seen him, but maybe he's the one that's been baptizing in Jordan."

The first said, "I suppose he's right about cleaning it up. All these animals do make a mess; but they bring in good revenue. I'm going to ask him what authority he has."

He went up to Jesus and said, "Show us something to prove you have authority to do this."

Jesus, with righteous anger, replied, "Destroy this temple and in three days I will raise it up." He was speaking of his body, as our bodies are temples.

The officer replied, "It took forty-six years to build this temple and will you build it in three days?"

Later, after he was resurrected, they remembered what he had spoken about his body, and they believed the scripture and what Jesus had said.

Those disciples who had been following him stood off to the side watching the proceedings. Andrew whispered to his brother, Simon, "Why doesn't anybody try to stop him?"

Simon whispered back, "Just look at him. He's a fierce man, angry and determined. Would you try to stop him?"

Andrew said, "You're right. I wouldn't, for sure!"

That evening, Simon said to Jesus, "Master, weren't you fearful when you were clearing the temple?"

Jesus said, "They all know what they are doing isn't right. They are afraid a prophet will come and destroy them for desecrating the temple, but I am not sent to destroy. I am sent to save and call all to repentance."

While he was at the Passover in Jerusalem, besides clearing the temple, *Jesus healed many people of various problems.* When they saw the miracles he did, many believed on him and followed him. But Jesus didn't commit to them, because he wanted those who would truly believe. He knew all people and didn't need anyone to tell him about them, because he knew what was in a person.[213]

Nicodemus, the Pharisee, and a ruler of the Jews, came to Jesus, this time by night, so as not to be seen. He called Jesus by the same title he was called. "Rabbi, we know you are a teacher come from God; for no man can do the miracles you do, unless God is with him."

Jesus answered, "Except a man is born again, he cannot see the kingdom of God."

---

[213] John 2:18-25

HIS DISCIPLES AND GALILEE

Nicodemus said, "How can a man be born when he is old? Can he enter the second time into his mother's womb and be born?"

Jesus said, "Except a man is born of water and of the Spirit, he cannot enter the kingdom of God. That which is born of the flesh is flesh; and that which is born of the Spirit is spirit. Don't marvel that I said, 'You must be born again.' The wind blows where it wants and you hear it, but cannot tell where it comes from or where it goes. So is everyone who is born of the Spirit."

Nicodemus said, "How can these things be?"

Jesus said, "Are you a master of Israel and don't know these things? I tell you, we speak the things we know and testify about those things we have seen; and you don't believe our witness. If I have told you earthly things and you don't believe, how shall you believe, if I tell you heavenly things? No man has gone up to heaven, but he who came down from heaven, even the Son of Man which is in heaven. As Moses raised the serpent in the wilderness, even so must the Son of Man be lifted up; that whoever believes in him should not perish, but have eternal life.

"For God so loved the world that he gave his only born Son, that whoever believes on him should not perish, but have everlasting life. God sent his Son into the world, not to condemn it; but that the world through him might be saved. He who believes on him is not condemned; but he who doesn't believe on him is already condemned, because he has not believed on the name of the only born Son of God.[214] This was preached before by the mouth of the holy prophets; for they testified of me.[215]

"And this is the condemnation, that light has come into the world and men love darkness rather than light, because their deeds are evil. For everyone who does evil hates the light, neither comes to the light, lest his deeds should be condemned.[216] But he who loves truth comes to the light that his deeds may be made manifest. And he who obeys the truth, his works are of God."[217]

Nicodemus said, "I love truth. That's why I am here--But you're not like what I thought the Messiah would be. I was there when John baptized you and I thought I heard a voice out of the sky say, 'You are my beloved Son, in whom I am well pleased.' When I talked to those I was with, nobody else heard it. Was there a voice from heaven?"

---

[214] John 3:1-18
[215] JST John 3:18
[216] John 3:19-20
[217] JST John 3:21

HIS DISCIPLES AND GALILEE

Jesus said, "As I said, 'If I tell you earthly things and you don't believe, how will you believe if I tell you heavenly things?' Why can't you believe what you hear? Are you afraid to put your shoulder to the wheel?"

Nicodemus stroked his beard and said, "I don't know. I am going to have to ponder on what you have told me. It has been very interesting. Thank you very much."

While Jesus was in Jerusalem, several disciples joined themselves to him. After the Passover, Jesus and his disciples went to the land of Judea and he remained there with them and baptized.

John also was baptizing in that area, because there was water there and he was not yet put in prison. There arose a question between some of John's disciples and the Jews about purifying.

John's disciples came to him and said, "Rabbi, he who was with you beyond Jordan, to whom you bore witness, is baptizing there and all the people come to him."

John said, "A man can receive nothing, except it be given him from heaven. You yourselves heard me say, 'I am not the Christ--I am sent before him.' He who has the bride is the bridegroom; but the friend of the bridegroom, who stands and hears him, greatly rejoices because of the bridegroom's voice. My joy, therefore, is full. He must increase, but I must decrease. He who comes from above is above all; he who is of the earth is earthly and speaks of the earth. He who comes from heaven is above all. He testifies of that which he has seen and heard, but not many receive his testimony. Those who have received his testimony declare God is true. For those whom God has sent, speak the words of God: God does not measure the Spirit to them. The Father loves the Son and has given all things into his hand. Those who believe on the Son have everlasting life. Those who don't believe the Son shall not have all of life; for the wrath of God is on them."[218]

After baptizing for several days, a disciple told Jesus, "I have a friend who is a Pharisee and he told me they are concerned about you, because you are baptizing more people than John. Actually, it is we that are doing the baptizing, but you know what I mean."

Jesus thought this over and, after praying, announced they would be going to Galilee. They would go through Samaria, rather than around it, as most Jews did. As they were walking there, several of the disciples were talking.

---

[218] John 3:22-36

HIS DISCIPLES AND GALILEE

One of the disciples said, as they approached Sychar, "I have never been in Samaria before. When we have gone to Jerusalem for Passover, we always took the long way around."

Another said, "The same with us. They're unclean people. Why do you suppose the master is going this way?"

The first said, "I have no idea, but we need to be careful about what we eat. Anything a Samaritan prepares is unclean."

A third said, "I have been to Samaria before and I have found them to be good people. They worship God and try to live good lives. Some of them are descendants of ours. When Assyria and then Babylon captured the area, most of our people were carried away. Some escaped and they brought some priests back to teach the people about the Lord. They have a temple, but I don't think they do the right things there, but they're not the bad people we make them out to be."

The first said, "You're the first I have heard say anything good about them. I anxious to see what the Master thinks of them."

When they got to Sychar, it was about noon, and Jesus sent his disciples into town to buy some food. He went and sat down by Jacob's well because he was tired from the trip.

A Samaritan woman came to draw some water, and Jesus, being thirsty, said to her, "Please draw some water for me to drink."

She said, "How is it that you, a Jew, ask me for a drink, when I am a Samaritan. The Jews have nothing to do with the Samaritans."

Jesus said, "If you knew the Lord's gospel and who you are speaking with, you would have asked me and I would have given you living water."

She said, "Sir, you have nothing to draw with and the well is deep. How would you get this living water? Are you greater than our father, Jacob, who gave us the well and drank from it himself, along with his children and cattle?"

Jesus said, "Whoever drinks from this well shall be thirsty again. But whoever drinks of the water that I shall give them, shall never be thirsty again; but the water I shall give them shall be a well of water springing up into everlasting life."

The woman said, "Sir, give me this water, so I don't get thirsty and have to come here to get water."

Jesus said, "Go get your husband and come back."

She said, "I don't have a husband."

Jesus said, "You have spoken the truth. You have had five husbands and the man you are living with is not your husband."

HIS DISCIPLES AND GALILEE

She said, "Sir, I see you are a prophet. Our fathers worshipped on this mountain, yet you Jews say Jerusalem is the place where people ought to worship."

Jesus said, "Woman, believe me, the time is coming when you shall neither on this mountain, nor in Jerusalem, worship the Father. You don't know who you worship; we know who we worship, for salvation is of the Jews. The time is coming and is now here, when the true worshippers shall worship the Father in spirit and in truth: For the Father seeks these to worship Him and to such has God promised his Spirit. They, who worship Him, must worship in spirit and in truth."

She said, "I know the Messiah, which is called Christ, is coming. When he comes, he will tell us all things."

Jesus said, "I am he," just as his disciples returned.

They were surprised to see him talking to a Samaritan woman, but were afraid to ask him why he was talking to her. When the disciples came, the woman left and went into town, leaving her water pot by the well.

She told the townspeople, "Come and see a man which told me all the things I ever did. Isn't he the Christ?" And she brought the people out to the well.

Meanwhile, the disciples were preparing food and urged Jesus to eat. He told them, "I have food to eat you don't know about."

The disciples asked one another, "Has someone brought him something to eat?"

Jesus said, "My food is to do the will of Him who sent me and to finish His work. People say, 'There are four months until harvest.' I say to you, 'Lift up your eyes and look at the fields; they are already white and ready to harvest.' They who reap will receive wages and gather fruit for eternal life; so those who sow and those who reap may rejoice together. One sows and another reaps. I sent you to reap on that which you had not labored: The prophets labored and you have made use of their labors."

When the Samaritans came who the woman had summoned, they asked him to stay with them a while, and they stayed two days. Many of the Samaritans believed on him because of what the woman said, "He told me all I ever did."

Others said, "We believe because we have heard him ourselves and know this is indeed the Christ, the Savior of the world."

After two days, they left for Galilee. Jesus said, "A prophet has no honor where he is raised."

HIS DISCIPLES AND GALILEE

When he came into Galilee, he was warmly received, because the people had gone to Jerusalem for the feast and saw what he did there. He came to Cana of Galilee, where he had turned the water into wine. There was a nobleman there, whose son was sick at Capernaum. When he heard Jesus had left Judea to come to Galilee, he came to him and asked him to come down to heal his son, who was at death's door.

Jesus said to him, "Unless you see signs and wonders, you will not believe."

The nobleman said, "Sir, come down before my son dies."

Jesus said, "Go on home; your son lives."

The nobleman believed what Jesus told him and left to go home. The next day, on his way home, he met his servants and they told him, "Your son lives."

He asked them when he recovered and they said, "Yesterday at one the fever left him."

The father knew it was the same time that Jesus had told him his son was healed. He believed and his whole house .[219]

Jesus continued to preach in Galilee and his fame spread throughout the region as he taught in their synagogues.

He finally decided it was time to go back to his hometown of Nazareth. On the Sabbath, he went into the Synagogue.

The eyes of the congregation were on him as he came in. They had heard of the miracles he did. In fact, many of them had been to Jerusalem for the Passover and had seen them in person.

One of the congregation leaned over and whispered to another, "I can't believe all the things I have been hearing about the miracles he is doing. How do you suppose he is tricking people into thinking they are cured? Are people so gullible, that if he says they are healed, they think they are?"

His companion said, "I don't have a clue. This is Joseph's son, our carpenter. He's thirty now; he's old enough to read and teach. I hope he reads and expounds on it. If he does, it will be interesting to hear what he has to say."

The other said, "I'm looking forward to that also, but I'm not expecting much."

When the service got to the point of reading the prophets, the minister handed Jesus the scroll of the book of the prophet Isaiah.

Jesus opened it to what is Isaiah 61:1-2. He read, "The Spirit of the Lord is on me, because he has anointed me to preach the gospel

---

[219] John 4

to the poor; he has sent me to heal the brokenhearted, to preach deliverance to the captives, recovering of sight to the blind, to set at liberty those who are bruised, and to preach the acceptable year of the Lord."

He closed the scroll and handed it back to the minister. The custom was the reader would explain what he had read, but he had to do it seated, so Jesus sat down.

He said, "Today this scripture is fulfilled. You surely will say to me this proverb, 'Physician, heal yourself'. The things you have done in Capernaum do also here. No prophet is without honor, except in his own town. But I will tell you a truth. There were many widows in Israel in the days of Elijah, when the heavens were shut up with no rain for three and a half years, causing a great famine throughout the land. To none of them was Elijah sent, but to Sarepta in Sidon, to a widow who was a Gentile. There were many lepers in Israel in the Prophet Elisha's time, but none of them were cured except Naaman, the Syrian, another Gentile."

When those in the Synagogue heard this, they were furious. Jesus saying he was the Messiah was not only ridiculous, but blasphemous, and comparing them to Gentiles, how could he do such a thing?

When he finished, they jumped up and grabbed him. Some of them wanted to stone him and others wanted to throw him off the cliff Nazareth is built close to. While they were arguing, Jesus walked away through the crowd and went to Capernaum on the northwest shore of the Sea of Galilee.

In Capernaum, he taught the people in the synagogue on the Sabbath days. The people were astonished at his doctrine, because he taught with power.

In the synagogue one Sabbath, there was a man which had a devil. He cried out with a loud voice and said, "Let us alone. What do you want? Have you come to destroy us? I know whom you are, the Holy One of God."

Jesus told him, "Be quiet and come out of him."

The devil threw the man on the ground and he came out of him, leaving the man uninjured. They were all amazed and said among themselves, "What is this! With authority and power, he commands the unclean spirits and they come out." The fame of him went everywhere in the vicinity.[220]

---

[220] Matthew 13:53-58 Luke 4: 14-37

HIS DISCIPLES AND GALILEE

From the synagogue, he went to Simon Peter's house. Simon's mother-in-law was sick and had a high fever. As soon as they told Jesus of her problem, he went to help her.

He came to her, took her by the hand, and lifted her up; immediately the fever left her. She immediately arose and served them. After the sun had set and the Sabbath was over, they brought all who were sick with various diseases to him and he healed them.

Almost the entire city was around their door. Devils came out of many saying, "You are Christ, the Son of God." He ordered them not to speak, because they knew he was Christ.

The next morning, he got up well before daybreak and went to a solitary place to pray. Simon and other of the disciples went after him.

When they found him, they said, "Everybody is looking for you."

Jesus said, "Let's go to the next towns, so I can preach there also. That is why I am here."

They left and he preached in their synagogues throughout Galilee and cast out devils. A leper came to him, kneeled, and said, "If you will, you can heal me and make me clean."[221]

By ritual law, the leper should not have approached Jesus, but he had faith and knew Jesus could heal him. A normal Jew, when approached by a leper, would have moved away, but not Jesus. Being healed by the Master was like being brought back from the dead.

Leprosy was then a living death. Under Mosaic Law, a leper must live outside the camp, cover the lip, have their head bare, wear ripped clothes, and if someone approached say, "Unclean, unclean."

The disease caused the hair to yellow and attacked joints, so fingers, toes, and limbs would rot and fall off. The Israelites considered the disease as punishment for sins of the worst kind. It was considered a disease of the dead. In the few cases where somebody was cured of the disease, the cleansing ceremony used the same symbols as that for touching a dead body.

When Aaron and Miriam, the sister of Moses, sinned, Miriam was punished with Leprosy. In Numbers 12:11-12, Aaron says to Moses, "I plead to you, don't lay on us this sin we so foolishly have done. Let her not be as one dead, whose flesh is half eaten when they are born." Moses prayed to the Lord in verse 13, saying, "Heal

---

[221] Mark 1:30-40; Matthew; 8:2; Luke 5:12

HIS DISCIPLES AND GALILEE

her now. O God, I pray." Miriam was put out of the camp for seven days and then healed.[222]

Jesus was filled with compassion and said, as he reached out his hand and touched him, "I will, be clean." As soon as he spoke, the leprosy left him and he was cleansed and made whole."

Jesus continued to speak and told him, "Go to where you live and show yourself to the priest and offer for cleansing those things which Moses commanded. See you don't tell anyone about this. *If you tell the priest or he finds out you were cleansed by me, there is some chance that being declared clean could be delayed."*

Still, when the man left, he told everybody what had happened, so Jesus could no longer go openly into the city because of the crowds following him. He had to go into the wilderness to get away from the crowds and to pray.

By disobeying Jesus and telling others of his healing, the leper, due to the large crowds caused by the notoriety, forced Jesus to go into the wilderness. They just exchanged places.[223]

After an absence, he returned to Capernaum, and immediately the word spread he was home. The crowd grew, he started teaching, and the crowd kept growing.

There was a group of four friends carrying their friend on a litter. Their friend was paralyzed and could not even talk. As they got to the area where the house was, one of them said, "This is one of the largest crowds I have ever seen here. Where did all these people come from? How on earth are we going to get our friend to where the Master can even see him?"

Another said, "I'm sure they will let us through when they see we are carrying somebody. Excuse us! Excuse us! We need to get through. Coming through. Coming through. Excuse us. Excuse us."

A second said, "This isn't working. Everybody is packed in too tight. Even if they want to move, there is no place for them to go."

Another looked around and said, "Let's walk around to the back of the house and see if we can get in there."

---

[222] Richard Trench, *Notes on the Miracles of Our Lord*, (1866) Second American Edition, D. Appleton & Co. New York, NY. Pg. 173-182; Charles Deems, *The Light of the Nations*, (1884) Gay Brothers & Co. New York, NY. Pg. 183-189; James Talmage, *Jesus the Christ*, (1981). The Church of Jesus Christ of Latter Day Saints, Salt Lake City, UT. Pg.199-200
[223] Mark 1:40-45 ; Matthew; 8:3-4; Luke 5:13-16

When they got to the back, there was no entrance, but they found a ladder and were able to get up on the roof. The roof was of tile and, by lifting the tile, they made a hole big enough to lower their friend through. The crowd was surprised to see a litter descending from the sky.

When their friend was safely on the floor, he looked up at Jesus and thought, "What am I doing here? This man seems to be reading my mind. If I had been doing what I knew was right, I wouldn't be lying here on this floor paralyzed. But I just had to be stupid and show off. I know he can heal me, if he wants to."

When Jesus saw them, he realized their faith from the effort they had made to get their friend to him. He also recognized their friend had faith to be healed, even though he had sinned.

He said to him, "Son, don't worry. Your sins are forgiven."

The scribes who were present thought to themselves, "This is blasphemy."

Jesus, knowing their thoughts, said, "Why do you think evil in your hearts? Is it easier to say, 'Your sins are forgiven; or to say, Get up and walk.' So you know the Son of Man has the authority on earth to forgive sins," he turned to the young man and said, 'Get up, take your litter, and go home.'"

With that, the man got up, picked up his litter and, with his friends, walked home.

The crowd was amazed and glorified God, saying, "We have never seen anything like this."[224]

One day, when Jesus was going to the seaside, he passed by a tax collector sitting where taxes are collected. He was Matthew, sometimes called Levi, the son of Alphaeus. Jesus said to him, "Come follow me."

He got up and followed Jesus.

Sometime later, he had Jesus and his disciples to dinner at his house. There were a lot of people there: Jesus with all of his disciples, Matthew's friends, and other tax collectors. The Jews did not like tax collectors, because they collected taxes for Rome and, since the tax collectors had to pay to have their position, many tax collectors were dishonest.

When Jesus arrived at Matthew's home, the difference between it, with its many rooms and servants and his small house, really struck him. He felt fortunate he had been able to work hard

---

[224] Matthew 9:2-8; Mark 2:1-12; Luke 5:17-26

HIS DISCIPLES AND GALILEE

and support the family after Joseph's death and even set aside money for his mother to live on while he was away on his ministry.

He looked at the faces of those assembled and could read what was in their hearts. Some, like Matthew, were good, honest men, concerned with keeping the law and doing good. Others were just interested in themselves. He then looked at some of the scribes and Pharisees and saw the hardness of their hearts. He wished there would be some way he could reach these people so they could feel the love of his Father and the sweet peace this love brings.

When the scribes and Pharisees saw all these people and Jesus eating with them, they asked his disciples, "Why is he eating with tax collectors and sinners?"

When Jesus heard it, he said, "They who are well don't need a doctor, but they who are sick: I came not to call the righteous to repentance, but sinners."

Since John the Baptist was imprisoned, his followers had no leader and some had joined with the Pharisees. They came to Jesus' disciples and asked, "Why do we and the Pharisees often fast and your disciples don't?"

When Jesus heard this, he said, "Do the friends of the groom mourn, as long as the groom is with them? The days will come when the groom will be taken from them and then they shall fast. Nobody sews a piece of new cloth on an old garment or else the new cloth will stress the old and the tear is made worse. Neither do people put new wine into old skins. If they do, the skins will break, the wine is lost, and the skins ruined. New wine is put into new skins and both are preserved. *Such is my gospel.*"[225]

Many of the disciples following Jesus came and left and came again. Some had families to be provided for and being a disciple was not an easy life.

One day, as he was preaching on the shore of the Sea of Galilee, there was a large crowd. So many people were trying to get close to him, the crowd was pressing on him from all sides. He needed to put some distance between himself and the crowd so he could talk and be heard.

He looked and saw two ships that the fishermen were out of while working on their nets. One of them was Simon Peter's. He got in and asked Peter to thrust out a little from shore. He sat down and taught the people out of the ship.

---

[225] Matthew 9:9-17; Mark 2:13-22; Luke 5:27-38; Talmage, James. (1981). *Jesus the Christ.* Salt Lake City, UT. The Church of Jesus Christ of Latter-day Saints. Pg.195-197

HIS DISCIPLES AND GALILEE

When he was finished, he asked Simon to go out to the deep water and let down their nets for a large haul.

Simon said, "Master we have worked all night long and have caught nothing. Nevertheless, I will do what you ask and let the net down."

When he did this, they caught a multitude of fish, so much that the net was in danger of breaking. They beckoned to their partners in the other ship to come and help. They came and filled both ships, so they began to sink.

When Peter saw this, he fell down at Jesus' knees and said, "Go away from me, Lord, for I am a sinful man."

James and John, the sons of Zebedee, were in the other boat; they were partners with Peter. They were all astonished at the haul of fishes they had taken.

Jesus said to Peter, "Don't worry; from now on you shall catch men." After this astonishing miracle, they left all they had and followed Jesus.[226]

Jesus and his disciples went back to Jerusalem for Passover, and on a Sabbath day, he went to a pool near the sheep market called Bethesda. There were five built-up areas around the pool for people to sit or lay in. It was evidently spring-fed and from time to time there would be some sort of spurt or moving of the water. It had the reputation that when this event occurred, the first person entering the water would be cured of whatever disease they had.[227]

A man was there who had an infirmity for thirty-eight years. When Jesus saw him lying there, he realized he had been there a long time and he asked him, "Would you like to be healed?"

The man said, "Sir, I have no one to put me in the pool, when the water is moved. While I am coming, another gets in before I can."

Jesus said to him, "Arise, pick up your bed, and walk." The man was made whole immediately, took up his bed, and walked.

The Jews saw him carrying his bed and asked him, "This is the Sabbath day and it's not lawful to carry your bed. Why are you doing it?"

He said, "The man who healed me, said, "Pick up your bed and walk."

They asked, "Who told you to do that?"

By this time, Jesus had left and the man couldn't see him, so he said, "I don't know who he is."

---

[226] Luke 5:1-11; Matthew 4:18-22; Mark 1:16-20
[227] John 5:1-4; Talmage, James. (1981). *Jesus the Christ*. Salt Lake City, UT. The Church of Jesus Christ of Latter-day Saints. Pg. 206

HIS DISCIPLES AND GALILEE

Later, Jesus saw the man in the temple and said, "Now you have been healed, sin no more." Jesus knew sin had been part of the problem for his condition.

The man then went and told the Jews it was Jesus who healed him. Because of this, the Jews sought how they could kill him for desecrating the Sabbath. When they spoke to him about it, Jesus said, "My Father works like this and so do I."

Thus, they sought the more to kill him, because he not only had broken the Sabbath, but made himself equal to God by saying God was his Father.

Jesus told them,

"Truly, the Son can do nothing of himself, but only what he sees the Father do: for whatever the Father does, so does the Son likewise. The Father loves the Son and shows him all the things He does and he will show him greater works than these that you may marvel for as the Father raises up the dead and quickens whom he will; so also, the Son quickens whom he will. The Father judges no one, but has given all judgment to the Son: that all should honor the Son, even as they honor the Father. Those who don't honor the Son, don't honor the Father, who has sent him.

"Truly I say to you, they who hear my word and believe on him that sent me, have everlasting life, and shall not be condemned; but are passed from death to life. The hour is coming, and now is, when the dead shall hear the voice of the Son of God and they who hear shall live. For as the Father has life in himself; so, has he given the Son to have life in himself; and has given him authority to judge, because he is the Son of Man. Don't marvel at this, for the hour is coming when all who are in the grave shall hear his voice and shall come forth; they who have done good, to the resurrection of life, but they who have done evil, to the resurrection of damnation.

"I can of my own self do nothing: as I hear, I judge and my judgment is just, because I seek not my own will, but the will of the Father who sent me. If I bear witness of myself, my witness is not true. There is another who bears witness of me and I know that the witness He bears of me is true. John was a burning and shining light and you were for a while willing to rejoice in his light. You went to him and he bore witness to the truth.[228] The testament of him was not from man, but of God. Since you say he is a prophet, you ought to receive that testimony, that you might be saved.[229]

"I have a greater witness than the testimony of John; for the works which the Father has given me to finish, the same works that I do, bear witness that the Father has sent me. The Father Himself, which has sent me, has borne witness of me. You don't have His word abiding in you; for you don't believe him whom He has sent.

"Search the scriptures, for in them you believe you have eternal life and they testify of me. You will not come to me that you might have life. I receive no honor from men, but I know you don't have the love of God in you. I am come in my Father's name and you don't receive me. How can you believe, which receive honor from one another and seek not the honor that comes from God only? Don't think I will accuse you to the Father; there is one that accuses you, even Moses, in whom you trust. If you had believed Moses, you would have believed me, for he wrote of me. If you don't believe his writings, how will you believe my words?"[230]

***

One Sabbath, Jesus and his disciples were walking through a wheat field. His disciples were hungry and, as they walked, they picked heads of grain and rubbed them in their hands, breaking out the kernels of wheat and blowing away the chaff. They were not stealing, because Mosaic law said it was proper when passing through a field to eat what was growing there to satisfy hunger, but you couldn't carry it away or use a sickle. There was a tradition that rubbing grains together in your hand was thrashing and blowing away the chaff was winnowing, which were illegal on the Sabbath. Some rabbis even held it was a sin to walk on grass on the Sabbath, because there might be grass seed that would be threshed by walking.[231]

---

[228] John 5:5-35
[229] JST John 5:34
[230] John 5:36-47
[231] Talmage, James. (1981). *Jesus the Christ*. Salt Lake City, UT. The Church of Jesus Christ of Latter-day Saints. Pg.212-213

HIS DISCIPLES AND GALILEE

There were Pharisees there watching, to catch Jesus doing something illegal. They said to him, "Your disciples are doing something that is not lawful to be done on the Sabbath."

Jesus said, "Haven't you read what David did when he and his men were hungry? He went into the house of God and ate the shewbread (twelve loaves of bread were set out every Sabbath and the old bread was eaten by the priests), which wasn't lawful for them to eat, only the priests. Haven't you read in the law how on the Sabbath the priests in the temple profane the Sabbath and are blameless? I say to you, that here right now is one greater than the temple. If you knew what this meant: 'I will have mercy and not sacrifice', you would not have condemned the guiltless; for the Son of Man is Lord even of the Sabbath."

For this reason, the disciples were not guilty of breaking the Sabbath, as they were serving the Lord, just as the priests in the temple do.

He left there and went into their synagogue. In there was a man, who had a withered hand. They asked him," Is it lawful to heal on the Sabbath?" that they might accuse him of abetting breaking of the Sabbath. They then watched to see what he would do.

He told the man, "Stand up," and the man stood up in their midst. Jesus said, "What man shall there be among you who has a sheep and, if it falls into a pit on the Sabbath, will not lift it out on the Sabbath? A man is much better than a sheep, thus it is lawful to do well on the Sabbath."

When he had looked around with anger at the hardness of their hearts, he said, "Stretch out your hand," and the man stretched it out and it was made whole, just like his other hand.

The Pharisees were filled with madness. They left and held a conference to discuss how they might destroy him.

When Jesus knew of this, he left and great crowds followed him. He healed all the ill and told them not to tell others about it, that it might be fulfilled which was spoken by Isaiah the prophet, "My Son, whom I have chosen, my beloved Son, in whom I am well pleased; I will put my spirit upon him and he shall show judgment to the Gentiles. He shall not struggle or cry for help, neither shall any man hear his voice in the streets and the Gentiles shall trust in his name."[232]

---

[232] Matthew 12:1-21; Mark 2:23-28; 3:1-8; Luke 6:1-11; Jesus the Christ, pg. 217-226

After this, Jesus went up on a mountain to pray and spent the whole night praying to his Father. When it was day, he called his disciples and, from them, he chose twelve, whom he ordained apostles. The twelve were Simon Peter and his brother, Andrew; the sons of Zebedee, James and John; Philip and Nathaniel (also known as Bartholomew); Matthew and Thomas; James, the son of Alphaeus; Simons Zelotes; Judas the brother of James (also known as Lebbeus or Thaddeus); and Judas Iscariot, who betrayed him.[233]

SERMON ON THE MOUNT AND CAPERNAUM

Jesus came down from the mountain toward the plain with his disciples. When they were almost down, a crowd met them. They were from Judea and Jerusalem, as well as Tyre and Sidon on the coast. They came to hear him and be healed of their diseases, and to have unclean spirits cast out. The whole crowd wanted to touch him, because power went out of him and healed them. When he was set, he looked at his disciples and spoke to them.

"Blessed are the poor in pride; for theirs is the kingdom of heaven. Blessed are they who mourn; for they shall be comforted. Blessed are the meek; for they shall inherit the earth. Blessed are they which do hunger and thirst after righteousness; for they shall be filled. Blessed are the merciful; for they shall obtain mercy. Blessed are the pure in heart; for they shall see God. Blessed are the peacemakers; for they shall be called the children of God. Blessed are they which are persecuted for righteousness' sake; for theirs is the kingdom of heaven. Blessed are you, when men shall revile you, persecute you, and shall say all manner of evil against you falsely, for my sake. Rejoice and be exceedingly glad; for great is your reward in heaven. The prophets which were before you, were also persecuted.

"You are the salt of the earth; but if the salt has lost its flavor, how shall it be salted? The salt then is good for nothing, but to be thrown away and trampled underfoot. You are the light of the world. A city that is set on a hill cannot be hidden. Neither do men light a candle and put it under a basket, but on a candlestick; and it gives light to all who are in the house. Let your light so shine before men,

---

[233] Matthew 10:1-4; Mark 3:13-19; Luke 6:12-15

SERMON ON THE MOUNT AND CAPERNAUM

that they may see your good works and glorify your Father which is in heaven.

"Think not I am come to destroy the law or the prophets; I am not come to destroy, but to fulfill. I say to you, 'Until heaven and earth pass, not one tiny thing shall pass from the law, until all is fulfilled.[234] Whoever shall break one of the least commandments, and shall teach others to do so, shall not be saved in the kingdom of heaven: but whoever shall do and teach these commandments of the law until it be fulfilled, the same shall be called great and shall be saved in the kingdom of heaven.'[235] I say to you, 'Except your righteousness shall exceed the righteousness of the scribes and Pharisees, you shall not enter into the kingdom of heaven.'

"You have heard it was said in old times, 'You shall not kill; and whoever shall kill shall be in danger of the judgment.' But I say to you, 'Whoever is angry with his brother without a cause shall be in danger of the judgment; and whoever shall insult his brother, shall be in danger of the council; but whoever shall say, 'You fool', shall be in danger of hell.'

"If you bring a gift to the altar and there remember your brother has something against you, leave your gift there and go on your way. First, be reconciled to your brother and then come and offer the gift. Agree with your adversary quickly, while you are with him; so your adversary doesn't deliver you to a judge and the judge give you to an officer and you be put in prison. You shall not get out until you have paid the last penny.

"You have heard it said in olden times, 'You shall not commit adultery.' Whoever looks at a woman to lust after her has already committed adultery with her in his heart. If your right eye causes you to stumble, cut it out and throw it away; for it is profitable for you that part of your body should perish that your whole body should not be cast into hell. If your right hand does evil, cut it off and throw it away; for it is profitable for you that part of your body should perish and not your whole body should be cast into

---

[234] Matthew 5:1-18; Luke 6:17-19
[235] JST Matthew 5:19

SERMON ON THE MOUNT AND CAPERNAUM

hell.[236] I have spoken these parables about your sins.[237] It has been said, 'Whoever shall not want his wife, should divorce her.' I say, 'Whoever shall put away his wife, except for fornication, causes her to commit adultery; and whoever shall marry her who is divorced, commits adultery.'

"You have heard it said in olden times, 'You shall not break an oath, but shall fulfill to the Lord your promises.' I say, 'Swear not an oath at all; neither by heaven, for it is God's throne; nor by the earth, for it is his footstool; nor by Jerusalem, for it is the city of the great King. Neither shall you swear by your head, because you cannot make one hair white or black. Let your communication be, Yes, yes, or No, no. Whatever is more than this is evil.'

"You have heard it has been said, 'An eye for an eye and a tooth for a tooth.' I say, 'You don't resist evil; but whoever shall hit you on your right cheek, turn to him the other also. If anyone will sue you and take away your coat, let them have your cloak also. Whoever shall compel you to go a mile, go with them two. Give to them who ask you and from them who would borrow from you, don't turn away.'

"You have heard it said, 'You shall love your neighbor and hate your enemy.' I say, 'Love your enemies, bless them who curse you, do good to them who hate you, and pray for them which despitefully use you and persecute you; that you may be the children of your Father which is in heaven. For he makes his sun to rise on the evil and the good, and sends rain on the just and on the unjust. If you love them which love you, what reward have you? Do not even sinners the same? Be perfect, even as your Father which is in heaven is perfect.'[238]

"Take heed you do not your alms before men, to be seen of them; otherwise you have no reward of your Father which is in heaven. When you do your alms, do not sound a trumpet before you, as the hypocrites do in the synagogues and in the streets, that they may have glory of men. I say to you, 'They have their reward.' When you give alms, let not your left hand know what your right hand does; that your

---

[236] Matthew 5:20-30
[237] JST Matthew 5:30
[238] Matthew 5:31-48

alms may be in secret, and your Father who sees in secret shall reward you openly.

"When you pray, you shall not be as the hypocrites; for they love to pray standing in the synagogues and on the corners of the streets that they may be seen of men. I say to you, 'They have their reward.' But when you pray, enter your closet and when you have shut the door, pray to your Father in secret and your Father who sees in secret shall reward you openly. Also, when you pray, do not use vain repetitions as the heathen do; for they think they shall be heard for their many words. Be not like them; for your Father knows what things you have need of before you ask Him.'

"Pray after this manner:

"Our Father, who art in heaven, hallowed be your name. Your kingdom come, your will be done on earth, as it is in heaven. Give us this day our daily bread and forgive us our trespasses, as we forgive those who trespass against us. And let us not be led into temptation, but deliver us from evil: For yours is the kingdom, and the power, and the glory forever. Amen.

"Remember prayer is communication and this prayer is a guide. Your prayer should be what you feel not some set prayer that is somebody else's. You are praying to your Father in heaven, so you should address it to Him as I did or in some similar fashion. Second, thank Him for your blessings. All you have comes from Him, so you need to thank Him for all the good you have. Third, ask for what you need and, if you are praying privately, pause and listen for His answer. It most often comes as a feeling. Last, close in my name, Jesus Christ. Amen.

"If you forgive men their trespasses, your Heavenly Father will also forgive you. But if you don't forgive others their trespasses, neither will your Father forgive your trespasses.

"When you fast, be not as the hypocrites, of a sad face; for they disfigure their faces so they may appear to men to fast. I say to you, 'They have their reward.' When you fast, anoint your head and wash your face; so you appear not to others to fast, but your Father, who sees in secret, shall reward you openly.

SERMON ON THE MOUNT AND CAPERNAUM

"Don't lay up for yourselves treasures on earth, where moth and rust destroy, and where thieves break in and steal. But lay up for yourselves treasures in heaven, where neither moth nor rust destroy, and where thieves don't break in and steal. For where your treasure is, there will your heart be also.

"The light of the body is the eye; if the eye be set on the glory of God, your whole body shall be full of light. But if your eye be set on evil; your whole body shall be full of darkness. If, therefore, the light that is in you is darkness, how great is that darkness!

"Nobody can serve two masters; for either he will hate one and love the other; or else he will hold to one and despise the other. You cannot serve God and riches. I say, 'Take no thought for your life, what you shall eat and drink; or for your body, what you shall put on. Is not life more than food and the body than clothing? See the birds of the air; they don't sow, nor reap, nor gather into barns, yet your Father in heaven feeds them. Aren't you much better than they?

"Which of you by thinking can add one foot to his height? Why think about clothing? Consider the lilies of the field, how they grow; they don't work, nor spin. Yet Solomon in all his glory was not dressed like one of these. If God so clothes what grows in the field, which is today and tomorrow is cast into the oven, shall he not much more clothe you, 'O ye of little faith?' Therefore, take no thought, saying, 'What shall we eat?; or 'What shall we drink?' or 'How shall we be dressed?' After all, these things the Gentiles seek. Your Heavenly Father knows you need these things. Seek first the kingdom of God and his righteousness, and all these things shall be added to you. Take no thought for tomorrow; for tomorrow shall take thought for itself. Sufficient to the day is the evil thereof."[239]

These are the words which Jesus taught his disciples they should say to the people.

"Judge not unrighteously, that you be not judged: but judge righteous judgment.[240] For with the judgment you

---

[239] Matthew 6
[240] JST Matthew 7:1

SERMON ON THE MOUNT AND CAPERNAUM

judge, you shall be judged; and with the measure you measure, it shall be measured to you again. Why do you see the speck that is in your brother's eye, but can't see the beam that is in your eye? How will you say to your brother, 'Let me get the speck out of your eye,' when you can't see for the beam in your eye? You hypocrite, first take out the beam that is in your eye and then you can see clearly to remove the speck from your brother's eye.

"Don't give that which is holy to the dogs, nor cast your pearls before swine, lest they trample them underfoot and turn again and rend you. For everyone who asks, receives, and they who seek, find. To him who knocks, it shall be opened. Or what man is there of you, whom if his son asks for bread will give him a stone? Or if he asks for a fish, will give him a serpent? If you then, being evil, know how to give good gifts to your children, how much more shall your Father which is in heaven give good things to them who ask him? Therefore, all things whatever you would have others do for you, do for others. This is the law and the prophets.

"Enter in at the narrow gate, for wide is the gate and wide is the way that leads to destruction and there are many which go in there. Because narrow is the gate and narrow is the way that leads to life; there are few who find it.

"Beware of false prophets, which come to you in sheep's clothing, but inwardly are ravening wolves. You shall know them by their fruits. Do men gather grapes of thorns or figs of thistles? Every good tree bears good fruit, but a corrupt tree bears bad fruit. Every tree that doesn't bear good fruit is cut down and put in the fire. By their fruits, you shall know them.

"Not everyone that says to me, "Lord, Lord," shall enter the kingdom of heaven, only they who do the will of my Father which is in heaven. Many will say to me then, 'Lord, haven't we prophesied in your name? And in your name cast out devils? And in your name done many wonderful works?' Then will I profess to them, 'I never knew you. Go away from me, you worker of evil.'

"Whoever hears these sayings of mine and does them, I will liken to a wise man, which built his house on a rock. The rain came down, the floods came, the winds blew, and all beat on that house. It fell not, for it was built upon a rock. Everyone who hears these sayings of mine and does them not, shall be likened to a foolish man, which built his house on the sand. The rain and the floods came, the winds blew, and beat on that house, which fell and great was the fall of it."

It came to pass, when Jesus had finished speaking to his disciples, the people who had heard him were astonished at his doctrine, for he taught them as one having authority and not as the scribes.[241]

When he was finished, he returned to Capernaum. There was a centurion whose servant was very dear to him. The servant was very sick and ready to die. When the centurion heard of Jesus, he sent to him the elders of the Jews to plead for him to come and heal his servant. When the elders came to Jesus, they immediately begged him to come, saying, "He is worthy for you to come. He loves our nation and has built us a synagogue."

Jesus went with them and, when he was not far from the house, the centurion sent friends to him, saying, "Lord, don't trouble yourself. I am not worthy that you should enter under my roof. Neither did I feel worthy to come to you, just say the word and my servant shall be healed. I also am a man set under authority, having soldiers under me. I say to one, 'Go,' and he goes. To another, 'Come' and he comes. To my servant, 'Do this,' and he does it."

When Jesus heard these things, he marveled, turned around, and said to the crowd following him, "I have not found such great faith, no, not in Israel."

When they who had been sent returned to the house, they found the servant well, who had been sick.[242]

The next day he went to Nain, along with many of his disciples and a big crowd. When they got close to the city gate, there was a dead man carried out. He was the only son of his mother and she was a widow. There also was a crowd with her. When the Lord saw her, he had compassion on her and said, "Don't weep." He came up and touched the bier the dead man was on. They who were carrying him stopped. He said, "Young man, arise."

He who was dead sat up and began to speak, and Jesus delivered him to his mother.

---

[241] Matthew 7:2-29; Luke 6:20-49
[242] Matthew 8:5-13: Luke 7:1-10

SERMON ON THE MOUNT AND CAPERNAUM

There came a fear on all who were there and they glorified God, saying, "A great prophet is risen up among us. God has visited his people." This story of him went throughout Judea and the entire region. The disciples of John told him of these happenings.[243]

John, the Baptist, knew his work was ended. So even though he knew Jesus was the savior, he sent two of his disciples to Jesus so they could see firsthand what was happening. He told them to ask Jesus, "Are you he who should come or should we look for another?"

When they came to Jesus, they said, "John, the Baptist, has sent us to you, saying, 'Are you he who should come or should we look for another?'"

While they were there, he cured many people of their infirmities, plagues, and evil spirits. To many who were blind, he gave sight. Jesus answered John's disciples, "Go tell John what things you have seen and heard. How the blind see, the lame walk, the lepers are cleansed, the deaf hear, the dead are raised, and the gospel is preached to the poor. Blessed are those who shall not be offended by me."

When the disciples of John had left, he began to speak to the people concerning John. "What did you go to the wilderness to see? A reed shaken with the wind? What did you go to see? A man clothed in soft raiment? They which are gorgeously dressed and live delicately are in kings' courts. What did you go to see? A prophet? Yes, and much more than a prophet. This is he of whom it is written, 'Behold, I send my messenger before your face, who shall prepare your way before you.' Among those who are born of women, there is not a greater prophet than John, the Baptist. But he who is least in the kingdom of God is greater than he. All the prophets and the law prophesied until John. If you will receive it, this is Elias, which was to come. He who has ears to hear, let him hear."

All the people and the tax collectors who heard him praised God, being baptized with the baptism of John. But the Pharisees and lawyers rejected the counsel of God against them, not being baptized of John.

The Lord said, "How shall I liken the men of this generation? To what are they like? They are like children sitting in the marketplace, saying, 'We have played for you and you have not danced. We have mourned to you and you have not wept.'

---

[243] Luke 7:11-17

"John, the Baptist, came neither eating bread nor drinking wine and you say, 'He has a devil.' The Son of Man came eating and drinking and you say, 'Behold a gluttonous man and a winebibber, a friend of tax collectors and sinners. Wisdom is proved by its deeds."[244]

Then he began to upbraid the cities where most of his mighty works were done, because they didn't repent. "Woe to you, Chorazin! Woe to thee, Bethsaida! If the mighty works, which were done in you, had been done in Tyre and Sidon, they would have repented long ago in sackcloth and ashes. I say, 'It shall be more tolerable for Tyre and Sidon at the day of judgment, than for you. Capernaum, you which are exalted to heaven, shall be brought down to hell. If the mighty works, which have been done in you, had been done in Sodom, it would have remained until this day. It shall be more tolerable for the land of Sodom in the day of judgment, than for you.'"[245]

DEATH OF JOHN THE BAPTIST AND PARABLES

It was shortly before the visit of John's disciples to Jesus that John was imprisoned. Herod had somewhat of a love/hate relationship with John.

Herod divorced his first wife, Phasaelis, and married Herodias, who had been married to his brother, Phillip. This was illegal under Jewish law, and John told Herod this publicly. This angered Herodias, who wanted Herod to kill John. Because Herod knew John was a holy man and a prophet, he listened to him gladly. But to please his wife, he imprisoned him.

Later, Herod had a party for his birthday and invited high captains and the chief people of Galilee. For entertainment, the daughter of Herodias came in and danced. Her dancing pleased Herod and the others, so Herod said to her, "I swear that whatever you ask me, I will give to you, to half of my kingdom."

She went to her mother and said, "What shall I ask?"

Her mother, of course, said, "Ask for the head of John, the Baptist."

---

[244] Matthew 11:2-19; Luke 7:18-35
[245] Matthew 11:20-24; Luke 10:12-16

DEATH OF JOHN THE BAPTIST AND PARABLES

She went right away to the king and said, "Give me the head of John, the Baptist, on a platter."

Herod was very sorry when he heard this, but for his oath's sake and because of those who were with them, he didn't want to turn her down. He ordered an executioner to behead John, and his head was brought in on a platter and given to Herodias' daughter, who gave it to her mother. John's disciples came and took his body and laid it in a tomb.[246]

One day, a Pharisee asked Jesus to his house to eat and, as they were eating, a woman of the city who was known to be a sinner came in. She had heard Jesus was there and brought an alabaster box of ointment. *The Jews ate in a Roman style, lying on their left side, perhaps on a couch or pillows, with their head toward the food and their feet behind.* She stooped or stood behind him at his feet, weeping, and began to wash his feet with her tears, wiped them with the hair of her head, kissed them, and anointed them with the ointment. When the Pharisee who had invited him saw this, he said to himself, "If this man were a prophet, he would know what sort of woman she is that is doing this, for she surely is a sinner."

Jesus, answering, said, "Simon I have something to ask you."

Simon said, "What is it?"

Jesus said, "A creditor had two debtors, the one owed five hundred dollars and the other fifty. When they couldn't repay the debt, he forgave them both. Which will love him the most?"

Simon said, "I suppose the one to whom he forgave the most."

Jesus said, "You have judged correctly."

Jesus turned to the woman and said to Simon, "See this woman? I came into your house and you didn't give me any water to wash my feet. She has washed my feet with her tears and wiped them with her hair. You didn't give me a kiss, but since I came in, this woman has not ceased to kiss my feet. You didn't anoint my head with oil, but this woman has anointed my feet with ointment. Therefore, I am going to forgive her sins, which are many, for she loved much and has repented. To whom little is forgiven, they show little love."

He turned to the woman and said, "Your sins are forgiven. Your faith has saved you, go in peace."

---

[246] Matthew 14:3-12; Mark 6:17-29

DEATH OF JOHN THE BAPTIST AND PARABLES

Those who were guests at the meal said to themselves, "Who is this that forgives sins?"[247]

A short time later, a man was brought to him who had a devil and was blind, deaf, and dumb. He healed him so the man could see, hear, and speak. All the people there were amazed and said, "Is this not the son of David?"

But when the Pharisees heard about it, they said, "This man casts out devils by Beelzebub, the prince of the devils."

Jesus knowing their thoughts said, "Every kingdom divided against itself is brought to ruin. Every city or house divided against itself shall not stand. If Satan casts out Satan, he is divided against himself. How shall his kingdom stand? If I, by Beelzebub, cast out devils, by whom do your children cast them out? They shall be your judges. If I cast out devils by the Spirit of God, then the kingdom of God has come to you. How can one enter a strong man's house and steal his things, unless he first ties up the strong man? Then he will be able to steal his things. He who is not with me is against me. He who doesn't gather with me, scatters abroad.

"All manner of sin and blasphemy shall be forgiven to men, but blasphemy against the Holy Ghost shall not be forgiven to men. Whoever speaks a word against the Son of Man shall be forgiven, but whoever speaks against the Holy Ghost, it shall not be forgiven him, neither in this world, nor in the world to come.

"Either make the tree good and its fruit good, or make the tree corrupt and its fruit corrupt; the tree is known by its fruit. O generation of vipers, how can you, being evil, speak good things? For out of the abundance of the heart, the mouth speaks. A good man, out of the good treasure of his heart, brings forth good things, and an evil man, out of the evil treasures, brings forth evil things. I say to you, 'Every idle word men shall speak, they shall give an account of at the day of judgment.' For by your words, you shall be justified, and by your words, you shall be condemned."

Then, a few of the scribes and the Pharisees said, "Master, we would like to see a sign from you."

He answered, "An evil and adulterous generation seeks after a sign, and there shall be no sign given to it, but the sign of the prophet Jonas. For, as Jonas was three days and three nights in the whale's belly, so shall the Son of Man be three days and three nights in the heart of the earth.

"The men of Nineveh shall rise in judgment with this

---

[247] Luke 7:36-50

DEATH OF JOHN THE BAPTIST AND PARABLES

generation and shall condemn it, because they repented at the preaching of Jonas, and a greater than Jonas is here. The queen of the south shall rise in the judgment of this generation and shall condemn it, for she came from the uttermost parts of the earth to hear the wisdom of Solomon and a greater than Solomon is here.

"When an unclean spirit is gone out of a person, it looks for good places to relocate. If it doesn't find any, it says, 'I will return to the person I came out of.' When it comes to that person, it finds the place swept and beautified. It then goes and finds seven other spirits more wicked than itself, and they enter in and live there. The last state of that person is worse than the first. This is the way it shall be for this wicked generation."

While he was talking to the people, his mother and brothers came and stood outside, wanting to speak with him. He was told about this and said, "Who is my mother? Who are my brothers?" He stretched out his hand toward his disciples and said, "See, my mother and my brothers. For whoever shall do the will of my Father which is in heaven, the same is my brother, sister, and mother."[248]

One day, as Jesus went out to teach the crowds, he noticed a large group of Pharisees. He sensed they were there to try to entrap him again, and decided to teach in parables. As was the usual case, as he walked to where he wanted to speak, the crowd thronged him. Many just wanted to touch him, as they thought that was all they needed to do to be healed.

He stopped and healed many who were asking for it. He came to where he wanted to speak, and got into a small boat along the shore. It was the only way he could escape being surrounded, so he could speak in a way the crowd could hear him. The boat pulled out slightly in a place where there was a steep drop-off, otherwise, the crowd would just wade out and he would not have gained a place from which to speak.

He said, "A sower went out to sow and, as he sowed, some fell by the roadside and was walked on. Some the birds ate. Some fell on rock and, as soon as it sprang up, it withered for want of moisture. Some fell among weeds and they choked it out. Some fell on good ground, grew, and bore fruit; some a hundredfold, some sixtyfold, and some thirtyfold."

Later, his disciples asked him, "What does this parable mean and why are you teaching this way?"

He said, "To you it is given to know the mysteries of the

---

[248] Matthew 12:22-50; Luke 8:19-21; 11:14-26;29-32

DEATH OF JOHN THE BAPTIST AND PARABLES

kingdom of heaven, but to them it is not given. For whoever has, to them shall be given, and they shall have more abundance: but whoever has not, from them shall be taken away even that they have. I speak to them in parables, that seeing they don't see and hearing they don't understand. In them is fulfilled the prophecy of Isaiah, that says, 'By hearing, you shall hear and not understand, and seeing you shall see and not perceive.' This people have hardened their hearts, their ears are hard of hearing, and their eyes are closed; lest at any time they should see with their eyes, hear with their ears, and understand with their heart and should be converted, that I should heal them.

"The parable is this, 'The seed is the word of God in man. Those seeds by the road side are those who hear, and then the devil comes and takes away the word out of their hearts, so they don't believe and are saved. Those who are on the rock are those which, when they hear the word, accept it with joy. They have no root, so for a while they believe, but in time with temptation, they fall away. That which falls among weeds are those, when they hear go forward, but are choked with the cares, riches, and pleasures of this life and don't bear any fruit. But the seed on the good ground are those which, with an honest and good heart, keep the word and bring forth fruit with patient endurance.

"No one when they have lighted a candle, covers it with a container or puts it under a bed, but they put it on a candlestick, so those who come in may see the light. Nothing is secret, that shall not be made public; neither anything hid, that shall not be known and be spread abroad. Take heed how you listen.[249] Whoever receives, to them shall be given and they shall have more, but whoever continues not to receive, from them shall be taken away that which they have."[250]

He gave the crowd another parable, "The kingdom of heaven is like a man which sowed good seed in his field, but while he slept, his enemy sowed tares among the wheat (tares look like wheat until the seed head is formed). When the seed grew and the heads formed, they recognized tares were mixed in among the wheat. The servants came to their master and asked him, 'Didn't you sow good seed in the field? If you did, where have all the tares come from?'

"He said, 'An enemy has done this.'

"His servants said, 'Should we go and gather the tares out of the wheat?'

---

[249] Matthew 13:3-23; Mark 4:2-25; Luke 8:5-18
[250] JST Matthew 13:10-11

DEATH OF JOHN THE BAPTIST AND PARABLES

"He said, 'No, because you may damage the wheat, gathering the tares. Let them grow together until the harvest, and then I will tell the reapers to first gather the tares, bundle them, and burn them. Then gather the wheat into my barn.'"

He told another parable, "The kingdom of heaven is like a grain of mustard seed, which a man took and planted in his field. It is one of the smallest seeds, but when it is grown; it is the largest of the herbs and becomes a tree that birds can lodge in."

And another, "The kingdom of heaven is like leaven, which a woman took and put in three measures of meal until all the meal was leavened."

He spoke in parables that it might be fulfilled which was spoken by the prophet, "I will open my mouth in parables and I will utter things which have been kept secret from the foundation of the world."

After Jesus sent the crowd away, his disciples asked him, "Explain the parable of the tares to us."

He said, "He that sows the good seed *is me,* the Son of Man, *with your help.* The field is the world. The good seed are the children of the kingdom, but the tares are the children of the devil and the devil is the enemy who sowed them. The harvest is the end of the world and the reapers are the angels. As the tares are gathered and burned in the fire, so shall it be at the end of this world. The Son of Man shall send forth his angels and they shall gather out of his kingdom all things that offend and they which do iniquity. They shall cast them into a furnace of fire and there shall be wailing and gnashing of teeth. Then shall the righteous shine forth as the sun in the kingdom of their Father. They, who have ears to hear, let them hear.

"Again, the kingdom of heaven is like a treasure hid in a field. When a man finds it, he hides it again and with joy, goes and sells all that he has and buys that field. Again, the kingdom of heaven is like a merchant, looking for good pearls. When he had found a pearl of a great price, he went and sold all that he had and bought it. Again, the kingdom of heaven is like a net that was cast into the sea and gathered of every kind. When it was full they drew it to shore and sat down. They gathered the good into vessels, but cast the bad away. So, shall it be at the end of the world. The angels shall come and remove the wicked from among the righteous. It will be like the wicked are thrown into a furnace. There will be wailing and gnashing of teeth."

DEATH OF JOHN THE BAPTIST AND PARABLES

Jesus asked his disciples, "Have you understood all I have said?"

They answered, "Yes, Lord."

He then said, "Every teacher of the law, which has become a disciple in the kingdom of heaven, is like a man who is a homeowner, who brings out of his storehouse old and new things."[251]

As the evening was coming, Jesus said to his disciples, "Let's go over to the other side of the sea."

After they had sent away the crowd, they went aboard a ship. There were several other little ships there. While they were going over, a great storm arose of wind and waves. The waves came into the ship and it was filled with water. Jesus was asleep on a pillow in the back of the boat. His disciples came to him and woke him up. They said, "Master, we are about to die; don't you care?"

Jesus got up, rebuked the wind, and said to the sea, "Be still." The wind ceased and it became very calm. He said, "Why are you so fearful? Why don't you have faith?"

His disciples were very afraid and said to one another, "What manner of man is this, that even the wind and the sea obey him?"[252]

When they arrived on the other side of the Sea of Galilee, they were in the country of the Gadarenes. A man met them, who for a long time had devils. He was naked and didn't live in a house, but in the tombs. He often had been caught and bound with chains, but they couldn't hold him, because he tore the chains apart. When he saw Jesus, he fell in front of him, and cried out in a loud voice, "Why are you doing this, Jesus, the Son of God, most high? Please don't bother me."

Jesus asked, "What is your name?"

He said, "Legion, for there are many of us."

Jesus said, "Come out of him."

The devils said, "Don't make us come out of him into the sea."

There was a large herd of pigs feeding close by on the mountain and they begged him he would allow them to enter the pigs that were there. Jesus allowed it and the devils came out and entered the pigs. They couldn't control them and the herd ran down the mountain, off a cliff, and drowned.

When those who were tending the pigs saw this, they fled, and went and told it in the city and in that area. Those who heard

---

[251] Matthew 13:24-52; Mark 4:26-34
[252] Matthew 8:23-27; Mark 4:35-41; Luke 8:22-25

DEATH OF JOHN THE BAPTIST AND PARABLES

about it came out to see what was done. When they came, they found the man, out of whom the devils were cast, sitting at the feet of Jesus, clothed, and in his right mind. Others who had seen it told them what had happened.

The whole group was afraid and begged Jesus to leave. The man who had the devils cast out asked Jesus to let him go with him, but Jesus sent him away, saying, "Return to your own house and show what remarkable things God has done for you."

He went his way and told them throughout the whole city what Jesus had done for him.

Jesus and his disciples returned to the other side and found the people waiting for him.[253] One of them was Jarius, one of the rulers of the synagogue. When he saw Jesus, he fell at his feet and said, "My little daughter is at the point of death. Please, please, I implore you come and lay your hands on her, that she may be healed, so she can live."

Jesus went with him and a crowd followed and thronged him as they were walking. There was a woman there who had a discharge of blood for twelve years and had seen many doctors, suffering much from their administrations without any improvement; in fact, getting worse. When she heard Jesus was there, she thought, "If I just touch his clothes, I shall be healed." She was in the throng behind him and came up and touched him.

As soon as she touched him, she felt she was healed. Jesus immediately knew he had been touched by someone wanting to be healed as he felt strength leave him. Even though people were thronging him on every side, he turned and looked around to see who had touched him and asked, "Who touched me?"

When all who were around him denied it, his disciples said, "What do you mean, who touched me? People are touching you on every side."

But the woman saw she had been discovered and, with fear and trembling, knowing she had been healed, came and fell in front of Jesus and told him what had happened. He said, "Daughter, your faith has made you whole. Go in peace and be healed of your problem."While they were talking, there came a man from the ruler of the synagogue's house who said, "Your daughter is dead, don't trouble the master anymore."

Jesus heard what was said and said to the ruler of the synagogue, "Don't be afraid, only believe."

---

[253] Matthew 8:28-34, 9:1; Mark 5:1-21; Luke 8:26-40

When they came to the ruler's house and saw all the goings on with the weeping and wailing, Jesus said, "Why are you carrying on so and weeping? The girl is not dead, but merely sleeping."

Those who were grieving laughed him to scorn, but he put them all out. He took the father and mother of the young girl and only Peter, James, and John, the brother of James, into where the girl was lying. He took her by the hand and said to her, "Young lady, arise."

Right away, she arose and walked. She was about twelve years of age. They were all astonished and amazed. He strictly charged them not to tell anyone about this, and told them to give her something to eat.[254]

After this, Jesus again returned home to Nazareth. *The last time he had been there, they had been determined to kill him, but he wanted to give those who he grew up with and loved another opportunity to accept him and his message. As was his custom, when he could, he taught them in their synagogues.* They were astonished at his teaching and said, "How did this man get this wisdom and these mighty works? Isn't this the carpenter's son and his mother Mary? Aren't his brothers James, Joses, Simon, and Judas? Aren't his sisters here with us? Then how can this man do all these things?"

Thus, they had no faith in him.

Jesus again said, "A prophet is not without honor, except in his own country, among his own family, and in his own house."

He was not able to do many great things there because of their unbelief, except he laid his hands on a few sick who believed in him and healed them. He marveled at their unbelief and went about the villages there teaching.[255]

THE TWELVE SENT OUT

Jesus decided it was time to give his disciples more experience. He called the twelve he had chosen *and conferred on them the Melchizedek Priesthood,* which gave them power and authority over devils and to cure diseases.[256]

Jesus said to the twelve:

---

[254] Matthew 9:18-25; Mark 5:22-43; Luke 8:41-56
[255] Matthew 13:53-58; Mark 6:1-6
[256] Hebrews 7:17-28

THE TWELVE SENT OUT

"Go out to preach in pairs, but don't go to the Gentiles or to any Samaritan city. Do go to the lost sheep of Israel. When you preach, say, 'The kingdom of heaven is at hand.' I give you authority to heal the sick, cleanse lepers, raise the dead, and cast out devils. Freely give as you have received. Don't take coin or currency with you, or two coats, or food, or a staff; for the worker is worth his wages. When you enter a town, ask who in it is worthy and stay there until you leave. When you come to a house, greet them and, if they be worthy, let your peace rest there, but if not, let your peace return to you. Whoever won't receive you, nor hear you, when you leave that house or city, shake the dust off your feet. I tell you, 'It shall be more tolerable for Sodom and Gomorrah on judgment day than for it.' I am sending you out as sheep amid wolves; be wise as serpents and harmless as doves.

"Beware of men; they will deliver you to councils and will scourge you in their synagogues. You shall be brought before governors and kings for my sake, for a testimony against them and the Gentiles. When you are delivered up, don't think how or what you shall say, but what to say will be given you when it is needed. You are not speaking, but the Spirit of your Father in Heaven. The brother shall deliver up his brother to death, and the father, the child. The children shall revolt against their parents and cause them to be put to death. You shall be hated by all people because of my name, but he that endures to the end shall be saved.

"When they persecute you in one city, flee to another. The disciple is not above his master, nor the servant above his lord. It is enough for the disciple to become like his master and the servant like his lord. If they have called the master of the house Beelzebub, what shall they call the members of his house? Fear them not, for there is nothing hidden that shall not be revealed, and hid, that shall not be known. What I tell you in darkness, speak you in light, and what you hear in your ear, preach upon the housetops.

"Don't fear them who kill the body, but are not able to kill the soul; but fear them who can destroy both soul and body in hell. Two sparrows are sold for little and one of them shall not fall to the ground without your Father in

THE TWELVE SENT OUT

heaven knowing it. Whoever will witness of me before men, they I will witness of before my Father in heaven. But whoever shall deny me before men, they I will also deny before my Father, which is in heaven.

"Don't think I am come to send peace on earth; I came not to send peace, but a sword. I am come to set a man at variance against his father, the daughter against her mother, and the daughter-in-law against her mother-in-law. A man's foes shall be they of his own household. They who love father or mother more than me are not worthy of me and they that love son or daughter more than me are not worthy of me. He that finds his life shall lose it and he that loses his life for my sake shall find it.

"He who receives a prophet in the name of a prophet shall receive a prophet's reward; he that receives a righteous man in the name of a righteous man shall receive a righteous man's reward. Whoever shall give a child only a drink of cold water in the name of a disciple shall in no way lose his reward."

The twelve went through the towns, preaching the gospel and healing everywhere. They cast out many devils and anointed with oil many that were sick and healed them.[257]

When the apostles returned, they told Jesus all they had done. He took them to a secluded wilderness area on a mountain near Bethsaida, on the north end of the Sea of Galilee. When this was told to the people of the city by some who saw him, a crowd began to gather. When Jesus saw the crowd, he had compassion for them, because they were as sheep without a shepherd, and began to teach them many things and to heal the sick.

When the day was almost over, his disciples came to him and said, "This is a wilderness area and it is getting late. It is time to send the crowd away so they can go to the towns around us and buy food, for they have nothing to eat."

Jesus asked Philip, "How are we going to buy food for them to eat?"

Jesus knew what he was going to do and said this to Philip to test him.

Philip answered, "Twenty thousand dollars' worth of food wouldn't be enough for everyone to have something to eat."

---

[257] Matthew 10:5-42; Mark 6:7-13; Luke 9:1-6

THE TWELVE SENT OUT

Andrew, Simon Peter's brother said, "There is a lad here who has five barley loaves and two small fish, but what is that among so many?"

Jesus commanded them to have the crowd sit down in companies by hundreds and fifties. When they had done that, Jesus took the five loaves and two fish, looked up to heaven and blessed and broke the loaves. He gave them to his disciples to give to the crowd and likewise divided the fish among them. They all ate and were filled. They collected the leftovers and filled twelve baskets. Not counting women and children, there were about five thousand men who were fed.

When those men saw the miracle Jesus did in feeding the crowd, they said, "Truly this is the prophet that was prophesied should come into the world."

Jesus perceived that they would come and take him by force to make him a king. He told his disciples, "I am going to leave now and go up on the mountain to pray. After I am gone, disperse the crowd. Take the ship to Gennesaret on the other side of the lake. I will join you later."

They asked him, "Master, how will you join us? There is no other boat."

He said, "I will join you; don't be concerned about it."

Reluctantly, they did as they were told. When they got to the boat, the wind was against them, so they started rowing. The rowing was difficult with the strong headwind and they weren't making much progress. They toiled through the night until almost morning, rowing, and had not gone very far when they saw Jesus walking on the sea. They thought he was a spirit and cried out in fear, but Jesus called to them, "Don't be afraid; it is I."

Peter answered, "Lord, if it is you, ask me to come to you on the water."

Jesus lifted his hand and said, "Come."

Peter got out of the boat and started walking on the water to Jesus. But when he looked around him with the strong wind and waves, he was afraid and began to sink. He cried out to Jesus, "Lord, save me!"

Immediately, Jesus reached out and caught him, saying, "Oh, you of little faith. Why did you doubt?"

When Jesus and Peter got into the ship, the wind stopped and those who were in the ship came and worshipped Jesus. Almost immediately, they reached land.

THE TWELVE SENT OUT

When those who were there saw Jesus, the word was spread that he had come, and they brought their sick to him to be healed. They asked if they could just touch his clothes, and those that did were healed. [258]

On the other side, those who were where the five thousand had been fed looked for Jesus and couldn't find him. They saw the disciples' boat was gone and knew Jesus had not gone with them. When they couldn't find him, they decided he must have also gone to the other side by some other means. They took boats over to the other side looking for him.

When they found him, they asked, "Master, how did you get here?"

He answered, "Truly, you seek me, not because you want to learn from my teaching or because you saw the miracles, but because you did eat of the food and were filled. Work not for food, which is soon gone, but for food which endures to everlasting life. That which the Son of Man shall give you, for him God, the Father, has sealed."

They asked him, "What shall we do, that we might work the works of God?"

Jesus answered, "This is the work of God, that you believe on him whom he has sent."

Still, they pressed him. "What sign will you show then, that we may see and believe you? What work do you do? Our fathers ate manna in the desert, as it is written, 'He gave them bread from heaven to eat.'"

Jesus said, "Truly, Moses didn't give you that bread from heaven, but my Father gave you the true bread from heaven. The bread of God is he who comes down from heaven and gives life to the world."

They said, "Lord, give us this bread forever."

Jesus told them, "I am the bread of life. He that comes to me shall never hunger and he that believes on me shall never thirst. But I said to you, 'That you also have seen me and don't believe.' All that the Father gives me shall come to me. They that come to me, I will in no way cast out, for I came down from heaven, not to do my own will, but the will of Him that sent me. This is the Father's will, who has sent me, that of all those He has given me I should lose none, but raise them up again at the last day. This is the will of Him that sent me, that every one which sees the Son and believes on him may have everlasting life, and I will raise him up at the last day."

---

[258] Matthew 14:13-36; Mark 6:30-55; Luke 9:10-17; John 6:5-21

THE TWELVE SENT OUT

The Jews murmured around him, because he said, "I am the bread which came down from heaven." They said to one another, "Isn't this Jesus, the son of Joseph, whose father and mother we know? How is it then that he says, 'I came down from heaven?'"

Jesus looked at them. "Don't murmur among yourselves. No man can come to me, except the Father, which has sent me, draws him. Then I will raise him up at the last day. It is written in the prophets, 'And they shall be all taught of God.' Therefore, everyone that has heard and has learned of the Father comes to me. Not that anyone has seen the Father, except they who are of God, they have seen the Father. Truly, I say to you, 'They who believe on me have everlasting life. I am that bread of life.' Your fathers did eat manna in the desert and are dead. This is the bread which comes down from heaven that a person may eat of and not die. I am the living bread which came down from heaven. If anyone eats of this bread, they shall live forever. The bread that I will give is my flesh, which I will give for the life of the world."

When the Jews heard this, they began arguing among themselves, saying, "How can this man give us his flesh to eat?"

Jesus said to them, "Truly, except you eat the flesh of the Son of Man and drink his blood, you have no life in you. Whoever eats my flesh and drinks my blood has eternal life. I will raise them up at the last day, for my flesh is meat indeed and my blood is drink indeed. They who eat my flesh and drink my blood dwell in me and I in them. As the living Father has sent me and I live by the Father, so they who eat me, even they shall live by me. This is the bread which came down from heaven; not as your fathers did eat manna and are dead. They who eat of this bread shall live forever."

Jesus said this in the synagogue in Capernaum. Many of his disciples, when they heard this, said, "This is a hard saying. Who can understand it?"

When Jesus knew that his disciples questioned it, he told them, "Does this offend you? What and if, you shall see the Son of Man ascend to where he was before? It is the spirit that quickens; the flesh does nothing. The words that I speak to you, they are spirit and they are life. There are some of you that don't believe."

Jesus knew from the beginning which of them didn't believe and who would betray him. He said, "No one can come to me, except it is given to them by my Father."

Many of his disciples went back to their lives and didn't follow him anymore. Jesus said to the twelve, "Will you also go away?"

Simon Peter answered, "Lord, to whom shall we go? You have the words of eternal life. We believe and are sure that you are the Christ, the Son of the living God."

Jesus nodded. "Have I not chosen you twelve and one of you is a devil?"

Jesus, of course, was speaking of Judas Iscariot, who should betray him.[259]

PASSOVER AGAIN AND TRANSFIGURATION

It was almost Passover time again. Jesus told his disciples, "I am not going to Passover in Jerusalem now. This next year, there will be a lot of persecution, with many groups of Pharisees and scribes trying to find things they can accuse us of doing wrong. Our crowds are going to be smaller, as more people make decisions on what they want to believe. But our preaching will go on and we will reach many people."

Shortly after telling his disciples this, a group of scribes and Pharisees came to Jesus and asked him, "Why do your disciples transgress the tradition of the elders by not washing their hands when they eat?"

Jesus answered, *"We do wash our hands, though we don't follow the ceremonial washing the elders do.* Why do you transgress the commandment of God by your traditions? God commanded, 'Honor your father and mother, for they that curse their father or mother shall surely die.' But you tell the children, 'If your father or mother ask anything of you, just tell them what you have is pledged to the Lord, and you can't help them. Thus, you are free.' You allow the children to not honor their parents. You have bypassed the commandment of God by your tradition. You hypocrites, well did Isaiah prophesy of you, saying, 'This people come close to me with their mouths and honor me with their lips, but their heart is far from

---

[259] John 6:22-71

PASSOVER AGAIN AND TRANSFIGURATION

me. In vain they worship me, teaching for doctrine the commandments of men.'"

He called the crowd to come hear him and said, "That which goes into your mouth doesn't defile you, but that which comes out of the mouth does."

His disciples came to him and said, "Don't you know that the Pharisees were offended when they heard this saying?"

He answered, "Every plant which my Father in heaven has not planted shall be rooted up. Let them alone; they are blind leaders of the blind. If the blind lead the blind, both shall fall into the ditch."

Peter said, "Explain this parable to us."

Jesus said, "Are you also without understanding? Don't you understand whatever goes in your mouth goes into your stomach and is then eliminated, but those things which come out of the mouth come from the heart and they defile the person? Out of the mouth come evil thoughts, murders, adulteries, fornications, thefts, false witness, and blasphemies. This is what defiles a person. But to eat with hands that haven't been washed ceremonially doesn't defile a person."

After this, they left Israel and went to Tyre and Sidon, perhaps to have some peace, but crowds met them there, also. A woman of Canaan was there. She called to him, pleading "Oh, Lord, Son of David, my young daughter is greatly vexed with a devil."

Jesus didn't answer a word to her, *but went right on talking to his disciples.*

She went up to Philip, who was off to one side and said, "Your master won't answer me. Please talk to him and plead my case to him. I have a daughter who is greatly vexed with a devil and it is destroying her. Please help me."

He said, "If my master doesn't want to talk to you, whatever I say won't change his mind."

The woman kept asking the disciples to help her. Finally, they went to Jesus and said, "Send this Canaanite away, for she is pestering us."

He said to her, "I am sent only to the lost sheep of the house of Israel, and you are of Canaan, not Israel."

Then she came and worshipped him, saying, "Lord, help me."

He said, "Let the children of Israel first be filled. It's not right to take the children's food and give it to the dogs."

PASSOVER AGAIN AND TRANSFIGURATION

She didn't lose her temper or composure at being called a dog, but said, "That's true, Lord. Yet the dogs under the table eat the children's crumbs."

Jesus answered, "Oh, woman. Great is your faith. Be it to you even as you want. The devil is gone out of your daughter."

When she went home, she found the devil gone out and her daughter lying on the bed.

They left Tyre and Sidon and went down through Decapolis to the Sea of Galilee. Jesus went up into the mountains and stopped there. A great crowd came up to him with those that were lame, blind, maimed, dumb, and with many other problems.

A man who was deaf and had a speech impediment was brought to him to be healed. He took him aside from the crowd and put his finger into his ears and touched his tongue. Looking up to heaven, he sighed, and said, "Be opened."

Right away, his ears were opened, his tongue was loosened, and he spoke plainly. He asked him to tell no one, but the more he asked, the more was it published.

They said, "He has done everything well. He makes both the deaf to hear and the dumb to speak."[260]

Jesus and his disciples stayed there teaching the crowd for three days. He called his disciples to him and said, "I feel sorry for these people. They have been here for three days and they have nothing to eat. I don't want to send them away fasting, as they may faint on the way. Many of them have come a long way."

His disciples said, "How could we get enough food in the wilderness to feed such a large crowd?"

Jesus said, "How many loaves do you have?"

They answered, "Seven and a few small fish."

He had the crowd sit down on the ground and took loaves and fish and gave thanks. He then broke the loaves and gave them to his disciples to give to the crowd. He also had his disciples distribute the fish. They all ate and were filled. Afterwards they filled up seven baskets with the leftovers. There were four thousand men that ate, plus women and children. He sent the crowd away, and they (he and his disciples?) went by ship to Magdala on the west side of the Sea of Galilee.

When they arrived, they found Pharisees and Sadducees there demanding to see a sign. It was unusual for the Pharisees and Sadducees to work together, as they were vying for political control.

---

[260] Matthew 15:1-31; Mark 7:1-37

PASSOVER AGAIN AND TRANSFIGURATION

Jesus said to them, "When it is evening, you say, 'It will be pleasant weather, because the sky is red.' In the morning, you say, 'It will be stormy weather, because the sky is dark and gloomy.' Oh, you hypocrites, you know the weather, but do you know the signs of the times? A wicked and adulterous generation seek a sign, but there shall no sign be given to it, except the sign of the prophet Jonah, who spent three days in the stomach of a whale."

He left them and got back in the ship and went over to the other side. He said to his disciples, "Beware of the leaven of the Pharisees and of the Sadducees."

They talked among themselves about what this meant and decided he was talking about there being no bread, because they had forgotten to get any and there was not more than one loaf.

When Jesus heard this, he said, "Why do you talk about not having bread? How can you not see and understand? Are your hearts still hardened? Having eyes, do you not see? Having ears, do you not hear? How do you not remember? When I broke the five loaves among the five thousand, how many baskets of leftovers were there?"

They said, "Twelve."

When the seven loaves among the four thousand were broken, how many baskets were filled?"

They said, "Seven."

He said, "How is it you do not understand that I spoke it not about bread, but that you should beware of the leaven of the Pharisees and of the Sadducees?"[261]

When they arrived at Bethsaida, a blind man was brought to him and they asked Jesus to heal him. He took the blind man by the hand and led him out of town. He put saliva on his eyes, put his hands on him, and asked, "How do you see?"

The man answered, "I see men walking like trees."

He again put his hand on his eyes and had him look up. His vision was restored and he could see clearly. He sent him away to his home and said, "Don't go into town or tell anybody about this."

He and his disciples went to the towns in Caesarea Philippi. On the way, he asked his disciples, "Who do men say I am?"

They answered, "Some say John, the Baptist, some say Elias, and some say one of the prophets."

He asked, "Who do you say I am?"

---

[261] Matthew 15:32-39; 16:1-12; Mark 8:1-21

PASSOVER AGAIN AND TRANSFIGURATION

Peter answered, "You are the Christ, the Son of the living God."

Jesus said to him, "Blessed are you, Simon, son of Jonah, for flesh and blood has not revealed it to you, but my Father which is in heaven. I also want to tell you that you are Peter (petros in Greek or small rock), and upon this rock (petra in Greek or bedrock), I will build my church and the gates of hell shall not prevail against it. I shall give you the keys of the kingdom of heaven and whatever you shall bind on earth, shall be bound in heaven and whatever you shall loose on earth, shall be loosed in heaven."

(What is being said here is that Peter (petros or little rock), through revelation, received the knowledge that Jesus was the Christ from God the Father and upon this rock (petra or the bedrock of revelation) the church of Jesus Christ would be built.)

He charged his disciples to tell no one he was Jesus the Christ. Then Jesus began to tell his disciples what would happen to him in the future. He said, "I must go to Jerusalem and suffer many things at the hands of the elders, chief priests, and scribes. I will be killed and will be raised again on the third day."

Peter took him to the side and began to rebuke him, "Lord, this shall not happen to you."

He said to Peter, "Get behind me, Satan. You are an offence to me, for you don't understand the things that are of God, but those that are of men."

Then he said to his disciples, "If any man will come after me, let him deny himself, take up his cross, and follow me. For whoever will save his life shall lose it, and whoever will lose his life for my sake, shall save it. What is a man profited, if he shall gain the world and lose his soul? Or what shall a man give in exchange for his soul? The Son of Man shall come in the glory of his Father with his angels and then he shall reward every person according to their works. I say, 'There are some standing here, who shall not taste of death, until they see the Son of Man coming in his kingdom.'"[262]

A week later, Jesus took Peter, James, and John and the four of them went up to the top of a high mountain and Jesus was transfigured before them. His clothing began shining and was extremely white, like pure snow; whiter than any whitening could make it. There appeared before them Elijah and Moses, and they talked with Jesus about his death, which should be accomplished at Jerusalem.

---

[262] Matthew 16:13-28; Mark 8:22-38, 9:1; Luke 9:18-27

PASSOVER AGAIN AND TRANSFIGURATION

Next, there was a cloud that came over them and a voice out of the cloud said, "This is my beloved Son, in who I am well pleased. Hear him."

Peter said to Jesus, "Master, it is good for us to be here. Let's make three tabernacles; one for you, one for Moses, and one for Elias." He said this because they were very afraid and didn't know what to do.

Jesus came over and touched them and told them to get up and not to be afraid. When they got up and looked around, suddenly there was nobody else there, except Jesus. As they came down from the mountain, he told them they shouldn't tell anyone what they had seen, until the Son of Man had risen from the dead. They kept this saying to themselves, questioning one with another what the rising from the dead should mean.

They asked Jesus, "Why do the scribes say that Elias must first come?"

He answered, "Elias truly must come first and prepare the way for the Son of Man, who must suffer many things and be considered of little worth. But Elias has already come and they have done to him whatever they wanted to do as it is written, 'He bore record of me and they didn't receive him.' Truly this was Elias."

Then the disciples understood he spoke to them of John, the Baptist.

When they came to the other disciples, they saw a big crowd around them and the scribes questioning them. As soon as the crowd saw him, they were surprised and ran to him, greeting him.

He asked the scribes, "What are you questioning them about?"

One of the crowd said, "Master, I have brought to you my son, who has a dumb spirit. Wherever he goes, the dumb spirit tears him, he foams and gnashes with his teeth, and he pines away. I spoke to your disciples that they should cast him out, but they couldn't."

He said, "Oh, faithless generation, how long shall I be with you? How long shall I suffer you? Bring him to me."

They brought the child to him and, when the dumb spirit saw Jesus, the spirit tore the child and he fell on the ground and rolled around foaming at the mouth. Jesus asked his father, "How old was the child when this started?"

The father said, "When he was young. Often the spirit has thrown him into fire and into water to destroy him. If you can do anything, have compassion on us and help us."

PASSOVER AGAIN AND TRANSFIGURATION

Jesus said to him, "If you can believe, all things are possible to those who believe."

Immediately, the father said, "Lord, I believe, but help my unbelief."

When Jesus saw the crowd come running, he rebuked the foul spirit, saying, "You, dumb and deaf spirit, I command you, come out of him and don't enter into him again."

The spirit cried out, tore him badly, and came out of him. The son lay on the ground as if he was dead; indeed, many said he was dead. But Jesus took him by the hand and lifted him up and he arose.

When Jesus came into his house, the disciples asked him, "Why couldn't we cast out the evil spirit?"

He said, "Because of your unbelief. If you have faith as a grain of mustard seed, you shall say to this mountain, 'Move over there,' and it shall move there. Nothing shall be impossible to you. However, this kind comes out only by prayer and fasting."

They left there and passed through Galilee. Jesus wanted some time to teach his disciples, so they walked in remote areas trying to keep away from crowds. Along the way, Jesus said to his disciples, "The Son of Man shall be betrayed into the hands of men. They shall kill him and, after he is dead, the third day he shall rise."

The disciples, when they heard this, were very sad. They weren't sure what he meant, but were afraid to ask him.

Later, those that received tribute money, which was paid for temple maintenance, asked Peter, "Does your master pay tribute?"

Without thinking, Peter said, "Yes."

A little later, as Peter was coming into the house, Jesus stopped him and asked, "What do you think, Simon? Of whom do the kings of the earth take tribute? Is it of their children or of strangers?"

Peter said, "Of strangers."

Jesus said, "Then the children are free and I don't owe anything. Nevertheless, lest we should offend them, go to the sea, cast in a fishing line, and take the first fish you catch. Open its mouth and you shall find a piece of money. Take it and give it to them for you and me."[263]

They went to Capernaum and, while there, he asked them, "What were you arguing about on the way here?"

---

[263] Matthew 17:1-27; Mark 9:2-32; Luke 9:28-45;

PASSOVER AGAIN AND TRANSFIGURATION

They told him, "It was nothing, we were just having fun." Actually, they had been arguing about who among them would be greatest.

Jesus sat down and called the twelve to him, took a child, and set the child down amid them. He said,

"Except you are converted and become as little children, you shall not enter the kingdom of heaven.[264] By this, I don't mean to be a child in understanding, but be humble and obedient as a child.[265] Whoever does this, the same is greatest in the kingdom of heaven. Whoever shall receive a child, such as this one, receives me. Whoever receives me, receives Him that sent me. If anyone desires to be first, they shall be last of all and servant of all. Whoever shall cause one of these children to stumble, it would be better for them that a millstone was hung about their neck and they were drowned in the depth of the sea.

"Woe to the world because of offenses. It needs to be that offenses come, but woe to those by whom they come. Thus, if your hand or foot is diseased, cut it off, so you don't die. It is better to be maimed or lame than to die with two hands and two feet. As it is with physical things, it is with spiritual things. Weed out the evil things, so you can have eternal life. If your eye troubles you, have it taken out. It is better to have one eye and live, than two eyes and die. The same with evil, dig it out, that you may have eternal life.

"Be careful that you care for these little ones, because in heaven, their angels do always see the face of my Father. For the Son of Man has come to save that which was lost[266] and to call sinners to repentance; but these little ones have no need of repentance, and I will save them.

"What do you think? If a man has one hundred sheep and one of them goes astray, doesn't he leave the ninety and nine, go into the mountains, and look for the one that has gone astray? Even so, it is not the will of your Father, who is in heaven, that one of these little ones should perish.[267]

---

[264] Matthew 18:1-3
[265] 1 Corinthians 14:20
[266] Matthew 18:4-14; Mark 9:33-37; Luke 9:46-48; 17:1-2
[267] JST Matthew 18:11

"Moreover, if your brother shall trespass against you, go tell him what has happened. If he will hear you, you have gained your brother. But if he won't hear you, then take two or three others, that in the mouth of two or three witnesses, every word may be established. If he won't hear them, tell it to the church, and if he won't hear the church, let him be to you as a heathen and a tax collector. Truly, I say to you, 'Whatever you shall bind on earth shall be bound in heaven and whatever you shall loose on earth shall be loosed in heaven.' I say, 'If two of you shall agree on earth about anything that you will ask, it shall be done for them of my Father which is in heaven.' For where two or three are gathered together in my name, there am I among them."

Then came Peter to him and asked, "Lord, how often shall my brother sin against me and I forgive him, seven times?"

Jesus said, "Not seven times, but until seventy times seven. The kingdom of heaven is like a certain king, which wanted to settle accounts with his servants. One of his servants was brought to him, who owed him one and a half million dollars. Because he had nothing to pay him with, his lord commanded him to be sold, along with his wife and children, and everything he had, for the payment. The servant fell down and worshipped him, saying, 'Lord, have patience with me and I will pay you all.' Then, the lord of that servant was moved with compassion, loosed him, and forgave him the whole debt."

"The same servant went out and found one of his fellow servants, who owed him, twenty-six hundred dollars and laid his hands on him, taking him by the throat, saying, 'Pay me all that you owe me.'"

"His fellow servant fell down at his feet and pleaded with him saying, 'Have patience with me and I will repay it all.' But he would not allow it and cast him into prison, until he would pay the debt."

"When his fellow servants saw what was done, they were very sorry and told their lord what was done. Then, his lord called him and said to him, 'You wicked servant, I forgave you all that debt, because you asked me. Shouldn't you also have had compassion on your fellow servant, even as I had pity on you?' His lord was angry and delivered him to the tormentors, until he would pay all that was owed.

"Likewise, shall my heavenly Father do to every one of you, if you don't forgive your brothers their trespasses."[268]

FEAST OF THE TABERNACLES

It was autumn and the Feast of the Tabernacles was coming. Jesus stayed in Galilee and didn't go into Judea, because the Jews wanted to kill him.

One day, Jesus left his disciples and joined his family. As he had before, he told his family how important baptism was and encouraged them again to be baptized. When he went to talk to his mother, his brothers, James, Joseph, Simon, and Judas, were talking among themselves.

Joseph said to them, "I am tired of Jesus making himself out to be a great prophet. I can't believe people fall for it. He does some amazing things, and I don't know how he does them, but he is just a guy, like the rest of us. I am tired of his always preaching to me."

Simon said, "I agree, if he was really a prophet he would go up to the Feast of the Tabernacles and show everybody miracles. He says the Jews are trying to kill him, but he just tells us that to make us think he is important."

The brothers all agreed.

Later, when Jesus returned, his brothers told him, "Go up to Jerusalem that your disciples may see the works you do. There is no one who does things in secret, when they want to be openly known. If you do things, show yourself to the world."

Jesus said to them, "It is not yet my time, but it is always your time. The world cannot hate you; but it hates me, because I testify that its works are evil. Go on up to this feast. I am not going yet, because my time has not fully come."

After his brothers went up, he also went up to the feast, not openly, but in secret. The Jews looked for him at the feast, but couldn't find him. There was a lot of discussion about him. Some said, "He is a good man," while others said, "No, he is a liar." The people didn't speak openly of Jesus because they were afraid of the Jews.

About the middle of the feast, Jesus went into the temple and taught. The Jews were amazed at his teaching, asking, "How did this man learn letters, never having been taught?"

---

[268] Matthew 18:15-35; Luke 17:3-4

FEAST OF THE TABERNACLES

Jesus answered them, "My doctrine is not mine, but His that sent me. If anyone will do His will, he shall know of the doctrine, whether it is of God, or whether I speak of myself. He that speaks of himself seeks his own glory; but he that seeks the glory for whoever sent him, the same is true and there is no unrighteousness in him. Didn't Moses give you the law, and yet none of you keep the law? Why are you trying to kill me?"

The people said, "You have a devil. Who is trying to kill you?"

Jesus said, "The last time I was in Jerusalem, I healed one man on the Sabbath and you all marveled that I did it on the Sabbath. Moses gave you circumcision and, on the Sabbath, you circumcise a male. If a male is circumcised on the Sabbath that the Law of Moses shouldn't be broken, why are you angry with me for healing a man on the Sabbath as I did? Don't judge by appearance but judge righteously."

Some of them said, "Isn't this he, whom they seek to kill? But, look, he is speaking boldly and they aren't saying anything to him. Do the rulers know this is the very Christ? However, we know where this man is from and, when Christ comes, no man will know where he is from."

Jesus cried out in the temple as he taught, "You both know me and know from where I am. I am not come of myself, but he that sent me is true, whom you don't know. But I know Him, because I am from Him and he has sent me."

Many of the people believed him and said, "When Christ comes, will he do more miracles than these which this man has done?"

The Pharisees heard the people were talking about these things concerning him and the Pharisees, and chief priests sent officers to take him.

Jesus said to them, "I am with you a little while, and then I will go to Him that sent me. You shall seek me and shall not find me, because where I am, you cannot come."

The Jews said, "Where will he go, that we shall not find him? Will he go to the dispersed among the Gentiles and teach the Gentiles? What is this he has said, 'You shall seek me and shall not find me, because where I am, you cannot come?'"

On the last day, the great day of the feast, Jesus stood and cried, "If anyone thirsts, let them come to me and drink. He that believes on me, as the scripture has said, 'Out of his belly shall flow rivers of living water.'"

FEAST OF THE TABERNACLES

He spoke this of the Spirit, which those that believe on him should receive, because the Holy Ghost was not yet given, because Jesus hadn't yet been glorified. (Ezekiel uses water in the same way to express the Spirit flowing out of the temple in Ezekiel 47:1-10)

Many of the people, when they heard this, said, "Truly, this is the Prophet." Others said, "This is the Christ." But some said, "Shall Christ be from Galilee? Don't the scriptures say, 'Christ will come of the seed of David and out of the town of Bethlehem, which is David's town.'" So, there was a division among the people, because of him. Some of them wanted to arrest him, but no one did.

The officers came to the chief priests and Pharisees, and they said to the officers, "Why haven't you brought him?"

The officers said, "Never has a man spoken like this man."

The Pharisees said, "Are you also deceived? Have any of the rulers or Pharisees believed on him? No, but the people who don't know the law are cursed."

Nicodemus, who was one of them, said, "Does our law judge any man before it hears him and knows what he does?"

They answered, and said to him, "Are you also of Galilee? Search the scripture and see; for out of Galilee there comes no prophet." This shut up Nicodemus and they all went home.[269] (The prophets Jonah, Nahum, and Hosea were all from Galilee).

After the feast, Jesus came again to the temple early in the morning, and the people came to him and he sat down and taught them. The scribes and Pharisees brought to him a woman taken in adultery. They sat her amid the group and said, "This woman was taken in the very act of adultery. Moses, in the law, commanded stoning for breaking this law. What do you say?"

They did this that they might accuse him of breaking the Law of Moses, for which the penalty was death, or the Roman law, which forbade them taking a life.

But Jesus stooped down and, with his finger, wrote on the ground, as though he had not heard them.

They continued asking him, and he stood up and said, "Let him that is without sin among you cast the first stone at her."

He again stooped down and wrote on the ground.

The woman's accusers, being convicted by their own conscience, left one by one, beginning at the eldest, down to the last. When Jesus was left alone with the woman, he said, "Woman, where are your accusers? Has no one condemned you?"

---

[269] John 7:1-53

FEAST OF THE TABERNACLES

She said, "No man, Lord."

Jesus said, "Neither do I condemn you: go and sin no more."

Returning to his teaching, he said, "I am the light of the world; those that follow me shall not walk in darkness, but shall have the light of life."

The Pharisees said to him, "Since you are bearing record of yourself, your record is not true."

Jesus said, "Though I bear record of myself, yet my record is true. For I know where I came from and where I am going. But you cannot tell where I came from or where I am going. You judge after the flesh, but I judge no one. Yet if I judge, my judgment is true: for I am not alone, the Father that sent me is with me. It is written in your law that the testimony of two men is true. I am one who bears witness of me and the Father that sent me bears witness of me, through all that I do."

Then, they asked, "Where is your Father?"

Jesus answered, "You don't know me, or my Father: if you knew me, you would know my Father, too."

Jesus spoke these things in the treasury. They wanted to arrest him, but they were afraid of the people and did not, because his time had not yet come.

Jesus went on speaking, "I will go on my way and you shall look for me and not find me. Thus, you shall die in your sin, because where I go, you cannot come."

The Jews discussed this among themselves, saying, "Will he kill himself? He says, 'Where I go, you cannot come.'"

Jesus said, "You are from beneath: I am from above. You are of this world, but I am not of this world. I said to you that you should die in your sins: for if you don't believe I am the savior, you shall die in your sins."

Then they said, "Who are you?"

Jesus said, "The same that I told you from the beginning. I have many things to say and to judge you from: but he that sent me is true and I speak to the world those things which I have heard from him."

Because of their animosity, they didn't understand he was speaking about the Father.

Jesus then said, "When you have lifted up the Son of Man, then shall you know that I am he and that I do nothing of myself; but as my Father has taught me, I speak those things. He that has sent me is with me: The Father has not left me alone; for I do always those things that please him."

FEAST OF THE TABERNACLES

As he said these things, many believed on him.

Then said Jesus to those Jews which believed on him, "If you continue in my word, then you are my disciples indeed, and you shall know the truth, and the truth shall make your free."

The Jews said, "We are the offspring of Abraham and were never in bondage to anyone. Why do you say, 'You shall be made free?'"

Jesus said, "Truly, I say to you that whoever commits sin is the servant of sin. A servant doesn't live in his master's house forever, but the Son does. Therefore, if the Son shall make you free, you indeed shall be free. I know you are the offspring of Abraham: but you are looking to kill me, because my word has no place in you. I speak about those things I have seen with my Father, and you about those things you have seen with your fathers."

They answered and said, "Abraham is our father."

Jesus said, "If you were Abraham's children, you would do the works of Abraham. But now you want to kill me, a man who has told you the truth, which I have heard from God. Abraham didn't do this. You do the deeds of your father."

They said, "We aren't bastards. We have one Father, even God."

Jesus said, "If God were your Father, you would love me, for I am of God and came from God. I didn't come of myself, but he sent me. Why don't you understand me? It's because you won't hear me. You are of your father the devil and will do the lusts of your father. He was a murderer from the beginning and doesn't follow truth, because there is no truth in him. When he speaks a lie, he speaks it of his own: for he is a liar and the father of it. Because I tell you the truth, you don't believe me. Which of you convicts me of sin? If I say the truth, why don't you believe me? He that is of God hears God's words: you don't hear them, because you are not of God."

The Jews said, "We have said you are a Samaritan and have a devil and it is true"

Jesus said, "I don't have a devil: but I honor my Father and you dishonor me. I don't seek my own glory; there is one that seeks and judges. I say to you that if a person will keep my sayings, they shall never see death."

The Jews said, "Now we know you have a devil. Abraham is dead and the prophets, and you say, 'If a person will keep my sayings, they shall never see death.' Are you greater than our father Abraham, who is dead? Who do you make yourself to be?"

FEAST OF THE TABERNACLES

Jesus said, "If I honor myself, my honor is nothing: it is my Father that honors me, whom you say is your God. Yet you have not known Him, but I know Him. If I should say I didn't know Him, I would be a liar like you, but I know Him and keep His sayings. Your father Abraham rejoiced to see my day, he saw it, and was glad."

The Jews said, "You aren't yet fifty years old and have you seen Abraham?"

Jesus said, "I tell you, before Abraham was, I was 'I am.'"

The Jews picked up stones to stone him with for calling himself "I am," a name for Jehovah. Jesus hid himself and left the temple, going through the midst of the Jews.[270]

Sometime later, as Jesus was walking through Jerusalem, he passed by a man who was blind from birth. His disciples asked him, "Master, who sinned, this man or his parents, that he was born blind?"

Jesus said, "Neither did this man sin, nor his parents, but that the works of God should be shown through him. I must do the works of Him that sent me, while it is day: the night is coming, when no one can work. As long as I am in the world, I am the light of the world."

He then spit on the ground, made clay of his saliva and anointed the eyes of the blind man with the clay. He told the man, "Go wash in the pool of Siloam."

The man went there, washed, and received his sight. Those who had seen him before said, "Isn't this the man that sat and begged?" Others said, "He looks like him."

But he said, "I am he."

They asked him, "How were your eyes opened?"

He said, "A man that is called Jesus made clay, anointed my eyes, and said to me, 'Go to the pool of Siloam and wash.' I did so and received my sight."

They asked, "Where is the man?"

He said, "I don't know."

He was brought to the Pharisees, and it was the Sabbath when this was done. They asked him, "How did you receive your sight?"

He said, "He put clay on my eyes, I washed, and now I can see."

Some of the Pharisees said, "This man is not of God, because he doesn't keep the Sabbath." Others said, "How can a man that is a

---

[270] John 8:1-59

FEAST OF THE TABERNACLES

sinner do such miracles?" Because of this, there was a division among them.

They said to him who had been blind, "What do you think of him who opened your eyes?"

He said, "He is a prophet."

The Jews didn't believe he was blind until they called his parents. They asked them, "Is this your son who was born blind? If so, how does he see?"

The parents said, "We know that this is our son and that he was born blind. How he sees now, we don't know. He is of age, ask him. He can speak for himself."

They said this because they feared the Jews. The Jews had already agreed that if anyone said he was Christ, they should be put out of the synagogue.

Thus, the parents said, "He is of age, ask him."

The Pharisees again called the man who was blind and said, "Give God the praise, for we know this man is a sinner."

He said, "Whether he is a sinner or not, I don't know. One thing I do know, I was blind and now I can see."

They said to him again, "What did he do? How did he open your eyes?"

He said, "I have told you already and you didn't hear. Why do you want to hear it again? Do you want to be his disciples?"

They reviled him and said, "You are his disciple; we are Moses' disciples. We know God spoke to Moses, but for this man, we don't know where he is from or what he is."

The man said, "Here is a marvelous thing. You don't know what this man is and yet he gave me sight. We know God doesn't hear sinners, but he hears those that worship God and do his will. Since the world began, it has never been heard that any man opened the eyes of one who was born blind. If this man were not of God, he could do nothing."

They answered, "You were born in sin and do you try to teach us?" and cast him out.

Jesus heard they had cast him out and went to find him. When he found him, he said, "Do you believe on the Son of God?"

He said, "Who is he, Lord, that I might believe on him?"

Jesus said, "It is I who is talking to you."

He said, "Lord, I believe," and worshipped him.

Jesus said, "For judgment I have come into this world, that they which see not, might see, and that they which see might be made blind."

Some of the Pharisees who were there heard him say this and said, "Are we blind also?"

Jesus said, "If you were blind, you should have no sin, but you say, 'We see.' Therefore, your sin remains."[271] Those who don't enter by the door into the sheepfold, but climb up some other way, are thieves and robbers. He who enters by the door is the shepherd of the sheep. The guard opens to him and the sheep know his voice. He calls them by name and leads them out. When he takes his sheep out, he goes before them and the sheep follow him, because they know his voice. They won't follow a stranger, but will run from him, because they don't know him."

Jesus spoke this parable to them, but they didn't understand what he was trying to tell them. He then said, "I am the door of the sheepfold. All who came before me were thieves and robbers and the sheep did not listen to them. I am the door and by me if anyone enters, they shall be saved. They shall go in and out and find pasture. The thief comes only to steal, kill, and to destroy. I am come that they might have life and have it more abundantly. I am the good shepherd. The good shepherd gives his life for the sheep. But he who is hired and not the shepherd, whose sheep they aren't, when he sees a wolf coming, leaves the sheep and flees. The wolf catches the sheep and scatters them. The hired hand flees, because he is just a hireling and doesn't care about the sheep.

"I am the good shepherd, know my sheep, and am known by them. As the Father knows me, even so I know the Father, and lay down my life for the sheep. Other sheep I have, which are not of this fold. Them also I must bring and they shall hear my voice. (Some of these other sheep are Nephites and Lamanites discussed later in the chapter "Christ and the Nephites"). There shall be one fold and one shepherd. Therefore, my Father loves me, because I lay down my life, that I might take it again. No man takes it from me, but I lay it down of myself and have power to take it again. This commandment have I received from my Father."

There was a division again among the Jews for these sayings. Many of them said, "He has a devil and is mad. Why listen to him?" Others said, "These are not the words of him that has a devil. Can a devil open the eyes of the blind?"[272]

After the Feast of the Tabernacles, Jesus left Jerusalem and returned to Galilee.

***

---

[271] John 9
[272] John 10:1-21

FEAST OF THE TABERNACLES

It was time for Jesus to leave Galilee for the last time; his ministry was ending. He knew in about six months he would have his last Passover and face crucifixion. As he was returning to Jerusalem, he decided to go through Samaria. He sent messengers before him to prepare a place for them to stay. When the messengers got to the village, they found they weren't wanted, because they were just stopping overnight on their way to Jerusalem, and didn't plan to stay.

When his disciples, James and John, found this out, they asked Jesus, "Lord, do you want us to command fire to come down from heaven and consume them as Elijah did?" (Elijah had called down fire from heaven to destroy his enemies as described in 2 Kings 1).

Jesus turned around and said, "Don't let your spirits be influenced by Satan. I am not come to destroy lives, but to save them."

They then went to another village.[273] On the way, a scribe said to Jesus, "I will follow you wherever you go."

Jesus said, "Foxes have dens and birds have nests, but the Son of Man has nowhere to lay his head."

He said to another who came to him, "Follow me."

But he said, "Lord, let me go first to bury my father."

Jesus said, "Let the dead bury their dead. You need to go and preach the kingdom of God."

Another told him, "Lord, I will follow you, but first let me go home and say farewell to my family."

Jesus said, "No man, having put his hand to the plow and then looking back, is fit for the kingdom of God."[274]

As time was growing short, Jesus appointed seventy men to serve as missionaries. He sent them in pairs before him, to those places he would go. This prepared his way and gave more men training. He told them, "The harvest is great, but the laborers are few. Pray to the Lord of the harvest, that he will send more laborers to his harvest. I send you forth as lambs among wolves. Don't carry a purse, money, or shoes. Don't stop to chat along the way, your message is urgent. Whatever house you enter in, first say, 'Peace be to this house.' If the son of peace be there, your peace shall rest on it. If not, it shall turn to you again.

"Stay in the same house, eating and drinking the things they give you. Laborers are worthy of their hire, so don't go from house

---

[273] Luke 9:51-56
[274] Matthew 8:19-22; Luke 9:57-62

FEAST OF THE TABERNACLES

to house. In whatever city you enter and they receive you, eat the things that are set before you. Heal the sick that are there and say to them, 'The kingdom of God has come near you.' Whatever city you enter and they don't receive you, go your way out into the streets of it and say, 'The very dust of your city, which clings to us, we do wipe off against you.' But be sure of this, the kingdom of God has come near to you."[275]

When the Seventy returned, they were joyful, saying, "Lord, even the devils are subject to us through your name."

Jesus said, "I beheld Satan as lightning fall from heaven. I give to you power to tread on serpents and scorpions, and over all the power of the enemy. Nothing in any way shall hurt you. Don't rejoice because the spirits are subject to you, but rather rejoice, because your names are written in heaven."

Jesus rejoiced at their return and prayed to his Father, "I thank you, O Father, Lord of heaven and earth, that you have hid these things from those who think they are wise and prudent, and have revealed them to babes, because, Father, it seemed good in your sight."

He turned to his disciples and said, "Blessed are the eyes which see the things you see. Many prophets and kings have desired to see and hear the things which you see and hear and have not seen and heard them. All things my Father has are given to me. No one knows the Son, but the Father and no one knows the Father, but the Son, and to whom the Son will reveal Him."

A lawyer stood up to test him and said, "Master, what shall I do to inherit eternal life?"

Jesus said, "What is written in the law? How do you understand it?"

He answered, "You shall love the Lord, your God, with all your heart, with all your soul, with all your strength, and with all your mind; and your neighbor as yourself."

Jesus said, "You have answered well. Do this and you shall live."

The lawyer, wanting to justify himself after answering his own question, asked, "Who is my neighbor?"

Jesus said, "A man went down from Jerusalem to Jericho and was attacked by thieves, who stripped him of his clothes, wounded him, and left, leaving him half dead. By chance, a priest came that way and, when he saw him lying on the roadside, went by

---

[275] Luke 10:1-11

him on the other side. Also, a Levite came to the place and looked at him, but also passed by on the other side. Next, a Samaritan on a journey came to the spot and, when he saw him, had compassion on him. He went to him and bound up his wounds, pouring in oil and wine. He set him on his own animal, brought him to an inn, and took care of him. The next day when he left, he gave the host two hundred dollars and said to him, 'Take care of him and whatever more you spend, I will repay you when I come again.'

"Now, which one of these do you think was neighbor to him that was attacked by the thieves?"

The lawyer said, "He that showed mercy on him."

Jesus said, "Go and do likewise."

Later, they went to Bethany, where a woman called Martha invited him into her house. She had a sister, Mary, who sat at Jesus' feet and listened to him. Martha was busy serving and came to him and said, "Lord, don't you care that my sister has left me to serve all by myself? Tell her to help me."

Jesus said, "Martha, Martha, you're worried about many things. But one thing is needed and Mary has chosen that good thing, which shall not be taken away from her."[276]

"Which of you shall have a friend and, if you go to him at midnight and say, 'Friend, lend me three loaves. A friend of mine in his journey has come to me and I have nothing to feed him.' He within his house will say, 'Don't bother me; the door is locked and my children and I are sleeping. I cannot get up and give them to you.' Though he doesn't want to get up and give them to him, because he is his friend, he will rise and give him as many as he needs. Ask and it shall be given you. Seek and you shall find. Knock and it shall be opened to you. For every one that asks, receives and they that seek shall find. To them that knock, it shall be opened."

"If a son shall ask bread of any of you that are fathers, will you give him a stone? Or if he asks for a fish, will you give him a serpent? Or if he asks for an egg, will you offer him a scorpion? If you, then, being evil, know how to give good gifts to your children, how much more shall your heavenly Father be willing to give the Holy Spirit to them that ask him?"

They brought a man to him who couldn't speak. He cast a devil out of him and, when the devil was gone, he spoke. The people were amazed at this, as they thought this was impossible. Some said

---

[276] Luke 10:17-42

FEAST OF THE TABERNACLES

it was by Beelzebub, the chief of the devils, that it was done. Some of them wanted a sign from him.

The scribes and Pharisees had said so many times it was through Beelzebub Jesus could cast out devils, the people believed it. He knew many were thinking this and, once again, said, "Every kingdom divided against itself is brought to desolation. A house divided against itself falls. You say I cast out devils through Beelzebub; if Satan is divided against himself, how shall his kingdom stand? If I by Beelzebub cast out devils, by whom do your sons cast them out? They shall be your judges. If I with the finger of God cast out devils, the kingdom of God has come to you."[277]

As he was talking, a woman in the group raised her voice and said, "Blessed is the womb that bore you and the breasts you sucked."

Jesus said, "Yes, but rather, blessed are they that hear the word of God and keep it."[278]

"No one, when they light a candle, puts it in a secret place, neither under a bushel, but on a candlestick, that they which come in may see the light. The light of the body is the eye. Therefore, when your eye is focused on right, your whole body is full of light, but when your eye is focused on evil, your whole body is full of darkness. Be careful the light which is in you isn't darkness. If your whole body is full of light, having no part dark, then the whole shall be full of light, as when the bright shining of a candle, gives you light."

As he spoke, a Pharisee asked him to dine with him. He went in without ceremonially washing his hands and sat down to eat. When the Pharisee saw it, he was amazed he had not ceremonially washed, as the custom was before eating. Jesus said, "You Pharisees clean the outside of the cup and the platter, but your inward part is full of plunder and wickedness. You fools, didn't He that made the outside, make the inside too? Wouldn't it be better to give charity and do right, that the inside would be clean, too? Woe to you Pharisees! You tithe mint, rue and all manner of herbs, but pass over judgment and the love of God. These you ought to have done, and not have left the other undone. Woe to you Pharisees! You love the best seats in the synagogues and greetings in the markets. Woe to you scribes and Pharisees, hypocrites! You are as graves which appear not, and those that walk over them are not aware of them."

---

[277] Luke 11:5-20
[278] Luke 11:27-28

FEAST OF THE TABERNACLES

One of the lawyers said, "Master, what you said is a denunciation of lawyers also."

Jesus said, "Woe to you also, you lawyers! For you load people with burdens grievous to be carried and you, yourselves, would not touch the burdens with one of your fingers. Woe to you! For you build the sepulchers of the prophets, and your fathers killed them. Truly, you bear witness that you approve of the deeds of your fathers. They, indeed, killed them and you build their sepulchers. The wisdom of God said, 'I will send them prophets and apostles. Some of them they will kill and some persecute, that the blood of all the prophets, which was shed from the foundation of the world, may be required of this generation.

"From the blood of Abel to the blood of Zacharias, *the father of John, the Baptist*, who perished between the altar and the temple, it shall be required of this generation. Woe to you lawyers! You have taken away the key of knowledge. You didn't accept the commandments of God and hindered those that wanted to learn and keep them."

As he said these things to them, the scribes and Pharisees began to get angry at him and tried to provoke him to say something, so they could accuse him.[279]

Meanwhile, a very large crowd had gathered, so large they were stepping on one another. As he took a break, he said to his disciples, "Beware of the leaven of the Pharisees, which is hypocrisy. There is nothing covered that shall not be revealed, neither hid, that shall not be known. Whatever you have spoken in darkness, shall be heard in the light, and that which you have spoken in the ear in closets, shall be proclaimed upon the housetops. I tell you, my friends, 'Be not afraid of them that kill the body, and after have no more they can do. But I warn you whom you shall fear: Fear them, which after they have killed, have power to cast into hell.' Yes, I tell you, 'Fear them.' Are not five sparrows sold for a dollar and a half and not one of them is forgotten before God? Even the very hairs of your head, are all numbered. Don't be afraid; you are more valuable than many sparrows. Also, whoever shall testify of me before men, they shall the Son of Man also testify of before the angels of God. But they, who deny me before men, shall be denied before the angels of God.

"Whoever shall speak a word against the Son of Man, it shall be forgiven them, if they repent. But to them that blasphemed against

---

[279] Luke 11:33-54

the Holy Ghost, it shall not be forgiven. When they bring you to the synagogues, to the magistrates, and other powerful people, don't take any thought about what you should answer or what you should say; for the Holy Ghost shall tell you in that time what you should say."

One of the group said, "Master, tell my brother to divide our inheritance with me."

Jesus said, "Who made me a judge or a divider over you?"

He spoke to the crowd, "Take care and beware of covetousness. A person's life is not about the things they have. A rich man had land that grew abundant crops. He thought to himself, 'What shall I do, because I have no room to store my crops?' He decided to pull down his barns and build bigger ones to hold all his crops and goods. He thought, I will say to myself, 'I have a lot of things saved for many years. I will take it easy and enjoy the good life, eating, drinking, and making merry.'"

"But God said to him, 'You fool, this night your soul shall be required of you. Then, whose shall those things be, which you have provided?' So it is with those that lay up treasure for themselves, and are not rich with God."

He said to his disciples, "I tell you to take no thought for your life, what you shall eat, neither for the body, what you shall put on. Life is more than food, and the body is more than clothing. Think about the ravens. They don't sow or reap and don't have a barn or storehouse. God feeds them. Aren't you much better than the fowls? Which of you by taking thought can add to his height one foot? If you can't do that small thing, why think about the rest? Look at the lilies, how they grow. They don't work or spin, yet I tell you that Solomon in all his glory was not dressed like one of these. If God clothes the grass, which today is in the field and tomorrow is cast into an oven, how much more will he clothe you? Oh, you of little faith.

"Seek not what you shall eat or what you shall drink. Don't let it worry you. For all these things do the nations of the world seek after, and your Father knows that you need these things.

"But rather seek you the kingdom of God and all these things shall be added to you. Don't be afraid, little flock; it is your Father's pleasure to give you the kingdom. Sell what you have and give charity; provide yourselves savings, which will not age, and a treasure in heaven that will last, where no thief will come and no moth will destroy it. For where your treasure is, there will your heart be also.

"Be dressed and ready with your lights burning, like those waiting for their lord when he will return from the wedding. That when he comes and knocks, they may open to him immediately. Blessed are those servants whom the lord, when he comes, shall find watching. I tell you that he shall dress and invite them to sit down to eat, and will come and serve them. If he comes at night or early in the morning before dawn, and finds them prepared, blessed are those servants. This know, that if the master of the house had known what hour the thief would come, he would have watched and not have suffered his house to be broken into. You be ready also, for the Son of Man comes at a time when you think he won't."

Peter said to him, "Lord, is this parable for us or for all?"

The Lord said, "Who then is that faithful and wise steward, whom his lord shall make ruler over his household, to give his servants their portion of food at the proper times? Blessed is that servant whom his lord, when he comes, shall find so doing. Truly I tell you that he will make him ruler over all that he has. But if that servant says in his heart, 'My lord delays his coming,' and shall begin to beat the servants and to eat and drink and be drunken, the lord will come in a day and hour when he doesn't expect him. He will fire him and appoint his portion with the unbelievers.

"The servant, who knew his lord's will and didn't prepare himself, nor did his will, shall be beaten with many stripes. But he that didn't know and did do things worthy of stripes shall be beaten with few stripes. For those to whom much is given, of them shall much be required, and to whom much has been committed, of them more will be asked.

"I am come to send fire on the earth; what do I care if it is already started? I came and was baptized for a purpose and I will accomplish that purpose, no matter how hard it is. Do you suppose I have come to bring peace on earth? I tell you, no; rather division. From now on, there shall be five in one house divided, three against two and two against three. The father shall be divided against the son and the son against the father; the mother against the daughter and the daughter against the mother; the mother-in-law against her daughter-in-law and the daughter-in-law against her mother-in-law."

He also said, "When you see a cloud rise out of the west, you right away say, 'A shower is coming,' and it does. When you see the south wind blow, you say, 'It will be warm,' and it is. You hypocrites, you understand the signs of the sky and the earth, how is it that you don't see the signs of these times today? Yes, and why don't even you judge what is right?

"When you go to the magistrate with your adversary, as you go, try hard to make an agreement with them. Otherwise, they may take you to a judge and the judge will deliver you to an officer, who will put you in prison. I say you shall not get out until you have paid the very last penny."[280]

ROMAN UPRISING

One of the crowd asked Jesus, "Did you hear about the demonstration they had at the temple last month? *It was put down by Roman soldiers. There were a few Galileans that were killed by the altar,* so their blood mingled with the blood of the animals being sacrificed."

Jesus said, "Do you suppose those Galileans were sinners above all the Galileans, because that happened to them? I tell you, no. But unless you repent, you all shall likewise perish. Or those eighteen, on whom the tower in Siloam fell and killed, do you think they were sinners above all those that live in Jerusalem? I tell you no, but unless you repent, you shall all likewise perish."

Next, he told them a parable, "A man had a fig tree planted in his vineyard and, when he came looking for fruit, there wasn't any. He said to the dresser of his vineyard, "Look, these last three years I have looked for fruit on this fig tree and there hasn't been any. Cut it down! Why should it take up space?"

His dresser said, "Lord, let it alone this year also, until I dig about it and fertilize it. If it bears fruit, it will be good. If it doesn't, cut it down."

Jesus was teaching in one of the synagogues on a Sabbath. There was a woman who had a spinal deformity for eighteen years. She was bent together and couldn't straighten up. When Jesus saw her, he called her to him and said, "Woman, you are released from your problem."

He laid his hands on her and immediately she was made straight and glorified God. The ruler of the synagogue was mad, because Jesus had healed her on the Sabbath day. He said to the people, "There are six days in which people ought to work. In them, come and be healed, and not on the Sabbath."

The Lord said, "You hypocrite! Doesn't each of you on the Sabbath free his ox or his ass from the stall and lead them away to

---

[280] Luke 12

water? Ought not this woman, being a daughter of Abraham, whom Satan has bound these eighteen years, be freed from the bond on the Sabbath?"

When he said this, all his adversaries were ashamed. All the people rejoiced for all the glorious things that were done by him.

He said, "What is the kingdom of God like? To what shall I liken it? It is like a grain of mustard seed, which a man took and planted in his garden. It grew and became a great tree and the fowls of the air nested in its branches." He said, "To what shall I liken it? It is like leaven, which a woman took and mixed in three measures of meal and the whole was leavened."

He went through the cities and villages, teaching as he journeyed to Jerusalem. Someone asked him, "Lord, are there few that are saved?"

He said, "Work hard to enter in at the narrow gate, for I tell you, many will try to enter in there and shall not be able. When the master of the house has risen and shut the door, you will come and begin to knock at the door, saying, ' Lord, Lord, open the door to us.' And he shall say, 'I don't know you.'"

"You shall say, 'We have dined with you and you have taught in our streets.'

"But he shall say, 'I tell you, I don't know you. Go away, all you workers of evil.'

"There shall be weeping and gnashing of teeth, when you shall see Abraham, Isaac, Jacob, and all the prophets in the kingdom of God and yourselves thrust out. They shall come from the east, the west, the north, the south, and shall sit down in the kingdom of God. Behold, there are last, who shall be first and there are first, who shall be last."

Some Pharisees came to him, saying "Go away from here, for Herod will kill you."

Jesus said, "Go tell that fox, 'I cast out devils and I do cures today and tomorrow, and the next day I shall be perfected. Nevertheless, I must walk today, tomorrow, and the next day; for it cannot be that a prophet will perish outside of Jerusalem.'

"Oh, Jerusalem, Jerusalem, which kills the prophets and stones them that are sent to you; how often I would have gathered your children together, as a hen gathers her brood under her wings and you wouldn't. See, your house is left to you empty and, truly, you shall not see me, until the time comes when you shall say, 'Blessed is he that comes in the name of the Lord.'"[281]

Later, he went into the house of one of the chief Pharisees to eat bread on the Sabbath, and they watched him to see what he would do.

There was a man there that had edema, a swelling of tissue. Jesus, knowing he was being set up, said to the lawyers and Pharisees, "Is it lawful to heal on the Sabbath?"

No one answered, so Jesus took him, healed him, and let him go.

He then said, "Which of you shall have an ass or an ox fall into a pit and will not right away pull it out on the Sabbath?"

Again, no one answered.

He noticed how those who were invited chose out the places of honor to sit and said, "When you are invited by someone to a wedding, don't sit down in the most honorable seat, in case a more honorable person than you has been invited. So, when the host and that person come, they don't say to you, 'Give this person your seat,' and you begin with shame to take the least honorable seat. But when you are invited, go and take the lowest seat, that when the host comes, they may say to you, 'Friend, take the higher seat.' Then you shall have honor from those who are sitting with you. Whoever exalts themselves shall be abased, and those who humble themselves shall be exalted."

Then Jesus said to his host, "When you have a dinner or a supper, don't call your friends, nor your brother, nor your relatives, nor your rich neighbors, that they don't invite you back and thus pay back the invitation. But when you make a feast, call the poor, the maimed, the lame, and the blind. Then you shall be blessed, for they cannot pay you back, but you shall be compensated at the resurrection of the just."

When one of them sitting at the meal heard these things, he said, "Blessed is he that shall eat in the kingdom of God."

Jesus said, "A man made a great supper and invited many. He sent his servant at supper time to say to them that were invited, 'Come, for all things are ready.' But they all began to make excuses not to come. The first said, 'I have bought some land and I have to go to look at it, please excuse me.' Another said, 'I bought five yokes of oxen and I need to prove them. Please excuse me.' Another said, 'I have just gotten married and cannot come.'

---

[281] Luke 13

"The servant reported these things to his lord who, being very angry, said to his servant, 'Hurry and go out into the streets and lanes of the city and bring here the poor, the maimed, the crippled, and the blind.' The servant did so and told his lord, 'I have done as you commanded and still there is room.'

"The lord said to the servant, 'Go out to the highway and pathways and urge those you find to come, that my house may be filled. I tell you that none of those that were invited shall taste of my supper.'"[282]

***

There was a great crowd and Jesus spoke to them, "If anyone comes to me and hates not their father, mother, wife, husband, children, brothers, sisters, and yes, their own life, or in other words, is afraid to lay down their life for my sake, they cannot be my disciple. Also, whoever does not bear their cross and come after me cannot be my disciple. Therefore, decide in your hearts that you will do the things which I shall teach and command you.[283]

"Which of you, intending to build something, doesn't first determine the cost, to see if you can afford to build it. That way, after you have started to build, you won't find that you don't have enough to finish it, and be mocked by all that see it unfinished, saying, 'These began to build, but didn't have enough to finish.'

"Or what king, going to war against another king, doesn't sit down first and decide whether he will be able, with ten thousand men, to meet those that are coming against him with twenty thousand? Or else, when the other is yet far away, he sends an ambassador and desires conditions of peace. Likewise, whoever it is, will not forsake all they have, cannot be my disciple.

"Salt is good, but if the salt has lost its taste, how will the food be seasoned? It is not fit for the land nor the dunghill, but men cast it out. They that have ears to hear, let them hear."[284]

The crowd drew near him, and there were tax collectors and sinners there. The Pharisees and scribes murmured and said, "This man receives sinners and eats with them."

Jesus said this parable to them, "Which one of you, having a hundred sheep, if you lose one of them, will not leave the ninety and nine in the wilderness, and go after that which is lost, until you find it? And when you find it, you put it on your shoulders rejoicing.

---

[282] Luke 14:1-25
[283] JST Luke 14:26-27
[284] Luke 14:28-35

When you come home, you call together your friends and neighbors, saying, 'Rejoice with me, for I have found my sheep which was lost.'

"I say to you, likewise joy shall be in heaven over one sinner who repents, more than over ninety and nine just persons which need no repentance.

"Either what woman having ten pieces of silver, if she loses one piece, doesn't light a candle and sweep the house, and seek diligently until she finds it? And when she has found it, she calls her friends and her neighbors together, saying, 'Rejoice with me, for I have found the piece which I had lost.'

"Likewise, I tell you, there is joy in the presence of the angels of God over one sinner who repents."

He also said,

"A man had two sons. The younger of them said to his father, 'Father, give me the portion of your goods that will be coming to me.' The father divided to him his portion. A short time later, the younger son gathered all his things and moved to a far country. There he wasted his inheritance with riotous living. When he had spent it all, there came a mighty famine in that land and he began to be in want. He took a job with a citizen of the country and his job was to go into the fields to feed swine. He was so hungry that he wanted to eat the pods the swine ate, but no one gave to him.

"When he came to himself, he said, 'How many hired servants of my father have food enough and to spare and I am dying with hunger? I will return to my father and will say to him, 'Father, I have sinned against heaven and against you. I am no longer worthy to be called your son. Make me as one of your hired servants.'"

"He returned to his father, but when he was still a long way off, his father, who continued daily to look for him, saw him and had compassion on him, and ran, and fell on his neck and kissed him.

"His son said to him, 'Father, I have sinned against heaven and in your sight. I am no longer worthy to be called your son.'

"But the father said, 'Bring out the best robe and put it on him. Put a ring on his hand and shoes on his feet. Bring forth the fatted calf and kill it, and let us eat and be merry: For this my son was dead and is alive. He was lost and is found.' And they began to be merry.

"His oldest son was in the field and, as he came near the house, he heard music and dancing. He called one of the servants and asked what was going on. The servant said, 'Your brother has come and your father has killed the fatted calf, because he is home safe and sound.'

"The oldest son was angry when he heard this and wouldn't go into the house. His father came out and asked him to come in. His son said, 'I have served you these many years and have not transgressed at any time what you asked me to do. Yet you have never given me as much as a kid, that I might make merry with my friends. But as soon as this son of yours was come, which has devoured your living with harlots, you have killed the fatted calf for him.'

"His father said, 'Son you are always with me and all that I have is yours. It was proper that we should make merry and be glad; for this your brother was dead and is alive, was lost and is found.'"[285]

That night, Simon said to Jesus, "Somehow it seems wrong that the prodigal son wasted his inheritance, yet he was able to come back into the family as though nothing happened."

Jesus said, "In my Father's kingdom, there is more than enough for all. All this you can have, but as in the case of the prodigal son, all that is lost one cannot have. All that the father has is the prodigal's brother's, except his love."

He said to his disciples, "There was a rich man, who had a steward and it was reported to him that his steward wasted his goods. He called in the steward and said, 'How is it I hear this account of you? Give me an account of your stewardship; perhaps you may no longer be my steward.'

"When the lord found out that his steward had been wasteful, he was going to put him out of his stewardship, just as soon as he could replace him. Knowing this, the steward said to himself, 'When my master takes away my stewardship, what shall I do? I don't want to dig ditches and I am ashamed to beg. Hmm, I know what I'm going to do. I will enrich his debtors, so they may want to hire me.'

"He called all his lord's debtors to him and said to the first, 'How much do you owe my lord?'

"The debtor said, 'One hundred measures of oil.'

---

[285] Luke 15

"The steward said, 'Take your bill, write fifty, and I will call it paid in full.'

"He said to another, 'How much do you owe?'

"That debtor told the steward, 'A hundred measures of wheat.'

"The steward said, 'Take your bill, write eighty, and I will call it paid in full.'

"His lord commended the unjust steward, because he had done wisely for himself."

Jesus said, "The worldly children of this generation are wiser than the righteous children. I tell you, make friends of the worldly, that when you fail, they will receive you into their everlasting habitations. Those that are faithful in that which is least, are also faithful in that which is much, and he that is unjust in the least, is unjust also in much. If you haven't been faithful in worldly things, who will commit to your trust the true riches of eternity? If you haven't been faithful in that which is another's, who shall give you that which is your own? No servant can serve two masters, for either they will hate the one, and love the other; or else they will love the one, and despise the other. You cannot serve God and money."

The Pharisees, who were lovers of worldly things, overheard him tell his disciples these things and derided him for it.

Jesus said, "You are those I am speaking about. You justify yourselves before the world, but God knows your hearts. That which is highly esteemed by the world, is an abomination in the sight of God."[286]

They said to him, "We have the law and the prophets. But you we will not receive to be our ruler, for you make yourself to be a judge over us."

Jesus said, "The law and the prophets testify of me. Yes, and all the prophets who have written, even until John, have foretold of these days. Since that time, the kingdom of God is preached and every man who seeks truth presses into it. It is easier for heaven and earth to pass, than for one title of the law to fail. Why do you teach the law and deny that which is written; and condemn him whom the Father has sent to fulfill the law, that you might all be redeemed?

"O fools! You have said in your hearts, 'There is no God.' And you pervert the gospel and the kingdom of heaven suffers violence, because of you. You persecute the meek, and in your

---

[286] Luke 16:1-15

violence, you seek to destroy the kingdom, and you take the children of the kingdom by force. Woe to you, you adulterers!"

They reviled him again, being angry at the saying that they were adulterers.

He continued, saying, "Truly I say to you, I will liken you to the rich man, who was clothed in purple and fine linen and fared sumptuously every day. There was also a beggar named Lazarus, who was laid at his gate, full of sores. He desired to be fed with the crumbs which fell from the rich man's table. Moreover, the dogs came and licked his sores. It came to pass the beggar died and was carried by angels into Abraham's bosom. The rich man also died and was buried. In hell, the rich man lifted up his eyes, being in torments, and saw Abraham far off, with Lazarus in his bosom. He called and said, 'Father Abraham, have mercy on me and send Lazarus, that he may dip the tip of his finger in water and cool my tongue; for I am tormented in this flame.'

"But Abraham said, 'Son, remember that you in your lifetime received good things and likewise Lazarus evil things, but now he is comforted and you are tormented. Beside all this, between us and you there is a great gulf, that they which would pass from here to you cannot. Neither can you come here.

"Then the rich man said, 'Please, Abraham, send to my father's house: for I have five brothers; that he may testify to them, lest they also come to this place of torment.'

"Abraham said, 'They have Moses and the prophets. Let them hear them.'

"He said, 'No, Father Abraham, if one went to them from the dead, they would repent.'

"Abraham said, 'If they will not hear Moses and the prophets, neither will they be persuaded, though one would rise from the dead.'[287]

"It is impossible that offenses won't come from sinners, but woe to those from whom they come. It would be better for them that a millstone was hung about their neck and they were cast into the sea, than that they should hurt one of these little ones," he said to his disciples as he pointed to a child.

"Take heed to yourselves. If your brother trespasses against you, rebuke him and, if he repents, forgive him. If he trespasses against you seven times in a day and seven times in a day turns again to you and says, 'I repent,' you shall forgive him."

---

[287] Luke 16:19-31

The apostles said to him, "Increase our faith."

The Lord said, "If you had faith as a grain of mustard seed, you might say to this sycamore tree, 'Be pulled up by the root and be planted in the sea, and it would obey you.'

"Which of you, having a servant plowing or feeding cattle, will say to them, by and by, when they have come from the field, 'Go and sit down to eat?'

"Would you not say to them, 'Make ready my supper, change your clothes, and serve me, until I have eaten and drunk, and afterward you shall eat and drink'?

"Will he thank that servant because he did the things commanded him? I don't think so. Likewise, you, when you have done all those things which the Lord commands you, you can say, 'We are unprofitable servants. We have done that which was our duty to do.'"

On his way to Jerusalem, Jesus passed through the midst of Samaria and Galilee. As he entered a village, ten men who were lepers stood far away. They called loudly, saying, "Jesus, Master, have mercy on us."

When he saw them, he said, "Go show yourselves to the priests."

It happened that as they went, they were cleansed. One of them, when he saw that he was healed, turned back and with a loud voice glorified God, fell at Jesus' feet, and thanked him, and he was a Samaritan.

Jesus said, "Weren't there ten cleansed? Where are the other nine? There are none found who returned to give glory to God, except this stranger."

He said to him, "Arise, go on your way. Your faith has made you whole."

The Pharisees demanded him to tell them when the kingdom of God should come. He said, "The kingdom of God doesn't come with observation. No one shall say, 'It is here,' or 'It is there,' for the kingdom of God is within you."

Jesus said to his disciples, "The days will come, when you shall desire to see one of the days of the Son of Man and you shall not see it. They shall say to you, 'See here,' or 'See there.' Don't go after them, nor follow them. For as lightning that lightens out of one part of the sky shines to another part of the sky, so shall the Son of Man be when he comes. But first, he must suffer many things and be rejected by this generation. As it was in the days of Noah, so shall it be in the days of the Son of Man. They ate, they drank, they married wives, and they were given in marriage, until the day Noah entered the ark. Then the flood came, and destroyed them all.

"Likewise, it was in the days of Lot. They ate, they drank, they bought, they sold, they planted, and they built. But the same day that Lot went out of Sodom, it rained fire and brimstone from heaven and destroyed them all. Thus, shall it be in the day when the Son of Man is revealed. In that day, those who shall be upon the housetop, with their things in the house, let them not come down to take them. Likewise, those that are in the field, don't return. Whoever shall seek to save his life shall lose it, and whoever shall lose his life shall preserve it. I tell you, in that night there shall be two in one bed; the one shall be taken and the other left. Two women shall be grinding together; the one shall be taken and the other left."

They said, "Where, Lord?"

He said, "Wherever the body is, there will the eagles be gathered."[288]

He spoke a parable to them to show that we always should pray and not despair, saying, "There was in a city a judge, which feared not God, nor regarded man. There also was a widow there and she came to him, saying, 'Give me justice against my adversary.'

"The judge would not for a while, but afterward he said to himself, 'Though I fear not God, nor regard man, yet I will give her justice as she wearies me by constantly coming to me and nagging me for justice.'"

Jesus said, "Pay attention to what the unjust judge said. Shall not God give justice to those that are his, who cry day and night to him, though it takes a long time? I tell you he will do it speedily. Nevertheless, when the Son of Man comes, shall he find faith on the earth?"

He spoke this parable for those which trusted in themselves that they were righteous and despised others, saying, "Two men went up to the temple to pray, one a Pharisee and the other a tax collector.

"The Pharisee stood and prayed as follows, 'God, I thank you that I am not as other men are, extortionists, unjust, adulterers, or even as this tax collector. I fast twice a week and give tithes of all that I have.'

"The tax collector, standing far away, would not lift up so much as his eyes to heaven, but struck his chest, saying, 'God be merciful to me, a sinner.'

---

[288] Luke 17

"I tell you, the tax collector went home to his house justified, rather than the Pharisee. Everyone that exalts themselves shall be abased, and they that humble themselves shall be exalted."[289]

A Pharisee, tempting him, asked, "Is it lawful for a man to divorce his wife for any cause?"

He answered, "Haven't you read, that he which made them at the beginning, made them male and female, and said, 'For this cause shall a man leave father and mother, shall stay fast by his wife, and the two of them shall be one flesh'? Therefore, they aren't two anymore, but one flesh. What God has joined together, let not man separate."

They asked, "Why did Moses then command to give a divorce, before separating?"

He said, "Because of the hardness of your hearts, he allowed you to divorce your wives. But from the beginning it wasn't that way. I tell you, whoever shall divorce his wife, except for fornication and shall marry another, commits adultery. Also, whoever marries her who is divorced, commits adultery."

Later, in the house, his disciples asked him about this, "If marriage is so strict, it sounds like one shouldn't marry."

He said, "All cannot do this, except those to whom it is given. There are some that are eunuchs who were born that way; some eunuchs were made eunuchs by others; some eunuchs made themselves eunuchs, for the kingdom of heaven's sake. Those that can receive it, let them receive it."[290]

They brought to him infants, that he would touch them, but when his disciples saw it, they rebuked them. But Jesus called them to him saying, "Allow little children to come to me and forbid them not; for of such is the kingdom of God. Truly I tell you, 'Whoever shall not receive the kingdom of God as a little child, shall in no way enter in there.'"[291]

A ruler asked him, "Good Master, what shall I do to inherit eternal life?"

Jesus said, "Why do you call me good? No one is good, except God. You know the commandments. Do not commit adultery. Do not kill. Do not steal. Do not bear false witness. Honor your father and mother."

The ruler said, "All these have I kept from my youth up."

---

[289] Luke 18:1-14
[290] Matthew 19:3-12; Mark 10:2-12
[291] Matthew 19:13-15; Mark 10:13-15; Luke 18:15-17

When Jesus heard this, he said, "Yet you lack one thing. Sell all that you have and distribute to the poor and you shall have treasure in heaven; and come, follow me."

When he heard this, the ruler was very sad, as he was very rich.

Jesus said to his disciples, "Truly I say that a rich man shall hardly ever enter into the kingdom of heaven. It is easier for a camel to go through the eye of a needle than for a rich man to enter into the kingdom of God."

When his disciples heard this, they were amazed and said, "Who then can be saved?"

Jesus said, "With men this is impossible, but with God all things are possible."

This prompted Peter to ask, "We have given up everything and followed you. What will we have for doing this?"

Jesus said, "I tell you that there is no one that has left house, or brothers, or sisters, or father, or mother, or spouse, or children, and lands for my sake and the gospel's, but they shall receive a hundredfold now in this time, houses, and brothers, and sisters, and mothers, and children, and lands, with their problems; and in the world to come eternal life. You shall sit upon twelve thrones, judging the twelve tribes of Israel.[292] But there are many who make themselves first, who shall be last and the last first." This he said, rebuking Peter.[293]

Jesus said, "The kingdom of heaven is like a man that owned a vineyard. He went out early in the morning to hire laborers to work in it. When he had agreed with the laborers for one hundred dollars a day, he sent them into his vineyard. He went out about nine am and saw others standing idle in the marketplace and said to them, 'Go also to my vineyard and whatever is right I will pay you.' So they went to the vineyard.

"Again, he went out about noon and about three pm and did likewise. About five pm he went out and found others standing idle and said to them, 'Why are you standing here all day idle?'

"They said, 'Because no one has hired us.'

"He said, 'Go to my vineyard, and whatever is right you shall receive.'

---

[292] Matthew 19:16-30; Mark 10:17-30; Luke 18:18-30
[293] JST Mark 10:31

"When evening came, the lord of the vineyard said to his steward, 'Call the laborers and give them their pay, beginning from the last to the first.' When those came who were hired the last hour, each received one hundred dollars. When the first came, they supposed that they would receive more, but they also received one hundred dollars. When they had been paid, they complained to the vineyard owner, saying, 'These last have only worked one hour and you have made them equal to us, which have borne the burden and the heat of the day.'

"He answered one of them, 'Friend, I did no wrong. Didn't you agree with me for one hundred dollars? Take what you earned and go on your way. I will pay the last, even as I did you. Is it not lawful for me to do what I will with my money? Is what you see evil, because I am good?'"

Jesus said, "The last shall be first and the first last. Many are called, but few are chosen."[294]

THE FEAST OF DEDICATION

Jesus went up to Jerusalem for the Feast of Dedication his last winter. As Jesus walked in the temple in Solomon's porch, the Jews thronged him and said, "How long will you make us doubt? If you are the Christ, tell us plainly."

Jesus said, "I told you and you didn't believe. The works I do in my Father's name, they bear witness of me. But you don't believe, because you are not of my sheep, as I told you. My sheep hear my voice and I know them and they follow me. And I give them eternal life and they shall never perish, neither shall any man pluck them out of my hand. My Father, which gave them to me, is greater than all and no one can pluck them out of my Father's hand. I and my Father are one (*meaning one in spirit*)."

The Jews took up stones again to stone him. Jesus asked them, "Many good works have I showed you from my Father. For which of those works do you stone me?"

They answered, "We don't stone you for a good work, but for blasphemy and because you, a man, make yourself God."

Jesus said, "Is it not written in your law, 'I said, "You are Gods?"' If he called them gods, to whom the word of God came and the scripture cannot be untrue; say you of him, whom the Father has

---

[294] Matthew 20:1-16

THE FEAST OF DEDICATION

sanctified and sent to the world, that he speaks blasphemy, because I said, 'I am the Son of God?' If I don't do the works of my Father, don't believe me. But if I do, though you don't believe me, believe the works; that you may know and believe, that the Father is in me and me in Him."

Therefore, they tried again to take him, but he escaped and went away again, beyond Jordan into the place where John at first baptized and there he lived. Many came to him and said, "John did no miracles, but all things that John spoke of this man are true." And many believed on him there.[295]

Jesus had lived there awhile when Martha and her sister Mary (who would anoint the Lord with ointment and wipe his feet with her hair) sent word to him. They said, "Our brother, Lazarus, whom you love is sick." For Jesus loved Martha, her sister, and Lazarus, who lived in Bethany.

When Jesus heard that, he said, "The sickness is not to death, but for the glory of God, that the Son of God might be glorified by it."

When he heard Lazarus was sick, he waited two days where he was. Then he told his disciples, "Let's go into Judea again."

His disciples said, "Master, the Jews just tried to stone you; why are you going there again?"

Jesus said, "Aren't there twelve working hours in a day? If anyone walks in the daylight, they don't stumble, because they have the light of this world. But if a person walks in the night, they stumble, because there is no light in them."

He said these things and afterwards, said, "Our friend Lazarus sleeps, but I go that I may awake him out of sleep."

His disciples said, "Lord, if he sleeps, he shall do well."

But Jesus spoke of his death, but they thought he had spoken of taking a rest in sleep.

Then said Jesus plainly, "Lazarus is dead. And I am glad for your sakes that I was not there, so you may believe. Nevertheless, let's go to him."

Then said Thomas, who is called Didymus by his fellow disciples, "Let us also go, that we may die with him."

When they arrived in Bethany at Martha's house, they found Lazarus had already been in the grave four days. Bethany was near Jerusalem, about two miles away. Many of the Jews came to Martha and Mary, to comfort them concerning their brother.

---

[295] John 10:22-42

THE FEAST OF DEDICATION

Martha, as soon as she heard that Jesus was coming, went and met him, but Mary stayed in the house. Martha said to Jesus, "Lord, if you had been here, my brother would not have died. But I know even now, whatever you will ask of God, God will give it to you."

Jesus said, "Your brother shall rise again."

Martha said, "I know he shall rise again in the resurrection at the last day."

Jesus said, "I am the resurrection and the life: those who believe in me, though they are dead, yet shall they live. And whoever lives and believes in me shall never die. Do you believe this?"

She said, "Yes, Lord. I believe you are the Christ, the Son of God, who should come into the world." She then went home and called Mary. her sister, secretly, saying, "The Master has come and is asking for you."

As soon as she heard that, she left and went to him. Jesus hadn't yet come into the town, but was in the place where Martha met him. The Jews who were with her in the house comforting her, when they saw Mary leave hastily, followed her, saying, "She is going to the grave to weep there."

When Mary came to Jesus and saw him, she fell at his feet, saying, "Lord, if you had been here, my brother wouldn't have died."

When Jesus saw her weeping and the Jews also weeping who came with her, he groaned in the spirit, was troubled, and said, "Where have you laid him?"

They said, "Come and see."

Jesus wept.

The Jews then said, "Look how he loved him!"

Some of them said, "Could not this man, which opened the eyes of the blind, have caused that even this man should not have died?"

Jesus, again groaning in himself, came to the grave. It was a cave and a stone lay before it.

Jesus said, "Take away the stone."

Martha said to him, "Lord, by this time he stinks, for he has been dead four days."

Jesus said, "Didn't I say to you that, if you would believe, you should see the glory of God?"

They then took away the stone from the place where the dead was laid. Jesus lifted up his eyes and said, "Father, I thank you that you have heard me. And I know you always hear me; but

THE FEAST OF DEDICATION

because of the people which stand nearby I said it, that they may believe you have sent me."

When he had said this, he said in a loud voice, "Lazarus, come out."

And he who was dead came out, bound hand and foot with grave clothes. His face was bound about with a cloth.

Jesus said to them, "Loose him and let him go."

Many of the Jews, which came to Mary and had seen the things which Jesus did, believed on him. But some of them went to the Pharisees and told them the things Jesus had done.

The chief priests and the Pharisees then held a council and said, "What are we to do? This man does many miracles. If we let him alone, all will believe on him and the Romans shall come and take away both our place and nation."

One of them, named Caiaphas, being the high priest that same year, said to them, "You know nothing at all, nor consider what is expedient for us, that one man should die for the people, so the whole nation doesn't perish."

This he spoke not of himself, but being high priest that year, he prophesied Jesus should die for that nation. And not for that nation only, but that also he should gather together in one the children of God that were scattered abroad. From that day forth, they took counsel together to put him to death.

Jesus, therefore, walked no more openly among the Jews, but went to an area near the wilderness, into a city called Ephraim and there stayed with his disciples.

The Jews' Passover was near, and many went out of the country up to Jerusalem before the Passover, to purify themselves. They looked for Jesus and talked among themselves in the temple, "What do you think? Will he come to the feast?"

Both the chief priests and the Pharisees had given a commandment, that, if any one knew where he was, they should tell them, that they might take him.[296]

After raising Lazarus, Jesus and his disciples returned to Perea, away from the Jews and Pharisees. On the way to Jerusalem, Jesus said, "In Jerusalem, the Son of Man shall be betrayed to the chief priests and the scribes, and they shall condemn him to death. He shall be delivered to the Gentiles to mock, to scourge, and to crucify. The third day he shall rise again."

---

[296] John 11:

THE FEAST OF DEDICATION

The mother of James and John, the sons of Zebedee, came to Jesus, worshipping him, and desiring a favor of him.

Jesus said, "What do you want of me?"

With her sons by her side, she said, "Grant that my two sons may sit, the one on your right hand and the other on the left, in your kingdom."

He said, "You don't know what you are asking."

To her sons he said, "Are you able to drink of the cup I shall drink of and be baptized with the baptism that I am baptized with?" *He said this thinking about what was soon going to happen to him, as he had just told his disciples.*

They said, "We are able to."

He said to them, "You shall indeed drink of my cup and be baptized with the baptism that I am baptized with. But to sit on my right hand and on my left is not mine to give, but it shall be given to them for whom it is prepared of my Father."

When the other ten disciples heard this, they were displeased with the two. But Jesus called them to him and said, "You know that the princes of the Gentiles exercise dominion over them and they who are great exercise authority over them. But it will not be so among you, but whoever will be great among you, let them be your minister. And whoever will be chief among you, shall be servant of all; even as the Son of Man came not to be ministered to, but to minister and to give his life a ransom for many."[297]

On the way to Jerusalem, they came to Jericho. As they passed through it, there was a man named Zaccheus. He wanted to have a look at Jesus but, because he was short and there was a big crowd, he couldn't see. He ran ahead of the crowd and climbed up a sycamore tree to see him as he passed.

When Jesus came to the place, he looked up and saw him. He said, "Zaccheus, hurry and come down, because today I must stay at your house."

He hurried and joyfully received him. When the crowd saw this, they murmured against Jesus, saying, "It is wrong for Christ to stay with a sinner." To Jews, all tax collectors were sinners, and Zaccheus was chief of the tax collectors and very rich.

Zaccheus stood and said, "Behold, Lord, half of my riches I give to the poor and if I have taken anything from any one by false accusation, I will restore it to them fourfold."

---

[297] Matthew 20:17-29; Mark 10:32-45; Luke 18:31-34

THE FEAST OF DEDICATION

Jesus said, "This day salvation has come to this house, as he also is a son of Abraham. For the Son of Man has come to seek and to save that which was lost."

As he spoke these things, Jesus added a parable, because they were close to Jerusalem, and they thought the kingdom of God should immediately appear. He said, "A nobleman went into a far country to receive for himself a kingdom and to return. He called his ten servants and gave each of them one pound of silver and told them to invest it until he returned.

"When he went to his kingdom, the citizens hated him and sent a message after him, saying, 'We will not have you reign over us.'

"When he returned, after having received the kingdom, he commanded his servants to whom he had given the money to give an accounting of it, so he would know how much each had made. The first came and said, 'Lord, your pound has gained ten pounds.'

"He said, 'Well done, good servant. Because you have been faithful in a very little, you will rule over ten cities.'

"The second said, 'Lord your pound has gained five pounds.'

"He said, 'You will be over five cities.'

"Another came saying, 'Lord, here is your pound, which I have kept wrapped up in a napkin. I feared you because you are a hard man, taking up what you have not laid down and reaping what you have not sown.'

"His lord said, 'I will judge you out of your own mouth, you wicked servant. You knew I was a hard man, taking up what I had not laid down and reaping what I had not sown. Why didn't you give the bank my money that when I came, I might have received my money with interest?'

"He said to those that stood by, 'Take from him the pound and give it to him that has ten pounds.'

"They said, 'Lord, he already has ten pounds.'

"The lord said, 'I say to everyone who has, will be given and from him who has not, even what he has will be taken away from him. Bring here my enemies, who didn't want me to reign over them and kill them in front of me.'"[298]

When they left Jericho, a large crowd followed Jesus. There was a blind man, Bartimaeus, the son of Timaeus, sitting by the

---

[298] Luke 19:1-27

THE FEAST OF DEDICATION

wayside. When he heard that Jesus was passing by, he cried out, saying, "Have mercy on me, Jesus, son of David."

The crowd told him to be quiet, but he cried out louder, "Have mercy on me, Jesus, son of David."

Jesus stopped and called to him, saying, "What do you want me to do for you?"

He said, "Lord, I want to receive my sight."

Jesus had compassion on him and said, "Go on your way; your faith has made you whole."

Immediately he received his sight and followed him.[299]

They continued and got to Bethany, where Lazarus was, who had been dead and whom Jesus raised from the dead. They had supper in the house of Simon, the leper, and Martha served, and Lazarus was one of them who sat at the table with him. Mary came in carrying an alabaster box, with a pound of spikenard ointment, very expensive. She broke the box and anointed the feet of Jesus with the ointment and wiped his feet with her hair. The house was filled with the odor of the ointment.

One of his disciples, Judas Iscariot, Simon's son, who would betray him, said, "Why was not this ointment sold and the money given to the poor. It's worth about a year's wages." He said this not because he cared for the poor, but because Judas was a thief and carried the purse for them. Some of the other disciples also murmured about it.

Jesus said, "Don't bother her; she has done a good work for me. You always have the poor with you, but you don't always have me. She has poured this ointment on my body, for my burial. Wherever this gospel shall be preached in the whole world, there shall also be what this woman has done. Let it be for a memorial for her." [300]

Many Jews were in Bethany, and thus, they knew that Jesus was there. Many came not only to see Jesus, but also to see Lazarus, whom he raised from the dead. The chief priests consulted how they might put Lazarus to death, because many believed on Jesus because of him.

As they approached Jerusalem and came to the Mount of Olives, Jesus told two disciples, "Go into the village ahead of you and right away you will find an ass tied and a colt with her. Untie

---

[299] Matthew 20:30-34; Mark 10:46-52; Luke 18:35-43
[300] Matthew 26:6-13; Mark 14:3-9; John 12:1-11

THE FEAST OF DEDICATION

them and bring them to me. If anyone says anything to you, say, 'The Lord has need of them, and right away they will allow it.'"[301]

All this was done that it might be fulfilled which was spoken by the prophet, saying, "O daughter of Jerusalem, behold, your King, who is just and has salvation, comes to you. He is lowly and riding on an ass and a colt the foal of an ass."[302]

His disciples went and did as Jesus commanded them. As they untied the ass and the colt, those that stood by asked, "What are you doing untying them?"

They answered as Jesus commanded and they let them go.

They put on them their clothes and Jesus sat on the colt. A great crowd spread their garments in the way. Others cut down branches from the trees and strewed them in the way. The crowds went before and followed them, crying, "Blessed is he that comes in the name of the Lord. Blessed be the kingdom of our father, David, that comes in the name of the Lord. Hosanna in the highest."

His disciples were also involved.

Some of the Pharisees in the crowd said to Jesus, "Master, rebuke your disciples."

He answered, "If these should be quiet, the stones would immediately cry out."

When he got to Jerusalem, the entire city was moved, saying, "Who is this?"

The crowd said, "This is Jesus, the prophet of Nazareth of Galilee."

At the time, his disciples didn't realize prophecy was being fulfilled here. But when Jesus was glorified, they realized this had happened. The people had heard of Lazarus being raised from the dead and the crowd wanted to see the man who had done this miracle.

The Pharisees said among themselves, "See how we don't prevail. The world has gone after him."

Jesus told his disciples, "The hour has come, that the Son of Man should be glorified, Truly, I say, 'Except a seed of wheat fall into the ground and die, it is alone. But if it dies, it brings forth much fruit. He that care only about his life shall lose it and he that is selfless in this world shall keep it to life eternal. If anyone serves me, let them follow me and where I am, there shall also my servant be. If anyone serves me, they my Father will honor. Now is my soul troubled and what shall I say? Father, save me from this hour, but

---

[301] Matthew 21:1-4; Mark 11:1-10; Luke 19:28-40
[302] Zechariah 9:9

THE FEAST OF DEDICATION

for this cause came I to this hour. Father, glorify your name. Then came a voice from heaven, saying, 'I have both glorified it and will glorify it again.'"

The people that stood by and heard it, said it thundered, others said an angel spoke to him. Jesus said, "This voice came not because of me, but for your sakes. Now is the judgment of this world and now shall the prince of this world be cast out. And I, if I be lifted up from the earth, will draw all to me."

He said this to signify how he would die.

The people answered him, "We have heard out of the law that Christ will live forever. Why do you say, 'The Son of Man must be lifted up'? Who is this Son of Man?"

Jesus said, "Yet for a little while the light is with you. Walk while you have the light, lest darkness comes upon you. For they that walk in darkness, don't know where they are going. While you have light, believe in the light, that you may be the children of light."[303]

After this, Jesus and his disciples returned to Bethany and he hid from the people.

Early the next morning, they returned into the city and Jesus was hungry. He saw a fig tree along the way and it had leaves. *The fruit of a fig tree comes first and then the leaves. Normally, if a fig tree has leaves, it will also have fruit, which may be eaten even if it is not fully ripe.* When they came to the tree, there were only leaves and no fruit. Jesus said, "Let no fruit grow on you hence and forever."

They continued into Jerusalem and, as they came in, Jesus wept and said, "If you only knew, even in this critical time, the things which bring you peace! But now they are hidden from you. The days will come that your enemies shall dig a trench around you and surround you on every side. They shall pull you down to the ground, with your children inside. They shall not leave one stone on another, because you didn't know the time of your visitation and hear my warning voice." (The Roman siege, which soon came).

When they arrived, Jesus went into the temple and began to cast out those that sold and bought. He said to them, "It is written, 'My house is the house of prayer, but you have made it a den of thieves.'"

After clearing the temple, he taught the people and healed the blind and lame who came. There were children there who, when

---

[303] Matthew 21:6-11; John 12:12-36

THE FEAST OF DEDICATION

they saw what was happening, cried out, "Hosanna to the Son of David."

When the chief priests and scribes heard him and saw the wonderful things happening, they were very unhappy. They said to Jesus, "Don't you hear what these children are saying?"

He said, "Yes. Have you never read, 'Out of the mouth of babes and sucklings you have perfected praise?'"

After that, they sought how they might destroy him, but they were afraid of the people.

When evening came, Jesus and his disciples left the city.[304]

The next day, they returned to the temple, passing by the fig tree that had been so full of promise the day before. Today, it was dried up from the roots.

Peter said, "Master, the fig tree which you cursed is withered away."

Jesus said, "Have faith in God. I tell you that whoever shall say to this mountain, be removed from here and put in the sea and not doubt in his heart, but shall believe those things which they ask shall happen, then they shall have whatever they ask. Therefore, I say, whatever you desire, when you pray, believe that you will receive them and you shall have them. When you pray, forgive, if you have anything against anyone, that your Father also which is in heaven may forgive you your trespasses. But if you do not forgive, neither will your Father which is in heaven forgive your trespasses."

When they reached Jerusalem, they went into the temple, where Jesus started teaching.

Overnight, the chief priests, scribes, and elders had been trying to decide what they should do to destroy him. They decided to ask him about his authority. If he stated plainly he was the Son of God, they could accuse him of blasphemy. If he wouldn't, they could remove him for not having authority.

As soon as they heard he was there, they came to him while he was teaching and said, "By what authority do you do these things and who gave you the authority?"

Jesus said, "I also will ask you one thing, which if you will tell me, I likewise will tell you by what authority I do these things. Was the baptism of John from heaven or of men? Answer me."

It was a common practice of the time to answer a question in this way. They reasoned with themselves, saying, "If we shall say, 'From heaven', he shall say, 'Why then did you not believe him?' But

---

[304] Matthew 21:12-19; Mark 11:11-19; Luke 19:41-48

THE FEAST OF DEDICATION

if we say, 'Of men', the people may riot, because the people believe John to be a prophet."

They said to Jesus, "We cannot tell."

Jesus said, "Neither will I tell you by what authority I do these things."

Jesus went on to tell several parables. He asked, "What do you think? A man had two sons. He went to the first and said, 'Son, go work today in my vineyard.'

"His son said, 'I will not', but later repented and did go.

"He went to the second son and said the same, 'Son, go work today in my vineyard.'

"He answered, 'Sir, I will go,' but didn't go.

"Which of the two did the will of his father?"

They said to him, "The first."

Jesus said, "I tell you that the tax collectors and the harlots will go into the kingdom of God before you. For John came to you in the way of righteousness and you didn't believe him, but the tax collectors and the harlots believed him. And when you saw it, you didn't repent afterwards, that you might believe him.

"Hear another parable. There was a man, who planted a vineyard, put a hedge around it, put in a winepress, built a tower, hired caretakers, and went to a far country. When harvest time was near, he sent his servants to the caretakers to pick the fruit so he could sell it. The caretakers took the owner's servants, beat one, killed another, and stoned a third one. The owner sent other servants, more than the first, and the same thing happened to them. Last of all he sent them his son, saying, 'They will reverence my son.'

"But when the caretakers saw the son, they said, 'This is the heir. Come, let us kill him and seize his inheritance.' They caught the son and killed him. When the lord of the vineyard comes, what will he do to those caretakers?"

They said, "He will destroy those wicked men and will let out his vineyard to other caretakers, which shall give him the fruits at harvest."

Jesus said, "Did you never read in the scriptures, 'The stone which the builders rejected, the same has become the cornerstone; this is the Lord's doing and is marvelous in our eyes?' Therefore, the kingdom of God shall be taken from you and given to a nation bringing forth the fruits thereof. Whoever shall fall on this stone shall

THE FEAST OF DEDICATION

be broken; but on whomever it shall fall, it will grind them to powder."[305]

Jesus continued, "The kingdom of heaven is like a certain king, who gave a wedding for his son. He sent out his servants to call them that were invited to the wedding, but they wouldn't come. Again, he sent out other servants, saying, 'Tell those who are invited I have prepared my dinner. My oxen and my fatlings are killed and all things are ready. Come to the wedding.' But they made light of it and went their separate ways; one to his farm and another to his merchandise. The others took his servants, mistreated some, and killed others. When the king heard of it, he was angry and sent his armies, destroyed the murderers, and burned their city.

"Then he said to his servants, 'The wedding is ready, but they who were invited were not worthy. Go into the highways and as many as you shall find, invite to the marriage.' The servants went out to the highways and gathered together as many as they found, both bad and good, and the wedding was furnished with guests. *As the guests came in, they were given wedding garments, and took their places.*

"When all was ready, the king came in to see the guests. He saw a man which did not have on a wedding garment. He said to him, 'Friend, how come you don't have on a wedding garment?' The man didn't reply *and the king realized he had sneaked in.*

"The king said to his servants, "Tie him hand and foot, take him away and cast him into outer darkness. There shall be weeping and gnashing of teeth. For many are called, but few are chosen."[306]

When the chief priests and Pharisees had heard his parables, they realized he spoke of them. When they sought to take him, they feared the crowd, because they took him to be a prophet.

After this, they watched him and sent spies, which feigned themselves just men, that they might twist his words and deliver him to the power and authority of the governor. They sent their disciples with the Herodians, supporters of the Herodian family, saying, "Master, we know you are true and teach the way of God in truth. Neither do you care what class a person is, but treat all the same. Then tell us what you think, is it lawful to give tribute to Cesar or not?"

Jesus saw their trickery and said, "Why do you tempt me, you hypocrites? Show me the tribute money." They brought him a penny and he said, "Whose image and writing is this?"

---

[305] Matthew 21:20-46; Mark 11:20-33, 12:1-12; Luke 20:1-18
[306] Matthew 22:1-14

THE FEAST OF DEDICATION

They said, "Cesar's."

He said, "Give, therefore, to Cesar the things which are Cesar's and to God the things that are God's."

When they heard this, they marveled at his words, because they couldn't twist them. They left and went on their way.

The same day, the Sadducees, who say there is no resurrection, came to him to try him and said, "Master, Moses said, 'If a man dies, having had no children, his brother shall marry his wife and raise children for his brother.' There were seven brothers and the first, after he married, died childless. The second brother took her to wife and he also died childless. The third took her and, in like manner, the seven also. They all left no children and all died. Last of all, the woman died. In the resurrection, whose wife shall she be, as all of the brothers had her?"

Jesus answered, "You err, not knowing the scriptures, or the power of God. The children of this world marry and are given in marriage. But they which shall be accounted worthy to obtain that world and the resurrection from the dead, neither marry there nor are given in marriage. Neither can they die any more, for they are equal to the angels and are the children of God, being the children of the resurrection. Now that the dead are raised, even Moses showed at the bush, when he called the Lord the God of Abraham, the God of Isaac, and the God of Jacob. For he is not a God of the dead, but of the living; for all live in him."

When the crowd heard this, they were astonished at his doctrine. But the Pharisees, when they heard the Sadducees silenced by him, met to make plans. One of them, a lawyer, asked him their question, testing him, "Master, which is the great commandment of the law?"

Jesus said, "You shall love the Lord, your God, with all your heart, with all your soul, and with all your mind. This is the first and great commandment. The second is like it. You shall love your neighbor as yourself. On these two commandments hang all the law and the prophets' teachings."

Jesus then, seeing all the Pharisees were gathered together, asked them, "What do you think of Christ? Whose son is he?"

They said, "The son of David."

He said, "How then does David, given by the spirit, call him Lord, saying, 'The Lord said to my Lord, "Sit on my right hand, until

THE FEAST OF DEDICATION

I make your enemies your footstool?'[307] If David called him Lord, how is he his son?"

No one could answer him a word and, from that time, they didn't dare question him.[308]

Jesus turned and spoke to his disciples, making sure the crowd with the scribes and Pharisees could hear him. He said, "The scribes and Pharisees sit in Moses' seat. Therefore, whatever they ask you to do, do. But don't do what they do; for they say and don't do. They take heavy burdens that are hard to carry and tie them onto people's shoulders. But they themselves would not move a burden with one of their fingers. All the works they do are so they can be seen. They make their phylacteries (amulets on the forehead) large and enlarge the borders of their garments. They love the best seats at feasts and the chief seats in the synagogues. They love being greeted in the markets and to be called by people, Rabbi, Rabbi (Meaning Master). But don't you be called Rabbi: for one is your Master, even Christ and you are all brothers. Call no man your father on the earth, for one is your Father, which is in heaven. Neither be called masters, for one is your Master, even Christ. But they that are greatest among you shall be your servant. Whoever shall exalt himself shall be abased and those that shall humble themselves shall be exalted.

"Woe to you, scribes and Pharisees, hypocrites! You shut up the kingdom of heaven against people; for you neither go in yourselves, nor allow those that want to enter to go in, because of your teaching. Woe to you, scribes and Pharisees, hypocrites! You devour widow's houses and for pretense make long prayers. Therefore, you shall receive the greater damnation. Woe to you, scribes and Pharisees, hypocrites! You travel across sea and land to make one proselyte, and when he is made, you make him two times more the child of hell than yourselves. (Due to their false teaching.)

"Woe to you, you blind guides which say, 'Whoever shall swear by the temple, it is nothing. But whoever shall swear by the gold of the temple, they are debtors!' You fools and blind. Which is greater, the gold or the temple that sanctifies the gold? And, 'Whoever shall swear by the altar, it is nothing. But whoever swears by the gift that is on it, they are guilty.' You fools and blind, which is greater, the gift or the altar that sanctifies the gift? Who therefore shall swear by the altar, swears by it and by all things thereon. And whoever swears by the temple, swears by it and he that dwells there.

---

[307] Psalm 110:1
[308] Matthew 22:15--46; Mark 12:13-37; Luke 20:19-44

THE FEAST OF DEDICATION

And those that swear by heaven swear by the throne of God, and him that sits on it.

"Woe to you, scribes and Pharisees, hypocrites! You pay tithe of mint, anise, cumin, and have omitted the weightier matters of the law, judgment, mercy, and faith. These you ought to have done and not leave the other undone. You blind guides, which strain at a gnat and swallow a camel.

"Woe to you, scribes and Pharisees, hypocrites! You make the outside of the cups and platters clean, but inside you are full of extortion and self-indulgence. You blind Pharisees, clean first that which is inside that the outside may be clean also.

"Woe to you, scribes and Pharisees, hypocrites! You are like whitewashed sepulchers, which indeed appear beautiful outwardly, but inside they are full of dead men's bones and of all uncleanness. Even so you also outwardly appear righteous to men, but within you are full of hypocrisy and iniquity.

"Woe to you, scribes and Pharisees, hypocrites! Because you build the tombs of the prophets and garnish the sepulchers of the righteous, and say, 'If we had lived in the days of our fathers, we would not have done what they did in killing the prophets. Therefore, you are witnesses to yourselves, that you are the children of them which killed the prophets. Do then as your fathers did. You serpents, you generation of vipers, how can you escape the damnation of hell?

"Thus, I send to you prophets, wise men, and scribes and some of them you shall kill and crucify, some of them you will scourge in your synagogues, and some persecute from city to city. That on you may come all the righteous blood that was shed upon the earth, from the blood of righteous Abel to the blood of Zacharias, son of Barachias *and father of John the Baptist,* whom you killed between the temple and the altar. Truly I say, 'All these things shall come upon this generation.'

"Oh, Jerusalem, Jerusalem, you that kill the prophets and stone them who are sent to you; how often would I have gathered your children together, even as a hen gathers her chickens under her wings and you would not! Behold, your house is left to you desolate. I tell you that you shall not see me now, until you shall say, 'Blessed is he that comes in the name of the Lord.'"[309]

Jesus sat by the treasury and watched how people put money into the treasury. Many who were rich put in a lot. There was there a poor widow and she put in two mites (about one dollar). He called

---

[309] Matthew 23:

THE FEAST OF DEDICATION

his disciples to him and said, "This poor widow has put more in than all they who have put into the treasury: for all they did put in of their abundance, but she of her want did put in all that she had, even all her living."[310]

As Jesus left the temple for the last time, he had a heavy heart. Though he had done many miracles among the people, they didn't believe on him. Thus, was the prophecy of Isaiah the prophet fulfilled, which he spoke, "Lord, who has believed our report? To whom has the arm of the Lord been revealed?[311] He has blinded their eyes and hardened their heart, that they should not see with their eyes nor understand with their heart and be converted, and I should heal them." Isaiah said this when he saw his glory and spoke of him.

There were many among the chief rulers that believed on him, but because of the Pharisees, they did not make it known, so they would not be put out of the synagogue; for they loved the praise of the world more than the praise of God. Jesus had called to them, saying, "Those that believe on me believe not on me, but on Him that sent me. And he that sees me sees Him that sent me. I have come to be a light to the world, that whoever believes on me should not live in darkness. If any one hears my words and believes not, I judge them not: for I came not to judge the world, but to save the world. He that rejects me and receives not my words has one that judges him: the word that I have spoken, the same shall judge him in the last day. For I have not spoken of myself, but the Father which sent me, He gave me commandment of what I should say and what I should speak. And I know that his commandment is life everlasting. Whatever I speak, therefore, even as the Father said to me, I speak."[312]

After Jesus was out of the temple, his disciples came to him to show him the buildings of the temple. Jesus said to them, "See all these buildings? I tell you there shall not be left here one stone upon another that shall not be thrown down."

On their way back to Bethany, Jesus and his disciples were all alone. They stopped on the Mount of Olives to enjoy the view and rest. His disciples came to him and asked, "When shall these things be? What shall be the sign of your coming and of the end of the world?"

Jesus said,

---

[310] Mark 12:41-44; Luke 21:1-4
[311] Isaiah 53:1
[312] John 12:37-50

THE FEAST OF DEDICATION

"Take care that no one deceives you. Many shall come in my name, saying, 'I am Christ,' and shall deceive many. You shall hear of wars and rumors of wars. See that you are not concerned; for all these things must come to pass, but the end is not yet. Nation shall rise against nation and kingdom against kingdom. There shall be famines, pestilences, and earthquakes in many places. All these are the beginning of sorrows.

"Then shall they deliver you up to be afflicted and they shall kill you. You shall be hated by all nations for my name's sake. Many shall be offended, shall betray one another, and shall hate one another. Many false prophets shall rise and shall deceive many. Because iniquity shall abound, the love of many shall wax cold. But he that shall endure to the end, the same shall be saved. The gospel of the kingdom shall be preached in all the world for a witness to all nations; and then the end shall come.[313] When you, therefore, shall see the abomination of desolation, spoken of by Daniel the prophet, stand in the holy place, then let them who be in Judea, flee to the mountains.

"Let those who are on the housetop not come down to take anything out of the house. Neither let them who are in the field return to take their clothes. Woe to them that are with child and to them that are nursing in those days! Pray that your flight be not in the winter or on the Sabbath day. For there shall be great tribulation, such as was not since the beginning of the world to this time, no, nor ever shall be. Except those days should be shortened, there should no one be saved. But for the elect's sake those days shall be shortened.

"If anyone shall say to you, 'Lo, here is Christ', or 'Lo, there is Christ,' don't believe it. For there shall arise false Christs and false prophets, and shall show great signs and wonders; so, if it were possible, they should deceive the very elect. I have told you before, if they say to you, 'Behold, he is in the desert,' don't go. If they say, 'Behold, he is in a secret place,' don't believe it. As the lightning comes out of the east and shines even to the west, so shall also the coming of the Son of Man be. Wherever the carcass is, there will the buzzards be.

---

[313] Matthew 24:1-15; Mark:1-14; Daniel 11:31; 12:11

THE FEAST OF DEDICATION

"Immediately after the trials of those days shall the sun be darkened, the moon shall not give her light, the stars shall fall from heaven, and the powers of the heavens shall be shaken. Then shall appear the sign of the Son of Man in heaven and all the tribes of the earth shall mourn. They shall see the Son of Man coming in the clouds of heaven with power and great glory. He shall send his angels with a great sound of a trumpet and they shall gather together his elect from the four winds, from one end of heaven to the other.

"Learn a parable of the fig tree. When its branches are yet tender and put forth leaves, you know that summer is nigh. Likewise, when you shall see all these things, know that it is near, even at the doors. I say this generation shall not pass, until all I have told you are fulfilled. Heaven and earth shall pass away, but my words shall not pass away.

"Of that day and hour no one knows, no, not even the angels of heaven, but my Father only. But as the days of Noah were, so also shall the coming of the Son of Man be. For as in the days that were before the flood, they were eating and drinking, marrying and giving in marriage, until the day Noah entered the ark. They didn't know until the flood came and took them all away; so shall the coming of the Son of Man be. There shall be two in the field, the one shall be taken and the other left. Two women shall be grinding at the mill; one shall be taken and the other left.

"Watch, therefore, for you don't know in what hour your Lord comes. But know this, that if the good-man of the house had known when the thief would come, he would have watched and would not have allowed his house to be broken into. Therefore, be ready, for in a time you think not, the Son of Man comes. Who then is a faithful and wise servant, whom his lord has made ruler over his household, to provide food at the proper time? Blessed are those servants, whom his lord when he comes shall find so doing. I say to you he shall make them rulers over all his goods.

"But if that evil servant shall say in his heart, 'My lord is delaying his coming;" the lord of that servant shall come in a day when he isn't expecting him and at time he is not planning on. He shall cut him asunder and appoint him

THE FEAST OF DEDICATION

his portion with the hypocrites. There shall be weeping and gnashing of teeth.'[314]

"I will give you another parable about the coming of the Son of Man. The kingdom of heaven is like ten young women, who took their lamps and went to meet the bridegroom. Five of them were wise and five were foolish. The foolish ones took their lamps, but did not take any extra oil. The wise ones took extra oil with their lamps.

"The custom was for the wedding party to travel from one house to another to meet the guests. The young women waited for the party to come, but it was later than they expected and they slept while waiting. About midnight they were awakened and told the party was coming. The young women trimmed their lamps and found they were out of oil. The foolish said to the wise, 'Give us of your oil, for ours are empty.' The wise said, 'We can't, because there may not be enough for all of us. Go to the store and buy some for yourselves.'

"While they were gone, the bridegroom's party came and those that were ready went into the wedding with him and the door was shut. When the other young women came, they knocked at the door, saying, 'Lord, Lord, open for us.' But he said, 'I don't know you.' Jesus said, "Watch, for you don't know the day or the hour when the Son of Man comes.

"I will tell you another parable of the coming of the Son of Man. The kingdom of heaven is as a man traveling to a distant country, who called his own servants and gave them his goods. To one he gave five talents, to another two, and to another one talent; according to their ability. He that received the five talents went and traded with them and made another five talents. Likewise, he that received two gained another two. But he that received the one hid his talent by burying it in the ground.

"After a long time, the lord of the servants returned and reckoned with them. He that received five talents came and brought another five talents, saying, 'Lord, you gave me five talents, see, I have gained you five more talents.' His lord said, 'Well done, my good and faithful servant. You

---

[314] Matthew 24:16-51; Mark 13:15-37

THE FEAST OF DEDICATION

have been faithful over a few things, I will make you ruler over many things. Enter into the joy of your lord.'

"He that had received two talents came and said, 'Lord, you gave me two talents, see I have gained you two more talents.' His lord said, 'Well done, my good and faithful servant, you have been faithful over a few things, I will make you ruler over many things. Enter into the joy of your lord.'

"He that had received the one talent came and said, 'Lord, I knew you were a hard man, reaping where you had not sowed and gathering where you had not scattered. I was afraid and hid your talent in the earth. Here it is.'

"His lord said, 'You wicked and slothful servant, you knew I reap where I have not sown and gather where I have not scattered. You should have given my money to the exchangers, so at my coming I would have received my money with interest. Take the talent from him and give it to him whom has ten talents. To everyone that has shall be given and they shall have in abundance. But from they that have not shall be taken away even what they have. Cast the unprofitable servant to outer darkness, there shall be weeping and gnashing of teeth.'

"When the Son of Man comes in his glory, with all the holy angels, then he will sit on the throne of his glory. Before him shall be gathered all nations and he shall separate them one from another as a shepherd divides his sheep from the goats. He shall set the sheep on his right hand, but the goats on the left. Then shall the King say to them on his right hand, 'Come, you blessed of my Father, inherit the kingdom prepared for you from the foundation of the world. I was hungry and you gave me food; I was thirsty and you gave me drink; I was a stranger and you took me in; naked and you clothed me; I was sick and you visited me; I was in prison and you came to me.'

"Then shall the righteous answer, saying, 'Lord, when did we see you hungry and fed you? Or thirsty and gave you drink? When were you a stranger and we took you in? Or naked and clothed you? Or when did we see you sick or in prison and came to you?'

"The King shall answer them, 'As you have done it to one of the least of these my brothers, you have done it to me.'

"Then he also shall say to those on the left hand, 'Depart from me, you cursed, into everlasting fire, prepared for the devil and his angels. I was hungry and you gave me no food. I was thirsty and you gave me no drink. I was a stranger and you didn't take me in. I was naked and you didn't clothe me. Sick and in prison and you did not visit me.'

"Then they shall say, 'Lord, when did we see you hungry, thirsty, a stranger, naked, sick, or in prison and didn't minister to you?'

"He shall answer them, 'As much as you didn't do it to one of the least of these, you didn't do it to me.' These shall go away to everlasting punishment, but the righteous into life eternal.

When Jesus had finished speaking to his disciples on the Mount of Olives, he said, "You know that in two days is the feast of the Passover and the Son of Man will be betrayed and be crucified."[315]

BETRAYED AND TRIAL

Two days before the feast of the Passover and unleavened bread, the chief priests, the scribes, and the elders of the people met in the palace of the high priest, who was Caiaphas. They consulted how they might take Jesus secretly and kill him. They decided not on the feast day, so there wouldn't be an uproar of the people. Then, being influenced by Satan, Judas Iscariot, of the twelve, went to the chief priests. He told them he would betray Jesus. They were glad and promised to pay him. He agreed and sought an opportunity to betray him to them in the absence of a crowd.

On the first day of unleavened bread, when they killed the Passover lamb, his disciples said to Jesus, "Where should we go and prepare to eat the Passover?"

In answer, he told Peter and John, "Go into the city and there you shall meet a man carrying a pitcher of water. Follow him. Wherever he goes in, say to the head of the house, 'The Master says, "Where is the guest chamber; where I shall eat the Passover with my

---

[315] Matthew 25, 26:1-2

disciples?" He will show you a large upper room furnished and prepared. There make ready for us."

His disciples went into the city, found it as he said, and they prepared the Passover. In the evening, Jesus came with the twelve and they sat down to eat.

As they ate, Jesus said, "With desire I have desired to eat this Passover with you before I suffer. I will not eat any more of it, until it is fulfilled in the kingdom of God."

He took the cup and gave thanks, saying, "Take this and divide it among yourselves. I will not drink of the fruit of the vine, until the kingdom of God shall come."

He took bread, gave thanks, broke it, and gave it to them, saying, "This is my body which is given for you. This do in remembrance of me."

Likewise, he also passed the cup, saying, "This cup is the new testament in my blood, which is shed for you."

He said, "One of you who are eating with me shall betray me. The Son of Man is going as it was determined, but woe to that man by whom he is betrayed. It would have been good for him if he had not been born."

His disciples became sorrowful and began to ask, "Is it I?"

Jesus said, "It is one of the twelve."

They continued to ask around the group, "Is it I?"

Finally, Judas asked, "Is it I?"

Jesus said, "It is you." *But his remark was lost to the others in conversations going on.*

There was a discussion among them about who would be the greatest.

Jesus said, "The kings of the Gentiles exercise lordship over them, and they who have this authority are called benefactors. But you shall not do this. He who is greatest among you, let him be as the younger, and he who is chief as he that serves. For who is greater, he who eats, or he who serves? Is not he who eats? But I am among you as he who serves. You are those who have continued with me in my temptations. I appoint to you a kingdom, as my Father has appointed to me. So, you may eat and drink at my table in my kingdom and sit on thrones judging the twelve tribes of Israel."[316]

After supper, Jesus took off his robe and tied a towel around him. He poured water in a basin and began to wash the disciples' feet. He wiped them with the towel he had around him. When he

---

[316] Matthew 36:13-29; Mark 14:10-25; Luke 22:1-30; John 13:1

BETRAYED AND TRIAL

came to Simon Peter, Peter said, "Lord, are you going to wash my feet?"

Jesus said, "What I do you don't know now, but you will know later."

Peter said, "You shall never wash my feet."

Jesus said, "If I don't wash you, you will have no part with me."

Peter said, "Lord, not my feet only, but also my hands and my head."

Jesus said, "He who is washed needs only his feet washed and is completely clean, but not all of you are clean." For he knew who should betray him. Therefore, he said, "You are not all clean."

After he had washed their feet and had put on his robe, he said, "Do you know what I have done to you? You call me Master and Lord and that is correct, for I am. If I then, your Lord and Master, have washed your feet, you also ought to wash one another's feet. For I have given you an example, that you should do as I have done to you. I say the servant is not greater than his lord, or he who is sent greater than he who sent him. If you know these things, happy are you if you do them.

"I speak not of you all; I know whom I have chosen, but that the scripture may be fulfilled, 'He who eats bread with me has lifted up his heel against me.' He who receives whomever I send receives me and he who receives me receives Him who sent me."

When Jesus said this, he was again troubled in spirit and testified, "I tell you one of you shall betray me."

The disciples looked around again, wondering about whom he was speaking. John, who Jesus loved, was leaning on Jesus' chest, so Simon Peter motioned to him, to ask who it was he was talking about. So John asked Jesus, "Lord, who is it?"

Jesus said, "He it is to whom I shall give a sop, when I have dipped it."

After he had given Judas the sop, Satan entered him and Jesus said, "What you do, do quickly."

Some of the disciples assumed, because Judas had the purse, Jesus had said to him, "Buy those things we need for the feast" or "Give something to the poor." In any case, Judas immediately left and went out into the night.

When he had left, Jesus said, "Now is the Son of Man glorified and God is glorified in him. If God be glorified in him, God shall also glorify him in Himself and shall immediately glorify him. Little children, for a little while I am with you. You shall seek me

BETRAYED AND TRIAL

and, as I said to the Jews, 'Where I go, you cannot come.' Now, a new commandment I give to you, 'That you love one another; as I have loved you, love one another.' By this shall all men know you are my disciples, if you have love one to another."

Simon Peter said to him, "Lord, where are you going?"

Jesus said, "Where I go, you cannot follow me now, but you shall follow me later."

Peter said, "Lord, why can't I follow you now? I will lay down my life for your sake."

Jesus said, "Simon, Simon, Satan has desired to have you, that he may sift you as wheat. But I have prayed for you, that your faith doesn't fail. When you are converted, strengthen your brothers."

Peter said, "Lord, I am ready to go with you, both to prison and to death."

Jesus said, "Peter, the rooster shall not crow today before you shall deny three times you know me."

He said to his disciples, "When I sent you without purse, money, and shoes, did you lack anything?"

They said, "Nothing."

He said, "Now, you who have a purse, let them take it. Likewise take your money and those who don't have a sword, let them sell their garment and buy one. I tell you what is written must yet be accomplished in me, 'He was reckoned among the transgressors.' The things concerning me have an end."

They said, "Lord, here are two swords."

He said, "It is enough.[317] Don't let your heart be troubled, but believe in God and believe in me. In my Father's house are many mansions. If this were not so, I would have told you. I go to prepare a place for you. And if I go and prepare a place for you, I will come again and receive you to myself. That where I am, you may be also. And where I go, you know, and the way you know."

Thomas said, "Lord, we don't know where you are going; how can we know the way?"

He said, "I am the way, the truth, and the life. No one comes to the Father, but by me. If you had known me, you should have known my Father also. From now on, you know Him and have seen Him."

Philip said, "Lord, show us the Father and it will suffice us."

Jesus said, "Have I been so long with you and yet you have not known me, Philip? Those who have seen me have seen the

---

[317] Matthew 26:31-35; Mark 14:27-31; Luke 22:31-38: John 13:4-38

Father. (*Jesus and his Father look alike.*) Why do you then say, 'Show us the Father?' Don't you believe I am in the Father and the Father in me? The words I speak to you I speak not of myself, but the Father who dwells in me, He does the works. Believe me that I am in the Father and the Father in me, or else believe me for the very works' sake. Truly I say, they who believe on me, the works I do, shall they do, because I go to my Father. Whatever you shall ask in my name, I will do, that the Father may be glorified in the Son. If you shall ask any thing in my name, I will do it.

"If you love me, keep my commandments. I will pray to the Father and he shall give you another Comforter, that he may abide with you forever, even the Spirit of Truth, whom the world cannot receive, because they don't believe in Him, nor know Him. But you know Him, for he dwells with you and shall be in you. I will not leave you comfortless. I will come to you. Yet a little while and the world will see me no more, but you will see me. Because I live, you shall also live. At that day, you shall know I am in my Father, and you in me, and I in you. They who have my commandments and keep them are they who love me, and they who love me shall be loved of my Father and I will love them, and will manifest myself to them."

Thaddeus said, "Lord, how will you manifest yourself to us and not to the world?"

Jesus said, "If someone loves me, they will keep my words and my Father will love them, and we will come to them and make our home with them. Those who don't love me, don't keep my sayings and the words which you hear are not mine, but the Father's, who sent me. These things have I spoken to you, being yet present with you. But the Comforter, who is the Holy Ghost whom the Father will send in my name, he shall teach you all things, and bring all things to your remembrance, whatever I have said to you. Peace I leave with you, my peace I give to you; not as the world gives, give I to you. Let not your heart be troubled, neither let it be afraid. You have heard how I said to you, 'I go away and come again to you.' If you loved me, you would rejoice, because I said, 'I go to the Father,' for my Father is greater than I. And now I have told you before it comes to pass, that when it comes to pass, you might believe. Hereafter, I will not talk much with you. For the prince of this world comes and has nothing in me. But that the world may know I love the Father and, as the Father commands me, even so I do."[318]

---

[318] John 14

They sang a hymn and went out to the Mount of Olives.[319] *On the way, they stopped to rest and Jesus taught them more.* He said,

"I am the true vine and my Father is the husbandman. Every branch in me that doesn't bear fruit, he takes away. Every branch that bears fruit, he purifies that it may bring forth more fruit. Now you are clean through the word which I have spoken to you. Abide in me and I in you. As the branch cannot bear fruit of itself, except it abides in the vine, no more can you, except you abide in me. I am the vine, you are the branches. Those who abide in me and I in them, the same bring forth much fruit. Without me you can do nothing. If a person abides not in me, they are cast off as a branch that is withered. People gather them and put them in the fire, and they are burned. If you abide in me and my words abide in you, you shall ask what you will and it shall be done to you.

"Herein is my Father glorified, that you bear much fruit, so shall you be my disciples. As the Father has loved me, so have I loved you; continue in my love. If you keep my commandments, you shall abide in my love, even as I have kept my Father's commandments and abide in his love. These things have I spoken to you, that my joy might be full. This is my commandment, 'Love one another, as I have loved you.' Greater love has no one than this, that they lay down their life for their friends. You are my friends, if you do whatever I command you. Hereafter I won't call you servants, for the servant doesn't know what his lord does. But I have called you friends, for all things I have heard of my Father, I have made known to you. You have not chosen me, but I have chosen you and ordained you to the priesthood to go and bring forth fruit. Whatever you shall ask of the Father in my name, he will give it to you."

He looked around at the disciples gathered at his feet.

"These things I command you, that you love one another. If the world hates you, you know it hated me before it hated you. If you were of the world, the world would love its own. But because you are not of the world, and I have

---

[319] Mark 14:26;

chosen you out of the world, therefore, the world hates you. Remember the word I said to you, 'The servant is not greater than his lord.' If they have persecuted me, they will also persecute you. If they have kept my sayings, they will also keep yours. But all these things will they do to you for my name's sake, because they don't know Him who sent me.

"If I had not come and spoken to them, they would have no sin, but now they have no cloak for their sin. He who hates me, hates my Father also. If I had not done among them the works which no other man did, they would have no sin; but now they have seen and hated both me and my Father. But this comes to pass, to fulfill what is written in their law, 'They hated me without a cause.' But when the Comforter is come, whom I will send to you from the Father, even the Spirit of Truth, which proceeds from the Father, he shall testify of me. And you also shall bear witness, because you have been with me from the beginning.[320]

"I have told you these things, that you won't be offended. They shall put you out of the synagogues; yes, the time is coming that whoever kills you will think he does God service. These things will they do to you, because they have not known the Father, or me. But these things have I told you, so when the time comes, you may remember I told you them. These things I said not to you at the beginning, because I was with you. But now I am going on my way to Him who sent me. But because I have said this to you, sorrow has filled your hearts. Nevertheless, I tell you the truth. It is expedient for you I go away, for if I don't go away, the Comforter will not come to you, but if I depart, I will send Him to you. I have many things to say to you, but you can't bear them now.

"But when the Spirit of Truth, comes, He will guide you to all truth. For he shall not speak of Himself, but whatever He shall hear, He shall speak, and He will show you things to come. He shall glorify me, for He shall receive of mine and shall show it to you. All things the Father has are mine. Therefore, I said He shall take of mine and shall show it to you. A little while and you shall not see me. And

---

[320] John 15

again, in a little while and you shall see me, because I go to the Father."

Some of the disciples said among themselves, "What is this he is saying to us, 'A little while and you shall not see me. And again, a little while and you shall see me, because I go to the Father?' What is he saying, ' A little while?' It doesn't make sense."

Jesus knew they wanted to ask him about it and said, "Are you asking among yourselves about what I said, 'A little while and you shall not see me and again, a little while and you shall see me? I tell you, you shall weep and lament, but the world shall rejoice. You shall be sorrowful, but your sorrow shall be turned to joy. A woman, when she is in labor, has sorrow because her time has come, but as soon as she has delivered the child, she doesn't remember the anguish, for the joy a child is born into the world. Now you, therefore, have sorrow, but I will see you again and your heart shall rejoice and the joy no one can take from you.

"In that day, you shall ask me nothing. Truly I say to you, 'Whatever you shall ask the Father in my name, he will give it to you.' Before this, you have asked nothing in my name. Ask and you shall receive, that your joy may be full. These things have I spoken to you in proverbs, but the time is coming, when I shall no more speak to you in proverbs, but I shall show you plainly of the Father. At that time, you shall ask in my name, and I won't need to pray to the Father for you, for the Father, Himself, loves you, because you have loved me and believed I came from God. I came from the Father and am come into the world. Again, I leave the world and go to the Father."

His disciples said, "Lo, now you speak plainly and don't speak in proverbs We are sure you know all things and explain so well no one needs to ask you anything. By this, we believe you came from God."

Jesus said, "Do you now believe? Behold, the time is coming, yes, has now come, that you shall be scattered, every one to his own, and shall leave me alone. Yet I am not alone, because the Father is with me. These things I have spoken to you, that in me you might have peace. In the world you shall have tribulation, but be of good cheer. I have overcome the world."[321]

Jesus spoke these words and lifted up his eyes to heaven and said, "Father, the hour is come, glorify your Son, that your Son also

---

[321] John 16

BETRAYED AND TRIAL

may glorify you. As you have given him power over all flesh, that he should give eternal life to as many as you have given him. This is life eternal, that they might know you are the only true God and Jesus Christ, whom you have sent. I have glorified you on the earth. I have finished the work which you gave me to do. And now, O Father, glorify me with your own self with the glory which I had with you before the world was. I have manifested your name to the men who you gave me out of the world. Yours they were and you gave them to me and they have kept your word. Now they have known all things, whatever you have given to me are from you. For I have given to them the words which you gave me and they have received them. They have surely known I came from you and they have believed you sent me. I pray for them. I pray not for the world, but for them which you have given me and I am glorified in them.

"Now I am no more in the world, but these are in the world, and I come to you. <u>Holy Father, keep through your own name those whom you have given me, that they may be one, as we are.</u> While I was with them in the world, I kept them in your name. Those you gave me I have kept, and none is lost but the son of perdition, that the scripture might be fulfilled. Now I come to you and these things I speak in the world, that they might have my joy fulfilled in themselves. I have given them your word and the world has hated them, because they are not of the world, even as I am not of the world. I don't pray that you should take them out of the world, but that you should keep them from the evil. They are not of the world, even as I am not of the world. Hallow them through your truth. Your word is truth. As you have sent me into the world, even so have I also sent them into the world. And for their sakes I hallow myself, that they also might be hallowed through the truth. Neither prey I for these alone, but for them also, who shall believe on me through their word. <u>That they all may be one, as you, Father, are in me and I in you, that they also may be one in us;</u> that the world may believe you have sent me.

"The glory which you gave me I have given them, that they may be one, even as we are one. I in them and you in me, that they may be made perfect in one and that the world may know you have sent me and have loved them as you have loved me. Father, I will that they also, whom you have given me, be with me where I am, that they may behold my glory, which you have given me, <u>for you loved me before the foundation of the world.</u> O righteous Father, the world has not known you, but I have known you and these have known you sent me. I have declared to them your name and will

BETRAYED AND TRIAL

declare it, that the love wherewith you have loved me, may be in them, and I in them."

After saying these things, Jesus went with his disciples over the brook Cedron into a place called Gethsemane, where there was a garden. Judas, who would betray him, knew the garden, because Jesus and his disciples often went there. [322] When they got to the garden, Jesus told them, "Sit here while I go and pray over there."

He said to Peter, James, and John, "Come with me. My soul is exceeding sorrowful even to death. Stay here and watch with me."

He went a little farther and fell on the ground face down and prayed, saying, "O my Father, if it be possible, let this cup pass from me; nevertheless, not as I will, but as you will."

After praying, he returned to Peter, James, and John and found them asleep. He said to Peter, "Could you not watch with me one hour? Watch and pray that you enter not into temptation. The spirit is willing, but the flesh is weak."

He went away the second time and prayed, saying, "Father, I know I must suffer for all the sins of each of your children, but all things are possible for you. Take away this cup from me; nevertheless, not my will, but your will be done."

He came again and found all the disciples sleeping, for their eyes were heavy. He left them again and prayed the third time, saying the same words.

An angel came to him from heaven, to strengthen him. Being in an agony, he prayed more earnestly and his sweat was big drops of blood falling to the ground.[323] When he rose from prayer and came to his disciples, he found them still sleeping, and said, "Sleep on and take your rest."

A short time later he came back and said, "The hour is at hand and the Son of Man is betrayed into the hands of sinners. Get up, he that betrays me is here."[324]

When Judas left the upper room earlier, he went to see his Sadducee contact, Hyman. When he had found him, he said, "I ate the Passover meal with Jesus this evening, and afterwards, I am sure he will go with his disciples to a garden on the Mount of Olives. It would be a good place to arrest him. I will identify him with a kiss, so you will know whom to arrest."

Hyman said, "I'll get word to Annas and we will get some soldiers to make the arrest."

---

[322] John 17, 18:1-2
[323] Matthew 26:36-41; Luke 22:43-46
[324] Matthew 26:45-46

BETRAYED AND TRIAL

Annas had been high priest previously, but had passed the title on to five of his sons, a grandson, and now it was held by his son-in-law, Caiaphas. Through his influence, he promoted his family to this office, and thus, he could enjoy the dignity and influence of the office, without the responsibility or the headaches it entailed. His influence with the Romans was due to his religious views, which supported the Roman regime, and his immense wealth, which came from the temple traffic and his cut of the booth profits. Of course, if Jesus had his way, the illegal traffic would cease.[325]

It took Annas some time to get a band of soldiers and other men together. They came with swords, staves, and torches, a great multitude, with Judas in the lead. He came up to Jesus to give him a kiss.

As he approached, Jesus said, "Are you going to betray the Son of Man with a kiss?"

When his followers saw this, they said, "Lord, shall we use our swords?"

Peter smote the servant of the high priest, Malchus, cutting off his right ear.

Jesus said to Peter, "Put up your sword. Don't you know I could pray to my Father and He would send more than twelve legions of angels? But how then could the scriptures be fulfilled? Thus, it must be."

Jesus then put forth his finger and healed the ear of Malchus.

The multitude stood still, watching all of this, as if they were waiting for permission from Jesus to arrest him.

Jesus said to them, "You have come out as if I'm a thief, with swords and staves to arrest me. I was with you daily in the temple teaching and you didn't arrest me, but the scriptures must be fulfilled."

When the disciples heard this, they all fled. *One of the disciples was a young man, Mark.* He had a linen cloth about his naked body. When they laid hold on him, he left the linen cloth and fled naked, saving himself.

Jesus said, "I have told you I am he; if you seek me, let these others go their way." He said this that the scripture, which says, "I have lost none of them which you gave me," might be fulfilled.[326]

---

[325] Bruce R. McConkie, *Doctrinal New Testament Commentary*, vol. I, (1974) Deseret Book Company, Salt Lake City, UT. pg. 784
[326] Matthew 26:47-56; Mark 14:43-52; Luke 22:47-53, 63-65, 67-71; John 18:3-11

BETRAYED AND TRIAL

John and Peter followed Jesus to the palace of Annas. John was known to the high priest and went in with Jesus, but Peter stood outside. John went out and spoke to the doorkeeper and brought Peter in. The young girl who kept the door said to Peter, "Aren't you one of this man's disciples?"

Peter said, "I'm not."

There was a fire of coals in the room, because it was cold, and the servants and officers were warming themselves. Peter stood with them and warmed himself.

One of them said, "Aren't you one of his disciples? You are a Galilean and your speech betrays you."

He began to curse and swear, saying, "I do not know him."

Another of the servants, who was kin to Malchus, said, "Didn't I see you in the garden with him."

Peter said, "No, I wasn't." and immediately the cock crowed.

Peter remembered the word of the Lord, how he said, "Before the cock crow you shall deny me three times" and Peter went out and wept bitterly.

Once in the palace, they took Jesus first to Annas, as he wanted to see Jesus, and then on to Caiaphas, the High Priest, his son-in-law, who also lived there. Caiaphas is the one who counseled the Jews that it was expedient one man should die for the people.

Caiaphas said to Jesus, "Tell us about your disciples and your doctrine."

Jesus said, "I spoke openly to the world. I taught in the synagogue and in the temple where the Jews were. In secret, I have said nothing contrary to what I have said in public. Why do you ask me? Ask them that heard me. *It is not lawful for one to incriminate himself."*

After he said this, one of the officers who stood by struck Jesus with the palm of his hand and said, "Why do you answer the high priest so?"

Jesus said, "If I have spoken evil, tell the court of the evil, but if I answered the question well, why do you hit me?"

The chief priests, elders and all the council had sought false witnesses against Jesus, so they could put him to death, but had found none.

Finally, they found two. They said, "We heard him say, 'I will destroy this temple that is made with hands and, within three days, I will build another made without hands.'"

The high priest arose and said, "Why do you not answer? Don't you know what these witness against you?"

But Jesus said nothing.

The high priest said to him, "I adjure you, by the living God, to tell us whether you are the Christ, the Son of God."

Jesus said, "What you said is correct. And hereafter, you shall see the Son of Man sitting on the right hand of power and coming in the clouds of heaven."

Then, the high priest rent his clothes and said, "Why do we need any more witnesses? You have heard the blasphemy; what do you think?"

The whole council condemned him to be guilty of death. Then, the men who held Jesus mocked him and hit him. They blindfolded him and hit him on the face, saying, "Prophesy who it is who hit you."[327]

After this, they led him to a holding cell, planning to take him to Pilate in the morning. Assembling the council and trying to find false witnesses had taken some time and dawn was about to break.

After Jesus was led out of the hall, Caiaphas addressed the council, "It has occurred to us we should meet a second time. After all, this is a capital crime and we want to do things correctly. We normally meet after the morning sacrifice and before the evening sacrifice. I know it is late and we are all tired, but we need to be back here just after the morning sacrifice. It also will give us an opportunity to find those council members we were not able to locate last night."

The whole trial was illegal. A capital trial was not supposed to be held at night or concluded within one day. Trials were not to be on the day preceding the Sabbath, on the first day of unleavened bread, or the eve of the Passover. A unanimous verdict on the day of trial has the effect of an acquittal. It also was illegal for a host of other reasons.[328]

John had stayed and saw the trial of Jesus. After the trial was over, he went to where the disciples were staying and told them, including Judas, what had happened. When Judas heard what had happened and Jesus was condemned, he began to repent. He went to the temple with the thirty pieces of silver he received and found one of the priests who he had talked to.

He said, "I have sinned because I betrayed an innocent man. Here are the thirty pieces of silver you paid me."

---

[327] Matthew 26:57-68; Mark 14:53-65: Luke 22:63-64
[328] James Talmage, *Jesus the Christ* (1981) The Church of Jesus Christ of Latter-day Saints, Salt Lake City, UT. Pg. 621-626

BETRAYED AND TRIAL

The priest said, "What is that to us? It's your sin."

When he heard that, Judas threw the silver pieces on the floor, stomped out, and went and hanged himself.

One of the priests said, as he stomped out, "I'm glad he's not my friend," and they all laughed. He continued, "Now, what are we going to do with these thirty pieces of silver? It's not lawful to put them in the treasury, because it's the price of blood."

One of them said, "We have talked about buying the field of the potter to bury strangers in. It's just the right price. Let's buy it with this silver." That is what they did and it was called, "The field of blood."

Thus, came to pass that which was spoken by Zechariah, "I said to them, 'If you think it good, give me my price; if not, don't.' So they weighed for my price, thirty pieces of silver. The Lord said to me, 'Give it to the potter, a goodly price, that I was appraised.' I took the thirty pieces of silver and cast them to the potter in the house of the Lord."[329]

Shortly after dawn, the chief priests met again with the elders, scribes and the whole council. They led Jesus into the council and said, "Are you the Christ? Tell us."

Jesus said, "If I tell you, you will not believe. Also, if I ask you, you will not answer me or let me go. Hereafter, you shall see the Son of Man sitting on the right hand of the power of God."

They then asked, "Are you the Son of God?"

He said to them, "I am."

They said, "What need we of any more witnesses? We have heard from his mouth."[330]

The whole crowd of them arose and led him from Caiaphas to the hall of judgment in Pilate's palace. It was early in the day, and they didn't go into the judgment hall, because they would have been defiled and they wanted to continue celebrating the Passover. During Passover, Jews were not to be in a home where there was leavened bread, and Pilate would have had leavened bread in his palace.

Pilate went out to them and said, "What accusation do you bring against this man?"

Caiaphas said, "If he were not a criminal, we would not have brought him to you."

Pilate said, "Take him and judge him by your law."

---

[329] Zechariah 11:12-13
[330] Luke 22:66-71, 23;1

BETRAYED AND TRIAL

Caiaphas said to Pilate, "It's not lawful for us to put any man to death, but he needs to die. We have already tried him. We found him perverting the nation, forbidding giving tribute to Caesar and saying he himself is Christ, a King.[331]"

Thus, it would be fulfilled, Jesus was crucified as he had prophesied.

Then Pilate came back into the judgment hall and said to Jesus, "Are you the King of the Jews?"

Jesus asked, "Are you asking for yourself or did others say to do so?"

Pilate said, "Am I a Jew? Your own nation and the chief priests have delivered you to me. What have you done?"

Jesus said, "My kingdom is not of this world. If my kingdom were of this world, then my servants would fight, so I would not be delivered to the Jews. But now my kingdom is not of this world."

Pilate said, "Are you a king then?"

Jesus said, "I am. To this end was I born and, for this cause, I came into the world, that I should bear witness of the truth. Everyone who is of the truth hears my voice."

Pilate said, "What is truth?"

Jesus said, "The truth I am concerned about is eternal life and the commandments of God."

Pilate went out to the Jews again and said, "I find no fault at all in him.[332]

When he said this, the Jews booed and screamed.

Caiaphas said above the roar, "He is stirring up the people. He has taught throughout Jewry, beginning at Galilee and coming to here."

Pilate asked, "Is he a Galilean?"

Caiaphas said, "Of course he is."

Pilate said, "Then I will send him to Herod. He's in Jerusalem now."

A servant came to Herod and told him a prisoner, Jesus, had been sent from Pilate and all the chief priests and scribes had come with him. He told the servant, "Have them come into the hearing chamber. I have wanted to see this Jesus for some time. Maybe he will do a miracle. That would be great to see. Also, make sure they know there is no leavening in my house, as I am a Jew."

---

[331] Luke 23:2-5; John 18:28-31
[332] John 18:32-38

Herod asked him lots of questions, but Jesus said absolutely nothing. The chief priests and scribes accused him of all kinds of crimes, but Jesus continued to say nothing.

When Herod saw Jesus wasn't going to say anything, he had his soldiers put on him a gorgeous robe and, along with them, he mocked and made fun of him. Herod sent him back to Pilate, and he and Pilate became friends, when previously they were not on good terms.[333]

When Jesus was sent back to Pilate, Pilate again called together the chief priests and rulers. When they were gathered, Pilate said, "You have brought this man to me, saying he is fomenting insurrection. I have examined him and have found no fault in this man concerning those things for which you have accused him, nor did Herod. I sent Jesus to him and Herod found he had done nothing worthy of death. Thus, I will chastise him and release him to you."

It was the custom at the Feast of Passover for a prisoner to be set free. The chief priests had been working to gather a crowd of supporters. They wanted them to ask for Barabbas, who for insurrection, robbery, and murder was imprisoned, and for Jesus to be crucified instead. So, when Pilate asked the crowd what they wanted, they said with one voice, "Away with this man; release Barabbas."

Pilate's wife sent him a note saying, "Have nothing to do with that just man. I have suffered many things this day in a dream because of him."

Pilate, wanting to release Jesus, said again, "I find no evil in this man."

Again, the crowd yelled, "Crucify him, crucify him."

At this point, Pilate was afraid that a riot was brewing and he could not prevail. He took water and washed his hands before the crowd and said, "I am innocent of the blood of this just person. This sin will be on you and not on me."

The people answered, "His blood is on us and our children."

He motioned a centurion over to him and said, "Release Barabbas and scourge their King. I would like to have released this man; he is not guilty of anything. The leaders are just jealous of him. Go ahead and scourge him as you normally would, but make sure you don't kill him. I don't know what the chief priests did to him, but he looks like he was roughed up pretty well already."

---

[333] Luke 23:6-12

The centurion said, "Yes, sir, I understand. You can trust me. We will do a good job of scourging, but we won't kill him. We'll do things that won't cause too much blood loss, but are painful. We'll pluck out part of his beard. It's painful and looks bad, but won't kill him. The men will have fun degrading him. Since he claims to be a king, we'll dress him in a purple robe that looks kingly and we'll do a crown of thorns on his head; it won't cause too much bleeding. It will look and feel bad. The soldiers will have fun with it. Trust me. We'll put on a good show. It ought to instill some pity in the throng, if they aren't too bloodthirsty."

The soldiers took Jesus into the common hall. They stripped him and scourged him. After scourging, they put the purple robe on him. They then platted a crown of thorns, put it upon his head and placed a reed in his right hand. They bowed their knees before him and mocked him, saying, "Hail, King of the Jews!" Then they spit on him, took the reed and hit him on the head with it, making the thorns dig into his head, causing pain and making his head bleed.

When they were done, Pilate took Jesus out to the crowd wearing the crown of thorns and the purple robe. They didn't pity him, but cried out, "Crucify him, crucify him."

Pilate said, "Take him then and crucify him, but I find no fault in him."

The Jews answered him and said, "We have a law and by our law he should die, because he made himself the Son of God."

When Pilate heard that, he was more afraid and went again into the judgment hall and said to Jesus, "Where are you from?"

But Jesus didn't answer him.

Then Pilate said, "Why don't you answer me? Don't you know I have power to crucify you or to release you?"

Jesus answered, "You could have no power at all against me, except it was given you from above. Thus, he who delivered me to you has the greater sin."

Pilate again sought to release him, but the Jews cried out, "If you let this man go, you are not Caesar's friend. Whoever says he is a king speaks against Caesar."

When Pilate heard this, he brought out Jesus and sat down in the judgment seat.

The Jews cried out, "Away with him, away with him, crucify him."

Pilate said, "Shall I crucify your King?"

The chief priests answered, "We have no king but Caesar."

Then Pilate had the soldiers dress Jesus in his own clothes and delivered him to the Jews to be crucified.[334]

As is the custom, they had the accused carry his own cross. They were going up to a place called Golgotha, which in Hebrew means "place of the skull." There were two criminals who were to be crucified along with Jesus. They were also carrying their crosses in the procession.

As Jesus walked, he tripped several times. After his suffering in Gethsemane and from the scourging, he was too weak to carry his cross; he simply could not walk and carry it.

They compelled Simon, a man of Cyrene, to carry it for him. A great crowd of people, crying and lamenting, followed him.

At one point, Jesus turned and said to them, "Daughters of Jerusalem, weep not for me, but weep for yourselves and your children. The days are coming when they shall say, 'Blessed are the childless, the wombs that never gave birth and the breasts that were never sucked.' Then they shall say to the mountains, 'Fall on us,' and to the hills, 'Cover us.'"

When they got to the place called Golgotha or Calvary, Simon laid down the cross he was carrying where the centurion in charge of the crucifixion showed him.

The centurion said, "Now the fun begins. Scipio, get the holes for the crosses ready. We'll do the king first."

He turned to Jesus and said, "You, the king! Lie down on that wood and stretch out your arms."

Jesus followed the instructions.

The centurion gave further orders. "Okay. Caius, you hold the hands. Paulus, you drive the nails."

Paulus drove the nails into the palms, while Jesus said nothing.

The centurion said, "Now, Caius, get his feet lined up with one on top so one nail will do it. . . . Come on, Paulus; hit the spike like you mean it."

When they were done, the centurion looked at their work. "I think the nails might pull out of his palms; let's put nails in the wrist, too."

Paulus picked up more spikes and drove one into each of Jesus' wrists.

---

[334] Matthew 27:15-31; Mark 15:6-20; Luke 23:13-25; John 18:39-46; 19:1-16

The centurion said, "Okay, guys, slide the cross down into the hole as you lift it up... Come on, lift! He's heavy, but not that heavy."

Finally, the wood cross slid into the prepared hole. Jesus' feet were about two feet above the ground, giving all the opportunity to hit and spit on him if they desired.

One of the women, to alleviate his pain, gave Jesus vinegary wine mixed with gall, but he wouldn't drink it.[335]

Jesus was placed in the middle, between the two criminals. Over his head they wrote his accusation, "THIS IS JESUS, THE KING OF THE JEWS" in Hebrew, Greek, and Latin.

Before nailing him to the cross, they'd stripped off his clothes. Later, they divided them along seams into four piles of fabric. His robe was one piece, woven without a seam. Paulus said, "Let's not tear it, but cast lots to see whose it will be." They all agreed, fulfilling Psalm 22:18, "They part my garments among them and cast lots on my robe."

Word had been sent to Annas and Caiaphas about the title that had been written. When they heard what it was, they were livid. They immediately went to Pilate and said, "You have written, 'THIS IS JESUS, THE KING OF THE JEWS.' Change it to, 'HE SAID, I AM KING OF THE JEWS.'"

Pilate said, "I am going to leave it the way I wrote it."[336]

Jesus was crucified about nine a.m.[337] There was a crowd that watched Jesus being nailed to the cross and continued watching his agony. It consisted of women who had followed him and some of his disciples. Also, there were some of the Jewish leadership.

The agony he was suffering was plain for all to see. There was no comfortable place to rest on the cross. There was a small projection that supported some of his weight, but it didn't help much. When he hung by his arms, because of the position, he had trouble breathing. When he tried to put weight on his feet, it tore his skin and muscles painfully.

Some of the Jewish leadership made fun of him and said, "He saved others, but he cannot save himself."

The soldiers also said, mocking him, "If you are the King of the Jews, save yourself."

---

[335] Luke 23:27, Psalm 69:21
[336] Matthew 27:32-38; Mark 15:21-28; Luke 23:26-31, 38; John 19:17-24
[337] Bruce R. McConkie, *Doctrinal New Testament Commentary,* (1974) Deseret Book Company, Salt Lake City, UT. Pg. 827

Of the soldiers, Jesus said, "Father, forgive them, because they don't know what they are doing."

Others said, wagging their heads, "You said you could destroy the temple and rebuild it in three days. Save yourself. If you are the Son of God, come down from the cross."

Still, others said, "He trusted in God; let Him deliver him now. If he will save him, let Him save him, for he said, I am the Son of God."

One of the criminals, who was crucified with him, railed on him and said, "If you are Christ, save yourself and us."

The other criminal said across Jesus, "Don't you fear God, since you are facing the same punishment. We are receiving punishment for what we have done, but this man has done nothing wrong."

He then looked at Jesus and said, *between gasps for air, "I truly am a thief. I liked to work in crowded areas. I would steal a man's purse without him ever knowing it. I liked to work in the temple, when it was crowded. I heard you speak there several times. I know you are the Son of God, as you claim. I was thinking about quitting, when I got caught. I'm worried about my wife and children. They don't even know I'm here.* Remember me when you come into your kingdom."

Jesus said, *"Your sins are forgiven.* Today, you will be with me in paradise."

Also, close to the cross of Jesus was Mary, his mother, her sister, the wife of Cleophas, Mary Magdalene, and his disciple John. Looking at his mother, then nodding to John, Jesus said, "Mother, see your son!"

Then he turned his head to John and said, "John, see your mother." From that point, John took her into his home as though she was his mother and cared for her.

When noon came, the sun dimmed and there was darkness over the whole land until three pm.

Jesus was spiritually attuned to his Father and could feel His presence. At about three, his Father withdrew His presence, leaving Jesus alone. At that time, Jesus cried out with a loud voice, saying, "My God, my God, why have you forsaken me?"

Some of them thought he was calling for Elias and said, "Let's see if Elias will come to take him down."

Jesus said, "I am thirsty."

One ran and got a sponge full of vinegar and gave it to him.

BETRAYED AND TRIAL

When he tasted it, he said, "It is finished; your will is done. Into your hands I commend my spirit," and died.[338]

When he died, there was an earthquake and the veil of the temple ripped in two, from the top to the bottom.

When the centurion saw the earthquake and what was done, he glorified God and said, "This certainly was a righteous man."[339] *He had seen many die, but this is the first time he had seen someone voluntarily give up his life as Jesus had done, commending his Spirit to the Father.*

The ripped temple veil was about sixty feet high, thirty feet wide, and four and a half inches thick.[340] It separated the Holy Place from the Holy of Holies. The Holy Place and the Holy of Holies or Most Holy Place made up what was called the inner temple. It was placed in the Court of the Priests.

The Holy of Holies is where God dwelled and only the High Priest could enter it once a year on the Day of Atonement. He went in carrying blood to atone for the people. *With the ripping of the veil, the Holy of Holies was open to the view of those in the Holy Place, signifying the blood of Christ had paid for the sin of man, so those who were holy could enter his presence. The paschal lambs being offered were killed at three in the afternoon, the same time Christ died.*

At his death, there were women looking on from a distance, among who was Mary Magdalene, Mary, the mother of James the younger, Joses, and Salome. When he was in Galilee, they followed Him and ministered to Him. There were also many other women who came with Him to Jerusalem.[341]

The Law of Moses says, "If a man has committed a crime worthy of death, you shall not leave his body overnight, but bury him that day."[342] Therefore, the Romans had granted the Jews permission that those who were crucified in their country could be taken off the cross and buried, though, in other places, the bodies were left to rot. Because the Sabbath was coming in a few hours and the Jews didn't want the bodies to remain on the cross, they asked Pilate to have their

---

[338] Matthew 38-50; Mark 15:29-37; Luke 23:32-37, 39-46; John 19:25-30
[339] Matthew 27:51, 54; Mark 15:38-39; Luke 23:46-47; John 19:30
[340] Alfred Edersheim, The Life and Times of Jesus the Messiah http://www.ccel.org/ccel/edersheim/lifetimes.html Publisher: Grand Rapids, MI: Christian Classics Ethereal Library Pg. 1414
[341] JST Mark 15:45
[342] Deuteronomy 21:22-23

legs broken. *When the legs are broken, the crucified hang only by their arms, which restricts their breathing, and they soon die.*

The soldiers came and broke the legs of the criminals crucified with Jesus, but when they came to Jesus, they saw he was already dead, so they didn't break his legs. One of the soldiers pierced his side with a spear and both blood and water came out.[343] Thus was fulfilled the scriptures which said, "A bone of him shall not be broken," and "They shall look on him whom they pierced."[344]

Joseph of Arimathea was a rich man and a disciple of Jesus, though secretly, for fear of the Jews. He was an honorable counselor and had not consented to the deeds done that day. That evening, he went to Pilate and asked for the body of Jesus.

Pilate was surprised he was dead and asked the centurion if it was true. When the centurion said it was, he gave the body to Joseph.

Nicodemus, who first came to Jesus at night, came also. He brought a mixture of myrrh and aloes. Joseph bought fine linen and the two of them took the body of Jesus and wrapped his body in the linen cloth and spices, as was the custom of the Jews.

They took the body down to Joseph's new sepulcher, which was in a garden close to where Jesus was crucified. It was hewn out of stone, where no one had been buried before.

Mary Magdalene and the other Mary followed them and watched to see where they laid Him.

After the men prepared Jesus' body, they rolled a large stone over the opening. Because the Jew's preparation day was about over and the Sabbath was fast approaching, they were in a hurry.[345] Thus was fulfilled the prophecy, "And he made his grave with the wicked and the rich upon his death, because he had done no violence, nor did he lie."[346]

The next day, Saturday the Sabbath, the Pharisees and chief priests together went to Pilate. *Pilate welcomed them and said, "I am surprised to see you today, it being your Sabbath. What's so important that you are here today?"*

Caiaphas said, "We remember the deceiver said, while he was still alive, 'After three days I will rise again.' Command his tomb be guarded until the third day, in case his disciples come by night

---

[343] Matthew 27:55-56; Mark 15:40-41, Luke 23;48-49; John 19:31-37
[344] Psalms 34;20 and Zechariah 12:10
[345] Matthew 27:57-61; Mark 15:42-47; Luke 23:50-56; John 19:38-42
[346] Isaiah 53:9

and steal his body and say to the people, 'He has risen from the dead.' Then this last error will be worse than the first."

Pilate said, "I will give you the guards, a centurion, and four soldiers. It's up to you to make the watch as secure as you can."

The Pharisees, chief priests, and some workers went with the soldiers to the tomb. When they arrived, Caiaphas, standing in front of the tomb, told the centurion, "We think the deceiver's disciples will come and try to steal his body. We are going to seal this tomb. This big stone that's in front of the opening is round and it's rolling on a level stone track, so it's easy to roll to the left. We're going to drive in metal wedges on that side of the round stone, so it can't be rolled. When we get it driven in, we will seal the stone all around with mortar. If his disciples are going to steal his body, they are going to have to work for it. All you need to do is keep somebody from undoing this work before Monday. You can handle that, can't you?"[347]

The centurion said, "No problem. I'll guarantee no one is getting into this tomb before Monday."

The centurion went back to his soldiers and repeated what he had been told. They watched the Pharisees and chief priests watching the workmen driving in the wedge and placing the mortar.

One of the soldiers said, "It seems strange to me the Jews make a lot of noise about not working on the Sabbath and here are their leaders, working hard on their holy day to seal a tomb. It doesn't make sense to me."

Another said, "You have that right. I don't know much about what they believe, but I do know they say not to work on the Sabbath. They must think that doesn't apply to them. It makes you wonder."

After the Jews left, the centurion told the soldiers, "This tomb is really secure. I think two of you on a watch, while two sleep, will do just fine. Make some beds underneath that tree. It gives all of us a good view of the tomb. Use some of those palm fronds and those pine branches and let's get this done."

---

[347] Matthew 27:62-66

CHRIST IN THE SPIRIT WORLD

As soon as Christ said, "It is finished, your will is done. Into your hands I commend my spirit," he died.

He found he was in a tunnel or cave as he could see light a short distance away. He walked toward light streaming in and came out into the open. There was gathered an innumerable crowd of men and women. When they saw Him come out, they all bowed.

He motioned to them to arise. He saw Joseph step out, who had raised Him and was a father to Him. Joseph hurried to him and gave him a hug. Christ noticed there was not a feeling of substance to the hug.

Joseph said, "I am so proud of you. You completed all you set out to do."

Christ looked around and the next person he saw was his cousin, John, the Baptist. Christ also gave John a hug and then John re-introduced Him to his father, Zacharias.

Christ looked around at the crowd and said, "Joseph, I have prayed hard to know where I would be going and what I should do. I assume Adam is in charge, as he is the eldest father. I would like to meet him."

"You will meet him. He's right here behind us," Joseph said as he turned around and gestured to a figure standing there.

Adam said, " We've been waiting for this time to come. All of us miss our bodies. Now you are here, you will be resurrected and we will be, too."[348]

Christ said, " My main task now is to organize an outreach for those in hell."

Adam said, "We know they are there, but there is an impassable gulf between us and we do not have any contact with them."

Christ said, "I know, but I have the keys that will allow those here in paradise to go to hell to preach to the spirits there. First, I would like to address those here in paradise."

Adam said, "We knew you were coming and are here waiting to hear from you."

Christ said, "That's good; let's get started."

He stood in front of the throng and said,

---

[348] D&C 138:16-18

CHRIST IN THE SPIRIT WORLD

"I have overcome death and am come to free you from the chains of death. All of you will soon be resurrected, combining your spirits and body, never to be separated again. You now know what it is like to live without a body and have really missed it.

"You have experienced physical death. Because Adam ate the forbidden fruit, he brought into the world physical death, the parting of the body and the spirit. We all lived in a pre-existence, with our heavenly parents. You don't remember that, just as I don't remember it. When we are resurrected, we will be able to remember that world.

"Heavenly Father gave us the Plan of Salvation. You were to leave the pre-existence, come to earth, receive a body and be tested. While on earth, you would be taught the gospel of Christ. If you did your best to obey the laws that were given and accepted me as your Savior, you would pass the test. All of you have passed the test, because you are here.

"Many have lived without knowledge of the gospel and Plan of Salvation. They are in hell. All must have knowledge of the Plan of Salvation and hear the gospel in its fullness. They then will have the opportunity to accept me as their Savior. [349]

"It is going to be up to all of you to take the gospel to those in hell. They must have the opportunity to hear it. If they learn of it, accept it and repent of their sins, they will join you here in paradise. I was crucified and have paid the price for their sins, but if they don't accept the gospel and repent,[350] they must suffer, even as I suffered.

"That caused me, even God, the greatest of all, to tremble because of pain, to bleed at every pore, and to suffer both in body and spirit. I didn't want to drink that bitter cup. Nevertheless, glory be to the Father, and I partook and finished what I was prepared to do for the children of men.[351]

"Adam, because he ate the forbidden fruit, brought death into the world. It's all part of the Plan of Salvation. When a person breaks one of my Father's laws, they sin and become unclean. No unclean thing can be in my Father's

---

[349] D&C 138;19
[350] True, but a compilation.
[351] D&C 19:16-19

kingdom. Because I lived a life free of sin, I did not need to die. I had the ability to come down off the cross. But I freely gave my life that all could live again. I know it is hard to understand, but because of my sacrifice, all who have lived will receive a body, even those who go to outer darkness or perdition.[352]

"Before being resurrected, you will be judged and receive a body based on the kingdom of glory you have earned. The celestial is the highest, where my Father lives; next the terrestrial, and the lowest is the telestial.[353]

"There is a gulf between you here in paradise and those in hell that separates you from them. It has been impossible for you to cross it. I have the keys to open a passage. Just as we don't remember living in the pre-existence, those who are in hell don't remember either. If they did, there would be no need for faith.

"They need to exercise faith, just as those still living in the world need to. Those who repent and ask forgiveness of their sins will be forgiven and can join you here in paradise. I have paid the price for their sins and all that is needed is for them to recognize they have sinned, to repent of that sin, and ask me in faith to forgive them. The price has already been paid."[354]

Christ selected Adam to lead the mission to teach the spirits in hell. Adam selected two others to assist him and began to form the spirits in Paradise into groups of men and women to teach those in hell. Jesus Christ led the first groups down to hell and started the missionary work there.

---

[352] True, but a compilation.
[353] I Corinthians 15:38-41; D&C 88:14-24
[354] True, but a compilation.

PART 4
AFTER THE RESURRECTION

THE RESURRECTED CHRIST

On Earth, it was now very early Sunday morning; dawn was just breaking. Two of the soldiers stood guard while the centurion and the other two were sleeping. An earthquake knocked the two who had been standing off their feet and awakened the others.

The centurion tried to scramble to his feet, but ended up on his knees with his hands on the ground to steady himself. He said, "What is going on!"

He glanced up at the tomb, his jaw dropped and he said, "Damn! Look! Who are they?"

The soldiers looked up at the tomb and saw two beings in snow white robes rolling back the stone. They looked right at the guards with a penetrating gaze that seemed to go right through the men.

The guards lay still, not knowing what to do, but not wanting to antagonize the beings, whoever they were. The angels, for that is what they were, jumped up and sat on the stone after they had rolled it out of the way.[355]

After a few minutes they disappeared.

Hesitantly, the centurion got to his feet and walked up to the tomb. He looked at the stone. To the side of the opening were the wedges and a pile of mortar, like someone had set them there. He walked into the tomb, but it was empty. He turned and came out, down to the others.

He said, "There is no body in there. Go see for yourselves."

The guards looked up the hill to the tomb, but only one of them went up, with trepidation. He looked around, then walked back and said, "Except for some linen clothes, it's empty. What do we do now? We could be in big trouble."

The centurion said, "I think we should go to Caiaphas and tell him what happened. No human rolled that stone away and no human stole that body. I doubt if Caiaphas would like us to tell what really happened here. If we agree to keep our mouths shut, we could be well rewarded."

One of the others said, "I like the idea, but what if they just do away with us."

The centurion said, "I think they need somebody to say the disciples stole the body; otherwise, they can make the case He came

---

[355] Matthew 28:2-4; IV Matthew 28:2-3

THE RESURRECTED CHRIST

back from the dead, like He said would happen. Doesn't it make sense? What do we have to lose?"

Another responded, *"Well, we could lose our lives, but I don't think we have any choice. They are going to find out about this sooner or later."*

They left to find Caiaphas.

When they found him, they recited what happened. Caiaphas was not happy. He went and got other of the chief priests and elders and they all met together. They decided to pay the guards a large sum of money.

They told the guards, "We will pay you this money if you say, 'His disciples came at night and stole his body while we were sleeping.' If Pilate hears about this, we will tell him what occurred so you will be protected."

The guards took the money and did as they were told. This saying is commonly reported among the Jews to this day.[356]

Early Monday morning, while it was still dark, Mary Magdalene, Salome and Mary, the mother of James, went to the tomb. They brought sweet spices so they could anoint Jesus. As they walked, they discussed how they were going to roll away the stone from the door of the tomb.

They arrived at the tomb just as the sun was rising. When they looked, they saw the huge stone was rolled away. They went into the tomb, but the body of Jesus was not there. They were puzzled and Mary Magdalene said, *"What do you suppose happened to Him? Did the gardener put Him someplace else?"*

The other Mary said, *"I don't know, it's really strange."*

As they were leaving, they saw two angels standing beside the stone dressed in long, white, shining garments. They were afraid and bowed their heads.

The angels said to them, "Why do you seek the living among the dead? You are looking for Jesus of Nazareth, who was crucified. He is not here for he is risen."

One pointed and said, "There is where they laid Him."

He continued, "Remember how he spoke to you when you were still in Galilee? He said, 'The Son of Man must be delivered into the hands of sinful men, be crucified and the third day rise again.' Go tell the disciples and Peter he will go before you into Galilee and you shall see Him there, as he told you."

---

[356] Matthew 28:11-15

They did remember Jesus' words, but they were scared and fled from the area, not knowing what to think of the situation.

After they ran a short distance, Salome said, "Stop. Why are we running? Those were angels. If they were going to do something to us, it already would have happened. Why would they have told us to tell the other disciples, if they didn't want us to go and tell them?"

"That's true," Mary Magdalene said.

They slowly walked a short distance lost in their thoughts, when she said, "I feel like I should go back and make sure Jesus isn't there some place."

The other Mary said, "If you want to go back, go back. I'm not going back. I don't like tombs and I don't want to see anymore strange people telling me what to do, even if they are angels like Salome thinks."

With that, Mary Magdalene turned back and left the other two talking. As she walked back, she was crying. She only walked back a short distance, when she saw Jesus standing, but didn't recognize Him.

He said, "Why are you weeping? Who are you looking for?"

She thought he was the gardener and said, "Sir, if you have taken Him somewhere else, tell me where and I will take Him away."

Jesus said, "Mary."

She turned toward him and, recognizing Him, said, "Master," as she started toward him.

He said, "Don't hold me because I have not yet ascended to my Father. Go to my brothers and tell them I am ascending to my Father and your Father; and to my God and your God."

She left and ran to catch up to the other women. As she came up to them, she called out, "I saw Him, I saw Him!"

They stopped and let her catch up. "You really did see Him?" they asked.

"Yes, yes!" she said breathlessly. "I thought he was the gardener at first. We talked and he said to tell his brothers he had to ascend to his Father and our Father and to my God and your God."

They went to John and Peter, and Mary Magdalene told them, "We went to the tomb while it was still dark and got there just at sunrise. The stone was rolled away and we went into the tomb. The body of Jesus wasn't there. We were perplexed and didn't know what to do.

"We walked out of the tomb and saw two angels. When they looked at us, it was like lightning and their clothing was white as

THE RESURRECTED CHRIST

snow. It was scary. The angels said to tell Peter and his disciples Jesus will go into Galilee and there you will see Him.

"We left to find you, *but after thinking about it for a few minutes, I decided I should go back and see what I could find. I saw someone and thought it was the gardener, but soon realized he was the Master.* He said to tell you he had to ascend to his Father and our Father and to his God and our God." [357]

Peter turned to John and said, "That doesn't make sense. Let's go see."

They ran to the tomb. John ran the fastest and got there first. He stooped down and looked in. He saw the linen clothes lying by themselves, but didn't go in. *He wanted to honor Peter and waited for him to arrive before going in.*

When Peter arrived, he went in and found the cloth that had been wrapped around Jesus' head, not lying with the linen clothes, but lumped in a ball by itself.

Then John went in to see for himself and saw and believed. They did not know yet the scripture he would rise from the dead. After this, Peter and John parted as they left to go to their own places.[358]

As Peter was walking toward where he was staying, he saw a figure approaching who looked familiar. As he got closer, he realized it was Jesus. He ran toward Him and fell on his knees before Him. "Master! Master!" he said.

Jesus said, "Yes, it is I. As you know, you are the one now in charge of the work here on earth. Don't despair. I will meet with you and the others and will teach you what to do. Go now and tell the others you have seen me. Meet in the upper room again tonight and discuss what needs to be done. I will be there to help."

Peter said, "Master, I will do what you ask. I promise I will do my best."

With that, Jesus, turned and walked away and, after a few steps, disappeared.[359]

After the resurrection of Christ, many graves were opened and those who had died were resurrected and went into Jerusalem.[360]

---

[357] Matthew 28:1, 5-10; Mark 16:1-10; Luke 24:1-10; John 20:11-18
[358] Luke 24:12; John 20:2-10
[359] Luke 24:34; 1 Corinthians 15:5
[360] Matthew 27:52-53

THE ROAD TO EMMAUS

After talking to Peter, Christ ascended to his Father. He passed through the gates of heaven with all the guardian angels bowing to Him. He was met by His Father and spiritual Mother. He hurried toward them and the three of them met in a big hug.

His Father said, "Son, I am so pleased with what you have done. I knew you would do it, but I am very happy it is behind you. It was quite an undertaking and we are thrilled with the love for your brothers and sisters you have shown."

His spiritual Mother said, "I, too, am so happy you have returned and now have a celestial body, like we have. Now, eternal happiness is yours."

Christ said, "Thank you, both of you. I am glad to have this celestial body, but my work is not done yet and I can't stay. I still have teaching I must do for the Nephites, as well as the Jews."

Elohim said, "That's true, so we won't keep you. The earthquakes and destruction in the Western Hemisphere are over and they are ready for you and need you. Go to them."

The three of them parted, and Christ went first on a walk to Emmaus, and then went to the Nephites. That day, two of the disciples were walking to the village of Emmaus, which was about seven miles from Jerusalem. They were discussing the events of the day when Jesus, whom they didn't recognize, caught up and walked along with them.

Jesus said, "What are you talking about as you walk that is making you sad?"

One of them was Cleopas (Cleophas), and he said, "Are you a stranger in Jerusalem and have not heard of the things which have happened in Jerusalem recently?"

Jesus said, "What things?"

They said, "Jesus of Nazareth was a wonderful prophet doing miracles before God and the people. The chief priests and our rulers delivered Him to the Romans, who condemned Him to death and have crucified Him. We believed it was He who would redeem Israel. This is the third day since these things were done. Some of the women who were part of our company have astonished us. They went to the tomb early today and found it empty, but also said they had seen a vision of angels, telling them He was alive. Some of them who were with us ran to the tomb and found it as the women had said, but didn't see Jesus."

Then this new companion said, "You should believe what the prophets have taught. Should not Christ have suffered these things to enter into his glory?[361] *If I may, let me explain the scriptures more fully to you.*

"Moses said, 'The scepter shall not depart from Judah, nor a lawgiver from between his feet, until Shiloh comes and to Him shall the gathering of the people be.'[362] *The scepter is the symbol of authority. Shiloh is the Messiah. Up until now, Israel has been able to make religious laws for themselves, but this will end.*

"Balaam, the son of Beor, said, when he was asked to curse Israel, 'There shall come a Star out of Jacob and a Scepter shall rise out of Israel.'[363] *It was the Messiah he saw.*

"Also, Moses said, 'The Lord, your God, spoke to me and said, 'I will raise up a prophet from among my people, like you. I, God, will put words in his mouth and he shall speak to them all I shall command Him.'[364] *The Lord is telling Moses about the Messiah.*

"Again, speaking of the Messiah, in the second Psalm David says, 'The Lord has said to me, "You are my Son; this day have I begotten you."'[365]

"In the 22nd Psalm, David starts it with, 'My God, my God, why have you forsaken me?', which is what Jesus said on the cross. The 16th verse says, 'They pierced my hands and my feet.' It goes on and in the 18th verse says, 'They part my garments among them and cast lots on my robe.' *All these things happened to Jesus at the crucifixion.*

"In the 20th verse of Psalms 34, it says, 'He keeps all his bones, not one of them is broken.' *It would have been normal for the soldiers to break Jesus' legs like they did of those who were crucified with Him. But they didn't, because He was already dead.*

"In the 69th Psalm, David says, 'For the zeal of your house has eaten me up . . .' *Jesus certainly showed this*

---

[361] Mark 16:12; Luke 24:13-26
[362] Genesis 40:10
[363] Numbers 24:15, 17
[364] Deuteronomy 18:15, 18
[365] Psalms 2:7

in the cleansing of the temple which he did on several occasions. And later in the Psalm he says, 'They gave me also gall for my meat and in my thirst, they gave me vinegar to drink.' *This was also accomplished while he was on the cross.*[366]

"David starts the 110th Psalm with, 'The Lord said to my Lord, "Sit at my right hand until I make your enemies your footstool."' *In other words, God the Father is saying to God the Son, sit at my right hand in the heavens.*[367]

"The 118th Psalm says, 'The stone which the builders refused has become the chief cornerstone. This is the Lord's doing. It is marvelous in our eyes.' [368] *In building, the chief cornerstone is the first stone put in and the rest of the building is measured from it.*

"Isaiah says, 'The Lord Himself shall give you a sign. Behold, a virgin shall conceive and bear a son and shall call his name Immanuel.'[369] *This is obviously talking about the birth of the Christ or Messiah.*

"Later he says, 'For to us a child is born. To us a son is given. The government shall be on his shoulder and his name shall be called Wonderful Counselor, The Mighty God, The Everlasting Father, The Prince of Peace. Of the increase of his government and peace, there shall be no end. He shall sit on the throne of David in his kingdom and order it and establish it with judgment and with justice from now even forever. The zeal of the Lord of hosts will perform this.'[370] *I think it is plain to understand.*

"*Isaiah goes on to talk about what the Messiah will do when He is on the earth.* 'And He shall be for a sanctuary, but also a stone of stumbling and for a rock of offense to Judah and Israel and for a gin and for a snare to the inhabitants of Jerusalem.' *He said it like it was. He taught the people they needed to be obedient to the Lord.*[371]

"Isaiah also says, 'The Lord God has given me the tongue of the learned. I gave my back to the whip and my

---

[366] Psalms 69:9, 21
[367] Psalms 110:1
[368] Psalms 114:22-23
[369] Isaiah 7:14
[370] Isaiah 9:6-7
[371] Isaiah 8:14

cheeks to them who plucked off the hair. I didn't hide my face from shame and spitting, for the Lord God will help me and I shall not be confounded. I have set my face like a flint and I know I shall not be ashamed.'[372] *As Christ was scourged, the soldiers whipped his back, a part of his beard was pulled out, he was spit on and they tried to shame Him, but he kept his head high.*

"Isaiah wrote over seven hundred years before Christ, 'Who has believed our report? To whom is the arm of the Lord revealed? He shall grow up before us as a tender plant and as a root out of a dry ground. He has no comeliness and when we shall see Him, there is no beauty we should desire Him. He is despised and rejected of men. A man of sorrows and acquainted with grief. We hid our faces from him. He was despised and we did not value him. He has carried our grief and sorrows and yet we didn't care He was stricken, smitten of God and afflicted. But, he was wounded for our transgression and bruised for our iniquities. The chastisement of our peace was upon Him and with his stripes we are healed. All we like sheep have gone astray and have turned everyone to his own way. The Father has laid on him the iniquity of us all. He was oppressed and afflicted, yet He opened not his mouth. He is brought as a lamb to the slaughter and as a sheep before her shearers is dumb, so he opened not His mouth. Yet it pleased the Father to bruise Him and put Him to grief. When you shall accept the offering He made of his soul for your sin, He shall be as your father. His days shall be prolonged and the pleasure of the Father shall prosper in his hand. The Father shall see the travail of His soul and shall be satisfied. By His knowledge shall the righteous servant justify many, for He shall bear their iniquities. Therefore, will the Father divide Him a portion with the great and He shall divide the spoil with the strong; because He has poured out his soul to death, was numbered with the transgressors, He bore the sin of many, and made intercession for the transgressors.'[373]

"Micah designates where Christ will be born. But you, Bethlehem Ephratah, though you are little among the thousands of Judah, yet out of you shall come to me He who

---

[372] Isaiah 50:4, 6-7
[373] Isaiah 53

is to be ruler of Israel. His doings are from long ago, from everlasting.'[374]

"Christ came into Jerusalem riding on an ass' colt, just as is said by Zechariah, 'Rejoice greatly, O daughter of Zion. Shout, O daughter of Jerusalem. Behold, your King comes to you. He is just and having salvation, lowly and riding on an ass, a colt, the foal of an ass.'[375]

"Also, Zechariah mentioned the betrayal of Jesus, 'I said to them, "If you think it good, give me my price; if not, don't." So they weighed for my price, thirty pieces of silver. The Lord said to me, "Give it to the potter, a goodly price that I was appraised." I took the thirty pieces of silver and cast them to the potter in the house of the Lord.'[376]

"Also, Zechariah describes the wounds Jesus will receive. 'What are these wounds in your hands?' Then he will answer, 'Those I was wounded with when in the house of my friends.'[377]

"Malachi foretells John, the Baptist's, coming as well as Jesus'. 'I will send my messenger and he shall prepare the way before me. The Lord, whom you seek, shall suddenly come to His temple, even the messenger of the covenant, whom ye delight in. Behold, He shall come, says the Lord of hosts.'"[378]

When their companion came to this point, they were close to the village where they were going. He made like he was going further. They asked Him, "Won't you stop with us? It is close to dark and the day is almost over."

He said, "If you wish, I'll stop with you," and He went in to stay with them. When they sat down to eat, He took bread, blessed it and broke it and gave to them. At this point, their eyes were opened and they recognized Him, but He vanished out of their sight.

One of them said, "Didn't our hearts burn, while He talked with us on the way and explained the scriptures to us. We need to tell the others He has risen."

They left immediately and returned to Jerusalem. They found ten of the apostles and others gathered together with the doors

---

[374] Micah 5:2
[375] Zechariah 9:9
[376] Zechariah 9:12-13
[377] Zechariah 13:6
[378] Malachi 3:1

THE ROAD TO EMMAUS

shut for fear of the Jews. They were discussing the fact Simon had seen the risen Lord.

Cleopas said, "We also have seen the risen Lord. As we were on our way to Emmaus, a stranger was also walking our way and joined us. It was Jesus, but we didn't recognize Him. He explained in the scriptures all the things pertaining to Himself. When we got to Emmaus, it seemed He was going to go on, so we asked Him to join us, which He did. As we started to eat, we recognized it was Christ when He broke the bread."[379]

As they were speaking, Christ himself stood amid them and said, "Peace be to you."

When they saw and heard him, they were frightened, thinking he was a spirit.

He said, "Why are you troubled? It is I, Myself. Touch me and see, for a spirit does not have flesh and bones, as you see I have."

He then showed them His hands and His feet.

They did not know what to believe and were wondering if it could be true, so He said, "Have you here any food?" *He did this to show them He had a real body, as spirits can't eat.*

They gave him a piece of a broiled fish and a honeycomb, which He took and ate before them. He said, "These are the words I spoke to you while I was still with you. All things must be fulfilled, which were written in the Law of Moses, in the prophets and in the psalms concerning me. *If you will study these, you will see all has been fulfilled as it was written.*"

He then went on to explain the scriptures to them and said, "Christ had to suffer and rise from the dead the third day for the remission of sins. Thus, you need to preach repentance and the remission of sins in, My name, among all nations beginning at Jerusalem. You are witnesses of these things."

Next, He said to them, "Receive the Holy Ghost. Whose sins you remit, are remitted for them and whose sins you retain are retained."[380]

The apostle, Thomas, was not with them when Jesus came. The other disciples told him, "We have seen the Lord."

But he said, "Except I shall see in His hands the print of the nails and put my finger into the print of the nails and thrust my hand into His side, I will not believe."

---

[379] Mark 16:13; Luke 24:27-32
[380] Mark 16:14; Luke 24:36-48; John 20:22-23

After eight days (as the Jews counted), again His disciples were together, and Thomas was with them. Jesus came, the doors being shut, and stood in the midst and said, "Peace be to you."

Then He said to Thomas, "See my hands. Put in here your finger. Put your hand here in My side and don't be faithless, but believing."

Thomas said, "My Lord and My God."

Jesus said, "Thomas, because you have seen me, you have believed. Blessed are they who have not seen and yet have believed."

Jesus did many other signs which are not written. But these are written, so you may believe Jesus is the Christ, the Son of God and believing you might have life through His name.[381]

CHRIST AND THE NEPHITES

After walking with His disciples and breaking bread, Christ went to the Nephites, in what would be the Americas, to teach them. They were primarily descendants of the tribe of Joseph. The family of Lehi, a prophet of the Lord and a contemporary of Jeremiah, left Jerusalem just before it was captured by the Babylonians. Lehi's family consisted of his wife Sariah, and four sons, the eldest Laman, then Lemuel, Sam, and finally Nephi, the youngest. Two more, Jacob and Joseph, were born to them later.

Lehi had a vision in which the Lord showed him Jerusalem would be destroyed and many other things pertaining to the salvation of man. After the vision, he testified to the people in Jerusalem of their wickedness and need for repentance, resulting in his life being threatened.

Later, he had another vision in which the Lord again told him Jerusalem would be destroyed and was commanded to leave all his gold, silver, and other possessions and flee into the wilderness with his family, which the family did.

Laman and Lemuel did not believe Jerusalem would be destroyed and did not want to be in the wilderness. Nephi prayed and received confirmation of what the Lord was asking and was told they would be led to a land of promise; a land choice above all other lands. He told his brothers about it and Sam believed him, while Laman and Lemuel did not.

---

[381] John 20:26-31

Lehi's sons were asked by the Lord to return to Jerusalem and get plates containing the writings of the prophets and the family's genealogy. They obtained the records, though Laban and Lemuel were not much help. After this, they returned to the wilderness and their parents.

They were asked to go back again and ask the family of Ishmael to join them in the wilderness, which they did. Joining the two families provided mates for the children, as Lehi had mostly sons, and Ishmael had all daughters.

While in the wilderness, Lehi had another vision in which he saw the tree of life. He was concerned about Laman and Lemuel, because they would not eat the fruit of the tree of life as the rest of the family did.[382]

When it was time to start for the land of promise, they were given the Liahona, a brass ball with spindles that pointed the way they should go. It worked by faith, and without faith it would not lead them where they wanted to go. Using it, they journeyed through the wilderness to the ocean and the land they named "Bountiful," because of the abundant fruit and wild honey.

There they built a ship following the design the Lord gave to Nephi. Laman and Lemuel would not help build the ship, because they did not think Nephi could do it. With help from the Lord, the two were persuaded to help and they built a good ship.

They prepared supplies and boarded the ship and set sail for the promised land. Laman and Lemuel rebelled against Nephi, tying him up. As soon as he was tied, a great storm arose and they could not steer the ship and were in danger of sinking. They released Nephi and, as soon as they did, the storm calmed and they could direct the ship as they had before. Shortly afterwards, they arrived at the promised land, somewhere in the western hemisphere. Nephi prepared plates of ore and kept a history of the people on the plates.[383]

Laman and Lemuel continued to be at odds with Nephi and his family. Upon the death of Lehi, Nephi and his family were warned by the Lord to take their things and flee into the wilderness, which they did. The two factions developed into two nations known as the Nephites and Lamanites, after their leaders, Nephi and Laman.[384] They had many wars, and usually the Nephites were more righteous than the Lamanites, but not always.

---

[382] BM 1 Nephi 1-8
[383] BM 1 Nephi 16-19
[384] BM 2 Nephi 5

CHRIST AND THE NEPHITES

About 600 years after leaving Jerusalem, there was a big storm and a large earthquake, with three days of complete darkness without any light, not even a fire. The most wicked of the people were killed and their cities were destroyed.

A voice from Heaven was heard and it said, "Behold my beloved son, in whom I am well pleased, in whom I have glorified my name---hear Him."

They saw a being descend in a white robe into the midst of them. He said, "I am Jesus Christ. Come forward and thrust your hands into my side and feel the nail holes in my hands and feet that you might know I am the God of Israel and the God of the whole earth and have been slain for the sins of the world."

He called Nephi and eleven others forward and gave them power to baptize and told them how to do it, so there would be no dispute. He ordained them apostles and spent several days teaching them to lead his church in that area. His disciples were baptized and given the Holy Ghost. They were given the sacrament and administered it to the people. He taught the same things he taught the Jews in the holy land, including the Sermon on the Mount and told them to be perfect, even as He or His Father in heaven were perfect.[385]

After teaching several days and organizing His church, He departed.

His disciples continued to teach and all were finally converted to his gospel and there were no more Lamanites. Until almost 200 AD, they lived in harmony, with no poor among them, and had all things in common. They prospered abundantly, becoming rich, and multiplied greatly until they covered the land.[386]

After this, pride developed and they no longer had things in common, and the Lamanites once more appeared. The Lamanites became more abundant and the Nephites lost their gospel focus, becoming more like the Lamanites.

From Lehi and Nephi's time, the Nephite prophets had kept numerous records on gold plates. About 322 AD, there was a ten-year-old boy named, Mormon. Ammaron, the prophet at the time, was getting old and he hid the plates so they would not be stolen for their gold. Ammaron was impressed with Mormon's demeanor and abilities, and told him where he hid the plates and told him when he was older, he should take charge of them.

---

[385] BM 3 Nephi 8-12
[386] BM 4 Nephi 1

About a year later, a war began between the Nephites and Lamanites. When Mormon was sixteen, he was given command of the Nephite army. Both the Lamanites and Nephites had become evil and there were very few righteous among them. Mormon preached to the people, but they would not listen to him. The Lamanites were more numerous than the Nephites and, while the Nephites won some battles, they began to be overcome by the Lamanites. There was blood and carnage spread throughout the land.

Mormon had a son, who was also a prophet and general with his father. During the years of war, there were times of peace and Mormon made an abridgement of the many plates he had. This abridgement is The Book of Mormon we have today, with a few chapters Moroni wrote after the death of his father.

When Mormon was about seventy-three years old, the war was still going on, with many thousands killed. He wrote the king of the Lamanites asking for a truce so he could gather all his people to the area of the hill Cumorah. The truce was granted and the Nephites gathered all their men, women, and children to the hill. There were about twenty-three generals, each with ten thousand troops. They saw the armies of the Lamanites marching toward them, and with that awful fear of death which fills the breasts of wicked, they waited to receive them.

The Nephites were wiped out, but there were twenty-four of them who had been wounded and were still alive among the dead, including Mormon and Moroni. Though they tried to hide from the Lamanites, all twenty-four were killed, except Moroni, who managed to hide for some years and continued to add more to what his father had written. Moroni hid the plates where Joseph Smith found them years later.[387]

JESUS IN GALILEE

After visiting the Nephites, Jesus came back to Galilee. The angels at the sepulcher and Jesus, Himself, told His disciples to go into Galilee and wait for Him there, so they did. Simon Peter, Thomas, Nathanael, James and John, the sons of Zebedee, and two others were there.

---

[387] BM Mormon 1-8

One day Peter said, "I am going fishing." The rest said they would go with him. They went into a boat, fished all night, and caught nothing.

When it was morning, Jesus stood on the shore, but His disciples didn't recognize Him.

Jesus said, "Do you have any fish?"

They said, "No."

Jesus said, "Cast the net on the right side of the boat and you will find them."

They did and now they couldn't draw the net in for the many fish there were.

John said to Peter, "It is the Lord."

When Simon Peter heard it was the Lord, he tied on his fisher's coat and jumped into the water and swam to the shore. The other disciples came in a rowboat, because they were not far from land, dragging the net with the fish. When they got to shore, they saw a fire of coals, with fish cooking on it, and bread.

Jesus said, "Bring some of the fish which you have caught."

Simon Peter went and drew the net to land full of large fish, a hundred and fifty-three. With all the large fish, the net was not broken.

Jesus said, "Come and eat.

None of the disciples dared to ask Him, "Who are you?," knowing it was the Lord.

Jesus came and gave them fish and bread. This is the third time Jesus showed Himself to his disciples as a group, after he had risen from the dead.

When they had dined, Jesus said to Simon Peter, "Simon, son of Jonas, do you love me more than these?"

Peter said, "Yes, Lord. You know I love you."

Jesus said, "Feed my lambs."

Jesus said to him the second time, "Simon, son of Jonas, do you love me?"

Peter said, "Yes, Lord. You know I love you."

Jesus said, "Feed my sheep."

Jesus said to him the third time, "Do you love me?"

Peter said, "Lord, you know all things. You know I love you."

Jesus said, "Feed my sheep. When you were young, you dressed yourself and walked where you wanted, but when you are old, you shall reach forward your hands and another shall dress you, and carry you where you don't want to go. Follow me."

Peter turned around and saw John. He asked Jesus, "What shall John do?"

Jesus said, "If I want him to stay until I come, what is that to you? Follow me."[388]

Jesus told his disciples to meet Him the next week on a mount in Galilee with all eleven and He would teach them.

When they came the next week to the mount, they found Jesus with food prepared for them. He served them and, as they ate, He spoke to them, saying,

"Before I sent you out two by two to preach and heal, I conferred on you the Melchizedek Priesthood. I want to talk about priesthood again. Abraham received this priesthood from Melchizedek, who received it through the lineage of his fathers all the way from Adam, the first man. It is without beginning of days or end of years.

"I confirmed a priesthood also on Aaron and his progeny, throughout all their generations, which priesthood also continues and abides forever with the higher priesthood which is after the holiest order of God. This higher priesthood administers the gospel and holds the key of the mysteries of the kingdom, even the key of the knowledge of God. Therefore, in its ordinances, the power of godliness is manifest. Without those ordinances and the authority of the priesthood, the power of godliness is not manifest to men in the flesh. For without this no man can see the face of God, even the Father and live.

"This Moses plainly taught to the children of Israel in the wilderness and sought diligently to hallow his people that they might behold the face of God. But they hardened their hearts and could not endure His presence. Therefore, I, the Lord, in my wrath, for my anger was kindled against them, swore they should not enter into My rest while in the wilderness, which rest is the fullness of My glory. Therefore, I took Moses out of their midst and the Holy Priesthood also.

"The lesser priesthood continued, which priesthood holds the key of the ministering of angels and the

---

[388] John 21:1-22

preparatory gospel. Which gospel is the gospel of repentance, and of baptism, and the remission of sins, and the law of carnal commandments, which I, the Lord, in my wrath, caused to continue with the house of Aaron among the children of Israel until John, whom I raised up, being filled with the Holy Ghost from his mother's womb.

"For he was baptized while he was yet in his childhood and was ordained by My angel at the time he was eight days old to this power, to overthrow the kingdom of the Jews and to make straight My way before the face of My people, to prepare them for the coming of the Son of Man, in whose hand is given all power.[389]

"Whoever is faithful to obtain the two priesthoods of which I have spoken and the magnifying of their calling, are sanctified by the Spirit to the renewing of their bodies. They become the sons of Moses and of Aaron and the seed of Abraham, and the church and kingdom, and the elect of God.

"Also, all they who receive this priesthood receive Me, for they who receive Me, receive My Father. And they who receive My Father, receive My Father's kingdom; therefore, all My Father has shall be given to them. This is by the oath and covenant which belong to the priesthood. Therefore, all those who receive the priesthood, receive this oath and covenant of My Father, which He cannot break, neither can it be moved.

"But whoever breaks this covenant after they have received it, and altogether turns away from it, shall not have forgiveness of sins in this world or in the world to come. Woe to all those who come not to this priesthood that you have received, which I have confirmed on all of you previously, by mine own voice. I have given the heavenly hosts and My angels charge concerning you.

"I now give to you a commandment to beware concerning yourselves, to give diligent heed to the words of eternal life. You shall live by every word that proceeds from the mouth of God. For the word of the Lord is truth, and whatever is truth is light, and whatever is light is Spirit, even My Spirit, the Spirit of Jesus Christ. And the Spirit gives light to every person who comes into the world, and the

---

[389] D&C 84:14-28

Spirit enlightens every person through the world, that listens to the voice of the Spirit. And everyone who listens to the voice of the Spirit comes to God, even the Father. The Father teaches them of the covenant which He has renewed and confirmed upon you, which is confirmed upon you for your sakes, and not for your sakes only, but for the sake of the entire world.

"You are My apostles, even God's high priests. You are they whom My Father has given me, you are My friends. Therefore, every soul who believes on your words, and is baptized by water for the remission of sins, shall receive the Holy Ghost. These signs shall follow them who believe. In My name; they shall do many wonderful works. In My name, they shall cast out devils. In My name, they shall heal the sick. In My name, they shall open the eyes of the blind, and unstop the ears of the deaf, and the tongue of the dumb shall speak. If anybody shall administer poison to them, it shall not hurt them and the poison of a serpent shall not have power to harm them.

"But a commandment I give to you, that you shall not boast yourselves of these things, neither speak them before the world, for these things are given to you for your profit and for salvation. From you, it must be preached to the entire world that they shall repent of their former evil works, for they are to be upbraided for their evil hearts of unbelief.

"Those who believe not on your words, and are not baptized in water in My name, for the remission of their sins, that they may receive the Holy Ghost, shall be damned, and shall not come into my Father's kingdom where My Father and I am.[390]

"This is My work and My glory --- to bring to pass the immortality and eternal life of man.[391] While I was with you, I said, 'All must be born of water and the Spirit or they cannot enter the kingdom of God.'[392] *Thus, unless you are born again through baptism by immersion in the similitude of rebirth and receive the Holy Ghost by the laying on of hands, you can't enter My Father's kingdom. You will*

---

[390] D&C 84:29-48, 63-76
[391] Moses 1:39
[392] John 3:5

receive these ordinances soon. Your forbearers also have not received them.

"All, must have the opportunity to partake of these ordinances. The gospel will be taught to all the world, the dead as well as the living.[393] *Since these ordinances have to be done by the living, the dead must receive them by proxy.* The first ordinances to be done for the dead are baptism and confirmation or the laying on of the hands for the Gift of the Holy Ghost.[394]

"*Marriage was instituted before the world was created.* As I said before, 'A man shall leave his father and his mother and shall hold to his wife and they shall be one flesh.' Therefore, they are no more two, but one flesh.[395] *A married couple will spend a lifetime becoming one, so it makes no sense for them to separate after death. To avoid this, they need to be married in the temple, by the authority of the Holy Priesthood. If you do not have a temple marriage while on this earth, you must be married and sealed by proxy after you have died.*

"*Families should be eternal.* Children need to be sealed to their parents and the parents to their children, so they can be together in the eternities. This is what Malachi meant when he said, 'Behold, I will send you, Elijah, the prophet, before the coming of the great and dreadful day of the Lord. He shall turn the heart of the fathers to the children and the heart of the children to their fathers, lest I come and smite the earth with a curse.'[396]

"*I will show Simon Peter plans for a temple and will teach you the ordinances that are needed to do the work in the temple, so when the temple is built, the work for the living and the dead can go forward.*"

After teaching them the temple ordinances, He said, "Besides temple work, you must go and preach to all the world. Next week, I want to meet you and the rest of My followers on the mount where we fed the five thousand. Please make the arrangements. I need to leave now."

With that, he walked away and disappeared.

---

[393] Isaiah 24:22; 42:6-7; 61:1
[394] 1 Corinthians 15:29
[395] Genesis 2:24; Matthew 19:5,6
[396] Malachi 4:5,6

JESUS IN GALILEE

The next week, a crowd of about five hundred was sitting on the mountainside where he had fed the five thousand. As they sat there, they saw a figure appear, walking down the mountain toward them, it was Jesus and they arose to greet Him.
He said,

"I am pleased all of you made the effort to come here. I want to start today with the plan of salvation. Before this world was, Father discussed with me and you, the plan for this world. He is the Father of our spirits and at that time we only had spirit bodies. Father had a physical body and we wanted one like He had, so we could be like Him. His plan gave us a physical body like His. But He told us this life would be a test and many of us would not get passing grades and would not be able to return to live with Him. A third of his spirit children rebelled and were cast down to this earth, out of His presence.[397] The rest of us, which includes all of you, were assigned times to come to this earth and were given tasks we might accomplish.

"Each one of us were given bodies and talents to go with them and each of us has had problems in this world. These problems came from three sources: Things we did, things others did to us, and acts of nature. Some of you had imperfect bodies when you were born, others developed imperfections with age, other imperfections came because of accidents and other things. Because Elohim and I want all to progress and become better, all living have their agency to make decisions for themselves.

"You have been given commandments to guide you in your decisions. You also have the Holy Ghost. It will guide you to make good decisions, if you seek it, and if you live the commandments, it will be easier to feel it. Because there is evil in the world and those who are evil also have their agency, bad things happen to good people. Compared to the eternities, your life on earth is but the blink of an eye. If everything was perfect, there would be little progress. You all need problems in life. Embrace them and move forward. Not everyone can live to old age. Death is sad for you here, but is joyful when you join those who have gone before.

---

[397] D&C 29:36; Revelations 12:4,9

"Adam and Eve were the first to come to this earth. They were commanded to be fruitful, multiply, and replenish the earth They were also told not to eat the forbidden fruit, which would make them wise, but would make them mortal and subject to physical death, but it would allow them to have children, so they could obey the commandment to multiply. They chose to eat the forbidden fruit and bring to pass the plan of salvation. They were given the law of sacrifice, and were told to sacrifice the best of their animals to their God. This was a similitude of My sacrifice and it was to point them to me.

"They did multiply and the earth was populated. There were many who were not righteous, and prophets were sent to preach repentance to them, but many did not repent. Finally, it got to the point where there were so few righteous, it was unlikely anyone who was born would have much chance to live a righteous life. Father decided to cause most of those then living to die. Noah built an ark and a few were saved to start life anew.

"Again, the world was populated. Abraham was born, and Father, knowing who he was from before, covenanted with him that I would be of his seed. Isaac and Jacob were born and Jacob's name was changed to Israel, and Father renewed His covenant with him. The twelve tribes of Israel were His children. Father sent Moses to Israel to free them from Egyptian bondage.

"Father wanted to give them the Melchizedek Priesthood, but they were not ready for it, so He gave them the Law of Moses instead, with the lesser or Aaronic Priesthood. I have restored the higher priesthood, which is My priesthood, but the scriptures will call it the Melchizedek Priesthood after the great High Priest, Melchizedek, King of Salem.[398]

"Since I have accomplished My sacrifice for sin on the cross and have restored the higher priesthood, the law of Moses is fulfilled. I have given you the two great commandments. The first is, 'You shall love the Lord, your God, with all your heart, all your soul, all your mind, and all your strength.' The second is, 'You shall love your neighbor as yourself.;[399] *The Ten Commandments and other*

---

[398] Genesis 14:18-20; Psalms 110:4; Hebrews 5:6; 7:1-4, 11, 15-17
[399] Mark 12:30, 31

commandments that are in the Law of Moses are part of 'Love your God and your neighbor.'

"I gave you the Ten Commandments, and it is important for you to continue to obey them. They are:
1. You shall have no gods before me.
2. You shall not make any image and bow down to it or worship it.
3. You shall not take the name of the Lord your God in vain.
4. Remember the Sabbath to keep it holy and don't do any work on that day.
5. Honor your father and mother, that your days may be long on the land the Lord gives you.
6. You shall not murder.
7. You shall not commit adultery.
8. You shall not steal.
9. You shall not give false witness.
10. You shall not covet anything of your neighbor's.[400]

"When you break these commandments, you need to repent. You should have a broken heart and a contrite spirit. That means a godly sorrow--a true repentance for your sins. This requires recognizing your sins, humbly asking forgiveness, and forsaking them in the future. If restitution can be made, it should be. Pride is the downfall of many.

"When one is prideful, they put themselves before God and are not obedient to the commandments. Commandments are given to you not to take joy from you, but to give you joy and eternal happiness. Keeping the commandments provides health and well-being, spiritually and physically. Your bodies are temples for your spirits and should be kept clean.

"I, God, have suffered and paid the price for your sins, so if you repent, you will not have to suffer. But if you will not repent, you must suffer even as I; which suffering caused me, even God, the greatest of all, to tremble because of pain, and to bleed at every pore, and to suffer both body and spirit--and would I might not drink the bitter cup, and

---

[400] Exodus 20:7-17

shrink. Nevertheless, glory be to the Father, and I partook and finished my preparations to the children of men.

"Wherefore, I command you again to repent; and confess your sins, lest you suffer these punishments of which I have spoken, of which in the smallest, yes, even in the least degree you have tasted at the time I withdrew my Spirit.[401]

"As I said before, one of the reasons we came here is to obtain bodies. Once we have our bodies, have learned how to use them, and have done what was asked, we can return and live with our Heavenly Parents. Not all will be able to do that. There are three degrees of glory: The celestial, terrestrial, and *telestial. The glory of the celestial is like the sun, the glory of the terrestrial is like the moon, and the glory of the telestial is like the stars.*[402]

"Those who are not able to keep celestial laws would not be comfortable living a celestial glory. Those who are not able to keep terrestrial laws would not be comfortable living a terrestrial glory. Those who are not able to keep telestial laws are not meet for a kingdom of glory.[403] *The decisions you make here on earth and what you do, determines who you will become in this life and in the eternities. I will be there to help you in those decisions, but you must knock so I can open.*

"A temple will be built in Galilee, where you will be able to be sealed (married) to your spouse and children for time and all eternity, so you can have an eternal family. After you have received your own ordinances, you can perform them by proxy for your ancestors, so they will also have an opportunity for eternal life.

"In my ministry, I was sent to the Jews, but I ask you to take My gospel to all nations.

"The purpose of temples has been to bring Father's children to Him. Since the Melchizedek Priesthood is once more on the earth, the use of temples changes. They will be a place to go to learn about your Heavenly Father and to receive the ordinances needed to be able to return to live with Him.

---

[401] D&C 19:16-20
[402] I Corinthians 15:40-41
[403] D&C 88:22-24

> "Since I have made my sacrifice, the Law of Moses is fulfilled, and there is no longer a need for blood sacrifice. Herod's temple will be destroyed and, hereafter, no temples will be constructed for blood sacrifice, but only to perform the saving ordinances. This will be to the Jews a symbol the Messiah has come."

Jesus continued teaching them many things on the mount. Finally, he told them to wait in Jerusalem for that which the Father had promised them, the Gift of the Holy Ghost. *He said, "Remember to keep the commandments, pray at least morning and evening to your Heavenly Father, study the teachings of the prophets daily, and attend your Sabbath meetings. Once you have the Gift of the Holy Ghost, this will allow you to have it as a constant companion on a daily basis." He then blessed them.*

While they looked, he was taken up into a cloud out of their sight. Two men stood by them dressed in white, who said, "You people of Galilee, why do you stand gazing up into heaven? This same Jesus, who is taken up from you into heaven, shall come in the same manner as you have seen Him go into heaven."[404]

THE APOSTLES AFTER THE ATONEMENT

Shortly after Jesus was taken up into Heaven, the apostles selected one to replace Judas. They selected two, Joseph Justus, called Barsabas, and Matthias. It was common for the Jews to cast lots to make a difficult decision. This time, they prayed and asked the Lord, who knows all men's hearts, to make the decision by making the lot fall on whom he would choose. After praying, they cast lots and the lot fell to Matthias.[405]

Fifty days after the Feast of Passover, the Feast of Pentecost was kept. It celebrated the harvest of grain. It lasted one day and that day was a day of holy convocation.[406] The apostles were meeting on this day in one place, when there came a sound from the sky as of a rushing, mighty wind. It filled the entire house where they were sitting. It looked like there were split tongues of fire sitting on each

---

[404] Acts 1:4, 5, 9-11
[405] Acts 1:23-26
[406] Bible Dictionary, *Feasts*, (1979). The Holy Bible, Authorized King James Version. Salt Lake City, UT. The Church of Jesus Christ of Latter-day Saints.

of them. All were filled with the Holy Ghost and began to speak with other tongues, as the Spirit dictated.

There was living in Jerusalem Jews, who were devout men from every nation. When word of this spread, a crowd came together and was confounded, because every man heard them speak in his own language. They were amazed and marveled, saying, "Aren't all who speak Galileans? Then how do we hear them speak in our native tongue? We are Parthians, Medes, Elamites, from Mesopotamia, Judea, Cappadocia, Asia, Phrygia, Pamphylia, Egypt, Libya, and Rome, yet we all hear them speak in our native tongue. What does this mean?"

Others, who were mocking, said, "These men are full of new wine."

Peter stood up, lifted his voice and said, "Men of Judea and all those who live in Jerusalem, listen to me: These are not drunken, as you suppose, seeing it is only nine in the morning, but this is what the prophet Joel said: 'God said, "It shall come to pass in the last days, I will pour out of My Spirit upon all flesh and your sons and daughters shall prophesy, your young men shall see visions, and your old men shall dream dreams. On My servants and on My handmaidens, I will pour out My Spirit and they shall prophesy."'

"Men of Israel, Jesus of Nazareth, a man approved of God among you, as shown by the miracles, wonders, and signs he did among you and of which you know, and who, being delivered by the plan of God, you have taken and by wicked hands have crucified and slain. God has raised Him up from the dead, because it was not possible for death to hold Him.

"David said concerning Him, 'I saw the Lord always near me, for He is on my right hand, that I should not be overcome. Therefore, I rejoiced and my soul was glad, for My body shall rest in hope, because you will not leave My soul in hell, as you didn't let your Holy One's body to see corruption. You have shown me the ways of life and will make me glad with your presence.'

"Men and brothers, let me speak to you of our patriarch David, who is dead and buried and whose sepulcher is with us today. He, being a prophet and knowing God had sworn with an oath to him, that of his offspring, he would raise up Christ to sit on his throne and, seeing this before, David spoke of the resurrection of Christ, that his soul was not left in hell, nor did his flesh see corruption. We are all witnesses God has raised up Jesus. Let all the house of Israel know God has made that same Jesus, whom you crucified, both Lord and Christ."

THE APOSTLES AFTER THE ATONEMENT

When the people heard this, they were pricked in their heart and said to Peter and the rest of the apostles, "What shall we do?"

Peter said, "Repent and be baptized in the name of Jesus Christ for the remission of sins and you shall receive the gift of the Holy Ghost. For the promise is to you and your children and to those far away, even as many as the Lord shall call."

With many words, he testified and exhorted them to save themselves.

Those who gladly received his word were baptized and that day about three thousand souls were added.[407]

The apostles continued to teach, the church grew, new positions were made, and apostles were replaced as some were killed. The Jews continued to persecute the church. One of those was Saul of Tarsus. The persecution was so bad the members were scattered throughout Judea and Samaria, except the apostles. Saul made havoc of the church, entering homes and taking men and women to prison.[408]

Saul went to the high priest and asked him to provide letters to the synagogues in Damascus, so he could go there and find members of the church and bring them to Jerusalem bound, whether they were men or women. As he went to Damascus and came close to it, suddenly there shone around him a light from heaven. He fell to the earth and heard a voice saying to him, "Saul, Saul, why do you persecute me?"

Saul said, "Who are you?"

He was answered, "I am Jesus whom you persecute. It is hard for you to kick against the pricks."

Saul trembling and astonished said, "Lord, what will you have me do?"

The Lord said, "Arise and go into the city and it shall be told you what you must do."

Those who journeyed with him stood speechless, hearing a voice, but seeing no one.

Saul arose, but when he opened his eyes, he could not see. They led him by the hand to Damascus. He was blind three days and did not eat or drink.

There was a disciple there, named Ananias. The Lord, in a vision, said, "Ananias."

Ananias said, "I am here, Lord."

---

[407] Acts 2: 1-41
[408] Acts 8: 1-4

THE APOSTLES AFTER THE ATONEMENT

The Lord said, "Go into the street called Straight and ask in the house of Judas for one called Saul of Tarsus. He is praying and has seen in a vision a man named Ananias coming in and putting his hand on him, that he might receive his sight."

Ananias answered, "Lord, I have heard from many of this man; how much evil he has done to your saints at Jerusalem. Here he has authority from the chief priest to put in prison all who call on your name."

The Lord said, "Go on your way, for he is a chosen vessel to me, to take my name before the Gentiles and kings, and the children of Israel. I will show him how great things he must suffer for my name's sake."

Ananias went there and into the house. He laid his hands on him and said, "Brother Saul, the Lord, even Jesus, who appeared to you in the way as you came, has sent me here so you could receive your sight and be filled with the Holy Ghost."

Immediately, something like scales fell from Saul's eyes and he received his sight. He arose and was baptized. After eating, he was strengthened and spent some days with the disciples, which were at Damascus. He went and preached Christ in the synagogues, saying He is the Son of God. All who heard him were amazed and said, "Is not this he who destroyed them which called on this name in Jerusalem and came here to do that also, bringing them bound to the chief priests?"

But Saul increased the more in strength and confounded the Jews who lived in Damascus, proving in truth, Jesus is Christ. After many days, the Jews counseled to kill him, but Saul knew of their plans. They watched the gates day and night to kill him, but the disciples took him by night and let him down by the wall in a basket.

When Saul came to Jerusalem, he wanted to join the disciples, but they were all afraid of him and didn't believe he was a disciple.

Barnabas took him and brought him to the apostles and declared how he had seen the Lord in the way, how the Lord had spoken to him, and how he had preached boldly at Damascus in the name of Jesus. Saul continued to preach and, when they again planned to kill him the brethren sent him to Tarsus.[409]

In Caesarea lived a centurion of the Italian band named Cornelius. He was a devout man and feared God with all his house, who gave many alms to the people and often prayed to God. About

---
[409] Acts 9:1-30

THE APOSTLES AFTER THE ATONEMENT

the middle of the afternoon, he had a vision in which an angel came to him and said to him, "Cornelius."

When he saw the angel, he was afraid and said, "What is it, Lord?"

The angel said, "Your prayers and your alms are known by God. Send men to Joppa and call for Simon Peter. He lives with Simon, a tanner, whose house is by the seaside. He will tell you what you should do."

When the angel left, Cornelius called two of his servants and a soldier that waited on him and told them what had happened and sent them to Joppa.

The next day, as they came close to Joppa, Peter went up to the housetop to pray about noon. He became very hungry and would have eaten but, while the food was being prepared, he fell into a trance. He saw heaven opened and a vessel descending to him, like a great sheet bound at the four corners. In it were all kinds of four-footed animals, wild beasts, creeping things, and fowls.

He heard a voice that said, "Rise, Peter; kill and eat."

Peter said, "Not so, Lord; I have never eaten anything that is common or unclean."

The voice said, "What God has cleansed, do not call common."

This was done three times and the vessel was taken up again into heaven. As Peter pondered what this should mean, the men sent by Cornelius came to Simon's house and stood at the gate. They called and asked whether Simon Peter was there. As Peter pondered, the Spirit said to him, "Three men are seeking you. Arise, go down, and go with them, doubting nothing, for I have sent them."

Peter went down, met them, and they spent the night. The next morning, Peter and some others from Joppa went with him. When they arrived in Caesarea, they found Cornelius was waiting for them with his relatives and some good friends.

As Peter came in, Cornelius met him and fell at his feet and worshipped him. But Peter took him up, saying, "Stand up. I myself am a man."

Peter talked to them and said, "You know it is unlawful for a Jew to keep company or come to one of another nation, but God has shown me I should not call any man common or unclean. Therefore, I came to you without asking any questions. Why have you sent for me?"

Cornelius said, "Four days ago, I was fasting and, about three in the afternoon, I prayed and a man stood before me in bright clothes. He said, 'Cornelius, your prayer is heard and your alms are had in remembrance in the sight of God. Send to Joppa and call Simon Peter. He is living in the house of Simon a tanner by the seaside. When he comes, he shall speak to you.' Thus, immediately I sent for you and now it is well you have come. We are all present here before God, to hear all things that are commanded you of God."

Peter said, "Of a truth, I see God is no respecter of persons. In every nation, he who hears Him and works righteousness is accepted with Him."

Peter then taught them of Christ. As he was teaching them, the Holy Ghost fell on all who heard the word. Those who came with Peter were astonished, because on the Gentiles also was poured out the gift of the Holy Ghost. For they heard them speak with tongues and magnify God.

Peter said, "Can anyone forbid water, that these should not be baptized, which have received the Holy Ghost, as well as we?" And he commanded them to be baptized in the name of the Lord.[410]

When Peter returned to Jerusalem, the Jewish members contended with him about his being with Gentiles. He told them about what happened with Cornelius. When they heard this, they held their peace and glorified God, saying, "Then has God also to the Gentiles granted repentance to eternal life."[411]

Herod, the king, killed James, the brother of John, with the sword. He saw it pleased the Jews and he proceeded to take Peter also. Peter was arrested and put in prison, with four detachments of four men each to keep him. Herod intended after Easter to bring him out to the people.

Peter was kept in prison, but prayer was made without ceasing by the church to God for him. The night, before Herod would have brought him out, Peter was sleeping between two soldiers, bound with two chains, while the keepers before the door kept the prison.

Behold, the angel of the Lord came to him and a light shone in the prison. He tapped Peter on the side and raised him up, saying, "Get up quickly."

As he did so, the chains fell off from his hands. The angel said, "Gird yourself and put on your sandals."

He did so and the angel said, "Put on your cloak and follow me."

---

[410] Acts 10
[411] Acts 11:1-18

THE APOSTLES AFTER THE ATONEMENT

Peter followed the angel out, not realizing it was real, but thinking it was a vision. When they came to the iron gate leading to the city, it opened of its own accord and they went out. As he walked through the street, the angel departed.

After he realized what had happened, he went to the house of John Mark, where many were gathered together praying. He knocked at the door of the gate and a young woman named Rhoda came to the door. When she knew Peter's voice, she didn't open the door, because she was so glad to hear his voice, but ran in and told the others how Peter was at the gate.

They told her she was mad, but she kept telling them it was true. Then they said, "It is his angel."

Meanwhile, Peter continued knocking and, when they finally opened the door and saw him, they were astonished.

But he motioned to them to be quiet and told them how the Lord had delivered him from prison. He said, "Go tell this to James and the brethren."

He then left and went elsewhere.

As soon as it was day, there was a big stir among the soldiers about what happened to Peter. When Herod sought for Peter and found he was gone, he examined the keepers and commanded they should be executed. He then left Judea for Caesarea.

One day, Herod made a speech to a group from Tyre and Sidon. He was dressed in royal apparel and sat on his throne.
The people gave a shout, saying, "It is the voice of a god and not of a man."

Immediately, the angel of the Lord struck him, because he gave not God the glory and he was eaten of worms and died.[412]

Certain prophets were at Antioch serving the Lord and, while they fasted, the Holy Ghost said, "Call Barnabas and Saul for the work we have to do." They laid their hands on them and sent them away.[413]

About this time Saul became known as Paul and was later called to be an apostle. He became noted for taking the gospel to the Gentiles.

---

[412] Acts 12
[413] Acts 13:1-3

APOSTASY AND RENAISSANCE

When Paul and others went to communities outside of Judea, they first took the gospel to the Jews. When the Jews would not accept Christ, they took the gospel to others. This caused conflict with the Jews.

Many of the non-Jewish communities worshipped idols. The manufacture of idols by craftsmen was a means of employment for many people. Many of these craftsmen felt threatened by the new theology that did not believe in idols and wanted them destroyed. They were a group that had political power and they used it to persecute Christians.

After Christ's resurrection, Peter was the prophet, guiding the church. He was assisted by James and John. All three of these, Peter, James, and John were apostles. When these three men were separated from the other apostles as leaders, three more apostles were chosen to make a body of twelve apostles. These twelve apostles were also a governing body to act when Peter, James, and John were not available and to call new apostles when one died.

Travel was slow and the apostles traveled long distances to preach. Several new apostles were called and set apart by the laying on of hands to replace those who were killed. The laying on of hands and ordaining them apostles gave them the right to call on God for divine help in doing their gospel work. Putting the hands on the head to ordain someone to a new position was a common practice by the Jews.[414]

The apostles were relying on revelation to make decisions. An example of this is Peter receiving the vision of animals let down in a sheet. That vision opened the preaching of the gospel to the Gentiles.[415] Revelation comes by dreams, visions, and occasionally an angelic visit, but usually it is a feeling or maybe a whisper in the ear. It comes through the Spirit which can be more easily felt if one is keeping God's commandments, attending church, and praying.

Because of the time it took to travel, the distances involved, and the persecution, it was hard for the apostles to correct the churches when problems developed. Most of Paul's writings to the various churches were to correct errors creeping in. When the persecution increased and the church lost its leaders, they were not

---

[414] Numbers 27:22-23; Deuteronomy 34:9; Acts 6:6, 13:3: 2 Timothy. 1:6: Hebrews 6:2
[415] Acts 10:9-17

able to reunite and call new apostles.

Without the leaders, the individual churches began to make their own decisions on questions of doctrine. As the churches grew and more churches were created, there was a lot of discussion on what was right and wrong. The churches in the larger towns had more political clout, because of their size.

Constantine I was the first Roman emperor to accept Christianity. He legalized it in his Edict of Milan in 313 AD and in 325 AD he called the First Council of Nicaea to decide on and solve some of the doctrinal problems that had developed. They came up with the Nicene Creed. This creed and its change over time became the basis for the beliefs of Christians and for the formation of the Roman Catholic Church.

With no prophet on the earth receiving revelation, the Spirit withdrew and the Dark Ages came upon the world. For centuries, the world lived in darkness, but around 1440 the printing press was invented by Gutenberg. He printed the Bible in Latin.

Shortly after 1500, Martin Luther translated the Latin Bible into German and printed it, making it possible for those, other than clergy, to know the word of God. In England, Tyndale and others printed the Bible in English and, for several, this work cost them their lives. As scriptures became more available and more people became familiar with them, the Spirit increased, giving the world the Renaissance. Science, arts, music, health, everything, improved.

Columbus discovered the Americas in 1492 and the colonization of the Americas by Europe began. This follows the Book of Mormon prophecy that this land, the Americas, are a choice land and will be a sanctuary for the people living in it if they are righteous, but when they forget their God and don't keep His commandments, it will be given to other people.[416]

Because of religious persecution and opportunities in this new world, many emigrated from Europe to this Promised Land. To reestablish His church, the Lord needed a place where there was religious freedom. He placed some of his strongest spirits in this land and gave them the opportunity to build a nation governed by the people with freedoms, particularly the freedom to worship as they pleased. If they were righteous they would prosper.

After the United States had been created and freedom of religion established, it was time for the Church of Jesus Christ to once again be on the earth. Joseph Smith was born December 23,

---

[416] BM Nephi 2:20-21; 13:13-14

1805 in Sharon, Vermont. He was preordained to establish and be the first prophet of the restored church. In 1811, the Smith family moved to Lebanon, New Hampshire, a very rural area.

In 1813, there was a typhoid fever epidemic in the area and several of the Smith children were sick, including Joseph. His leg became infected and the infection settled in his leg bone, causing severe pain. Today, this is known as osteomyelitis.

Until the discovery of antibiotics, the usual cure for this was to amputate the leg. Dr. Stone was called in to treat Joseph, but two operations were unsuccessful. The doctor recommended amputation, Joseph's mother wanted to have another opinion and insisted on a "council of surgeons."

Dr. Nathan Smith, the founder of the Dartmouth Medical School, came with Dr. Cyrus Perkins, a former student of his and now his partner, along with several medical students. Dartmouth was only about five miles from the Smith home. Around 1798, Dr. Smith pioneered what is now called a sequestrectomy, where the diseased and dying bone is removed.

In 1827, Dr. Smith published the procedure, but it was not until about 1847 that it became the recognized procedure. Dr. Smith operated on Joseph's leg and it healed, but for three years, he used crutches, and he walked with a limp the rest of his life.[417]

Some might say this was a coincidence, but there are too many such things related to Joseph. If his leg had been amputated, it would have been much more difficult for him to have accomplished all he did. Years before he was born, his grandfather prophesied, "It has been borne in upon my soul that one of my descendants will promulgate a work to revolutionize the world of religious faith."[418]

Joseph's family left Sharon, where he was born, because of crop failures. They kept moving west looking for better opportunities until they arrived in Palmyra, New York. Crop failures were a real trial for the Smith family, but it brought Joseph to the place where the Lord wanted him.

---

[417] Leroy S. Wirthlin, *Joseph Smith's Surgeon* (Nov. 1978). Liahona Magazine, The Church of Jesus Christ of Latter-day Saints, Salt Lake City, UT.

[418] Joseph Fielding Smith, *Essentials in Church History,* Classics in Mormon Literature, Salt Lake City: Deseret Book Co., 1979, p. 25.

There was a religious revival in the area with the Methodists, Presbyterians, and the Baptists vying for members. Joseph was confused by the various ministers preaching different things because he didn't know which was right. As he was reading the Bible, he came across James 1:5, which says, "If any of you lack wisdom, let him ask of God, who gives to all men liberally, and doesn't upbraid; and it shall be given him."

This scripture came to him very powerfully and he reflected on it again and again, so he decided to ask God and went into the woods to pray. He had never made such an attempt and was nervous. It was a beautiful morning, but as he knelt to pray, he was seized upon by some unseen power. He was almost ready to abandon himself to destruction, when he saw a pillar of light exactly over his head. Two Personages appeared whose brightness and glory defied all description. One of them spoke to him, calling him by name and said, pointing to the other, "This is My Beloved Son. Hear Him!"

Joseph asked them which church he should join and was told to join none of them, as they drew near to the Lord with their lips, but their hearts were far from Him and they teach for doctrines the commandments of men, having a form of godliness, but they deny the power thereof.

Later, the angel Moroni came to him at night and showed in a vision where some gold and brass plates were hidden, that contained a history of Jews who had traveled to the Western Hemisphere from Jerusalem. He was told in a few years he would be able to translate some of them into English by the using the Urim and Thummim that was in the box with the plates.[419] Through this process, The Book of Mormon was written and then published. It is a second Testament of Jesus Christ (the Bible is the first).

In 1830, The Church of Jesus Christ of Latter-day Saints was established with a handful of members and, even though there had been and continued to be persecution, the church grew and flourished and today, under the direction of Christ, it is a world-wide church with about 16 million members.

THE SECOND COMING AND MILLENNIUM

For a long, long time, the prophets have foretold of the second coming of Jesus Christ. Some of them tell of good things and

---

[419] PGP Joseph Smith---History 1: 1-59

THE SECOND COMING AND MILLENNIUM

some of wars, famines, pestilence, and other disasters. No one knows when the second coming will take place, but we can see some of the prophecies are coming true now.

The scattering and gathering of Israel: Moses said, "And the Lord shall scatter you among all people, from one end of the earth to the other . . ."[420] Jeremiah said, "I will gather the remnant of my flock out of all countries where I have driven them and will bring them again to their homes and they shall be fruitful and increase."[421] Today, Israel has been reestablished as a country and Jews from all over the world have moved there and are still moving there.

The coming forth of The Book of Mormon is itself a sign of the second coming. Isaiah tells us, "Jerusalem shall be brought down, but it will speak out of the ground." Jerusalem was destroyed, but some Jews fled and their story is told in The Book of Mormon, which was taken out of the ground.

There were many wars and earthquakes which Isaiah mentions. Isaiah also says, "The vision of all is to you as the words of a book that is sealed, which men deliver to one who is learned, saying, 'Read this, please.' But he says, 'I cannot, for it is sealed.' So it is delivered to one that is not learned, and he says, 'I am not learned.'

The Lord said, "I will do a marvelous work among this people, even a marvelous work and a wonder, for the wisdom of their wise men shall perish and the understanding of their prudent men shall be hidden. In that day, shall the deaf hear the words of the book and the eyes of the blind shall see out of obscurity and of darkness."[422] (This is describing the coming forth of the Book of Mormon.)

The word of the Lord came to Ezekiel, "Take one stick (scroll) and write on it for Judah and the children of Israel, his companions and take another stick (scroll) and write on it for Ephraim of Joseph and for all the house of Israel his companions. Join them together so they are one stick in your hand. That the sticks are one in your hand shall be seen by the house of Israel."[423]

The Jews have been looking forward to the coming of Elijah for centuries. He came to Joseph Smith and Oliver Cowdery on April 3, 1836. He said he came to turn the hearts of the fathers to the

---

[420] Deuteronomy 28:64
[421] Jeremiah 23:3
[422] Isaiah 29:4-6; 11-18
[423] Ezekiel 37:15-20

THE SECOND COMING AND MILLENNIUM

children and the children to the fathers, lest the whole earth be smitten with a curse. By this you may know the great and dreadful day of the Lord is near.[424]

Christ told us, "You shall hear of wars and rumor of wars; don't let that bother you, for all these must come, but the end is not yet. Nation shall rise against nation and kingdom against kingdom, and there shall be famines, pestilences, and earthquakes in various places. All these are the beginning of sorrows."[425]

Daniel tells of this, "And at that time shall Michael stand up, the great prince which stands for the children of your people, it shall be a time of trouble, such as never was since there was a nation.[426]

Also, Malachi says, "For, behold, the day is coming, that shall burn as an oven; and all the proud, yes, and all who are wicked, shall be stubble, for the day that comes shall burn them up, says the Lord, that it shall leave them neither root nor branch."[427]

This is not a time for the righteous to worry. The Lord tells us, "And it shall come to pass, they who fear me shall be looking for the great day of the Lord to come, even for the signs of the coming of the Son of Man. They shall see signs and wonders, for they shall be shown forth in the heavens above, and in the earth beneath. They shall behold blood, fire, and smoke.

"Before the day of the Lord shall come, the sun shall be darkened, and the moon be turned to blood, and the stars fall from heaven. The remnant shall be gathered to a safe place and look for me. Behold, I will come and they shall see me in the clouds of heaven, clothed with power and great glory, with all the holy angels. They who don't watch for me shall be cut off. But before the arm of the Lord shall fall, an angel shall sound his trumpet, and the saints who have slept shall come forth to meet me in the cloud. Wherefore, if ye have slept in peace, blessed are you, for as you now behold me and know I am, even so shall ye come to me and your souls shall live, your redemption shall be perfected, and the saints shall come forth from the four quarters of the earth."[428]

The righteous will be saved, and this brings us into the Millennium, a thousand years of peace, when Satan is bound and cannot lead mankind to do evil. The world shall beat their swords

---

[424] D&C 110:13-16
[425] Matthew 24:6-8
[426] Daniel 12:1
[427] Malachi 4:1
[428] D&C 45:39-45

THE SECOND COMING AND MILLENNIUM

into plowshares and their spears into pruning hooks, because one nation shall not fight against another nation and they shall not learn war any longer.

A child will be born and grow to old age, because there will be no death as we know it. When someone dies, it won't be until old age and when they do die, they will be changed in an instant to a resurrected being and continue doing as they had before. Because there is no death, there will be no sorrow. Outside of these things, life will be much like it is now. We will eat, work, plant, harvest crops, marry, and have children.[429]

Christ said, "Unless you are born of the water (baptism) and the spirit (gift of the Holy Ghost), you cannot enter the kingdom of God." He also said, "Marriages need to be performed by the living." Paul told us baptisms for the dead were being done by the saints in the early church.[430] *What kind of God would damn a person to a hell because no one ever taught them about Him? These baptisms, marriages, and other ordinances done for the dead are sacred and need to take place in a suitable place. For this reason, temples have been built and these ordinances are being done there. Genealogy is the tool that is being used to find those who need this work done.*

The Millennium will be a time to do this temple work and to teach the gospel of Jesus Christ. The Millennium is suited for temple work, because the living and angels will be able to talk to one another and obtain information from the dead so their temple work can be done.

When the work is done and the Millennium is finished, Satan will be freed for a short time. He will deceive the world and will bring followers from all over the world to fight against Michael and his angels, but Satan and his armies will be defeated. Then the final judgment will take place, and the world will be judged.[431] The Lord said, "If you keep my commandments and endure to the end, You shall have eternal life, which gift is the greatest of all the gifts of God."[432]

---

[429] Isaiah 2:4; 65:20-23; D&C 101:26-34
[430] John 3:5; Matthew 22:30; 1 Corinthians 15:29
[431] Revelation 20
[432] D&C 14:7

EPILOGUE

I hope this book has increased your knowledge of the Savior, has given you a better understanding of His ministry and who he is. I also hope you felt the Spirit as you read about Him. People feel the Spirit differently, but many say it is like a warm feeling that permeates the soul from the top to the bottom. In any case, it is a good feeling one wants to continue feeling.

If you aren't convinced that your Heavenly Father is real, now would be the best time to pray and ask if what you have read is true. Find a quiet place and kneel or sit down, bow your head in reverence and pray. Call Him by name, such as Father in Heaven. Next, thank him for the good you have. It could be family, a comfortable house, your job, etc. Then ask for the knowledge you wish. Wait for an answer. Then close in the name of Jesus Christ, amen. If you don't get an answer, pray again the next day, and the next, and the next. You need to exercise faith. Try it for ten days, if necessary. You will get an answer if you sincerely want to know.

How does one maintain a closeness to the Savior, so you can continue to feel the Spirit? The scriptures are important in doing so. There is magic in them. Well, not really magic, but there is something about reading them daily that gives you a boost; making life seem better. If you read at a normal speed and read just fifteen or twenty minutes a day, in a year, you will be able to go through the Bible and the Book of Mormon as well.

Besides the scriptures, one needs to attend church on a weekly basis. Of course, none of this does much good if you are not keeping the commandments: The Ten Commandments, other basic commandments, as well as doing good to others.

How did I gain my testimony of Jesus Christ, my Savior? I had questions and no answers. I attended many denominations and read about others and I could not find good answers. I gave up and thought there were none, but I kept reading and praying. My sister and family joined the LDS church and sent me a copy of "A Marvelous Work and Wonder," which tells about The Church of Jesus Christ of Latter-day Saints. I put it on my bookshelf and didn't read it.

I took a new job with a new company and one of my assistants was LDS. We would sometimes eat lunch together and he told me about his church. The more I heard, the more interested I became, so I started reading "A Marvelous Work and Wonder," the book my sister had sent me. It answered all the questions I had been

EPILOGUE

asking and I joined the LDS Church. It was like going from a dark room into a bright room. The world seemed to be changed and all this light poured into my life. I read the Book of Mormon and other LDS scripture, prayed about it, and was told they were true.

The world of today does everything in its power to take God out of it. There is no prayer in schools and most workplaces. Most people are afraid to bring God into everyday conversations, as somebody might be offended. The Bible doesn't address evolution, but I don't think it rules it out. It says the world was made in seven days, but it does not say they are earth days on this planet. There are a lot of questions about how things are done I can't answer, but that doesn't mean God doesn't exist.

I was attending a fundraiser for our District Attorney, who was running for re-election. Shortly before the drawing, I was told I would win the drawing. It wasn't a voice, but the knowledge was given to me; it was a strange feeling. The drawing was for a barbeque grill, which I didn't need because we had just purchased a new one. Knowing I would be the winner gave me time to decide what I would do when my winning number was called. When it was called, I told the auctioneer I didn't need the BBQ and to auction it off to raise additional funds. From this, as well as many things others have told me, I know the future can be foreseen, at least a short distance into it. I know from the scriptures, prophets can see a long way into the future. If the future can be known, there must be something out there that is much like God.

When I pray, I get answers on an individual basis. The answers are for me, just for me. God knows me!

How is this possible? I don't know. I just know it is true. The Book of Mormon wasn't translated and copied as many times as was the Bible, so there is less chance of error. Whatever scriptures you use, read and study them daily.

Much of the world thinks that Mormon's don't believe in the Bible because they have The Book of Mormon. Of course, that is not true, in fact, we believe The Book of Mormon is another testament to Jesus Christ, the Bible being the first.

Probably the biggest difference between Mormon's and most other mainline Christian Churches is our view of God, Jesus Christ, and the Holy Ghost or Holy Spirit. These three are often called the Trinity. The scriptures time after time refer to these three as being one.

How are they one? Most Christian Churches believe they are one in being, reflecting different sides of their being, while

Mormons believe they are separate entities with one purpose. Jesus is the literal physical son of God. That is why it was so important that Mary was a virgin. She is the mother of Jesus, while God the Father, is the father of Jesus' physical body. In the Bible, Jesus is often called the Son of God. He also is referred to as the Son of man. In this case, it means the same as Son of God as in this usage man is a synonym for God.

How can God the Father and God the Son be two beings if there is only one God? Would that not make two Gods? God's family is a patriarchal family and we are all members. The patriarch is God and those who are doing His will, are one in purpose with Him. They might be called Gods while doing His work, but the real God is God the Father, the one God Almighty.

There is one more major difference. We have a prophet to guide us and give us revelation just as was done before Christ. The Church of Jesus Christ of Latter-day Saints relies on revelation and it is how the members and leaders function daily. Those teaching a class or speaking may be given guidelines but are expected to rely on revelation to know what to teach and say. Revelation is the answer we get when we pray if we are open to the Spirit.

Mormons also believe they were born spiritually before they were born to their earthly parents and lived with their Heavenly spiritual parents before being born here on earth, just like Jesus was. That is why John 1:1, Ephesians 3:9, Colossians 1:16, and Hebrews 1:2 all tell us that Jesus Christ was the creator of the world and everything in it. He did all of this as a spirit and most of us helped Him do it.

In Jeremiah 1:5 it says, "Before I formed you in the womb, I knew you...." Jeremiah must also have been alive before he was born, showing we existed before we came to earth to gain a body. Romans 8:29 says, "For whom he knew before, he also determined to be in his image and be the firstborn of many brothers." I think this means Christ was the firstborn of God's spiritual children. He gained a physical body when he was born of Mary, just like we gained a physical body from our parents, to go with the spirit body we had from God the father of our spirits.

There continue to be catastrophes around the world such as earthquakes, fires, hurricanes, along with wars and rumors of wars. Christ spoke of the signs of the second coming and told the righteous they don't have to worry.[433]

---

[433] Matthew 23:6-8; Mark 13:7-8; Luke 21:10-11

EPILOGUE

    None of us know when the second coming will take place, but for any of us, tomorrow may be the day we meet our Savior. If you want to feel the peace the Lord promises each of us and increase your knowledge of the gospel, even though it takes work. I highly recommend "The Book of Mormon." To receive a free copy, call 877-537-0003 or just Google "free copy of Book of Mormon."

www.ingramcontent.com/pod-product-compliance
Lightning Source LLC
LaVergne TN
LVHW051108080426
835510LV00018B/1955